i-Ready® Classroom Mathematics

Grade 4 • Volume 2

Curriculum Associates®

978-1-4957-8039-4

North Billerica, MA 01862

13 14 15 22

BTS22

802706

Contents

UNIT 1

Whole Numbers
Place Value, Comparison, Addition, and Subtraction

UNIT 2 Operations

Multiplication, Division, and Algebraic Thinking

UNIT 3

Multi-Digit Operations and Measurement

Multiplication, Division, Perimeter, and Area

Fractions, Decimals, and Measurement
Addition, Subtraction, and Multiplication

UNIT 5

Geometry and Measurement
Figures, Classification, and Symmetry

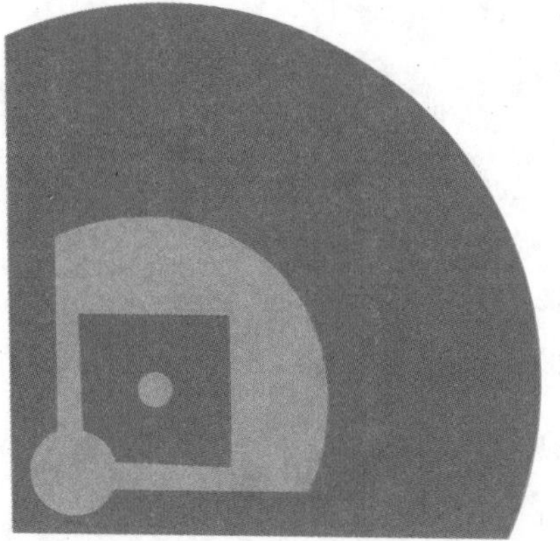

UNIT

4

Fractions, Decimals, and Measurement

Addition, Subtraction, and Multiplication

SELF CHECK

Before starting this unit, check off the skills you know below. As you complete each lesson, see how many more skills you can check off!

I can . . .	Before	After
Compare fractions with unlike denominators.	☐	☐
Add and subtract fractions and mixed numbers.	☐	☐
Add and subtract fractions in line plots.	☐	☐
Multiply a fraction by a whole number.	☐	☐
Write decimals as fractions and write fractions as decimals.	☐	☐
Compare decimals.	☐	☐
Solve problems about time and money.	☐	☐
Solve problems about length, liquid volume, mass, and weight.	☐	☐

UNIT 4

Build Your Vocabulary

REVIEW

denominator numerator
equation unit fraction

Math Vocabulary

Define the review words. Then work with your partner to clarify.

Review Word	Current Thinking	Revise Your Thinking
unit fraction		
equation		
numerator		
denominator		

Academic Vocabulary

Put a check next to the academic words you know. Then use the words to complete the sentences.

☐ connection ☐ observe ☐ predict ☐ reasonable

1. The answer is .... It makes sense.
2. When there is a .... between numbers, they have something in common.
3. A magnifying glass helps you .... objects in greater detail.
4. When I ...., I say what I think will happen next.

Understand Equivalent Fractions

Dear Family,

This week your child is exploring equivalent fractions.

You can show the **equivalent fractions** $\frac{2}{3}$, $\frac{4}{6}$, and $\frac{8}{12}$ with models.

The model at the right is divided into 3 equal parts. The shaded section shows the fraction $\frac{2}{3}$.

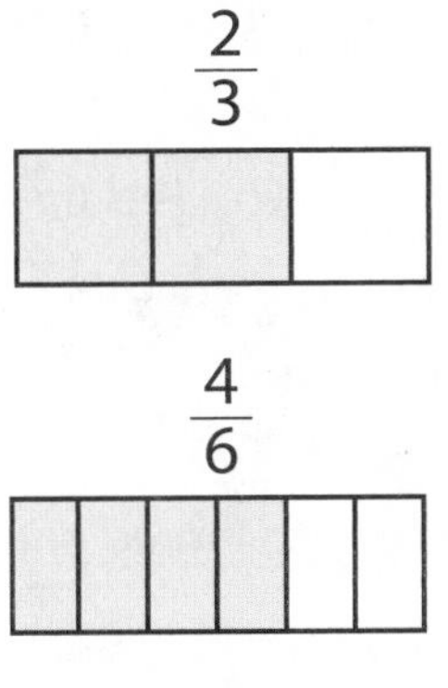

The same model can be divided into 6 equal parts. It has 2 times as many parts shaded and 2 times as many equal parts. The shaded section shows the fraction $\frac{4}{6}$.

The same model can be divided again into 12 equal parts. Now it has 4 times as many parts shaded and 4 times as many equal parts. The shaded section shows the fraction $\frac{8}{12}$.

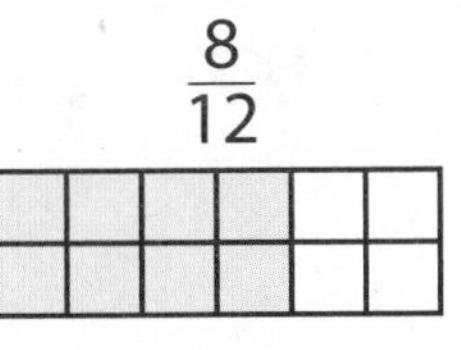

Another way to find equivalent fractions is to multiply both the **numerator** and **denominator** of a fraction by the same number. This is the same as multiplying by 1 because $\frac{2}{2} = 1$ and $\frac{4}{4} = 1$.

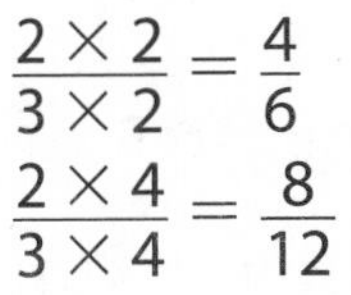

$$\frac{2 \times 2}{3 \times 2} = \frac{4}{6}$$
$$\frac{2 \times 4}{3 \times 4} = \frac{8}{12}$$

Invite your child to share what he or she knows about equivalent fractions by doing the following activity together.

ACTIVITY EQUIVALENT FRACTIONS

Do this activity with your child to explore equivalent fractions.

Materials $\frac{1}{8}$-cup measuring cup, soup pot, ingredients shown in the recipe (all optional)

Look at the recipe below for bean soup. Then follow the steps below to find equivalent fractions.

- Suppose the only measuring cup available is a $\frac{1}{8}$-cup measuring cup. Rewrite the recipe so all the ingredients can be measured using only the $\frac{1}{8}$-cup measuring cup. (This means that you will find equivalent fractions with 8 as the denominator.)
- Discuss how the numerator relates to using the $\frac{1}{8}$-cup measuring cup to measure each ingredient. (The numerator is the number of times the measuring cup is filled.)
- Make the recipe for your family to enjoy.

Bean Soup

Ingredients

$\frac{4}{4}$ cup stewed tomatoes

$\frac{3}{4}$ cup canned black beans with liquid

$\frac{1}{2}$ cup cooked rice

$\frac{1}{4}$ cup salsa

Directions

Mix all the ingredients together in a soup pot. Stir.
Heat and serve. Enjoy!

Explore Equivalent Fractions

What is really going on when fractions are equivalent?

Learning Target

- Explain why a fraction $\frac{a}{b}$ is equivalent to a fraction $\frac{(n \times a)}{(n \times b)}$ by using visual fraction models, with attention to how the number and size of the parts differ even though the two fractions themselves are the same size. Use this principle to recognize and generate equivalent fractions.

SMP 1, 2, 3, 4, 5, 6, 7

MODEL IT

Complete the problems and models below.

1 Look at the area models below.

a. Write the fraction of each model that is shaded.

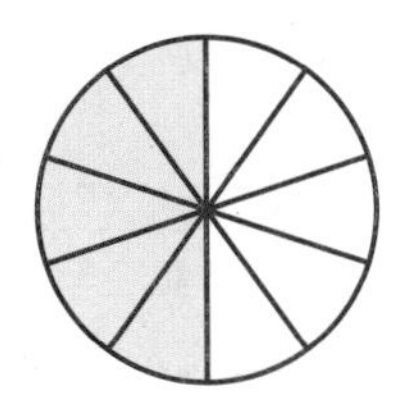

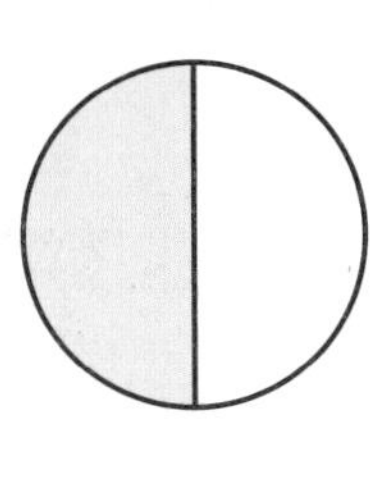

....

b. How are the models of the fractions the same? How are they different? Explain.

2 Equivalent fractions name the same part of a whole. Shade the models to show fractions equivalent to $\frac{1}{2}$. Then name the fractions.

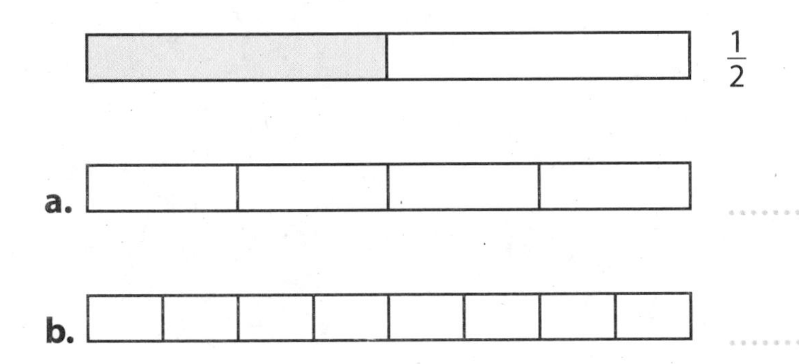

DISCUSS IT

- What is the same about the models for the equivalent fractions in problem 2? What is different about the models?
- I think equivalent fractions show the same amount in different ways because . . .

MODEL IT

Complete the models and answer the questions below.

3 Shade each model to represent the fraction shown.

$\frac{1}{3}$

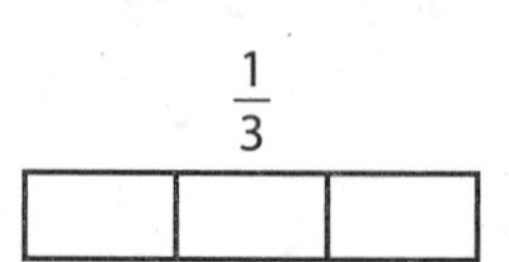

a. Is the size of the area you shaded in each model the same? ....

b. How do you know that $\frac{1}{3}$, $\frac{2}{6}$, and $\frac{4}{12}$ are equivalent fractions?

$\frac{2}{6}$

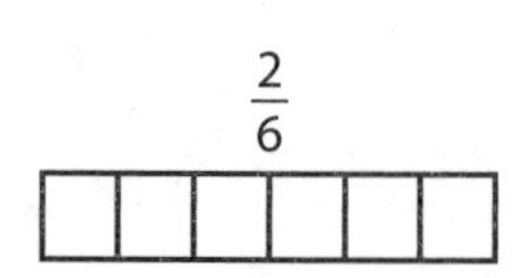

c. Compare the models. How many times as many equal parts and shaded parts does each model have than the model above it?

$\frac{4}{12}$

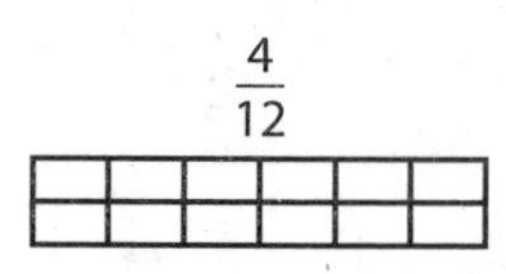

4 You can also multiply the numerator and denominator of a fraction by the same number to get an equivalent fraction.

a. Write the missing numbers to complete the equation.

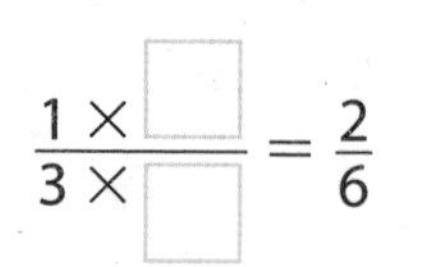

$\frac{1 \times \square}{3 \times \square} = \frac{2}{6}$

b. How many times as many is the numerator and denominator in $\frac{2}{6}$ as in $\frac{1}{3}$?

c. Write the missing numbers to show a different equivalent fraction for $\frac{1}{3}$.

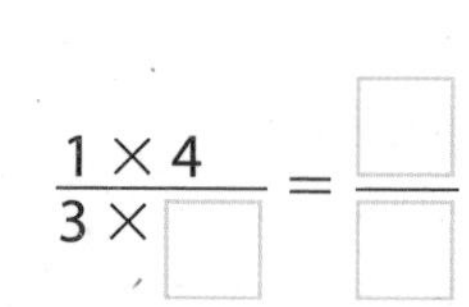

$\frac{1 \times 4}{3 \times \square} = \frac{\square}{\square}$

DISCUSS IT

- How could you and your partner use multiplication to find another equivalent fraction for $\frac{1}{3}$?
- I think models and equations can help you understand equivalent fractions because . . .

5 REFLECT

Explain how you can divide a rectangle into equal parts to show equivalent fractions.

....

....

....

Name: ______________________________

Prepare for Equivalent Fractions

1 Think about what you know about equivalent fractions. Fill in each box. Use words, numbers, and pictures. Show as many ideas as you can.

What Is It?	What I Know About It

equivalent fractions

Examples	Examples	Examples

2 Shade the models to show fractions equivalent to $\frac{1}{2}$. Then name the fractions.

$\frac{1}{2}$

....

....

Solve.

3. Shade each model to represent the fraction shown.

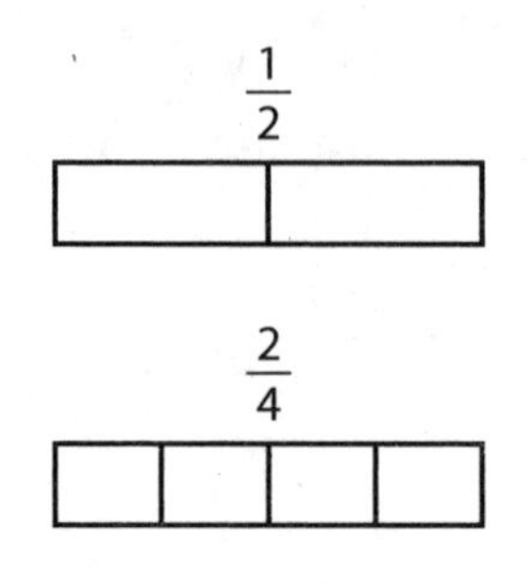

a. Is the size of the area you shaded in each model the same?

b. How do you know that $\frac{1}{2}$, $\frac{2}{4}$, and $\frac{4}{8}$ are equivalent fractions?

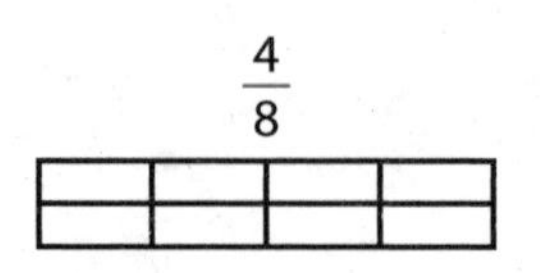

c. Compare the models. How many times as many equal parts and shaded parts does each model have than the model above it?

4. You can also multiply the numerator and denominator of a fraction by the same number to get an equivalent fraction.

a. Write the missing numbers to complete the equation.

$$\frac{1 \times \square}{2 \times \square} = \frac{2}{4}$$

b. How many times as many is the numerator and denominator in $\frac{2}{4}$ as in $\frac{1}{2}$?

c. Write the missing numbers to show a different equivalent fraction for $\frac{1}{2}$.

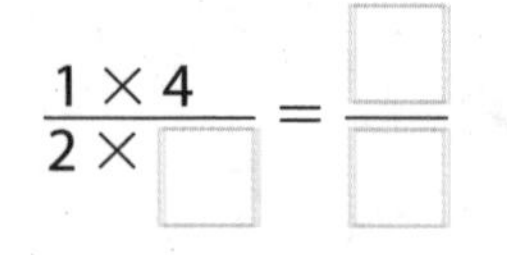

Develop Understanding of Equivalent Fractions

MODEL IT: AREA MODELS

Try these two problems.

Use the model at the right.

a. Shade the model to show the unit fraction $\frac{1}{4}$.

b. Show 8 equal parts in the model and write the equivalent fraction. ....

c. How do the number and size of the parts compare in the equivalent fractions?

2 Use the model at the right to show $\frac{2}{5}$. Then divide the model into a different number of parts to show an equivalent fraction.

a. What equivalent fraction is shown?

b. How many times as many shaded parts and equal parts are in the equivalent fraction as are in $\frac{2}{5}$?

DISCUSS IT

- Compare your model in problem 2 to your partner's model. How are the models the same? How are the models different?
- I think area models help me understand equivalent fractions because . . .

MODEL IT: EQUATIONS

Use equations to help you think about equivalent fractions.

3 Write the missing numbers to find a fraction equivalent to $\frac{5}{6}$ using multiplication.

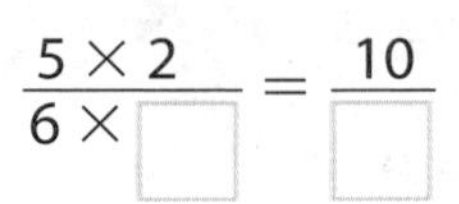

4 **a.** Write the missing numbers to find a fraction equivalent to $\frac{4}{6}$ using multiplication.

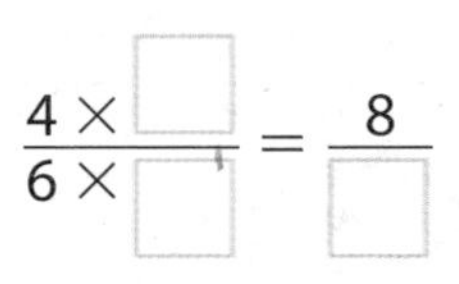

b. What happens if you divide both the numerator and denominator in $\frac{4}{6}$ by 2?

5 To find a fraction equivalent to $\frac{6}{8}$, Beth divided by 2 to get 4 in the denominator. What should Beth do to find the numerator? What are the equivalent fractions?

DISCUSS IT

- Look at problems 4a and 5. How did you know what number to multiply or divide by?
- I think using multiplication or division equations can help me find equivalent fractions because . . .

CONNECT IT

Complete the problems below.

6 How can you use area models and equations to make equivalent fractions?

7 Choose any model to find two fractions equivalent to $\frac{2}{6}$.

Practice with Equivalent Fractions

Study how the Example shows one way to model equivalent fractions. Then solve problems 1–8.

EXAMPLE

A model can show equivalent fractions.

The model has 5 equal parts. It shows $\frac{3}{5}$.

Divide the model into 10 equal parts to show an equivalent fraction.

The model shows $\frac{6}{10}$.

$\frac{3}{5} = \frac{6}{10}$

1. Divide the model below to show $\frac{1}{2} = \frac{5}{10}$.

2. Draw a model to show $\frac{1}{6}$. Then divide the model into twice as many parts to find an equivalent fraction.

   $\frac{1}{6} =$ ....

3. Multiply the numerator and denominator of $\frac{1}{6}$ by 2. $\frac{1 \times 2}{6 \times 2} =$ ....

4. Why does it make sense that the fraction you wrote in problems 2 and 3 is the same?

5 Write the missing numbers to find two equivalent fractions to $\frac{4}{5}$.

$\frac{4 \times \square}{5 \times 2} = \frac{\square}{10}$ $\frac{4 \times 20}{5 \times 20} = \frac{\square}{100}$

6 Shade the model below to show $\frac{1}{5}$. Then show 10 equal parts and write an equivalent fraction.

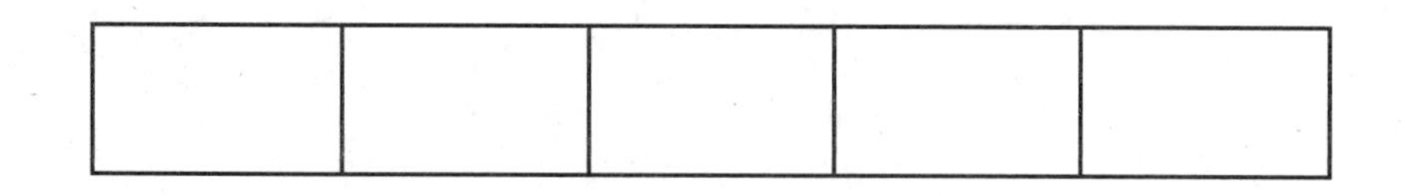

7 Shade the model below to show $\frac{2}{3}$. Then show 12 equal parts and write an equivalent fraction.

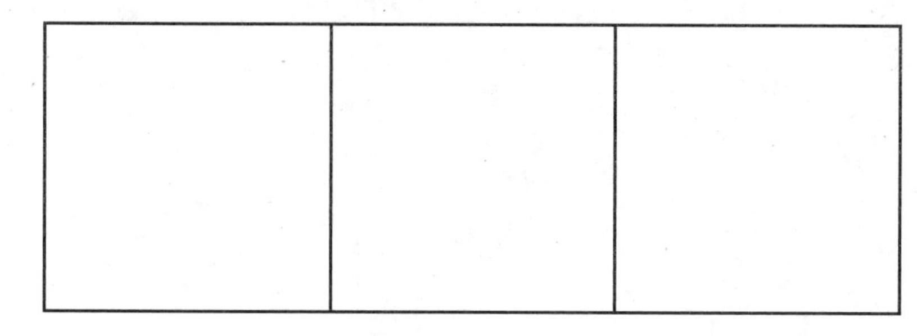

8 Chris said that a fraction equivalent to $\frac{9}{12}$ is $\frac{3}{6}$. Is Chris correct? Explain.

Vocabulary

denominator the number below the line in a fraction that tells the number of equal parts in the whole.

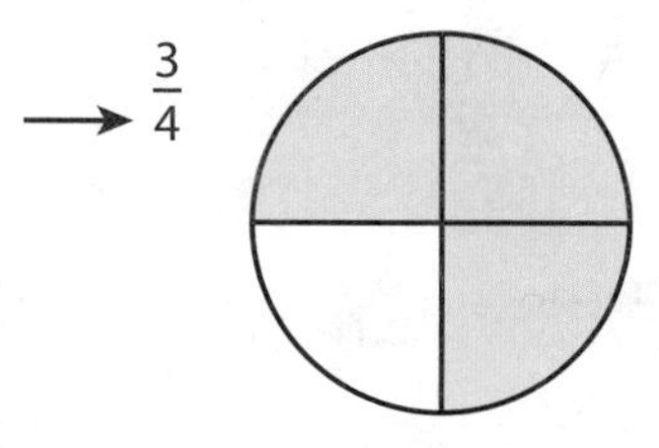

4 equal parts

equivalent fractions two or more different fractions that name the same part of a whole or the same point on a number line.

numerator the number above the line in a fraction that tells the number of equal parts that are being described.

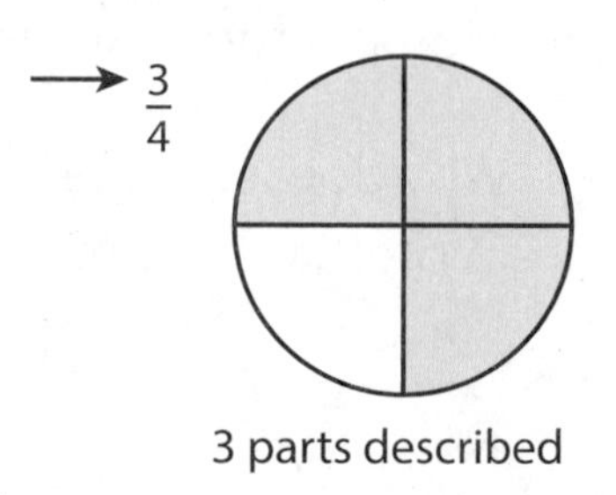

3 parts described

Refine Ideas About Equivalent Fractions

APPLY IT

Complete these problems on your own.

1 COMPARE

Use different methods to find two fractions that are equivalent to $\frac{3}{3}$.

2 ILLUSTRATE

Explain why you can multiply both the numerator and denominator by the same number to make an equivalent fraction. Draw a model to show an example.

3 CHOOSE

Fia needs $\frac{3}{4}$ of a cup of brown sugar. She only has a $\frac{1}{3}$-cup measuring cup and a $\frac{1}{8}$-cup measuring cup. Which should she use and why?

PAIR/SHARE

Discuss your solutions for these three problems with a partner.

APPLY IT

Use what you have learned to complete problem 4.

4 **Part A** The shaded part of each rectangle models a fraction. Draw lines to match the fraction model on the left with an equivalent fraction on the right.

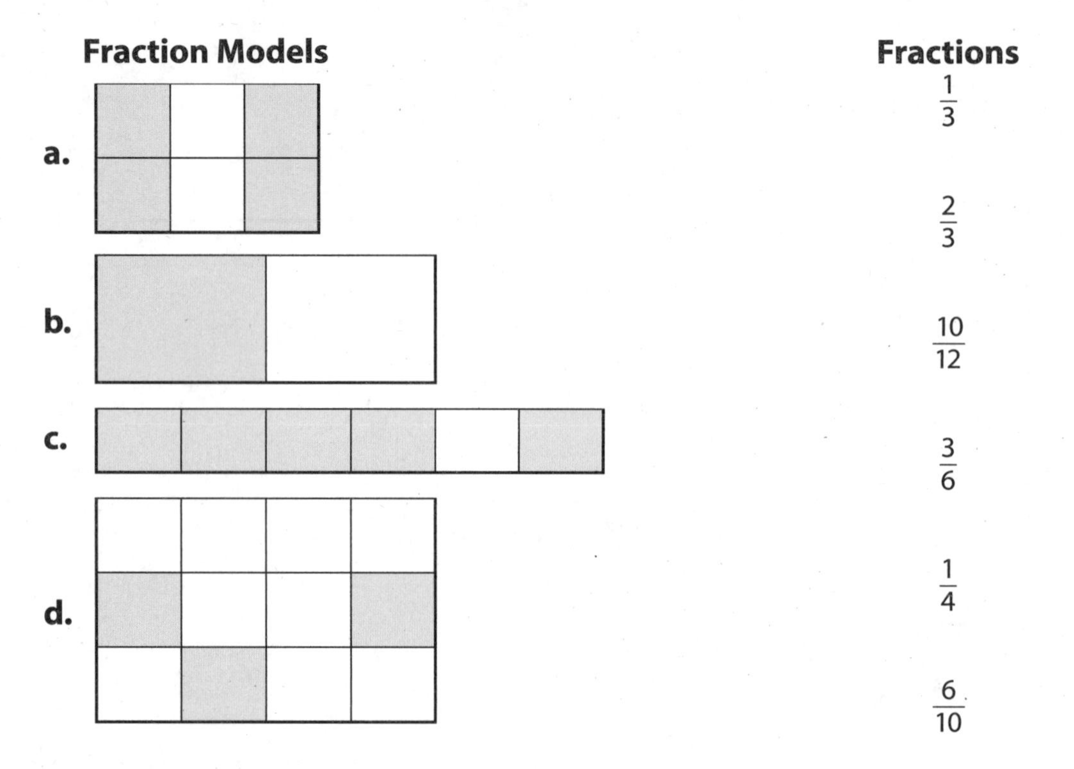

Part B Choose one of the fraction models in Part A. Explain how to use multiplication or division to check the equivalent fraction. Why does this work?

MATH JOURNAL

Explain why $\frac{3}{4}$ is equivalent to $\frac{9}{12}$.

Compare Fractions

LESSON 18

Dear Family,

This week your child is learning to compare fractions.

There are different ways to compare fractions.

One way to compare fractions, such as $\frac{3}{5}$ and $\frac{3}{6}$, is to use models. You must use the same-sized whole for both. If the wholes are different sizes, it does not make sense to compare the parts. Each whole model below is the same size.

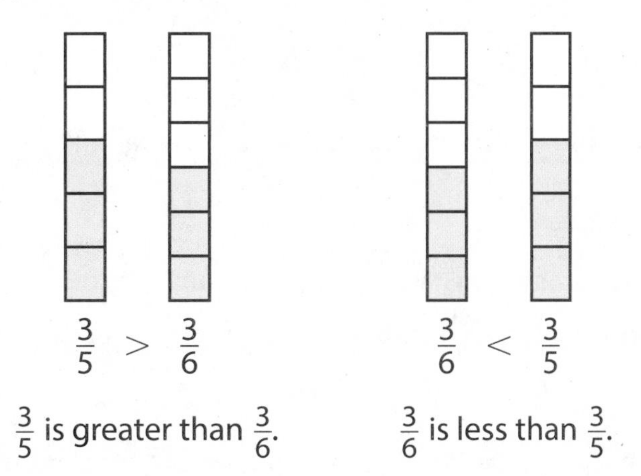

$\frac{3}{5} > \frac{3}{6}$ $\qquad$ $\frac{3}{6} < \frac{3}{5}$

$\frac{3}{5}$ is greater than $\frac{3}{6}$. $\qquad$ $\frac{3}{6}$ is less than $\frac{3}{5}$.

Another way to compare fractions is to write equivalent fractions with the same denominators. Using the same denominators means that there are the same number of parts in each whole. Then you can compare the numerators to find which fraction has a greater number of parts.

$$\frac{3 \times 6}{5 \times 6} = \frac{18}{30} \qquad \frac{3 \times 5}{6 \times 5} = \frac{15}{30}$$

$$\frac{18}{30} > \frac{15}{30}, \text{ so } \frac{3}{5} > \frac{3}{6}.$$

Your child might also use a number line to compare fractions by comparing each fraction to a **benchmark fraction,** such as $\frac{1}{2}$.

Invite your child to share what he or she knows about comparing fractions by doing the following activity together.

ACTIVITY COMPARING FRACTIONS

Do this activity with your child to compare fractions.

Materials 4 same-sized clear glasses, colored liquid

- Fill one glass to the top with colored liquid. This glass represents 1 whole. Fill another glass half full to represent $\frac{1}{2}$. Leave a third glass empty to represent 0.
- Pour any amount of liquid into the fourth glass. Compare the fourth glass to the full glass and the empty glass to determine if the amount of liquid represents a fraction that is closer to 0 or to 1.
- Then determine if the amount of liquid in the fourth glass represents a fraction that is greater than or less than $\frac{1}{2}$. You can check your answer by comparing the fourth glass to the glass that is half full.
- Now empty the fourth glass. Take turns filling it with various amounts of colored liquid and describing the quantity as representing a fraction that is greater than or less than $\frac{1}{2}$.
- Talk with your child about why it is important that the four glasses are the same size and shape. (Half of a tall glass is a different amount of liquid than half of a short glass.)

Explore Comparing Fractions

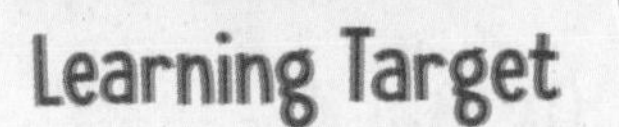

Learning Target

- Compare two fractions with different numerators and different denominators. Recognize that comparisons are valid only when the two fractions refer to the same whole. Record the results of comparisons with symbols >, =, or <, and justify the conclusions.

SMP 1, 2, 3, 4, 5, 6, 7

Previously, you learned to compare fractions using models. Use what you know to try to solve the problem below.

Adriana and June have granola bars that are the same size. Adriana eats $\frac{2}{4}$ of her granola bar. June eats $\frac{2}{5}$ of her granola bar. Which girl eats more of her granola bar?

TRY IT

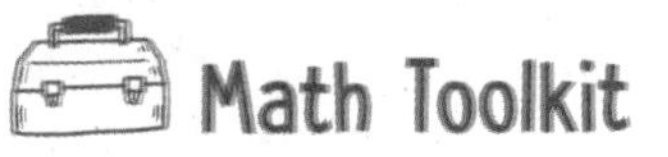

Math Toolkit

- fraction circles
- fraction tiles
- number lines
- fraction bars
- index cards
- fraction models

DISCUSS IT

Ask your partner: Do you agree with me? Why or why not?

Tell your partner: I agree with you about . . . because . . .

CONNECT IT

1 LOOK BACK

Who eats more of her granola bar, Adriana or June? Explain.

2 LOOK AHEAD

Deciding who eats more of her granola bar means comparing the fractions $\frac{2}{4}$ and $\frac{2}{5}$. To compare fractions, you must use the same-sized whole.

a. Suppose you have two more granola bars that are the same size. Compare the fractions $\frac{3}{4}$ and $\frac{3}{5}$ using the area models to know who ate more. Use $>$, $<$, or $=$ to compare, just as with whole numbers.

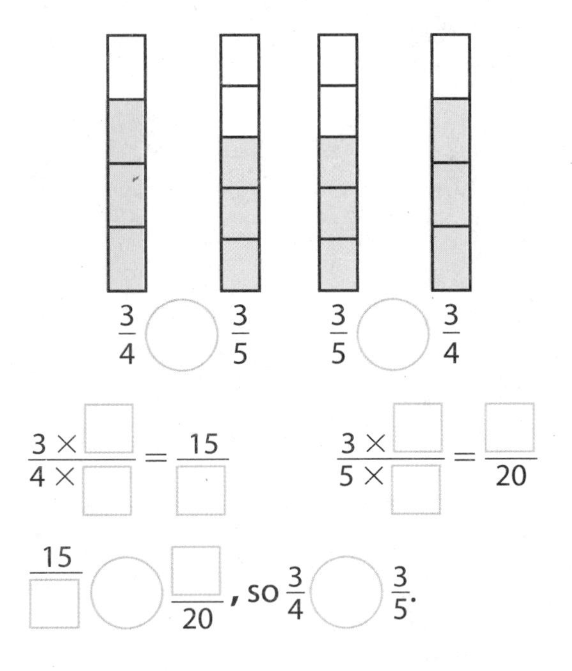

b. You can use equivalent fractions to compare fractions with different denominators. Compare $\frac{3}{4}$ and $\frac{3}{5}$. Rewrite one or both of the fractions so they have the same denominator, or a **common denominator**. Use $>$, $<$, or $=$ to compare.

3 REFLECT

Suppose the granola bars were different sizes. Could you still compare $\frac{3}{4}$ and $\frac{3}{5}$ in the same way? Explain.

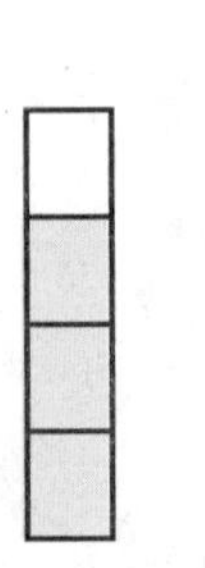

Name: ________________________

Prepare for Comparing Fractions

1 Think about what you know about common denominators. Fill in each box. Use words, numbers, and pictures. Show as many ideas as you can.

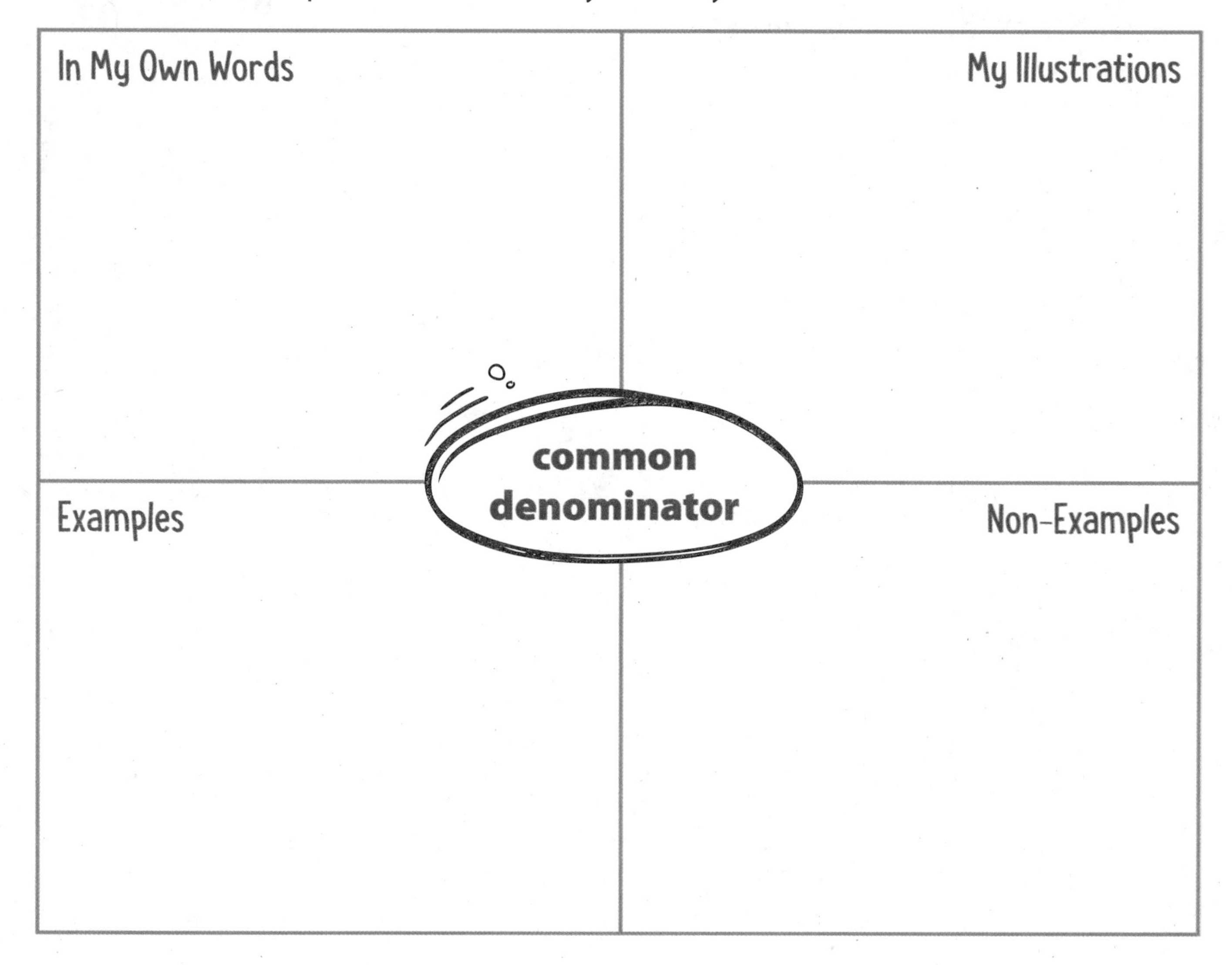

2 Compare $\frac{2}{3}$ and $\frac{2}{5}$. Rewrite the fractions so they have a common denominator.

Use >, <, or = to compare.

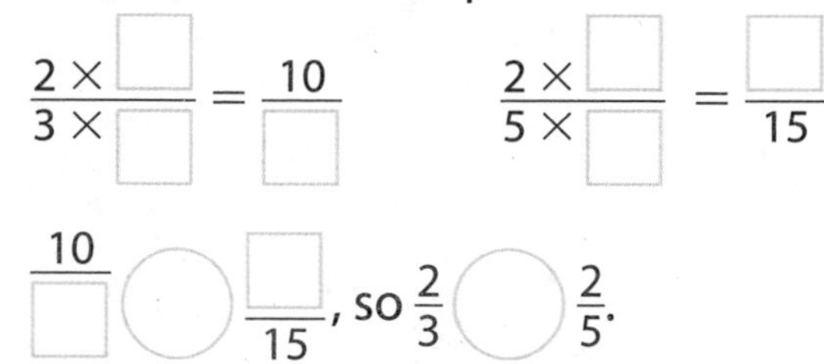

3 Solve the problem. Show your work.

Donato and Aman have bottles of juice that are the same size. Donato drinks $\frac{3}{4}$ of his juice. Aman drinks $\frac{3}{6}$ of his juice. Which boy drinks more juice?

Solution ....

4 Check your answer. Show your work.

Develop Using Common Numerators and Denominators

Read and try to solve the problem below.

A grasshopper weighs $\frac{2}{100}$ of an ounce. A beetle weighs $\frac{8}{10}$ of an ounce. Which weighs more?

TRY IT

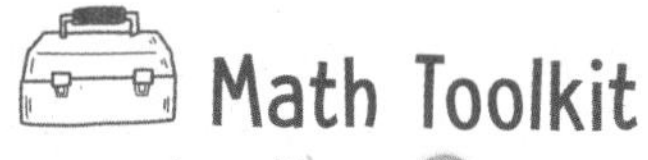

- number lines
- hundredths grids
- tenths grids
- index cards
- fraction models

Ask your partner: How did you get started?

Tell your partner: I started by . . .

Explore different ways to understand comparing fractions.

A grasshopper weighs $\frac{2}{100}$ of an ounce. A beetle weighs $\frac{8}{10}$ of an ounce. Which weighs more?

MODEL IT

You can use models to help compare fractions.

The models show the fractions of an ounce that the grasshopper and beetle weigh.

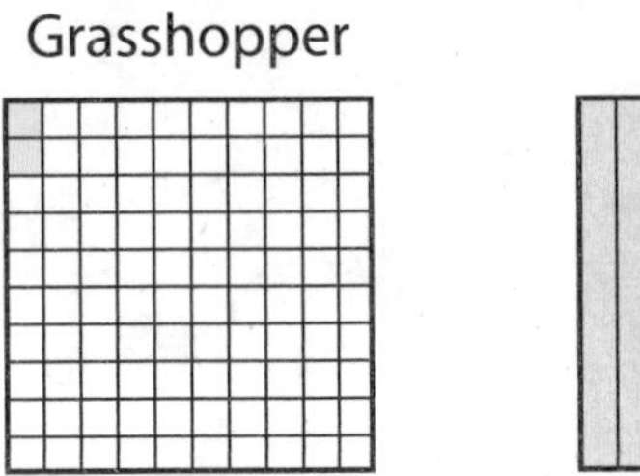

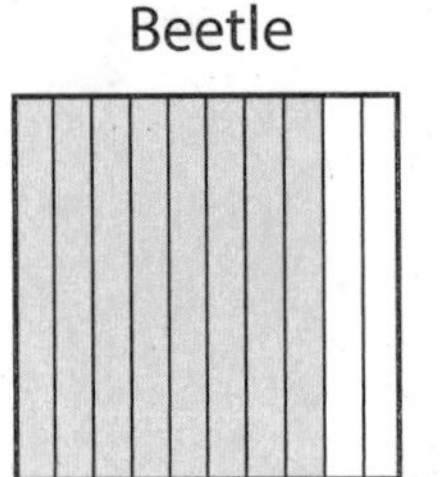

MODEL IT

You can use a common denominator to help compare fractions.

When you compare two fractions, it helps if they have a common denominator. Fractions with the same denominator are made up of parts of the same size. The numerators tell how many of those parts each fraction has. When two fractions have the same denominator, you can compare the numerators.

Compare $\frac{2}{100}$ and $\frac{8}{10}$.

The fractions are not written with a common denominator. Find a fraction equivalent to $\frac{8}{10}$ that has a denominator of 100.

$$\frac{8 \times 10}{10 \times 10} = \frac{80}{100}$$

Now, compare the numerators of $\frac{2}{100}$ and $\frac{80}{100}$.

$$80 > 2$$

So, $\frac{80}{100} > \frac{2}{100}$ and $\frac{8}{10} > \frac{2}{100}$.

CONNECT IT

Now you will use the problem from the previous page to help you understand how to compare fractions by finding a common numerator.

1. What is an equivalent fraction for $\frac{2}{100}$ that has a numerator of 8? ....

2. One model is divided into 400 equal parts, and the other is divided into 10 equal parts. Which model has smaller parts?

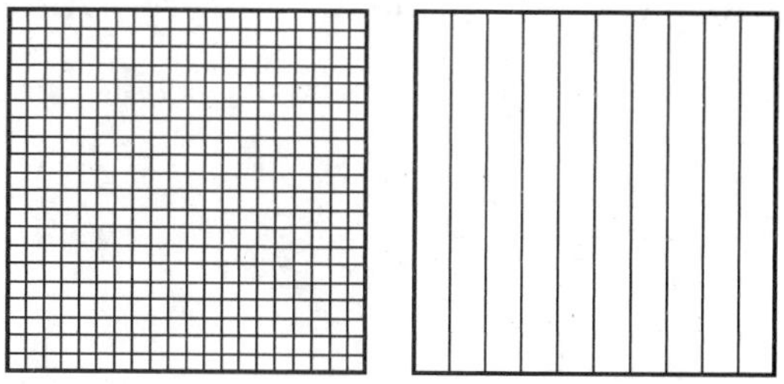

3. Shade 8 parts of each model.

4. Which model has a greater area shaded?

5. Which fraction is greater, $\frac{8}{400}$ or $\frac{8}{10}$? ....

6. Which weighs more, the grasshopper or the beetle? ....

7. Look at the denominators of $\frac{8}{400}$ and $\frac{8}{10}$. When two fractions have the same numerator and different denominators, how do you know which fraction is greater? Explain.

8. ## REFLECT

Look back at your **Try It**, strategies by classmates, **Model Its**, and the **Connect It** problems on this page. Which models or strategies do you like best for comparing fractions? Explain.

....

....

....

APPLY IT

Use what you just learned to solve these problems.

9. Mel's tomato plant is $\frac{8}{12}$ of a foot tall. Her pepper plant is $\frac{3}{4}$ of a foot tall. Compare the heights of the plants using $<$, $>$, or $=$. Use a model to show your comparison. Show your work.

Solution ....

Compare the fractions $\frac{4}{6}$ and $\frac{2}{5}$ using $<$, $>$, or $=$. Use a model to show your comparison. Show your work.

Solution ....

11. Morgan has the two fraction models shown. Morgan shades Model B to show a fraction less than the fraction shown by Model A. How many parts of Model B could she have shaded? Explain.

Model A

Model B

Name: ____________________

Practice with Common Numerators and Denominators

Study the Example showing how to compare fractions by finding a common denominator. Then solve problems 1–7.

EXAMPLE

A length of ribbon is $\frac{3}{4}$ of a foot. Another length of ribbon is $\frac{5}{6}$ of a foot. Compare the lengths using a symbol.

Find a common denominator. $\frac{3 \times 3}{4 \times 3} = \frac{9}{12}$ $\frac{5 \times 2}{6 \times 2} = \frac{10}{12}$

Write the equivalent fractions. $\frac{3}{4} = \frac{9}{12}$ $\frac{5}{6} = \frac{10}{12}$

Compare the numerators. $\frac{9}{12} < \frac{10}{12}$

Since $9 < 10$, that means $\frac{9}{12} < \frac{10}{12}$.

$\frac{3}{4} < \frac{5}{6}$

1 Shade the models to show $\frac{3}{4}$ and $\frac{5}{6}$. Compare the fractions. Write <, >, or =.

$\frac{3}{4}$ ◯ $\frac{5}{6}$

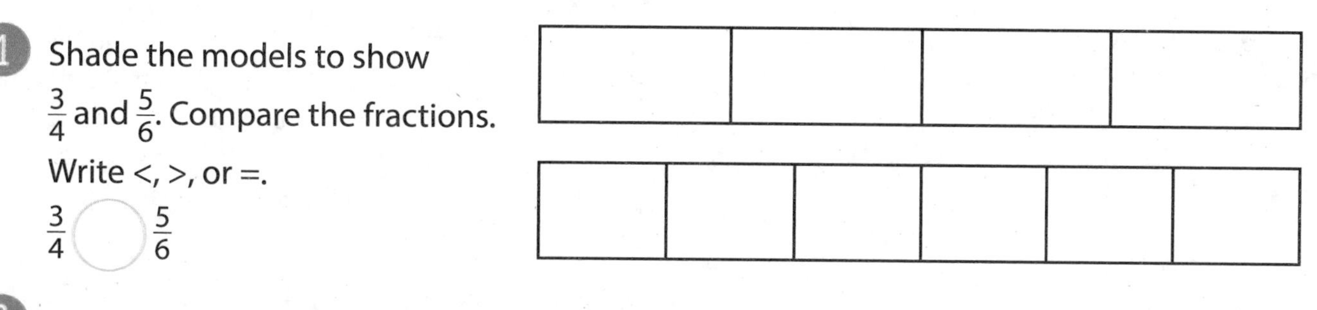

2 Divide each model in problem 1 into 12 equal parts to show an equivalent fraction. Write the equivalent fractions and symbol to show the comparison.

$\frac{\square}{12}$ ◯ $\frac{\square}{12}$

3 Compare $\frac{2}{3}$ and $\frac{9}{12}$ by finding a common denominator.

a. Write a fraction equivalent to $\frac{2}{3}$ with a denominator of 12.

$\frac{2 \times \square}{3 \times \square} = \frac{\square}{12}$

b. Compare the fractions.

$\frac{\square}{12}$ ◯ $\frac{9}{12}$. So, $\frac{2}{3}$ ◯ $\frac{9}{12}$.

4 Compare $\frac{1}{5}$ and $\frac{2}{12}$ by finding a common numerator.

a. Write a fraction equivalent to $\frac{1}{5}$ with a numerator of 2.

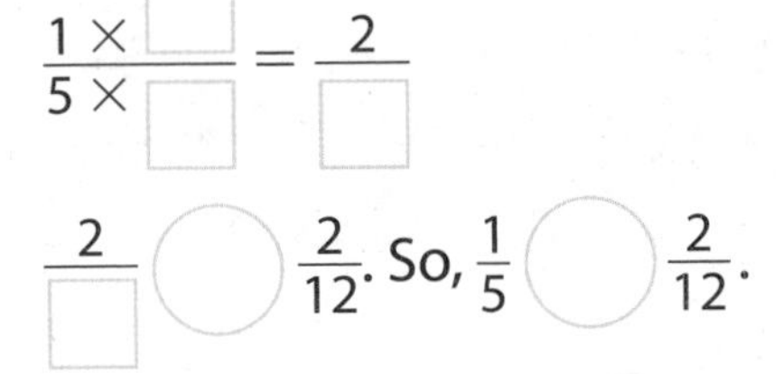

$\frac{1 \times \square}{5 \times \square} = \frac{2}{\square}$

b. Compare the fractions.

$\frac{2}{\square} \bigcirc \frac{2}{12}$. So, $\frac{1}{5} \bigcirc \frac{2}{12}$.

5 Compare the fractions. Use the symbols <, >, and =.

a. $\frac{2}{5} \bigcirc \frac{8}{10}$

b. $\frac{5}{12} \bigcirc \frac{1}{3}$

c. $\frac{3}{5} \bigcirc \frac{60}{100}$

d. $\frac{9}{100} \bigcirc \frac{9}{10}$

6 Tell whether each comparison is *True* or *False*.

	True	False
$\frac{2}{3} > \frac{5}{6}$	Ⓐ	Ⓑ
$\frac{4}{10} < \frac{4}{5}$	Ⓒ	Ⓓ
$\frac{70}{100} = \frac{7}{10}$	Ⓔ	Ⓕ
$\frac{1}{3} > \frac{3}{1}$	Ⓖ	Ⓗ
$\frac{3}{4} < \frac{2}{3}$	Ⓘ	Ⓙ

Vocabulary

common denominator a number that is a common multiple of the denominators of two or more fractions.

denominator the number below the line in a fraction that tells the number of equal parts in the whole.

numerator the number above the line in a fraction that tells the number of equal parts that are being described.

7 Can two fractions with the same numerator and different denominators be equal? Use words and numbers to explain.

Develop Using a Benchmark to Compare Fractions

Read and try to solve the problem below.

Jasmine's swimming lesson lasts for $\frac{2}{3}$ of an hour. It takes her $\frac{1}{6}$ of an hour to do her homework. Does Jasmine spend more time on her homework or at her swimming lesson?

TRY IT

Math Toolkit
- fraction circles
- fraction tiles
- number lines
- fraction bars
- index cards
- fraction models

DISCUSS IT

Ask your partner: Why did you choose that strategy?

Tell your partner: I knew . . . so I . . .

Explore different ways to understand using benchmarks to compare fractions.

Jasmine's swimming lesson lasts for $\frac{2}{3}$ of an hour. It takes her $\frac{1}{6}$ of an hour to do her homework. Does Jasmine spend more time on her homework or at her swimming lesson?

MODEL IT

You can use a number line to help you compare fractions.

The number line shows where the fractions $\frac{2}{3}$ and $\frac{1}{6}$ are compared to 0 and 1.

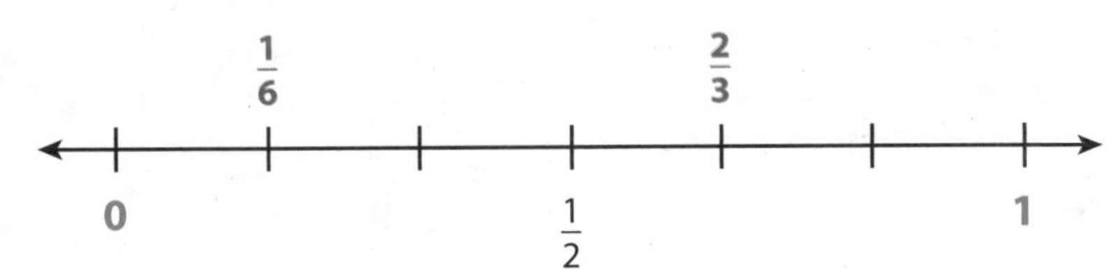

The number line shows that $\frac{1}{6}$ is closer to 0 than $\frac{2}{3}$ is.
It also shows that $\frac{2}{3}$ is closer to 1 than $\frac{1}{6}$ is.
This means that $\frac{1}{6} < \frac{2}{3}$ and $\frac{2}{3} > \frac{1}{6}$.

SOLVE IT

You can use a benchmark fraction to solve the problem.

Another way to compare fractions is by using a benchmark fraction.
Use $\frac{1}{2}$ as a benchmark to compare $\frac{1}{6}$ and $\frac{2}{3}$.

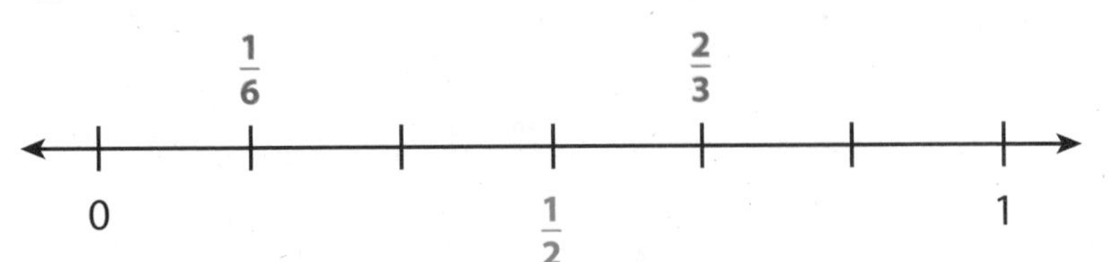

The number line shows that $\frac{1}{6}$ is less than $\frac{1}{2}$ and $\frac{2}{3}$ is greater than $\frac{1}{2}$.
So, $\frac{1}{6} < \frac{2}{3}$ and $\frac{2}{3} > \frac{1}{6}$.

Jasmine spends more time at her swimming lesson than on homework.

CONNECT IT

Now you will solve a similar problem using 1 as a benchmark. Think about the two fractions $\frac{11}{10}$ and $\frac{7}{8}$.

1. Which fraction, $\frac{11}{10}$ or $\frac{7}{8}$, is greater than 1? ....

2. Which fraction, $\frac{11}{10}$ or $\frac{7}{8}$, is less than 1? ....

3. Which fraction, $\frac{11}{10}$ or $\frac{7}{8}$, is greater? Explain.

4. Write $<$, $>$, or $=$ to show the comparison. $\frac{11}{10}$ ◯ $\frac{7}{8}$

5. Explain how you can use benchmarks to compare fractions.

REFLECT

Look back at your **Try It**, strategies by classmates, and **Model It** and **Solve It**. Which models or strategies do you like best for using benchmarks to compare fractions? Explain.

....

....

....

....

APPLY IT

Use what you just learned to solve these problems.

7 Tell which fraction is greater, $\frac{4}{8}$ or $\frac{3}{4}$. Use the benchmark fraction $\frac{1}{2}$ to explain your answer. Show your work.

Solution ....

8 Nathan walks $\frac{10}{10}$ of a mile. Sarah walks $\frac{11}{12}$ of a mile. Who walks a greater distance? Explain. Use a benchmark number in your explanation.

Solution ....

....

....

9 Use the benchmark fraction $\frac{1}{2}$ to compare the two fractions below.
Which symbol correctly compares the fractions?

$\frac{4}{6} \bigcirc \frac{3}{8}$

Ⓐ $<$

Ⓑ $>$

Ⓒ $=$

Ⓓ $+$

Name: ______________________________

Practice Using a Benchmark to Compare Fractions

Study the Example showing how to use 1 as a benchmark to compare fractions. Then solve problems 1–4.

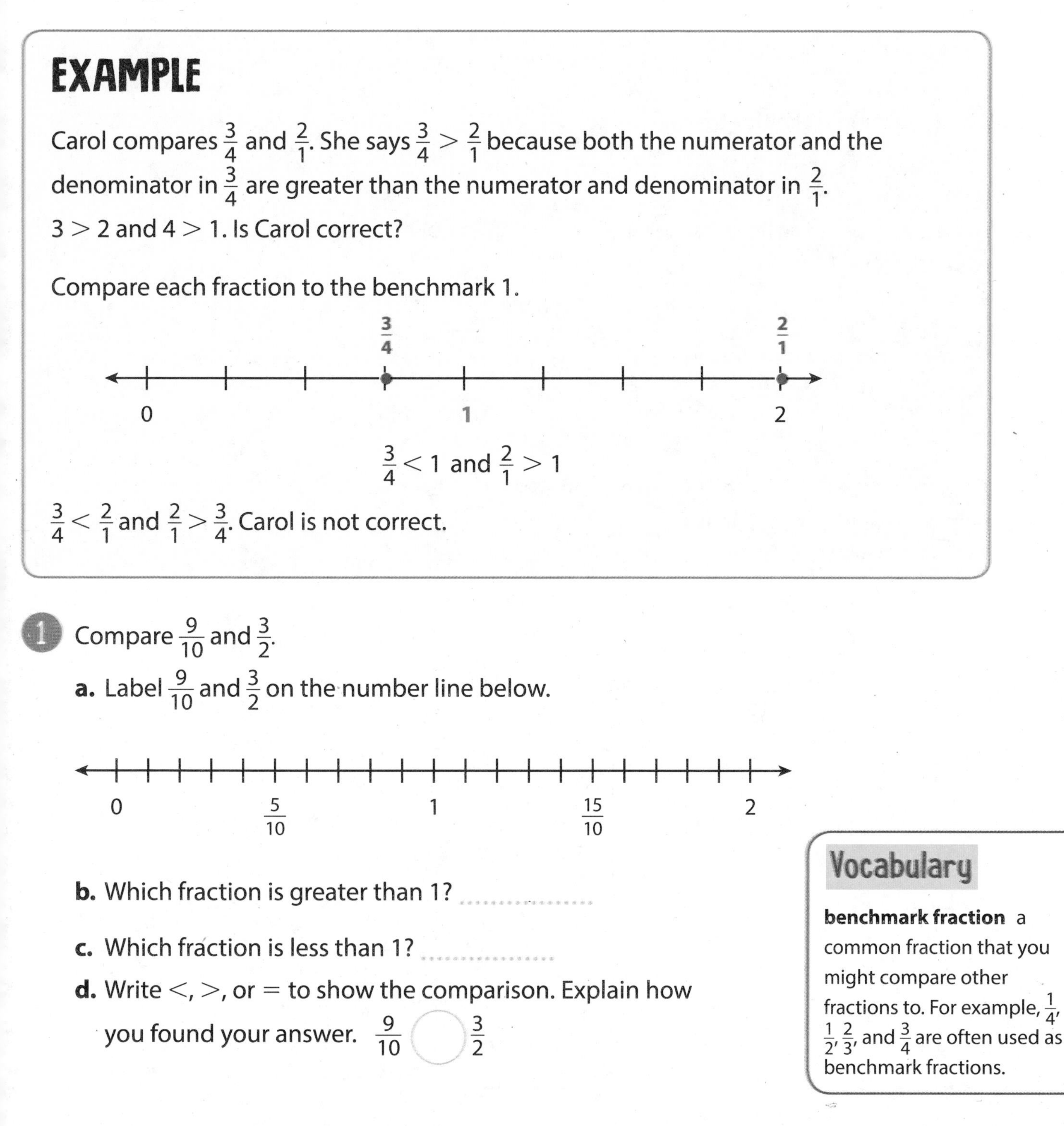

EXAMPLE

Carol compares $\frac{3}{4}$ and $\frac{2}{1}$. She says $\frac{3}{4} > \frac{2}{1}$ because both the numerator and the denominator in $\frac{3}{4}$ are greater than the numerator and denominator in $\frac{2}{1}$. $3 > 2$ and $4 > 1$. Is Carol correct?

Compare each fraction to the benchmark 1.

$\frac{3}{4} < 1$ and $\frac{2}{1} > 1$

$\frac{3}{4} < \frac{2}{1}$ and $\frac{2}{1} > \frac{3}{4}$. Carol is not correct.

1 Compare $\frac{9}{10}$ and $\frac{3}{2}$.

a. Label $\frac{9}{10}$ and $\frac{3}{2}$ on the number line below.

b. Which fraction is greater than 1? ....

c. Which fraction is less than 1? ....

d. Write $<$, $>$, or $=$ to show the comparison. Explain how you found your answer. $\frac{9}{10}$ ◯ $\frac{3}{2}$

Vocabulary

benchmark fraction a common fraction that you might compare other fractions to. For example, $\frac{1}{4}$, $\frac{1}{2}$, $\frac{2}{3}$, and $\frac{3}{4}$ are often used as benchmark fractions.

2 Compare $\frac{5}{6}$ and $\frac{1}{3}$ using the benchmark fraction $\frac{1}{2}$.

a. Label $\frac{5}{6}$ and $\frac{1}{3}$ on the number line below.

0 $\frac{1}{2}$ 1

b. Which fraction is greater than $\frac{1}{2}$? ....

c. Which fraction is less than $\frac{1}{2}$? ....

d. Write $<$, $>$, or $=$ to show the comparison. Explain how you found your answer.

$\frac{5}{6}$ ◯ $\frac{1}{3}$

3 Use a benchmark fraction to compare the fractions $\frac{7}{10}$ and $\frac{5}{12}$. Explain how you found your answer.

4 Write *True* or *False* for each comparison. Then write the benchmark you could use to compare the fractions.

	True* or *False	**Benchmark**
$\frac{9}{8} > \frac{11}{12}$		
$\frac{2}{5} < \frac{5}{6}$		
$\frac{7}{10} < \frac{2}{4}$		
$\frac{4}{5} > \frac{2}{2}$		
$\frac{3}{2} < \frac{9}{10}$		

Refine Comparing Fractions

Complete the Example below. Then solve problems 1–9.

EXAMPLE

Becker catches a fish that is $\frac{3}{12}$ of a yard long. The fish has to be longer than $\frac{1}{3}$ of a yard in order to keep it. Can Becker keep the fish?

Look at how you could show your work using a number line.

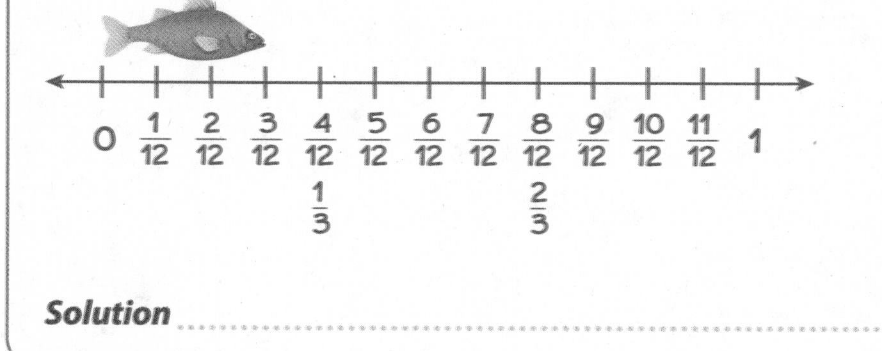

Solution ....

It is important that both measurements use the same unit!

PAIR/SHARE
How else could you solve this problem?

APPLY IT

1 Myron and Jane work on the same set of homework problems. Myron finishes $\frac{5}{6}$ of the problems, and Jane finishes $\frac{2}{3}$ of the problems. Who finishes more of their homework problems? Show your work.

Solution ....

Which strategy for comparing do you think works best with these fractions?

PAIR/SHARE
How did you and your partner decide what strategy to use to solve the problem?

2 Compare the fractions $\frac{3}{10}$ and $\frac{7}{12}$ using the benchmark fraction $\frac{1}{2}$. Show your work.

You already know about how big $\frac{1}{2}$ is!

Solution

PAIR/SHARE
Draw a model to check your answer.

3 Janelle walks $\frac{3}{6}$ of a mile. Pedro walks $\frac{6}{10}$ of a mile. Which statement shows how to find the greater fraction?

There are several ways to compare fractions!

Ⓐ $\frac{3}{6} = \frac{6}{12}$ and $\frac{6}{12} < \frac{6}{10}$

Ⓑ $\frac{3}{6} = \frac{6}{12}$ and $\frac{6}{12} > \frac{6}{10}$

Ⓒ $\frac{6}{10} = \frac{3}{5}$ and $\frac{3}{5} < \frac{3}{6}$

Ⓓ $\frac{3}{6} < \frac{1}{2}$ and $\frac{6}{10} > \frac{1}{2}$

Tina chose Ⓑ as the correct answer. How did she get that answer?

PAIR/SHARE
How can you find the answer using a benchmark fraction?

4 Grant uses $\frac{2}{3}$ of a cup of raisins and $\frac{3}{4}$ of a cup of almonds to make trail mix. Which statement can be used to find out if there are more raisins or almonds in the trail mix?

Ⓐ $\frac{2}{3} = \frac{8}{12}$ and $\frac{3}{4} = \frac{9}{12}$

Ⓑ $\frac{2}{3} = \frac{4}{6}$ and $\frac{3}{4} = \frac{4}{5}$

Ⓒ $\frac{2}{3} = \frac{6}{9}$ and $\frac{3}{4} = \frac{6}{12}$

Ⓓ $\frac{2}{3} = \frac{6}{9}$ and $\frac{3}{4} = \frac{6}{7}$

5 Select $>$, $<$, or $=$ to complete a true comparison for each pair of fractions.

	$>$	$<$	$=$
$\frac{8}{3} \square \frac{9}{4}$	Ⓐ	Ⓑ	Ⓒ
$\frac{7}{10} \square \frac{7}{8}$	Ⓓ	Ⓔ	Ⓕ
$\frac{1}{2} \square \frac{3}{8}$	Ⓖ	Ⓗ	Ⓘ
$\frac{2}{4} \square \frac{4}{6}$	Ⓙ	Ⓚ	Ⓛ
$\frac{7}{5} \square \frac{140}{100}$	Ⓜ	Ⓝ	Ⓞ

6 Sam's music teacher tells him to practice his trombone for $\frac{5}{10}$ of an hour. Sam practices for $\frac{2}{6}$ of an hour. Does he practice long enough? Show your work.

Sam .... practice long enough.

7 Compare the fractions $\frac{5}{10}$ and $\frac{5}{8}$. Write the symbol $>$, $<$, or $=$.

$\frac{5}{10}$ ◯ $\frac{5}{8}$

8 Rachel and Sierra have the same number of boxes of fruit to sell for a fundraiser. Each box is the same size. Rachel sells $\frac{9}{10}$ of her boxes, and Sierra sells $\frac{5}{8}$ of her boxes. Which girl sells a greater fraction of her boxes of fruit? Draw a model to show your answer. Show your work.

.... sells a greater fraction of her boxes of fruit.

MATH JOURNAL

Jeff says $\frac{3}{4}$ of a small pizza is more than $\frac{1}{3}$ of a large pizza. Alicia disagrees. Who is right? Do you have enough information to know who is right? Explain.

☑ **SELF CHECK** Go back to the Unit 4 Opener and see what you can check off.

Understand Fraction Addition and Subtraction

LESSON 19

Dear Family,

This week your child is exploring fraction addition and subtraction.

Adding fractions means joining or putting together parts of the same whole. When you add $\frac{3}{4}$ and $\frac{2}{4}$, you are putting one-fourths together.

- You can use a number line to show $\frac{3}{4} + \frac{2}{4} = \frac{5}{4}$.

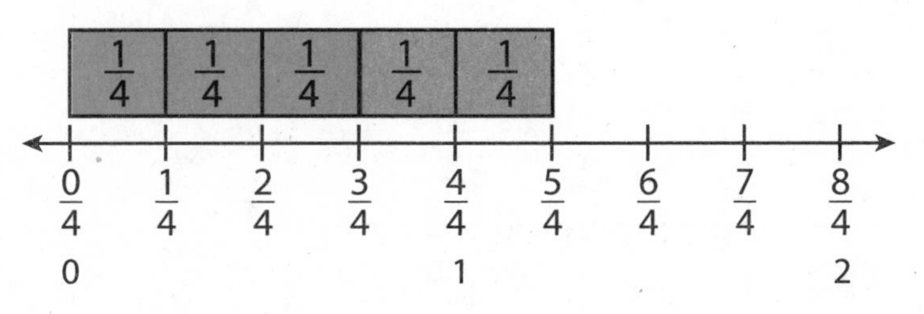

Subtracting fractions means separating or taking away. When you subtract $\frac{3}{4}$ from $\frac{5}{4}$, you are taking away one-fourths.

- You can use a number line to show fraction subtraction, too.

The number line below shows $\frac{5}{4} - \frac{3}{4} = \frac{2}{4}$.

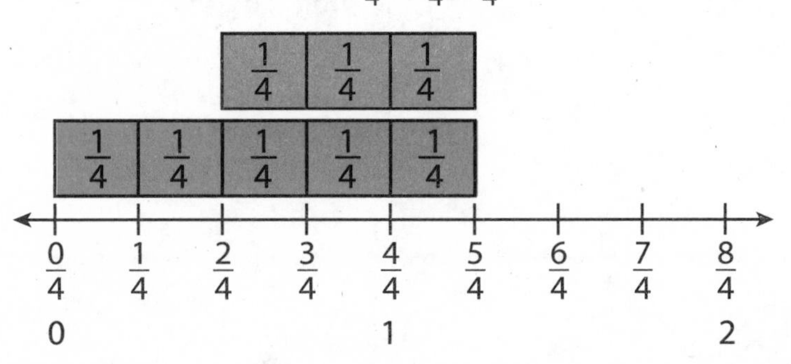

Adding and subtracting fractions is just like adding and subtracting whole numbers. When the denominators of the fractions are the same, you can just add or subtract the numerators.

Invite your child to share what he or she knows about fraction addition and subtraction by doing the following activity together.

ACTIVITY FRACTION ADDITION AND SUBTRACTION

Do this activity with your child to explore adding and subtracting fractions.

Materials 1 piece of fruit (or a picture of 1 piece of fruit)

- Cut the fruit (or the picture of fruit) into sixths.

  Explain that the 6 pieces should be the same size, so each piece is $\frac{1}{6}$ of the whole.

- Have your child take some of the pieces.
  You take some of the pieces.

- Now talk about putting your pieces of fruit together.
  Ask: *How much of the whole fruit do you have together?*

  Example: Your child takes $\frac{2}{6}$. You take $\frac{3}{6}$.

  Together you have $\frac{5}{6}$ of the fruit.

- Put your and your child's pieces of fruit together and look at the total.
  Have your child take some of the pieces.
  Ask: *How much of the whole fruit is left?*

  Example: Your child takes 3 pieces.

  Start with $\frac{5}{6}$. Take away $\frac{3}{6}$.

  That means $\frac{2}{6}$ of the fruit is left.

- Look for other real-life opportunities to explore adding and subtracting fractions with your child.

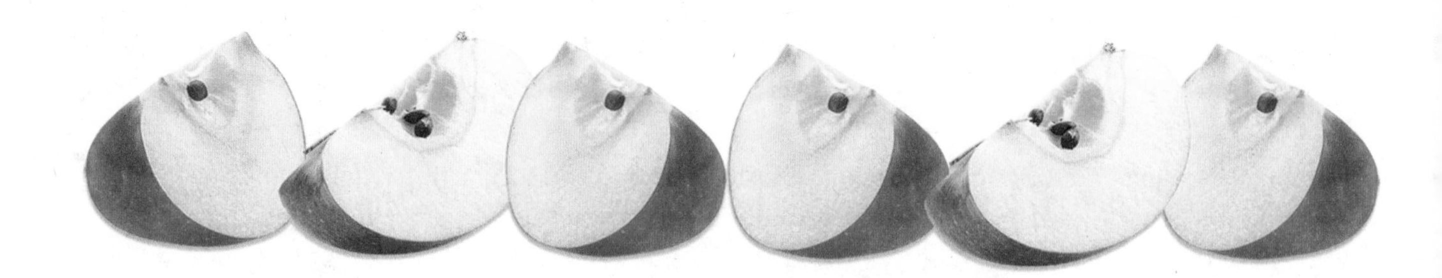

Explore Fraction Addition and Subtraction

What is really going on when you add and subtract numbers?

Learning Target

- Understand a fraction $\frac{a}{b}$ with $a > 1$ as a sum of fractions $\frac{1}{b}$.
  - Understand addition and subtraction of fractions as joining and separating parts referring to the same whole.

SMP 1, 2, 3, 4, 5, 6, 7, 8

MODEL IT

Complete the models below.

1. Show how to find 2 + 3 using a number line.

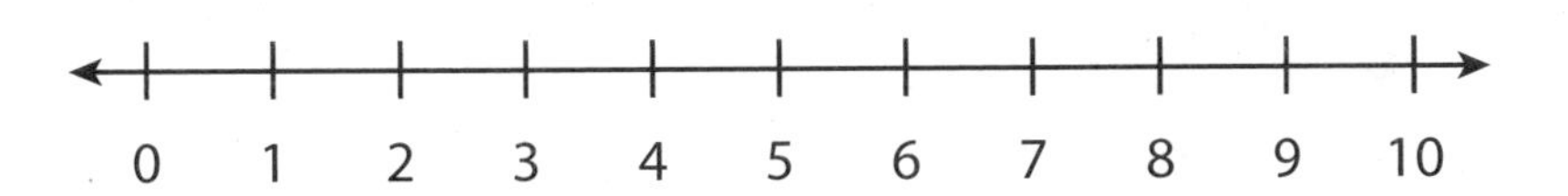

2. Think about how you could show $\frac{2}{4} + \frac{3}{4}$ on the number line.

   Show your work.

$\frac{0}{4}$ $\frac{1}{4}$ $\frac{2}{4}$ $\frac{3}{4}$ $\frac{4}{4}$ $\frac{5}{4}$ $\frac{6}{4}$ $\frac{7}{4}$ $\frac{8}{4}$

0 1 2

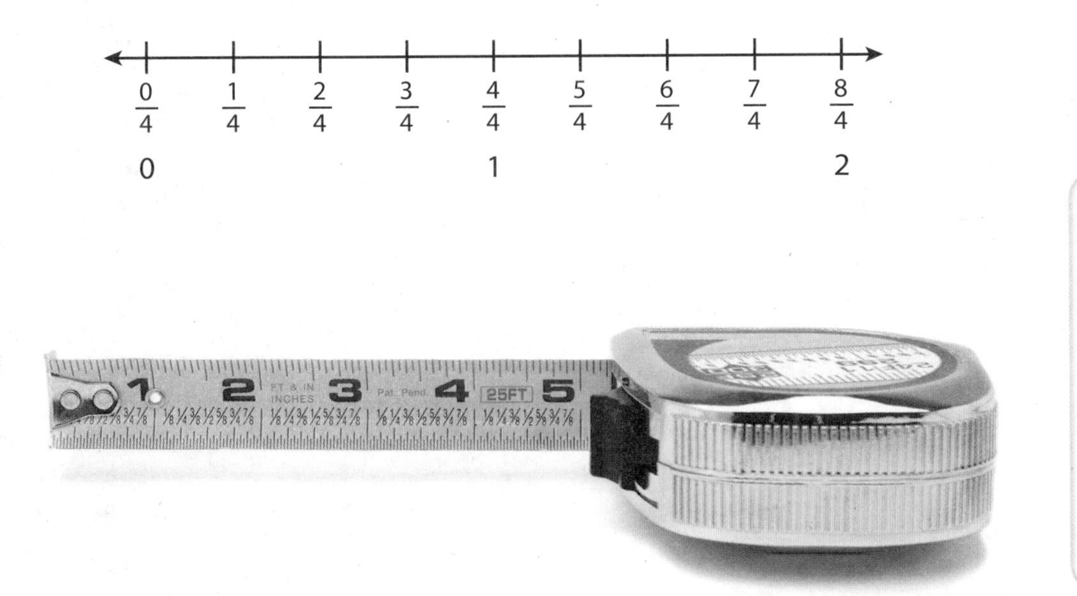

DISCUSS IT

- Compare your number lines to your partner's number lines. Are they the same?
- I think adding fractions is like adding whole numbers because . . .

MODEL IT

Complete the models below.

3 Draw to show 5 − 2 on the number line.

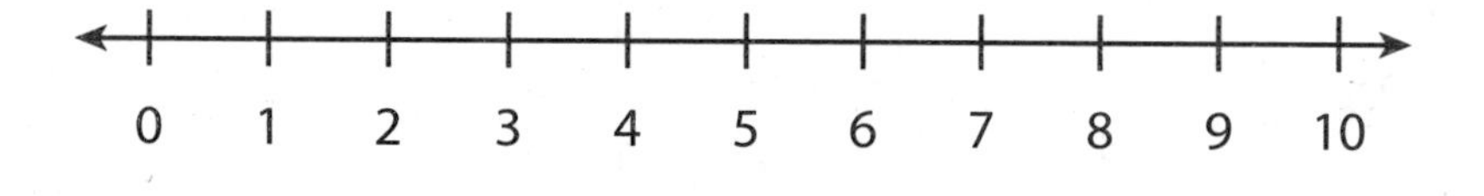

4 Think about how to show $\frac{5}{4} - \frac{2}{4}$ on the number line.

Show your work.

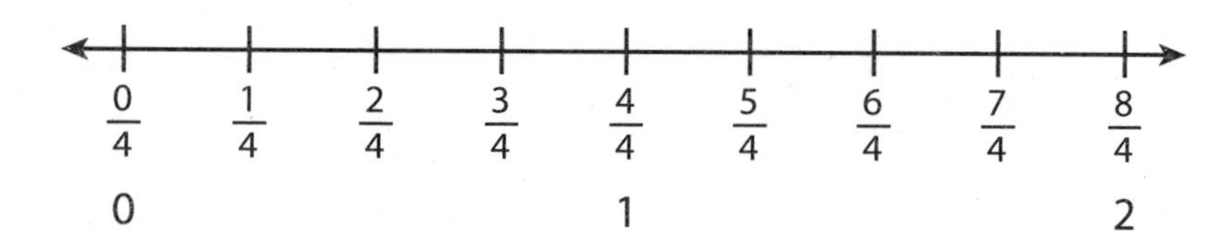

DISCUSS IT

- How did you and your partner decide which fraction to start with?
- I think subtracting fractions is like subtracting whole numbers because . . .
  I think subtracting fractions is different from subtracting whole numbers because . . .

5 REFLECT

Compare a number line model for adding whole numbers and a number line model for adding fractions. How are they the same? How are they different?

Name: ______________________________

Prepare for Fraction Addition and Subtraction

1. Think about what you know about unit fractions. Fill in each box. Use pictures, words, and numbers. Show as many ideas as you can.

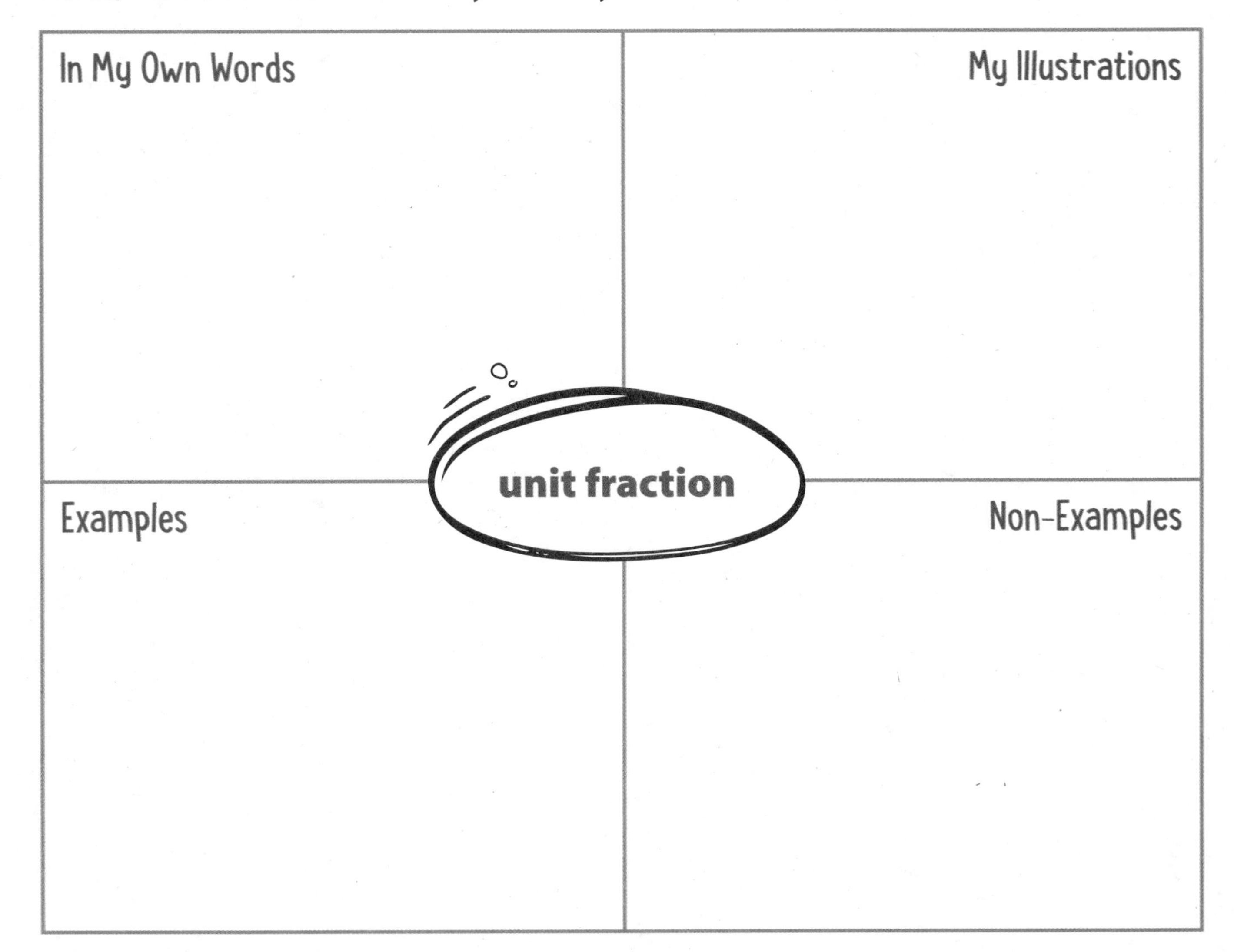

2. Show $\frac{3}{8}$ using unit fractions.

Solve.

3. Show 3 + 4 and $\frac{3}{6} + \frac{4}{6}$ on the number lines below.

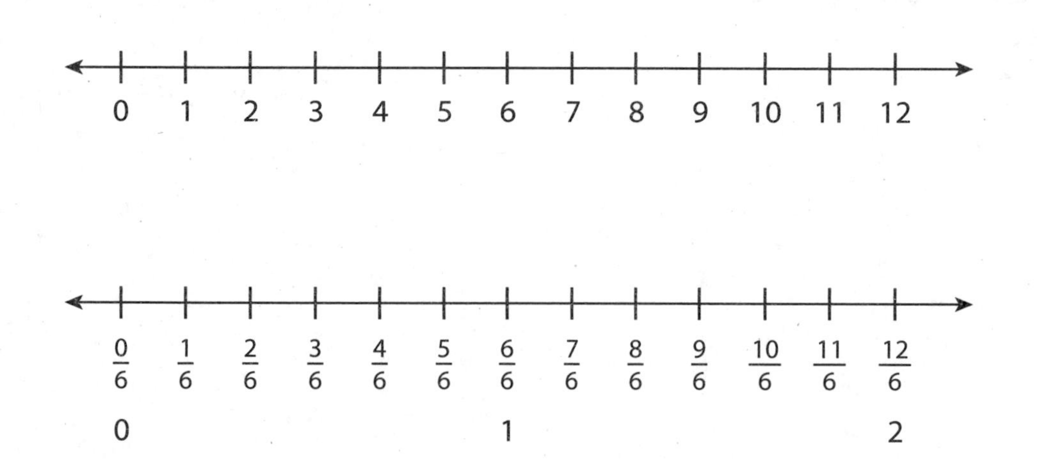

4. Look at problem 3. How are adding whole numbers and adding fractions alike? How are they different?

5. Show $\frac{7}{5} - \frac{5}{5}$ on the number line below.

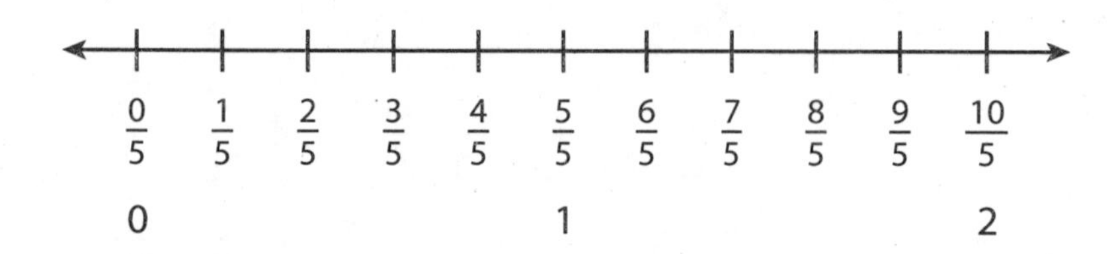

Develop Understanding of Fraction Addition and Subtraction

MODEL IT: NUMBER LINES

Try these two problems.

1 Label the number line below and use it to show $\frac{2}{4} + \frac{1}{4}$.

Write the sum. ....

DISCUSS IT

- Did you and your partner show adding and subtracting on the number lines the same way?
- I think number lines model adding and subtracting with fractions because . . .

2 Label the number line below and use it to show $\frac{4}{5} - \frac{2}{5}$.

Write the difference. ....

MODEL IT: AREA MODELS

Use the area models to show adding or subtracting fractions.

3 Show $\frac{1}{8} + \frac{2}{8}$.

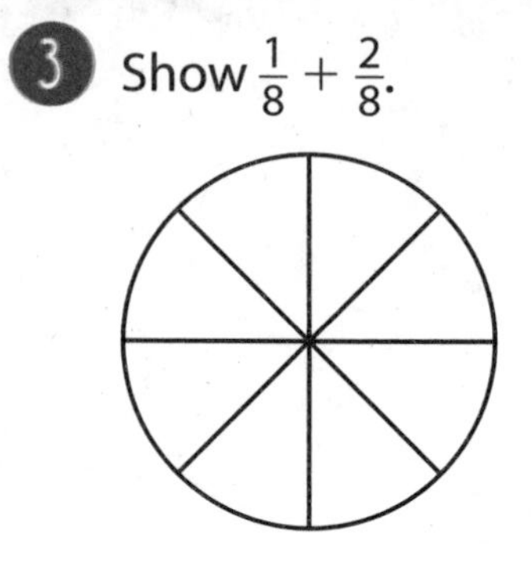

4 Show $\frac{6}{10} - \frac{2}{10}$.

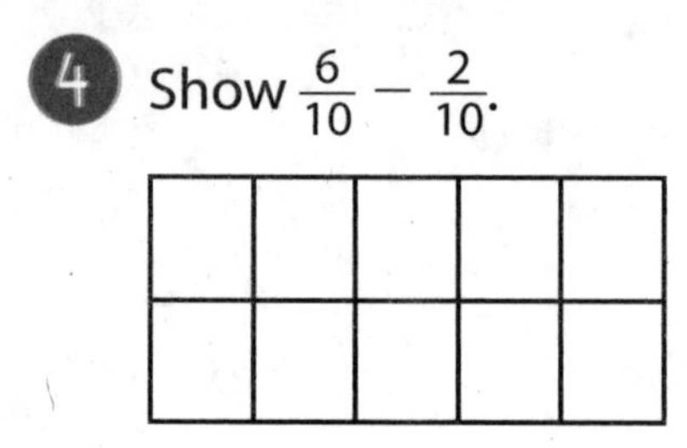

DISCUSS IT

- How did you know how many equal parts to show in each model?
- I think the two different area models show fractions because . . .

CONNECT IT

Complete the problems below.

5 How are the number lines and the area models alike? How are they different?

6 Choose any model you like to show $\frac{5}{10} - \frac{3}{10}$.

Name: ______________________________

Practice Fraction Addition and Subtraction

Study how the Example shows adding fractions.
Then solve problems 1–12.

EXAMPLE

You can count on or count back to add or subtract whole numbers. You can do the same to add or subtract fractions.

To add fourths, use a number line that shows fourths.

Add $\frac{3}{4}$ and $\frac{2}{4}$.

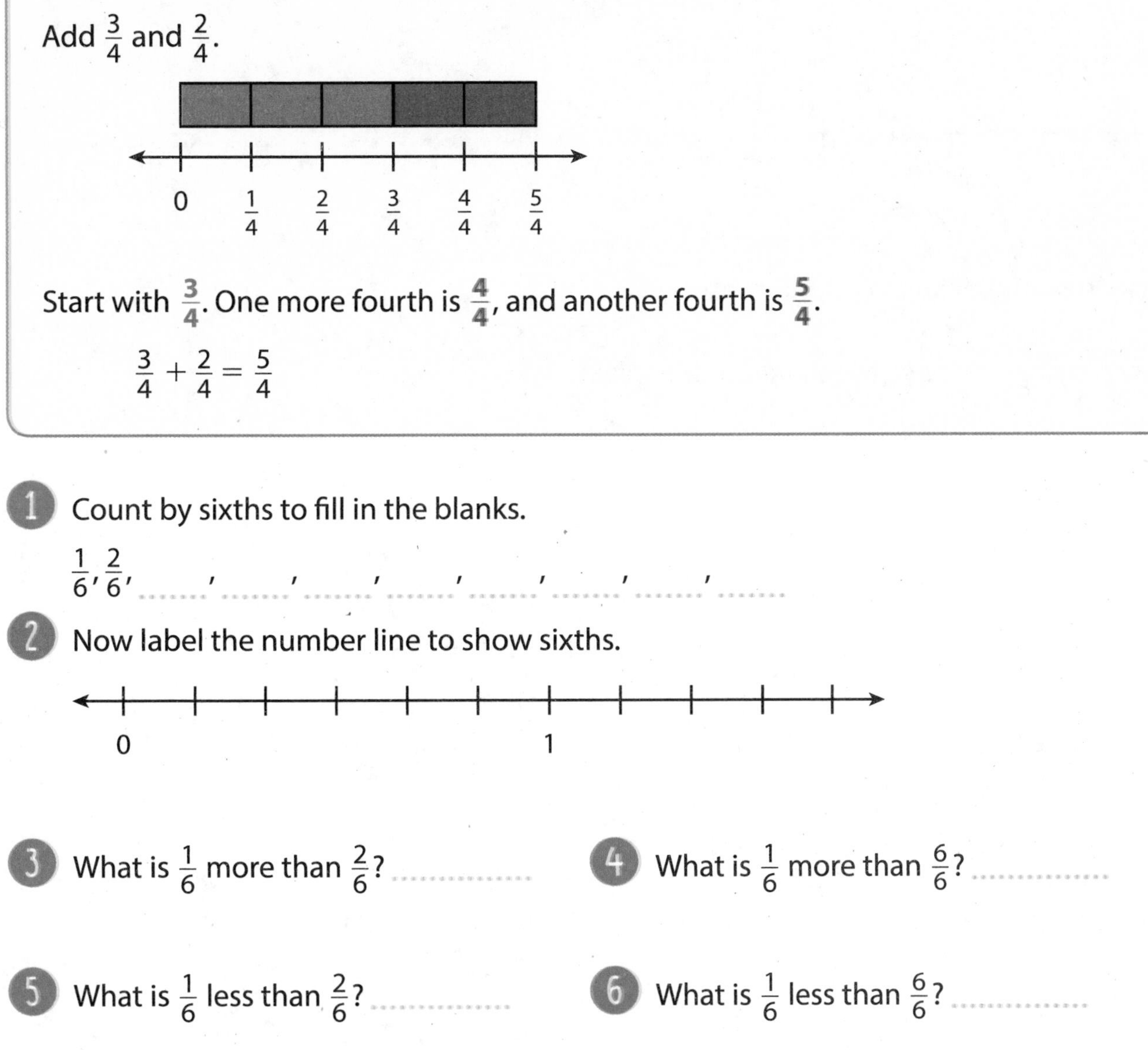

Start with $\frac{3}{4}$. One more fourth is $\frac{4}{4}$, and another fourth is $\frac{5}{4}$.

$$\frac{3}{4} + \frac{2}{4} = \frac{5}{4}$$

1. Count by sixths to fill in the blanks.

   $\frac{1}{6}$, $\frac{2}{6}$, ______, ______, ______, ______, ______, ______, ______, ______

2. Now label the number line to show sixths.

   0   1

3. What is $\frac{1}{6}$ more than $\frac{2}{6}$? ______

4. What is $\frac{1}{6}$ more than $\frac{6}{6}$? ______

5. What is $\frac{1}{6}$ less than $\frac{2}{6}$? ______

6. What is $\frac{1}{6}$ less than $\frac{6}{6}$? ______

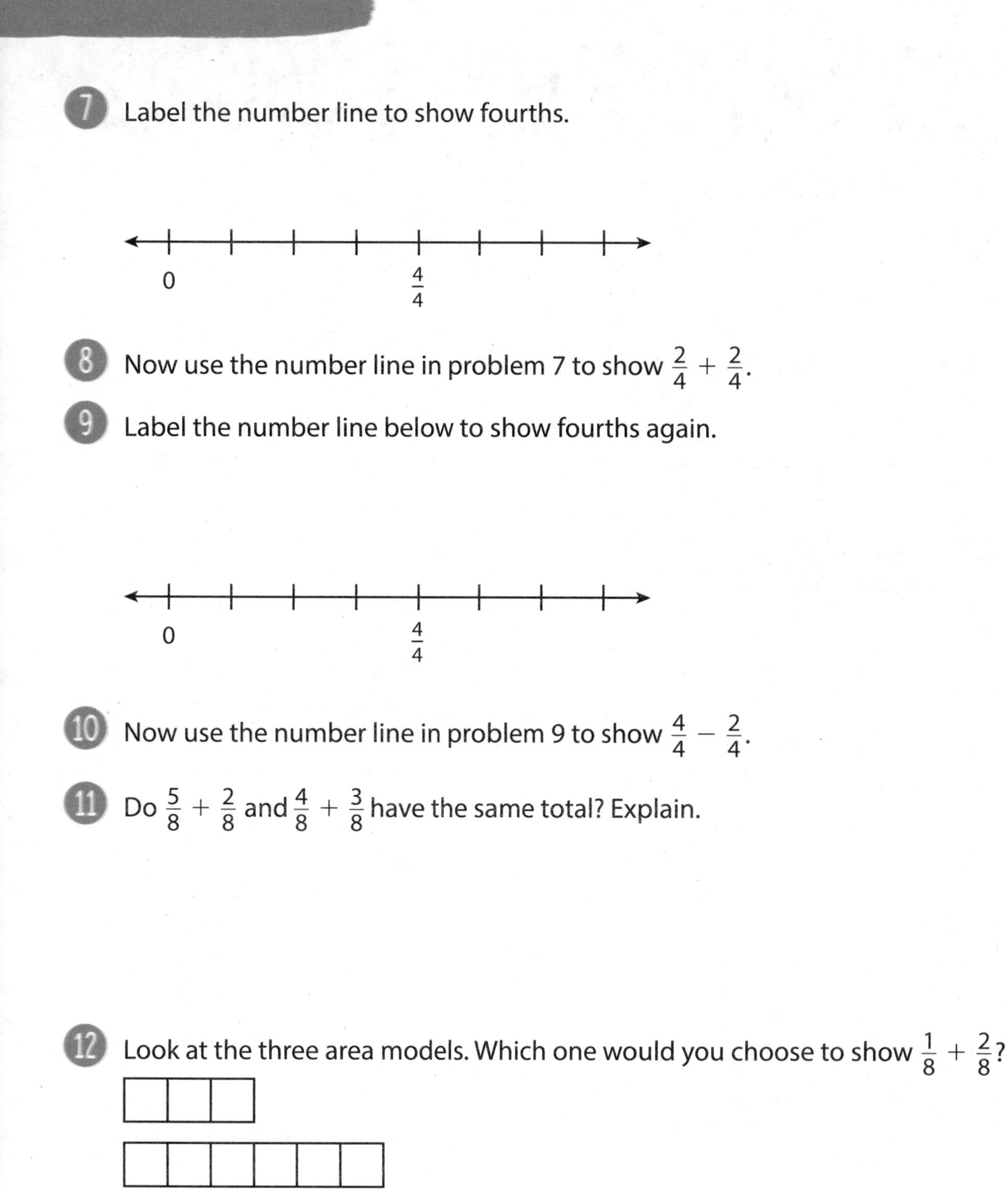

7 Label the number line to show fourths.

8 Now use the number line in problem 7 to show $\frac{2}{4} + \frac{2}{4}$.

9 Label the number line below to show fourths again.

10 Now use the number line in problem 9 to show $\frac{4}{4} - \frac{2}{4}$.

11 Do $\frac{5}{8} + \frac{2}{8}$ and $\frac{4}{8} + \frac{3}{8}$ have the same total? Explain.

12 Look at the three area models. Which one would you choose to show $\frac{1}{8} + \frac{2}{8}$?

Explain how the denominator of the fraction helps you choose the model.

Refine Ideas About Fraction Addition and Subtraction

APPLY IT

Complete these problems on your own.

1 COMPARE

Draw two different models to show $\frac{2}{3} - \frac{1}{3}$.

2 EXPLAIN

Rob has a large pizza and a small pizza. He cuts each pizza into fourths. He takes one fourth from each pizza and uses the following problem to show their sum: $\frac{1}{4} + \frac{1}{4} = \frac{2}{4}$. What does Rob do wrong?

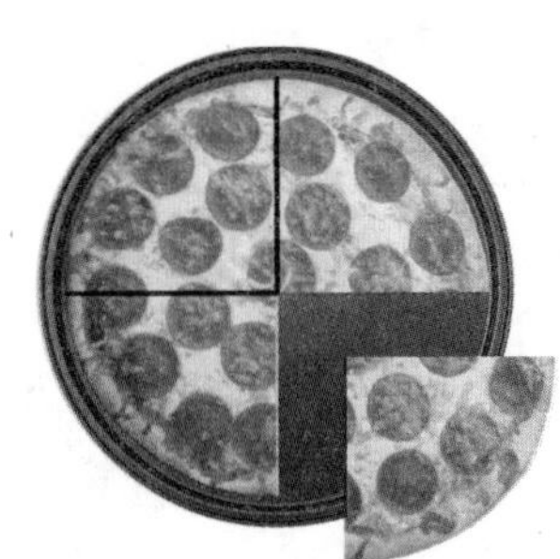

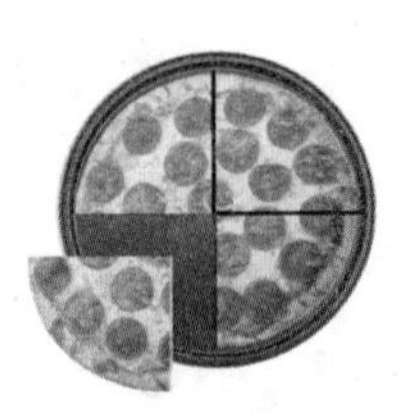

3 DEMONSTRATE

Think about how you add three whole numbers. You start by adding two of the numbers. Then you add the third number to that sum. You add three fractions the same way.

Use the number line and area model below to show $\frac{1}{10} + \frac{3}{10} + \frac{4}{10}$.

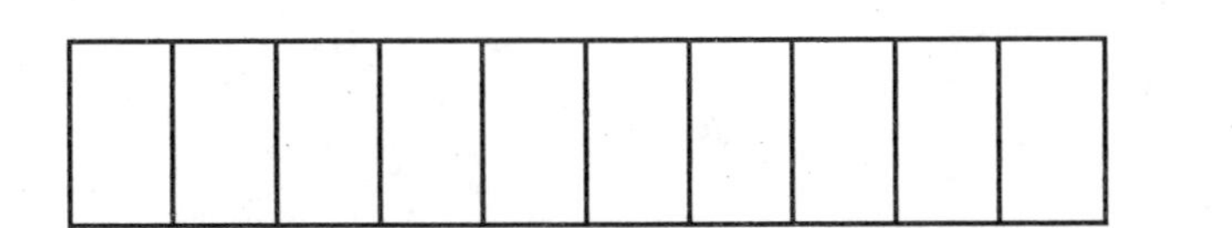

PAIR/SHARE

Discuss your solutions for these three problems with a partner.

Use what you have learned to complete problem 4.

4 Jen has $\frac{4}{10}$ of a kilogram of dog food. Luis has $\frac{3}{10}$ of a kilogram of dog food. A large dog eats $\frac{2}{10}$ of a kilogram in one meal.

Part A Write two different questions about this problem that involve adding or subtracting fractions.

Question 1:

Question 2:

Part B Choose one of your questions to model. Circle the question you choose. Show the addition or subtraction using a number line and an area model.

MATH JOURNAL

5 Look at the expression $\frac{1}{8} + \frac{1}{8} + \frac{1}{8} + \frac{1}{8} + \frac{1}{8}$. Is this sum greater than, less than, or equal to $\frac{5}{8}$? Explain how you know.

Add and Subtract Fractions

LESSON 20

Dear Family,

This week your child is learning how to add and subtract fractions with like denominators.

Fractions with the same number below the line have like denominators.

like denominators: $\frac{1}{4}$ and $\frac{3}{4}$ unlike denominators: $\frac{1}{2}$ and $\frac{3}{4}$

To find the sum of fractions with like denominators, understand that you are adding like units. Just as 3 apples plus 2 apples is 5 apples, 3 eighths plus 2 eighths is 5 eighths. Similarly, when you take away, or subtract, 2 eighths from 5 eighths, you have 3 eighths left.

$\frac{3}{8} + \frac{2}{8} = \frac{5}{8}$

You can also use a number line to understand adding and subtracting like fractions.

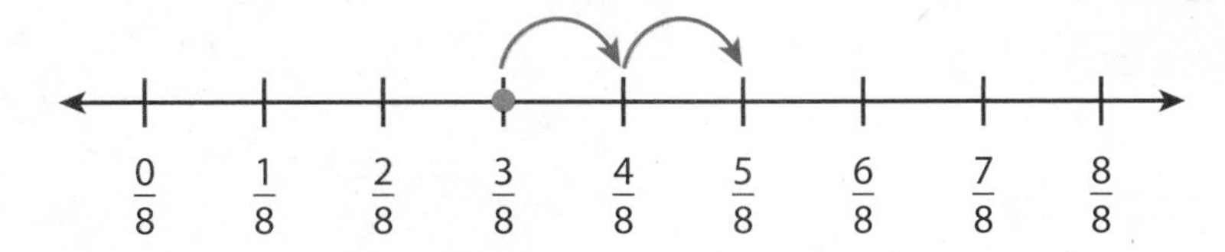

Remember that the denominator names units the same way that "apples" names units.

So, when you add two fractions with like denominators, the sum of the numerators tells how many of those units you have.

When you subtract two fractions with like denominators, the difference of the numerators tells how many of those units you have.

Invite your child to share what he or she knows about adding and subtracting fractions by doing the following activity together.

ACTIVITY ADDING AND SUBTRACTING FRACTIONS

Do this activity with your child to add and subtract fractions.

Materials bowl, measuring cup, ingredients shown in the recipe

Follow the recipe below to make a creamy cracker spread or veggie dip.

Creamy Spread

Ingredients

$\frac{5}{8}$ cup cream cheese

$\frac{2}{8}$ cup sour cream

herbs

crackers or veggies

Directions

Mix the cream cheese, sour cream, and herbs together in a medium bowl. Serve immediately with crackers or sliced fresh veggies. Enjoy!

After you have made the spread, ask your child questions such as these:

1. *What fraction of a cup is the total amount of spread?*
2. *If you spread $\frac{1}{8}$ of a cup on crackers or veggies, how much spread is left?*

Make up a simple recipe using fractions for someone else in the family to make!

Answers: **1.** $\frac{7}{8}$ cup; **2.** $\frac{6}{8}$ cup

Explore Adding and Subtracting Fractions

Previously, you learned that adding fractions is similar to adding whole numbers. Use what you know to try to solve the problem below.

Learning Targets

- Decompose a fraction into a sum of fractions with the same denominator in more than one way, recording each decomposition by an equation. Justify decompositions, e.g., by using a visual fraction model.
- Solve word problems involving addition and subtraction of fractions referring to the same whole and having like denominators.

SMP 1, 2, 3, 4, 5, 6, 7

Lynn, Paco, and Todd share a pack of 12 cards. Lynn gets 4 cards, Paco gets 3 cards, and Todd gets the rest of the cards. What fraction of the pack does Todd get?

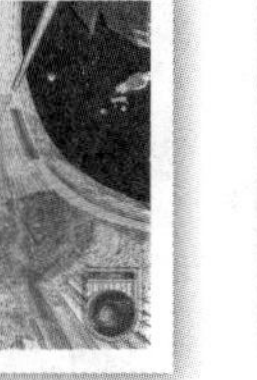
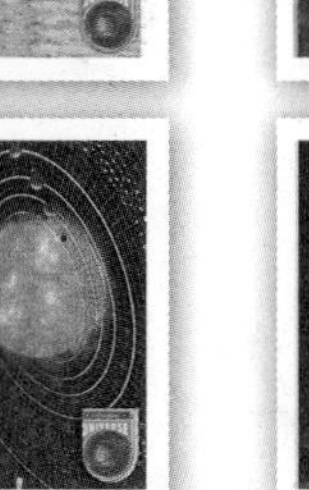

TRY IT

Math Toolkit

- counters
- fraction circles
- fraction tiles
- fraction bars
- number lines
- fraction models

DISCUSS IT

Ask your partner: Why did you choose that strategy?

Tell your partner: At first, I thought . . .

CONNECT IT

1 LOOK BACK

Explain how you can find the fraction of the pack that Todd gets.

2 LOOK AHEAD

In the problem on the previous page, the whole is the pack of cards. Since there are 12 cards in the pack, each card represents $\frac{1}{12}$ of the whole. Look at the whole shown here. The whole is the pizza. It is a single object.

a. How many equal parts are shown in the pizza? ....

b. What fraction can you use to describe each piece of pizza? ....

c. What fraction can you use to describe the whole? ....

d. What fraction can you use to describe the 3 pieces being taken away? ....

3 REFLECT

How does knowing about equal parts help you add and subtract fractions?

....

....

....

....

....

Name: ______________________________

Prepare for Adding and Subtracting Fractions

1 Think about what you know about fractions. Fill in each box. Use words, numbers, and pictures. Show as many ideas as you can.

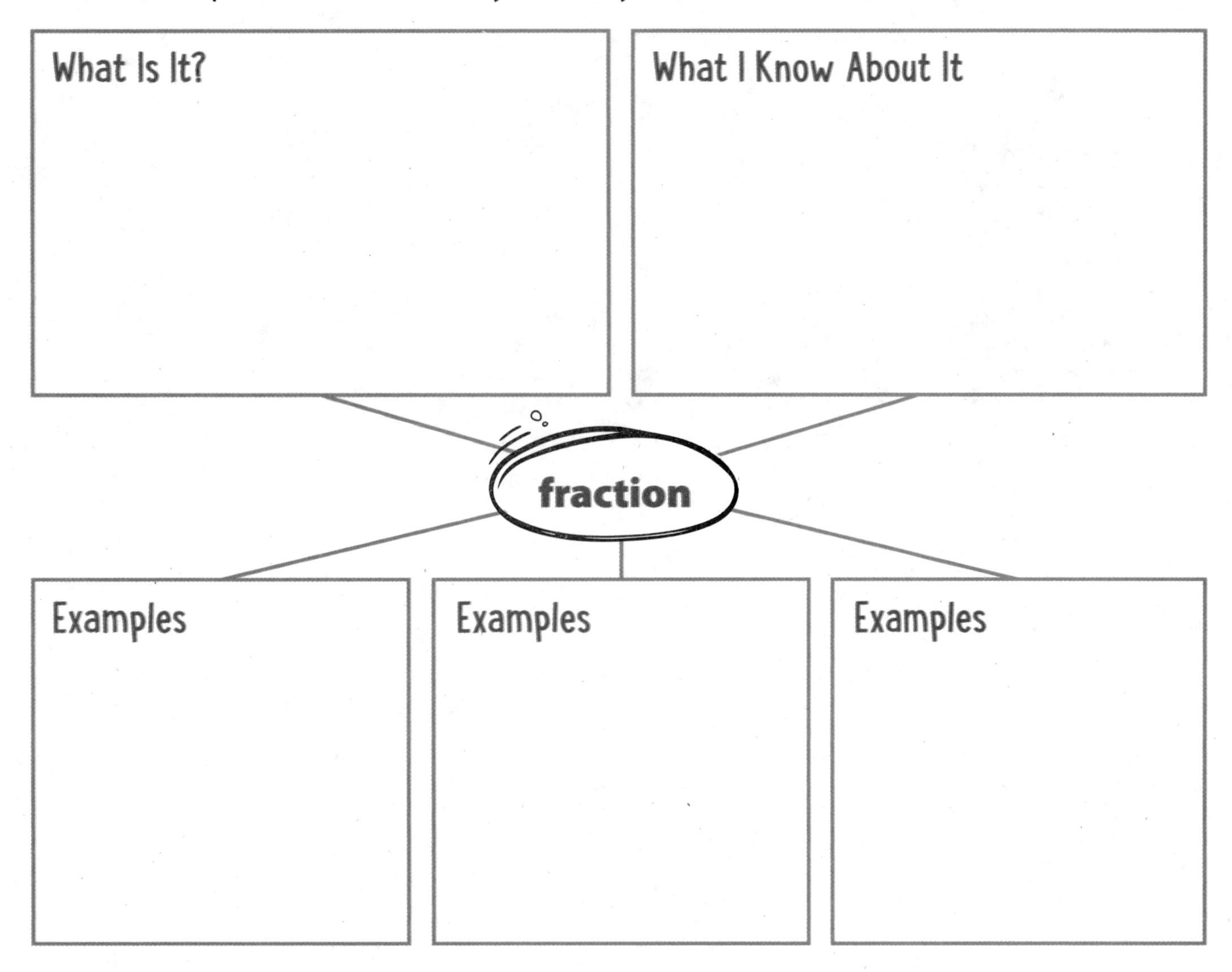

2 Does the model below show eighths? Why or why not?

$\frac{1}{8}$	$\frac{1}{8}$	$\frac{1}{8}$	$\frac{1}{8}$	$\frac{1}{8}$	$\frac{1}{8}$	$\frac{1}{8}$	$\frac{1}{8}$

3 Solve the problem. Show your work.

Maria, Jon, and Kara share a set of 10 animal stickers. Maria gets 2 stickers, Jon gets 4 stickers, and Kara gets the rest of the stickers. What fraction of the stickers does Kara get?

Solution ....

4 Check your answer. Show your work.

Develop Adding Fractions

Read and try to solve the problem below.

Josie and Margo are painting a fence green. Josie starts at one end and paints $\frac{3}{10}$ of the fence. Margo starts at the other end and paints $\frac{4}{10}$ of it. What fraction of the fence do they paint altogether?

TRY IT

Math Toolkit

- fraction circles
- fraction tiles
- fraction bars
- number lines
- index cards
- fraction models

DISCUSS IT

Ask your partner: How did you get started?

Tell your partner:
A model I used was . . .
It helped me . . .

Explore different ways to understand adding fractions.

Josie and Margo are painting a fence green. Josie starts at one end and paints $\frac{3}{10}$ of the fence. Margo starts at the other end and paints $\frac{4}{10}$ of it. What fraction of the fence do they paint altogether?

PICTURE IT

You can use a picture to help understand the problem.

Think what the fence might look like if it has 10 equal-sized parts.

Each part is $\frac{1}{10}$ of the whole.

The girls paint 3 tenths and 4 tenths of the fence.

MODEL IT

You can also use a number line to help understand the problem.

The number line below is divided into tenths with a point at $\frac{3}{10}$.

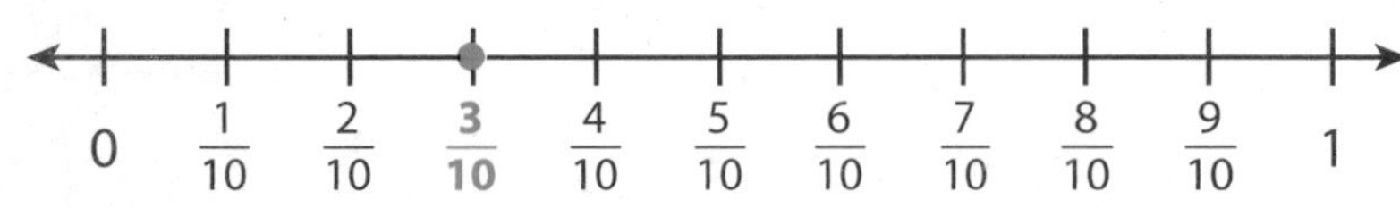

Start at $\frac{3}{10}$ and count 4 tenths to the right to **add** $\frac{4}{10}$.

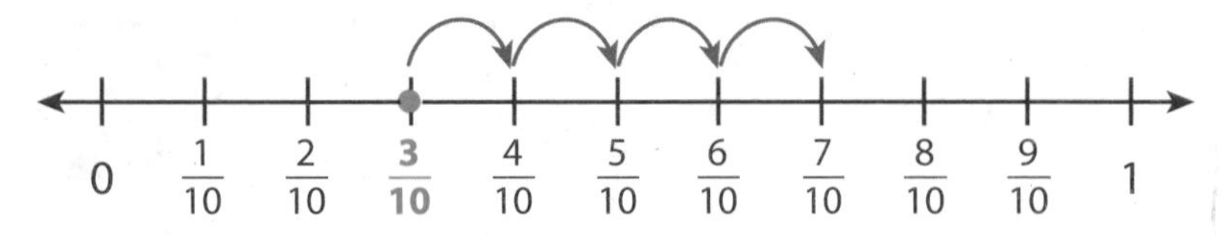

CONNECT IT

Now you will use the problem from the previous page to help you understand how to add any two fractions that have the same denominator.

1. Look at **Picture It**. How do you know that each section of fence is $\frac{1}{10}$ of the whole fence?

2. What do the numerators, 3 and 4, tell you?

3. How many tenths of the fence do Josie and Margo paint altogether? ....

4. Complete the equations to show what fraction of the fence Josie and Margo painted altogether.

Use words:	**3 tenths**	+	**4 tenths**	=	...... tenths
Use fractions:	$\frac{3}{10}$	+	$\frac{4}{10}$	=	$\frac{\square}{10}$

5. What would be the sum if the fractions were $\frac{3}{10}$ and $\frac{5}{10}$? ....

6. Explain how you add fractions that have the same denominator.

7. ## REFLECT

Look back at your **Try It**, strategies by classmates, and **Picture It** and **Model It**. Which models or strategies do you like best for adding fractions? Explain.

....

....

....

....

APPLY IT

Use what you just learned to solve these problems.

8 Lita and Otis help their mom clean the house. Lita cleans $\frac{1}{3}$ of the house. Otis cleans $\frac{1}{3}$ of the house. What fraction of the house do Lita and Otis clean altogether? Show your work.

Solution ....

9 Mark and Imani use string for a project. Mark's string is $\frac{1}{5}$ of a meter long. Imani's string is $\frac{3}{5}$ of a meter long. How long are the two strings combined? Show your work.

.... of a meter

Paola makes a fruit smoothie. She uses $\frac{2}{8}$ of a pound of strawberries and $\frac{4}{8}$ of a pound of blueberries. How many pounds of fruit does she use? Show your work.

Solution ....

Name: ____________________

Practice Adding Fractions

Study the Example showing one way to add fractions. Then solve problems 1–9.

EXAMPLE

Shrina has a muffin pan that holds 12 muffins. She fills $\frac{3}{12}$ of the pan with carrot muffin batter. Then she fills $\frac{6}{12}$ with pumpkin muffin batter. What fraction of the pan does she fill?

$$\frac{3}{12} + \frac{6}{12} = \frac{9}{12}$$

So, she fills $\frac{9}{12}$ of the muffin pan.

$\frac{3}{12}$ $\frac{6}{12}$

1. Sam fills $\frac{2}{12}$ of another pan with banana muffin batter. Shade $\frac{2}{12}$ of the muffin pan diagram at the right.

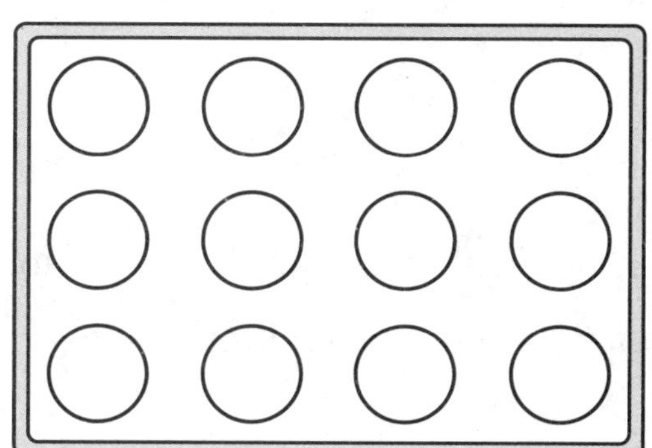

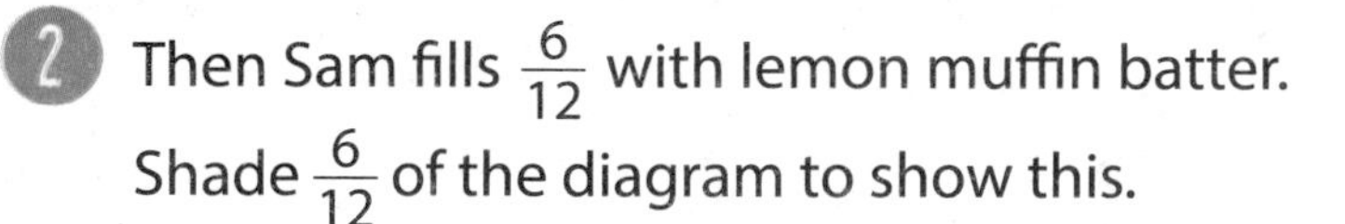

2. Then Sam fills $\frac{6}{12}$ with lemon muffin batter. Shade $\frac{6}{12}$ of the diagram to show this.

3. In problem 2, what fraction of the pan in all is filled now? ....
Write an equation for this problem that includes your answer.

Kay runs $\frac{6}{8}$ of a mile and rests. Then she runs another $\frac{6}{8}$ of a mile.

4 Divide the number line below to show eighths.

0 1 2

5 Label $\frac{6}{8}$ on the number line above.

6 Use arrows to show $\frac{6}{8} + \frac{6}{8}$ on the number line.

7 What is the total distance Kay runs? ....

8 Write an equation for this problem that includes your answer.

9 Jin cleans $\frac{1}{10}$ of the patio before lunch and $\frac{9}{10}$ of the patio after lunch. What fraction of the patio does Jin clean altogether? Show your work.

Solution ....

Develop Subtracting Fractions

Read and try to solve the problem below.

Alberto's water bottle has $\frac{5}{6}$ of a liter of water in it. He drinks $\frac{4}{6}$ of a liter. What fraction of a liter of water is left in the bottle?

TRY IT

Math Toolkit

- fraction circles
- fraction tiles
- fraction bars
- number lines
- index cards
- fraction models

DISCUSS IT

Ask your partner: Can you explain that again?

Tell your partner: I disagree with this part because . . .

Explore different ways to understand subtracting fractions.

Alberto's water bottle has $\frac{5}{6}$ of a liter of water in it. He drinks $\frac{4}{6}$ of a liter. What fraction of a liter of water is left in the bottle?

PICTURE IT

You can use a picture to help understand the problem.

The picture shows the whole liter divided into 6 equal parts.

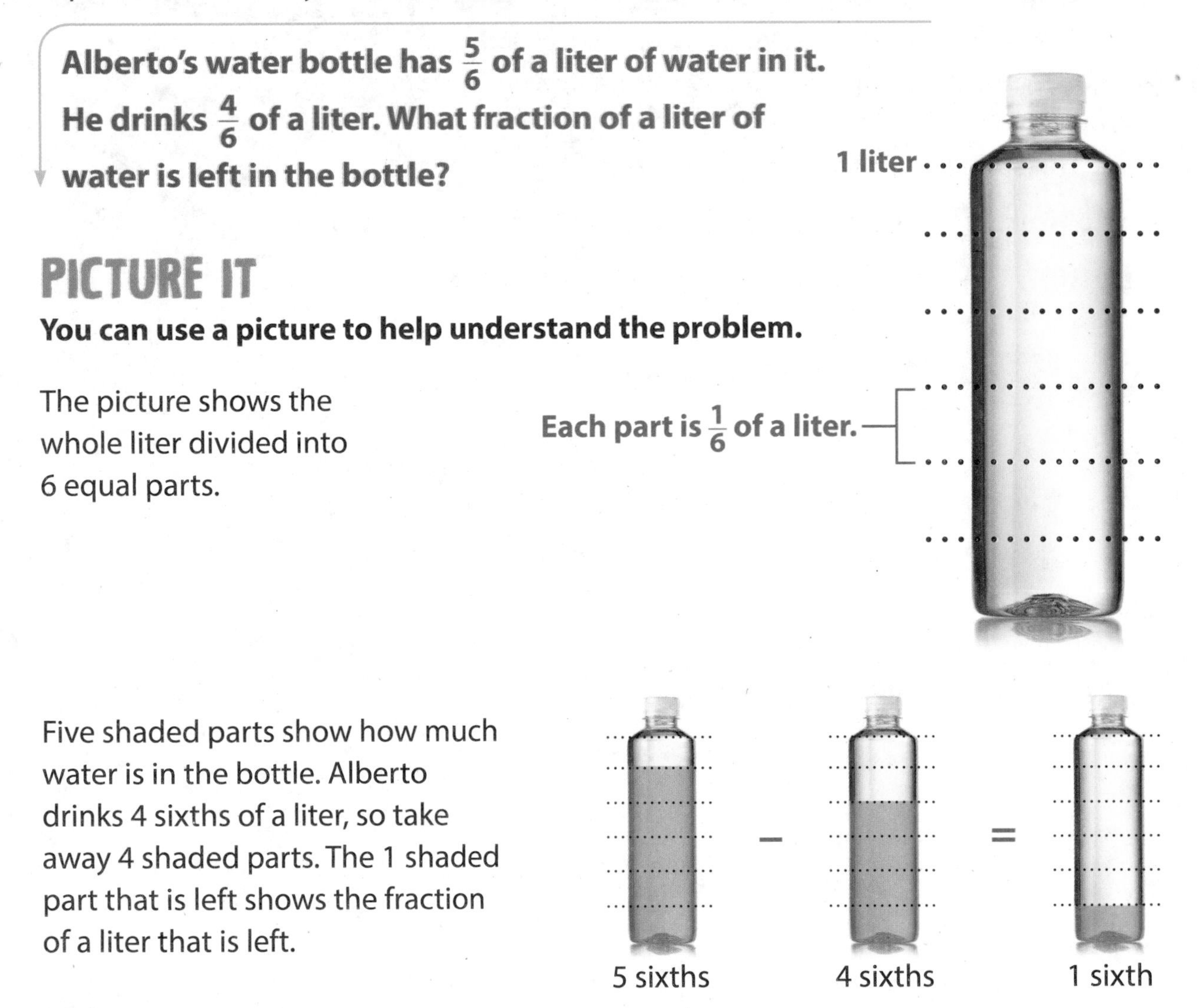

Five shaded parts show how much water is in the bottle. Alberto drinks 4 sixths of a liter, so take away 4 shaded parts. The 1 shaded part that is left shows the fraction of a liter that is left.

MODEL IT

You can also use a number line to help understand the problem.

The number line at the right is divided into sixths, with a point at $\frac{5}{6}$.

Start at $\frac{5}{6}$ and count back 4 sixths to **subtract** $\frac{4}{6}$.

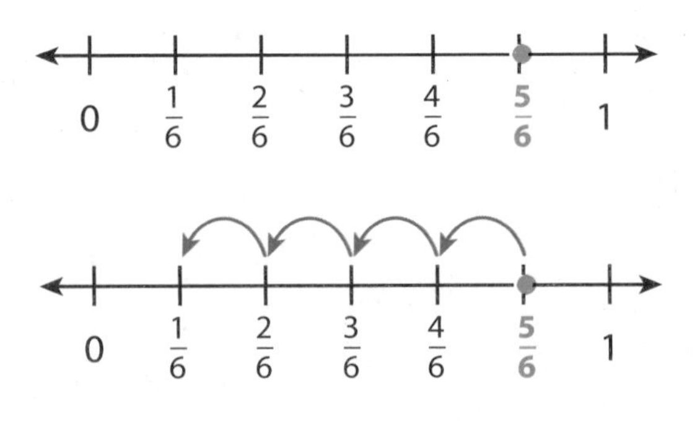

CONNECT IT

Now you will use the problem from the previous page to help you understand how to subtract any two fractions that have the same denominator.

1. In **Picture It**, why does $\frac{1}{6}$ represent 1 of the equal parts of the liter?

2. What do the numerators, 5 and 4, tell you?

3. How many sixths of a liter are left in the bottle after Alberto drinks 4 sixths? ....

4. Complete the equations to show what fraction of a liter is left in the bottle.

Use words: **5 sixths** − **4 sixths** = ... sixth

Use fractions: $\frac{5}{6} - \frac{4}{6} = \frac{\square}{6}$

5. Explain how you subtract fractions with the same denominator.

REFLECT

Look back at your **Try It**, strategies by classmates, and **Picture It** and **Model It**. Which models or strategies do you like best for subtracting fractions? Explain.

....

....

....

....

APPLY IT

Use what you just learned to solve these problems.

7. Carmen has $\frac{8}{10}$ of the lawn left to mow. She mows $\frac{5}{10}$ of the lawn. Now what fraction of the lawn is left to mow? Show your work.

Solution ....

8. Mrs. Kirk has $\frac{3}{4}$ of a carton of eggs. She uses some for baking and has $\frac{2}{4}$ of the carton left. What fraction of the carton does she use? Show your work.

Solution ....

9. Badru reads $\frac{4}{8}$ of a book. How much of the book does he have left to read?

   Ⓐ $\frac{1}{8}$

   Ⓑ $\frac{2}{8}$

   Ⓒ $\frac{4}{8}$

   Ⓓ $\frac{6}{8}$

Name: ______________________________

Practice Subtracting Fractions

Study the Example showing one way to subtract fractions. Then solve problems 1–7.

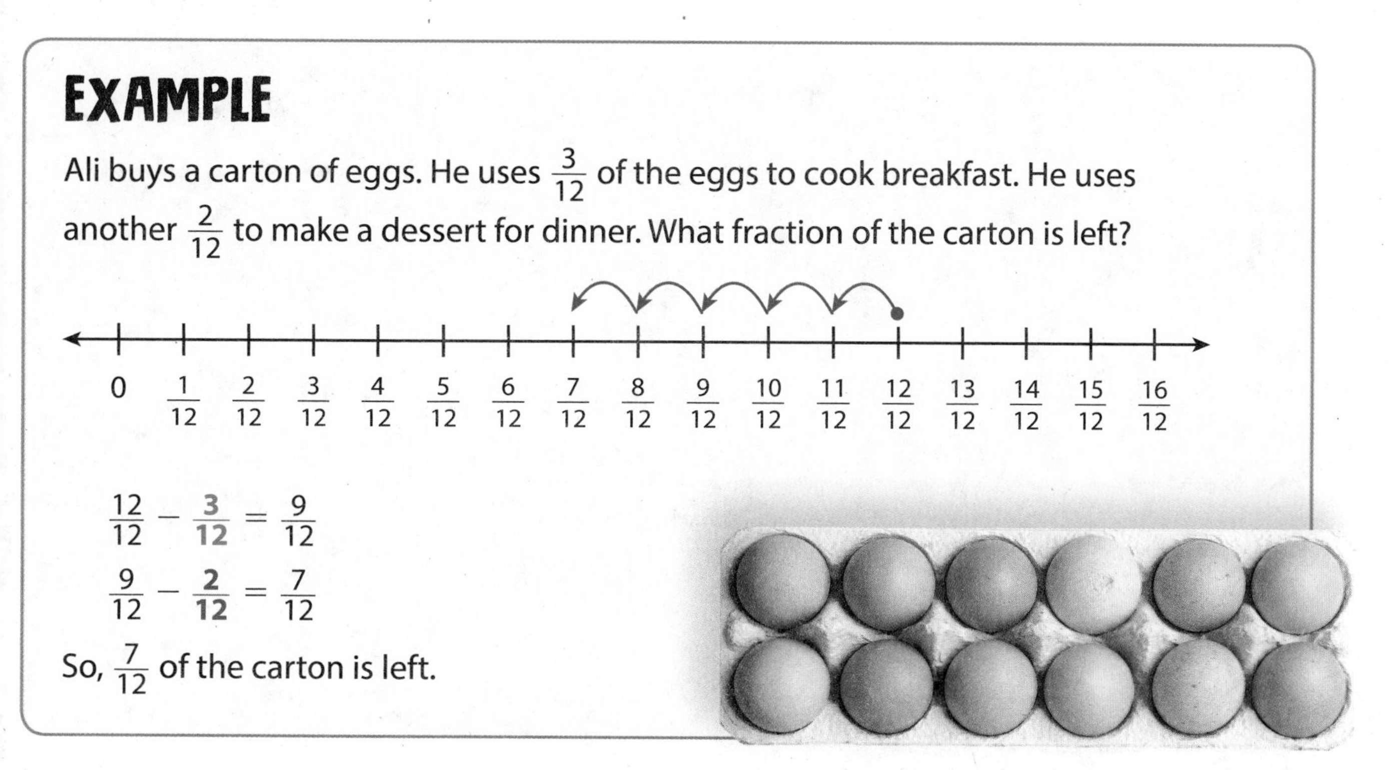

EXAMPLE

Ali buys a carton of eggs. He uses $\frac{3}{12}$ of the eggs to cook breakfast. He uses another $\frac{2}{12}$ to make a dessert for dinner. What fraction of the carton is left?

$$\frac{12}{12} - \frac{3}{12} = \frac{9}{12}$$

$$\frac{9}{12} - \frac{2}{12} = \frac{7}{12}$$

So, $\frac{7}{12}$ of the carton is left.

Keisha is at her friend's house. Her friend's house is $\frac{8}{10}$ of a mile from Keisha's home. Keisha walks $\frac{3}{10}$ of a mile toward home. Then her mother drives her the rest of the way home.

1. Divide the number line below to show tenths. Then label each tick mark.

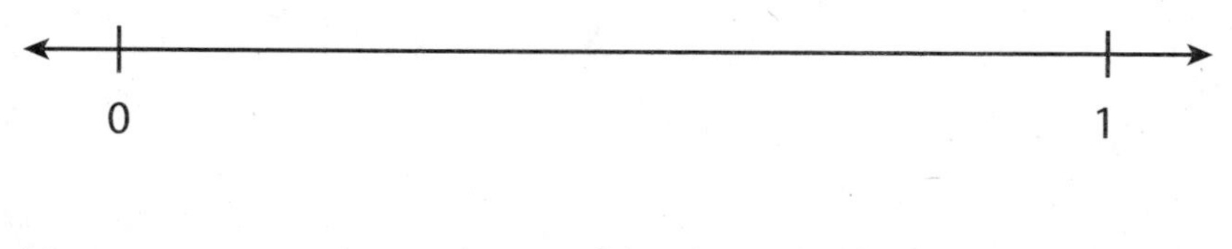

2. Use arrows to show the problem on the number line you labeled in problem 1.

3. How far does Keisha's mother drive her? ....

4. Write an equation for this problem that includes your answer.

5 Anna makes a quilt by sewing together green, white, and yellow fabric. When she finishes, $\frac{2}{6}$ of the quilt is green, and $\frac{3}{6}$ is yellow. The rest is white. What fraction of the quilt is white? Show your work.

Solution ....

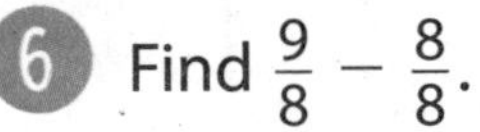

6 Find $\frac{9}{8} - \frac{8}{8}$.

Use a number line or an area model to show your thinking.

Solution ....

7 Shanice has 1 whole pizza. She eats some of it and has $\frac{4}{6}$ of the pizza left. What fraction of the pizza does she eat? Show your work.

Solution ....

Develop Decomposing Fractions

Read and try to solve the problem below.

Dan has $\frac{5}{6}$ of his reading left to complete for the week. He plans to complete his reading on two or more days of the week from Monday to Friday. What are two different ways he could plan to complete his reading? Use a fraction to describe the part of his reading he does each day.

TRY IT

Math Toolkit

- counters
- fraction circles
- fraction tiles
- fraction bars
- number lines
- fraction models

DISCUSS IT

Ask your partner: Do you agree with me? Why or why not?

Tell your partner: I do not understand how . . .

Explore different ways to understand decomposing fractions.

Dan has $\frac{5}{6}$ of his reading left to complete for the week. He plans to complete his reading on two or more days of the week from Monday to Friday. What are two different ways he could plan to complete his reading? Use a fraction to describe the part of his reading he does each day.

MODEL IT

You can use models to show how to decompose a fraction in different ways.

When you decompose a fraction, you break it into parts.

The models show two ways to decompose $\frac{5}{6}$.

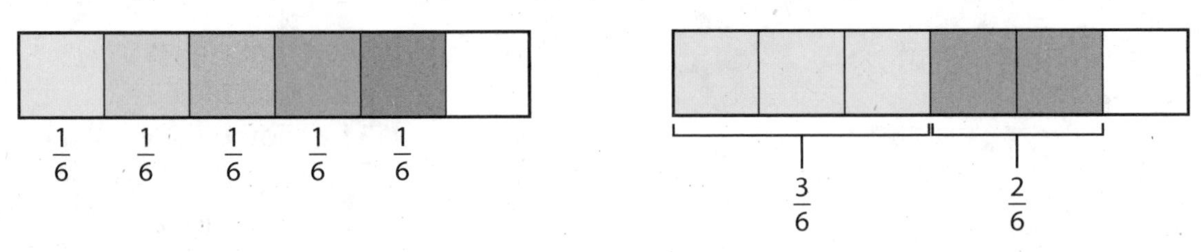

MODEL IT

You can also use equations to decompose a fraction in different ways.

You can list different ways to add fractions to make $\frac{5}{6}$.

$\frac{5}{6} = \frac{1}{6} + \frac{1}{6} + \frac{1}{6} + \frac{1}{6} + \frac{1}{6}$

$\frac{5}{6} = \frac{1}{6} + \frac{1}{6} + \frac{1}{6} + \frac{2}{6}$

$\frac{5}{6} = \frac{1}{6} + \frac{2}{6} + \frac{2}{6}$

$\frac{5}{6} = \frac{3}{6} + \frac{1}{6} + \frac{1}{6}$

$\frac{5}{6} = \frac{3}{6} + \frac{2}{6}$

$\frac{5}{6} = \frac{4}{6} + \frac{1}{6}$

CONNECT IT

Now you will use the problem from the previous page to help you understand how to decompose a fraction in different ways.

1. Look at the first **Model It**. How many equal parts are in each model? ....

   How many shaded parts are in each model? ....

2. Look at the equations in the second **Model It**. How can you tell if two or more fractions add to make $\frac{5}{6}$?

3. What is the greatest amount of his reading that Dan could do in one day?

4. What are two different ways that Dan could do his reading?

5. Explain how to find all the different ways to decompose a fraction.

6. REFLECT

   Look back at your **Try It**, strategies by classmates, and **Model Its**. Which models or strategies do you like best for decomposing a fraction? Explain.

   ....

   ....

   ....

   ....

APPLY IT

Use what you just learned to solve these problems.

7 Find three ways to decompose $\frac{7}{8}$ into a sum of other fractions. Draw a model for each way to show how you know the way is correct. Show your work.

Solution ....

8 Complete the equations to show a way to decompose each fraction.

a. $\ldots\ldots + \frac{1}{4} + \frac{3}{4} = \frac{5}{4}$

b. $\frac{3}{4} = \frac{1}{4} + \ldots\ldots$

c. $\frac{9}{12} = \frac{3}{12} + \frac{3}{12} + \ldots\ldots$

9 Draw a diagram to justify your answer to problem 8b.

Name: ______________________

Practice Decomposing Fractions

Study the Example showing how to decompose a fraction in different ways. Then solve problems 1–5.

EXAMPLE

Sarah's family has $\frac{4}{8}$ of a cherry pie left over. Sarah and her sister share the leftover pie. What are two different ways that Sarah and her sister can each get some of the pie?

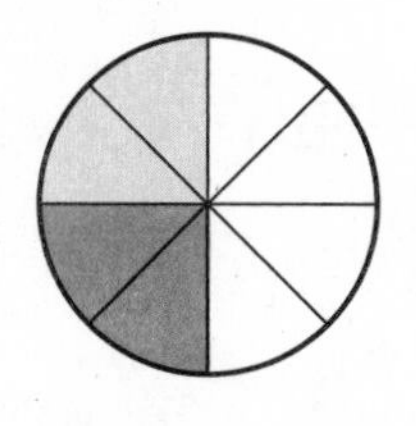

$\frac{2}{8} + \frac{2}{8} = \frac{4}{8}$

Sarah and her sister each get $\frac{2}{8}$ of the pie.

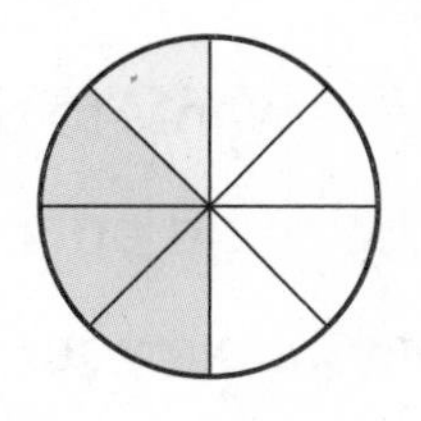

$\frac{1}{8} + \frac{3}{8} = \frac{4}{8}$

Sarah gets $\frac{1}{8}$ of the pie, and her sister gets $\frac{3}{8}$ of the pie.

1 Complete the equations to show how to decompose $\frac{3}{5}$ in two different ways.

a. $\frac{3}{5} = \frac{1}{5} +$ ....

b. $\frac{3}{5} = \frac{1}{5} +$ .... $+ \frac{1}{5}$

2 Shade the area model below to show the equation in problem 1a.

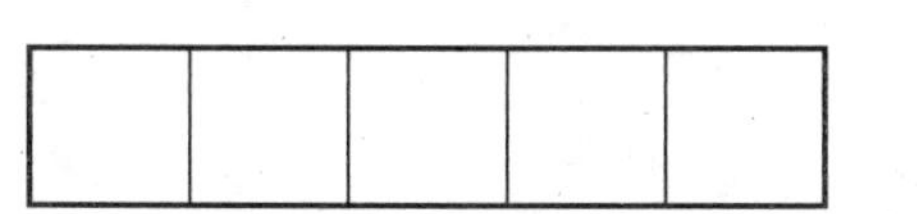

3 Select all the equations that show a correct way to represent $\frac{7}{10}$.

Ⓐ $\frac{1}{10} + \frac{5}{10} = \frac{7}{10}$

Ⓑ $\frac{2}{10} + \frac{5}{10} = \frac{7}{10}$

Ⓒ $\frac{1}{10} + \frac{2}{10} + \frac{4}{10} = \frac{7}{10}$

Ⓓ $\frac{1}{10} + \frac{4}{10} + \frac{3}{10} = \frac{7}{10}$

Ⓔ $\frac{1}{10} + \frac{1}{10} + \frac{1}{10} + \frac{1}{10} + \frac{1}{10} + \frac{1}{10} + \frac{1}{10} = \frac{7}{10}$

4 Vijay has $\frac{6}{6}$ of a cup of raisins. He wants to put the raisins into three snack bags. What are two different ways he could put raisins into three snack bags?

Use a model to show each way. Show your work.

Solution

5 Is $\frac{7}{12} + \frac{1}{12}$ equivalent to $\frac{4}{12} + \frac{4}{12}$? Explain your answer.

Refine Adding and Subtracting Fractions

Complete the Example below. Then solve problems 1–9.

EXAMPLE

Jessica hikes $\frac{2}{5}$ of a mile on a trail before she stops to get a drink of water. After her drink, Jessica hikes another $\frac{2}{5}$ of a mile. How far does Jessica hike in all?

Look at how you could show your work using a number line.

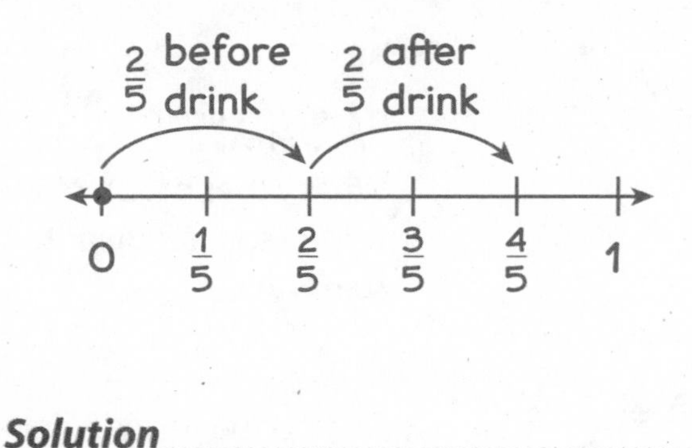

Solution ....

The student used labels and "jump" arrows to show each part of the hike on a number line. It is just like adding whole numbers!

PAIR/SHARE
How else could you solve this problem?

APPLY IT

1 Ruth makes 1 fruit smoothie. She drinks $\frac{1}{3}$ of it. What fraction of the fruit smoothie is left? Show your work.

Solution ....

What fraction represents the whole fruit smoothie?

PAIR/SHARE
How did you and your partner decide what fraction to start with?

2 Mr. Chang has a bunch of balloons. $\frac{3}{10}$ of the bunch is red. $\frac{2}{10}$ of the bunch is blue. What fraction of the bunch is not red or blue? Show your work.

I think that there are at least two different steps to solve this problem.

Solution ....

PAIR/SHARE
What other problem in this lesson is similar to this one?

3 Emily eats $\frac{1}{6}$ of a bag of carrots. Nick eats $\frac{2}{6}$ of the same bag of carrots. What fraction of the bag of carrots do Emily and Nick eat altogether?

Ⓐ $\frac{1}{6}$

Ⓑ $\frac{1}{3}$

Ⓒ $\frac{3}{6}$

Ⓓ $\frac{3}{12}$

Rob chose Ⓓ as the correct answer. How did he get that answer?

To find the fraction of the bag Emily and Nick ate together, should you add or subtract?

PAIR/SHARE
Does Rob's answer make sense?

4 Lin buys some cloth. He uses $\frac{5}{8}$ of a yard for a school project. He has $\frac{2}{8}$ of a yard left. How much cloth does Lin buy?

Ⓐ $\frac{3}{8}$ of a yard

Ⓑ $\frac{7}{16}$ of a yard

Ⓒ $\frac{7}{8}$ of a yard

Ⓓ $\frac{8}{8}$ of a yard

5 Carmela cuts a cake into 12 equal-sized pieces. She eats $\frac{2}{12}$ of the cake, and her brother eats $\frac{3}{12}$ of the cake. What fraction of the cake is left?

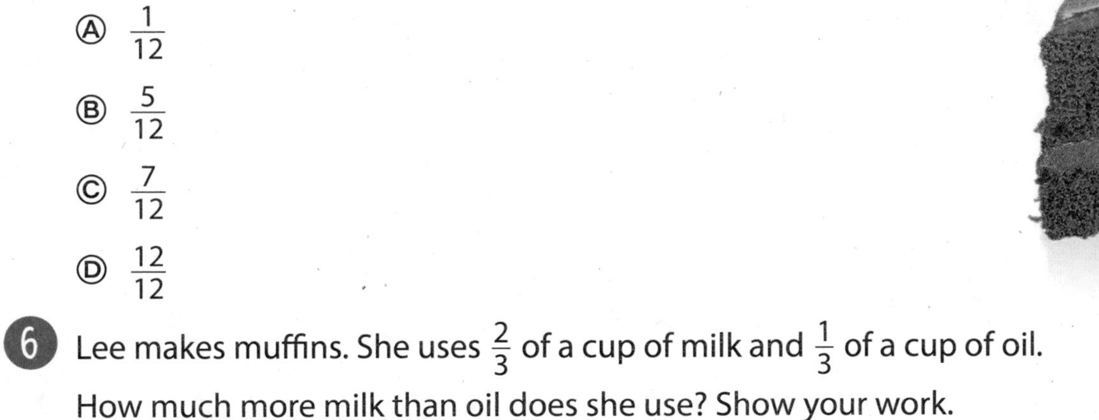

Ⓐ $\frac{1}{12}$

Ⓑ $\frac{5}{12}$

Ⓒ $\frac{7}{12}$

Ⓓ $\frac{12}{12}$

6 Lee makes muffins. She uses $\frac{2}{3}$ of a cup of milk and $\frac{1}{3}$ of a cup of oil. How much more milk than oil does she use? Show your work.

Solution ....

7 Lucy and Melody work together to paint $\frac{6}{8}$ of a room. Which models could be used to show how much of the room each girl paints?

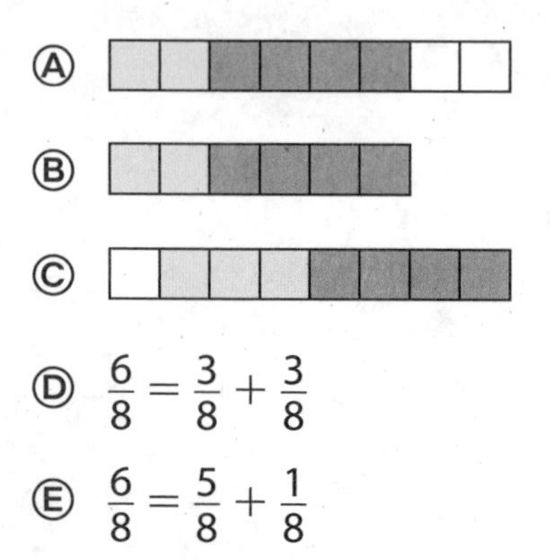

Ⓐ

Ⓑ

Ⓒ

Ⓓ $\frac{6}{8} = \frac{3}{8} + \frac{3}{8}$

Ⓔ $\frac{6}{8} = \frac{5}{8} + \frac{1}{8}$

8 Cole and Max pick $\frac{9}{10}$ of a bucket of blueberries in all. Cole picks $\frac{3}{10}$ of a bucket of blueberries. What fraction of a bucket of blueberries does Max pick? Show your work.

Solution ....

9 MATH JOURNAL

Ms. Jones cuts an apple into eighths. She eats $\frac{3}{8}$ of the apple and gives the rest to her son and daughter. Describe two different ways her son and daughter can share the rest of the apple if they each have some of the apple.

☑ SELF CHECK Go back to the Unit 4 Opener and see what you can check off.

Add and Subtract Mixed Numbers

LESSON 21

Dear Family,

This week your child is learning to add and subtract mixed numbers.

A mixed number is a number with a whole-number part and a fractional part.

Using models can help your child add mixed numbers, such as $1\frac{2}{6} + 1\frac{5}{6}$.

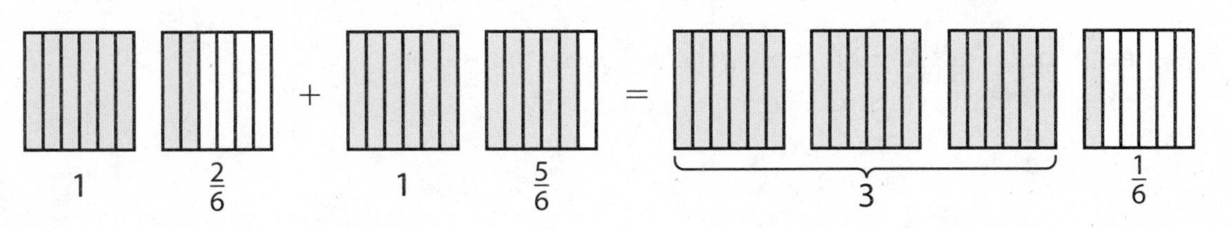

The model shows that you can add the wholes, $1 + 1 = 2$.

Then you can add the parts, $\frac{2}{6} + \frac{5}{6} = \frac{7}{6}$.

The fraction $\frac{7}{6}$ is another whole, $\frac{6}{6}$ or 1, and $\frac{1}{6}$.

The model shows the sum is 3 wholes and $\frac{1}{6}$ of a whole.

So, $1\frac{2}{6} + 1\frac{5}{6} = 3\frac{1}{6}$.

Invite your child to share what he or she knows about adding and subtracting mixed numbers by doing the following activity together.

ACTIVITY ADDING AND SUBTRACTING MIXED NUMBERS

Do this activity with your child to add and subtract mixed numbers.

Materials construction paper $\left(8\frac{1}{2} \times 11 \text{ inches or } 9 \times 12 \text{ inches}\right)$, magazine or newspaper with pictures (or a picture of your own), scissors, ruler, glue or tape

- Use a sheet of construction paper to make a paper frame for a fun photo. Choose a picture from a newspaper or a magazine or use a photo of your own. Choose a picture that is smaller than 5 inches by 8 inches.
- Measure the length and width of your picture to the nearest $\frac{1}{8}$ of an inch.
- Add 2 inches to the length and 2 inches to the width of your picture. That will be the size of the construction paper you need.

  Example: The length of your picture is $5\frac{7}{8}$ inches. $5\frac{7}{8} + 2 = 7\frac{7}{8}$ inches

  The width of your picture is $3\frac{3}{8}$ inches. $3\frac{3}{8} + 2 = 5\frac{3}{8}$ inches
- Subtract your totals from the construction paper's width and length. That is how many inches to cut off the length and width of the construction paper.
- Measure and cut your construction paper to size. Then center the photo and attach it so that there is a 2-inch frame all around the photo.

Look for other real-life opportunities to add and subtract mixed numbers with your child.

Explore Adding and Subtracting Mixed Numbers

Learning Target

- Add and subtract mixed numbers with like denominators.

SMP 1, 2, 3, 4, 5, 6, 7

Previously, you learned about adding and subtracting fractions. In this lesson, you will learn about adding and subtracting whole numbers and fractions. Use what you know to try to solve the problem below.

Raquel measures milk with a $\frac{1}{2}$-cup measuring cup. She fills the cup 5 times and pours each $\frac{1}{2}$ of a cup of milk into a bowl. How much milk does Raquel pour into the bowl?

TRY IT

Math Toolkit

- fraction circles
- fraction tiles
- number lines
- index cards
- fraction models

DISCUSS IT

Ask your partner: How did you get started?

Tell your partner: I started by . . .

CONNECT IT

1 LOOK BACK

Explain how you found the total amount of milk Raquel pours into the bowl.

2 LOOK AHEAD

Suppose Raquel has another bowl with $2\frac{3}{4}$ cups of milk. She then pours $1\frac{3}{4}$ cups of milk into this bowl. How much milk is in this bowl now?

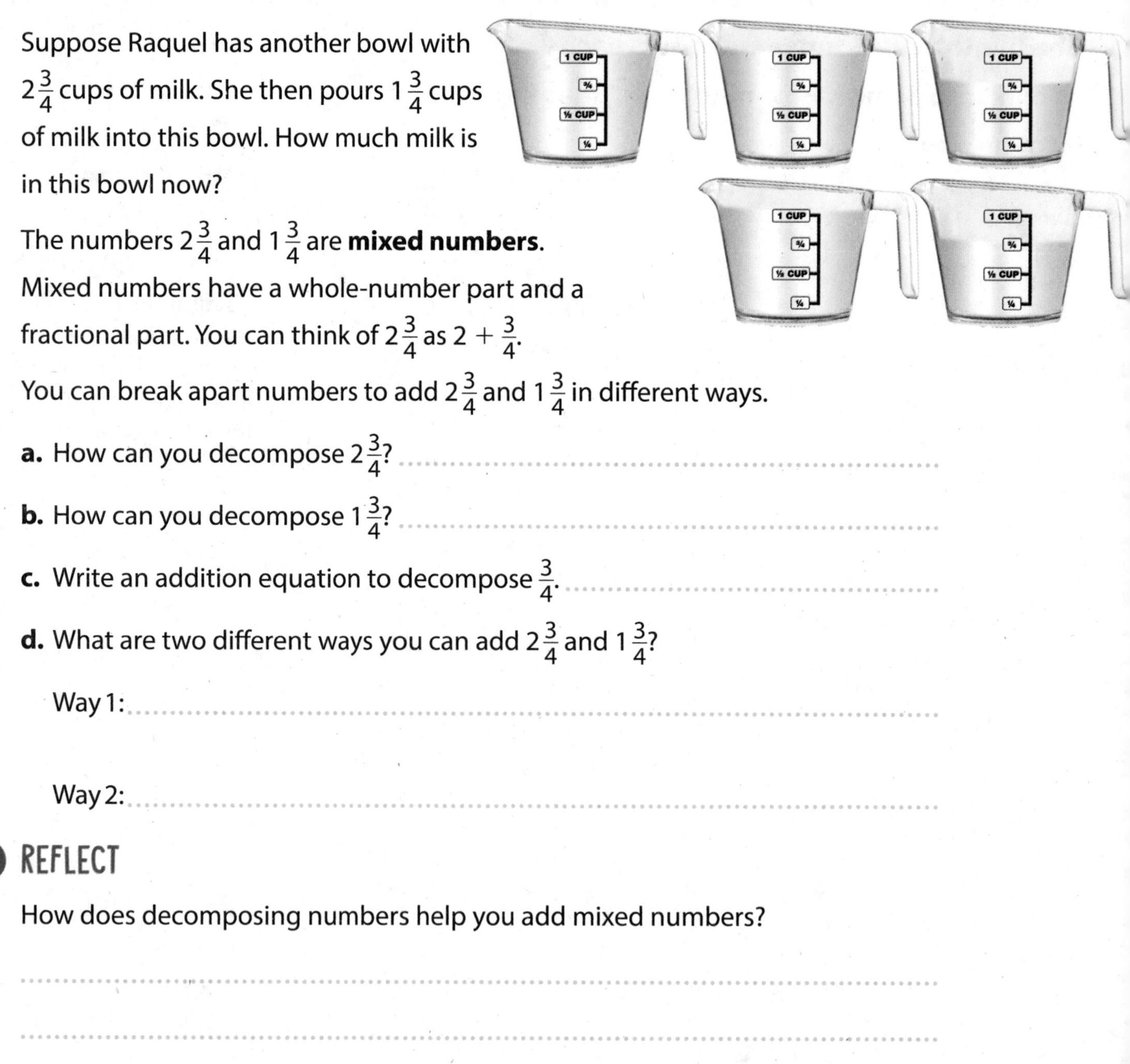

The numbers $2\frac{3}{4}$ and $1\frac{3}{4}$ are **mixed numbers.** Mixed numbers have a whole-number part and a fractional part. You can think of $2\frac{3}{4}$ as $2 + \frac{3}{4}$.

You can break apart numbers to add $2\frac{3}{4}$ and $1\frac{3}{4}$ in different ways.

a. How can you decompose $2\frac{3}{4}$? ....

b. How can you decompose $1\frac{3}{4}$? ....

c. Write an addition equation to decompose $\frac{3}{4}$. ....

d. What are two different ways you can add $2\frac{3}{4}$ and $1\frac{3}{4}$?

Way 1: ....

Way 2: ....

3 REFLECT

How does decomposing numbers help you add mixed numbers?

....

....

Prepare for Adding and Subtracting Mixed Numbers

1 Think about what you know about mixed numbers. Fill in each box. Use words, numbers, and pictures. Show as many ideas as you can.

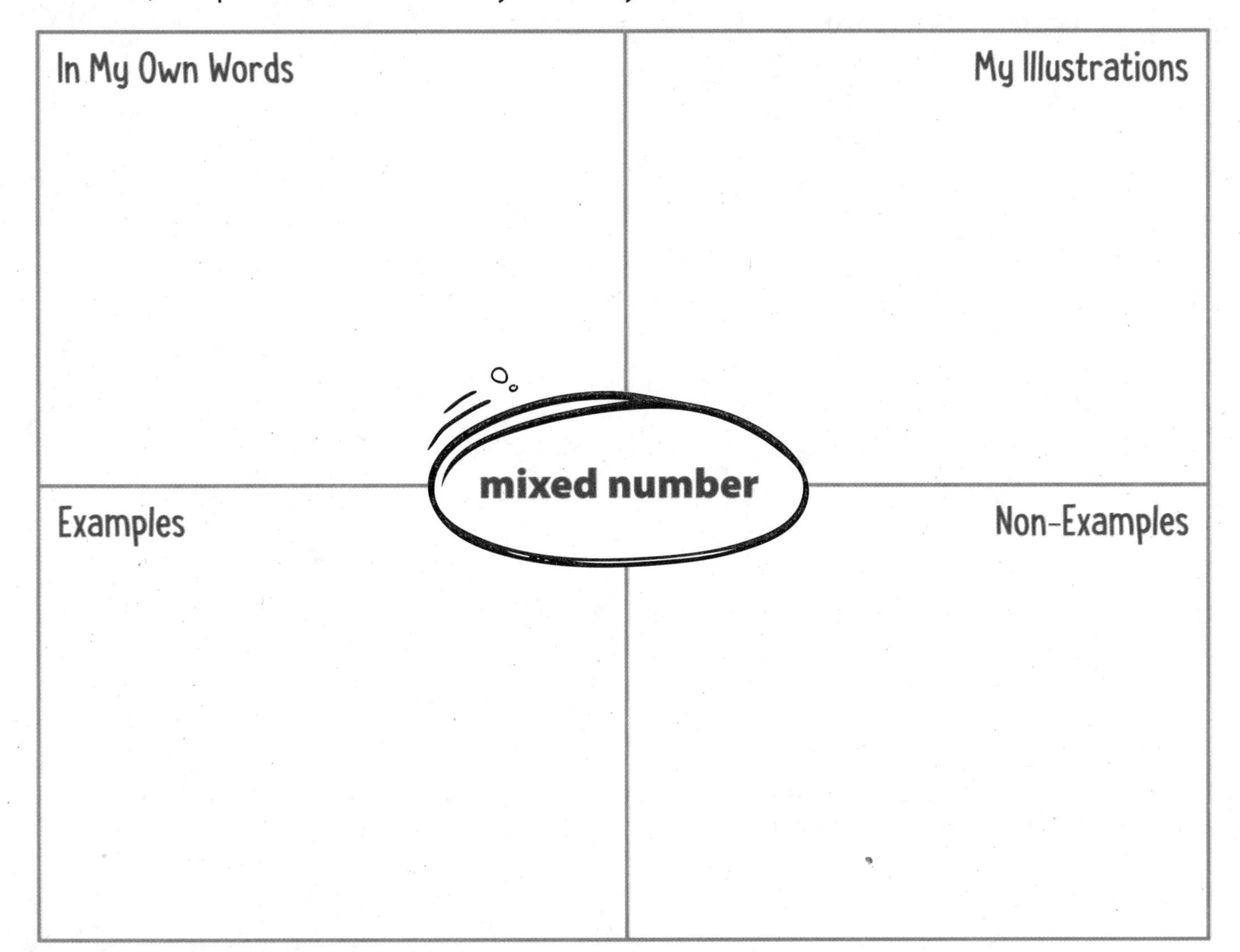

2 **a.** Is $1\frac{2}{5}$ a mixed number? Explain.

b. How can you decompose $1\frac{2}{5}$?

3 Solve the problem. Show your work.

Paco measures water with a $\frac{1}{4}$-cup measuring cup. He fills the cup 7 times and pours each $\frac{1}{4}$ of a cup of water into a bowl. How much water does Paco pour into the bowl?

Solution ....

4 Check your answer. Show your work.

Develop Adding Mixed Numbers

Read and try to solve the problem below.

Markers come in boxes of 8. For an art project, one group of students uses $1\frac{5}{8}$ boxes of markers, and another group uses $1\frac{6}{8}$ boxes. How many boxes of markers do the two groups use altogether?

TRY IT

Math Toolkit

- fraction circles
- fraction tiles
- number lines
- index cards
- fraction models

DISCUSS IT

Ask your partner: Why did you choose that strategy?

Tell your partner: At first, I thought . . .

Explore different ways to understand adding mixed numbers.

Markers come in boxes of 8. For an art project, one group of students uses $1\frac{5}{8}$ boxes of markers, and another group uses $1\frac{6}{8}$ boxes. How many boxes of markers do the two groups use altogether?

PICTURE IT

You can use pictures to help add mixed numbers.

The picture shows the boxes of markers. Each marker is $\frac{1}{8}$ of the whole box.

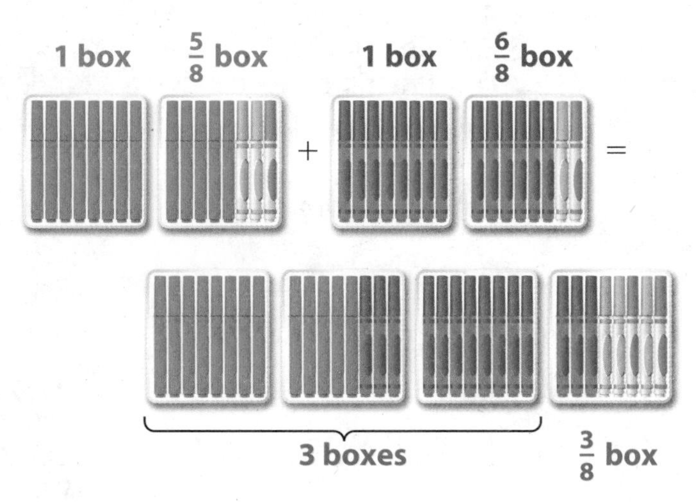

MODEL IT

You can also use a number line to help add mixed numbers.

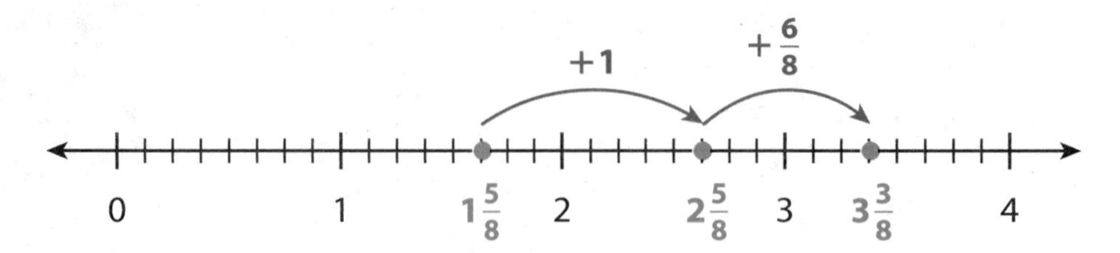

Remember that 1 whole box is 8 markers, or $\frac{8}{8}$ of a box.

CONNECT IT

Now you will use the problem from the previous page to help you understand how to add mixed numbers.

1 What is the sum of just the whole-number parts of $1\frac{5}{8}$ and $1\frac{6}{8}$? ....

2 What is the sum of just the fractional parts of $1\frac{5}{8}$ and $1\frac{6}{8}$? ....

3 Think about how many wholes are in $\frac{11}{8}$ and how many extra eighths there are. Complete the equations below.

$\frac{11}{8} = \frac{8}{8} + \frac{\square}{8}$ $\quad\quad$ $\frac{8}{8} =$ .... $\quad\quad$ So, $\frac{11}{8} = 1 + \frac{\square}{8}$.

4 Now add the sum of the whole numbers to the sum of the fractions.

$2 + 1 + \frac{3}{8} =$ ....

5 Explain how you add mixed numbers.

REFLECT

Look back at your **Try It**, strategies by classmates, and **Picture It** and **Model It**. Which models or strategies do you like best for adding mixed numbers? Explain.

APPLY IT

Use what you just learned to solve these problems.

Mrs. Suarez sells pies at a fair. She sells $3\frac{5}{6}$ pies the first day and $1\frac{3}{6}$ pies the second day. How many pies does she sell in all? Show your work.

Solution ....

8 Show two different ways to add $3\frac{2}{5} + 2\frac{1}{5}$. Show your work.

9 Beth goes on vacation for $4\frac{1}{2}$ days in June and $8\frac{1}{2}$ days in July. How many days is Beth on vacation in June and July altogether? Show your work.

Solution ....

Name: ______________________

Practice Adding Mixed Numbers

Study the Example showing a way to add mixed numbers. Then solve problems 1–5.

EXAMPLE

Aaron uses $2\frac{1}{4}$ cups of flour to make muffins and another $1\frac{3}{4}$ cups of flour to make pancakes. How many cups of flour does he use altogether?

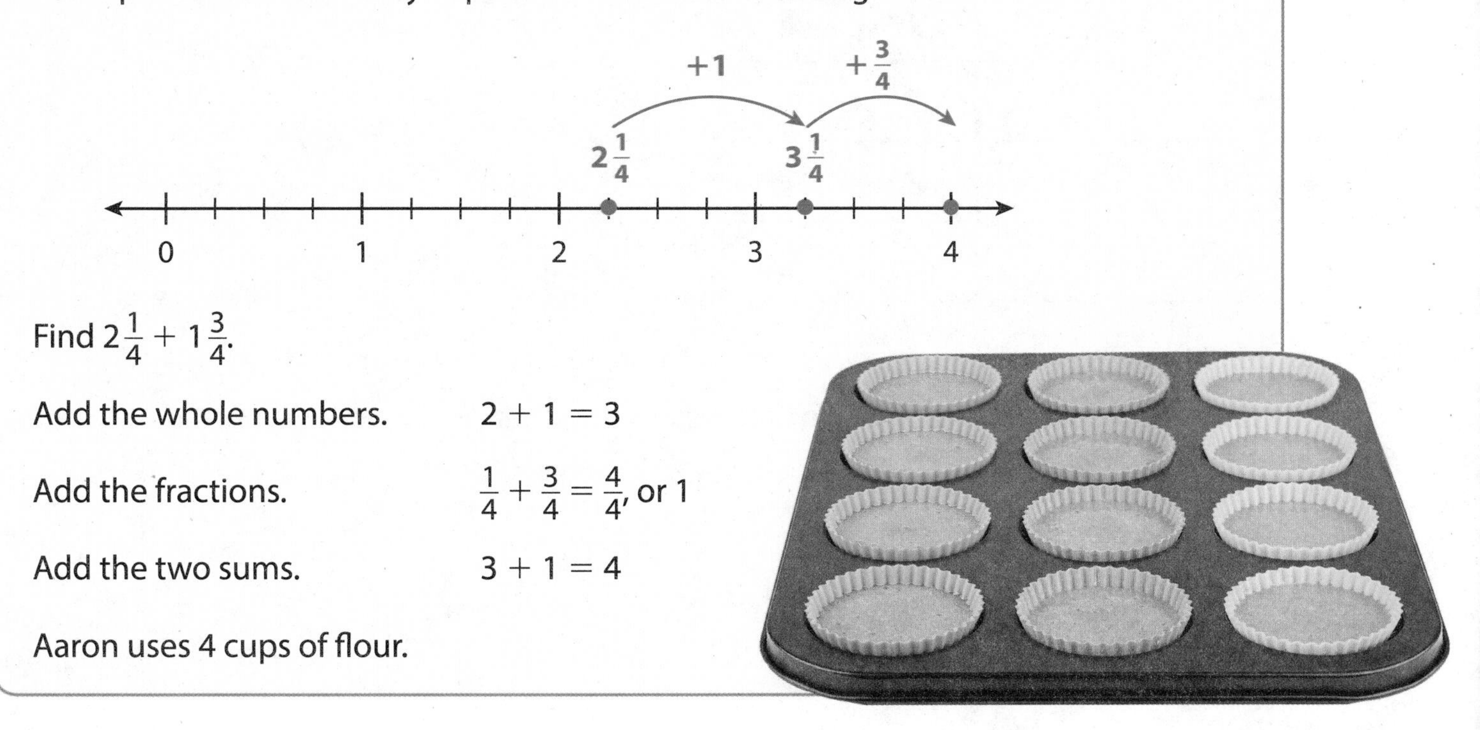

Find $2\frac{1}{4} + 1\frac{3}{4}$.

Add the whole numbers. $2 + 1 = 3$

Add the fractions. $\frac{1}{4} + \frac{3}{4} = \frac{4}{4}$, or 1

Add the two sums. $3 + 1 = 4$

Aaron uses 4 cups of flour.

1 Marissa uses $3\frac{1}{3}$ cups of oats to make oatmeal and $2\frac{1}{3}$ cups of oats to make snack bars. How many cups of oats does Marissa use in all?

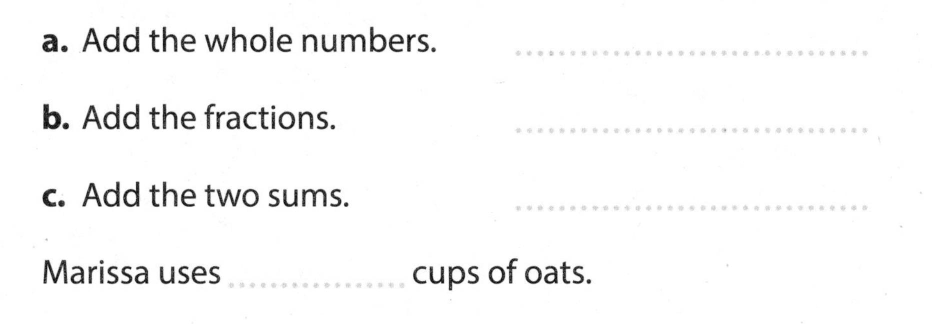

a. Add the whole numbers. ....

b. Add the fractions. ....

c. Add the two sums. ....

Marissa uses .... cups of oats.

Vocabulary

mixed number a number with a whole-number part and a fractional part.

$2\frac{1}{4}$ and $1\frac{3}{4}$ are mixed numbers.

2. Draw and label a number line to show $1\frac{1}{4} + 2\frac{2}{4}$.

3. Tell whether each addition equation is *True* or *False*.

	True	False
$10\frac{2}{5} + 5\frac{1}{5} = 15\frac{3}{10}$	Ⓐ	Ⓑ
$5\frac{3}{8} + 3\frac{5}{8} = 9$	Ⓒ	Ⓓ
$8\frac{3}{4} + 1\frac{2}{4} = 9\frac{1}{4}$	Ⓔ	Ⓕ
$3\frac{2}{3} + 2\frac{1}{3} + 1 = 7$	Ⓖ	Ⓗ

4. Tim uses $4\frac{1}{2}$ cups of oranges, $3\frac{1}{2}$ cups of apples, and $5\frac{1}{2}$ cups of pears in a fruit salad. How many cups of fruit does Tim use altogether? Show your work.

Solution ....

5. Jerry and two friends take a trip together. Jerry drives $80\frac{7}{10}$ miles. Arthur drives $60\frac{5}{10}$ miles. Charlie drives $40\frac{8}{10}$ miles. How many miles do they drive in all? Show your work.

Solution ....

Develop Subtracting Mixed Numbers

Read and try to solve the problem below.

Ursula picks carrots and radishes from her garden. She picks $4\frac{1}{4}$ pounds of carrots and $1\frac{3}{4}$ pounds of radishes. How many more pounds of carrots does she pick than radishes?

TRY IT

Math Toolkit
- fraction circles
- fraction tiles
- number lines
- index cards
- fraction models

DISCUSS IT

Ask your partner: Do you agree with me? Why or why not?

Tell your partner: I agree with you about … because …

Explore different ways to understand subtracting mixed numbers.

Ursula picks carrots and radishes from her garden. She picks $4\frac{1}{4}$ pounds of carrots and $1\frac{3}{4}$ pounds of radishes. How many more pounds of carrots does she pick than radishes?

PICTURE IT

You can use a picture to help subtract mixed numbers.

This picture shows $4\frac{1}{4}$ pounds of carrots.

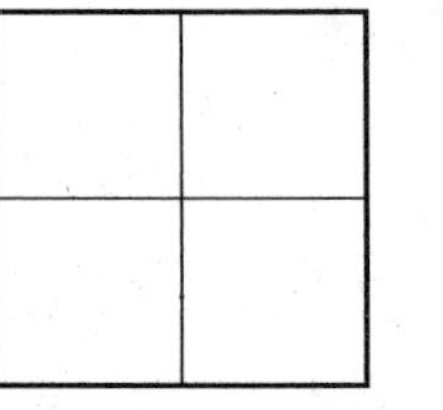
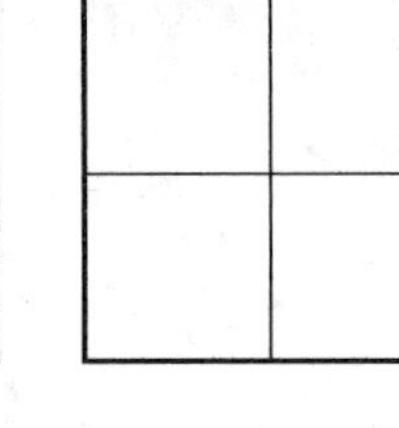
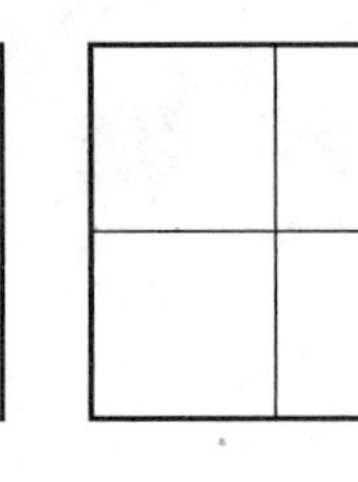
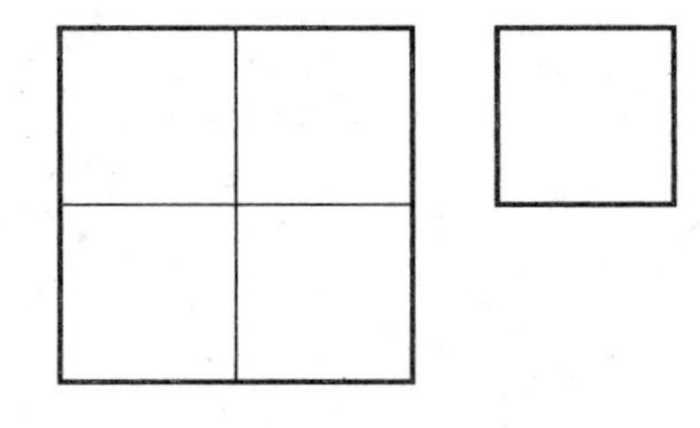

This picture shows $4\frac{1}{4}$ pounds of carrots minus $1\frac{3}{4}$ pounds of radishes.

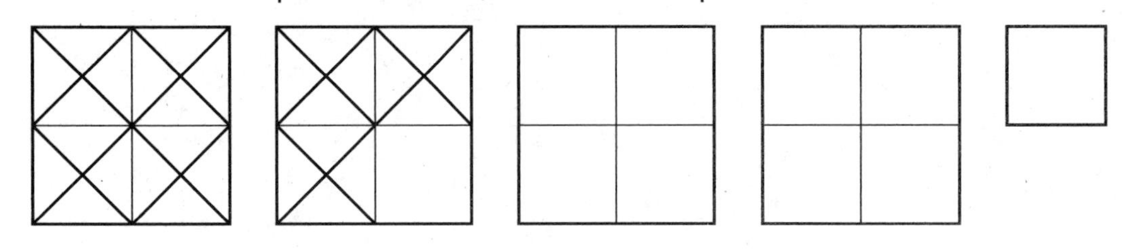

$4\frac{1}{4} - 1\frac{3}{4} = ?$

MODEL IT

You can also use a number line to help subtract mixed numbers.

To subtract using a number line, start at the number you are subtracting from and move left the amount you are subtracting.

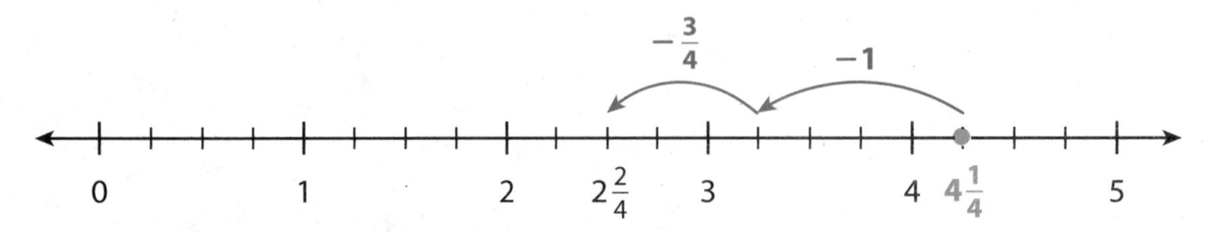

CONNECT IT

Now you will use the problem from the previous page to help you understand how to subtract mixed numbers.

Find the difference: $4\frac{1}{4} - 1\frac{3}{4}$.

1. Complete the equations to write $4\frac{1}{4}$ as a fraction greater than 1.

   $4\frac{1}{4} = \frac{16}{\square} + \frac{1}{4}$ So, $4\frac{1}{4} = \frac{\square}{4}$.

2. Complete the equations to write $1\frac{3}{4}$ as a fraction greater than 1.

   $1\frac{3}{4} = \frac{\square}{4} + \frac{3}{4}$ So, $1\frac{3}{4} = \frac{\square}{4}$.

3. Subtract the fractions. Write an equation that shows the difference.

4. How many more pounds of carrots does Ursula pick than radishes?

5. Explain how you can use fractions greater than 1 to subtract mixed numbers.

6 REFLECT

Look back at your **Try It**, strategies by classmates, and **Picture It** and **Model It**. Which models or strategies do you like best for subtracting mixed numbers? Explain.

APPLY IT

Use what you just learned to solve these problems.

7 Monica rides her bike $3\frac{1}{4}$ miles on Monday. She rides $2\frac{2}{4}$ miles on Tuesday. How much farther does Monica ride on Monday than on Tuesday? Show your work.

Solution ....

8 Look at problem 7. Monica wants to ride $8\frac{2}{4}$ miles in all. How many more miles does she need to ride? Show your work.

Solution ....

9 What is the difference of $8\frac{1}{3}$ and $5\frac{2}{3}$? Write your answer as a fraction and a mixed number. Show your work.

Solution ....

Name: ______________________________

Practice Subtracting Mixed Numbers

Study the Example showing a way to subtract mixed numbers. Then solve problems 1–7.

EXAMPLE

On a holiday, Sara's family drives $3\frac{2}{4}$ hours to her cousin's house. The drive usually takes $2\frac{3}{4}$ hours. How much longer does the drive take on the holiday?

Find $3\frac{2}{4} - 2\frac{3}{4}$.

$3\frac{2}{4} - 2\frac{3}{4} = \frac{3}{4}$

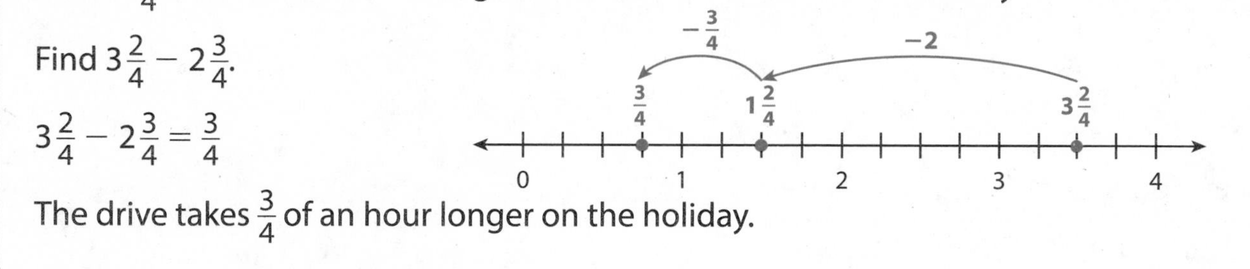

The drive takes $\frac{3}{4}$ of an hour longer on the holiday.

Steve makes $9\frac{3}{6}$ cups of pancake batter on a weekend camping trip. He uses $3\frac{4}{6}$ cups of batter for breakfast on Saturday.

1. Write each mixed number as a fraction greater than one.

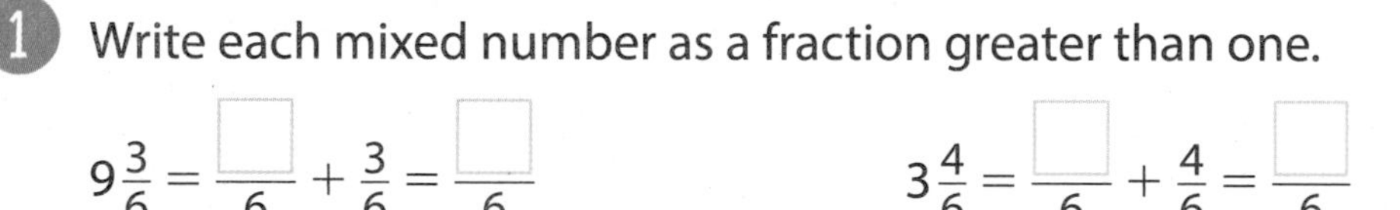

$9\frac{3}{6} = \frac{\square}{6} + \frac{3}{6} = \frac{\square}{6}$ $3\frac{4}{6} = \frac{\square}{6} + \frac{4}{6} = \frac{\square}{6}$

2. Subtract the fractions to find how many cups of batter are left for breakfast on Sunday.

$\frac{\square}{6} - \frac{\square}{6} = \frac{\square}{6}$

3. Write the difference as a mixed number.

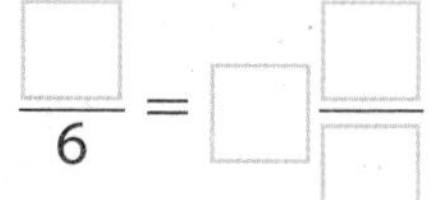

$\frac{\square}{6} = \square\frac{\square}{\square}$

4. Use addition to check the answer.

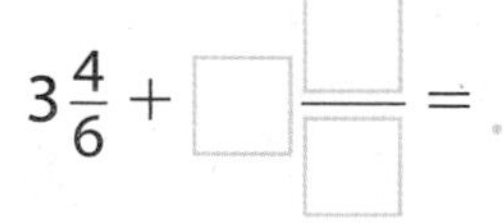

$3\frac{4}{6} + \square\frac{\square}{\square} =$ ....

5 Which expressions have the same value as $7\frac{5}{6} - 2\frac{3}{6}$?

Ⓐ $10\frac{2}{6}$

Ⓑ $\frac{47}{6} - \frac{15}{6}$

Ⓒ $(7 - 2) + \left(\frac{5}{6} - \frac{3}{6}\right)$

Ⓓ $5\frac{2}{6}$

Ⓔ $9\frac{2}{6}$

6 Helen buys 5 pounds of oranges. She slices $2\frac{3}{10}$ pounds of oranges to bring to a party. How many pounds of oranges does Helen have left that are not sliced? Show your work.

Solution ....

7 Kira reasons that $6\frac{1}{4} - 2\frac{3}{4} = 4\frac{2}{4}$ because the difference between 6 and 2 is 4 and the difference between $\frac{1}{4}$ and $\frac{3}{4}$ is $\frac{2}{4}$. Is Kira's reasoning correct? Explain.

Refine Adding and Subtracting Mixed Numbers

Complete the Example below. Then solve problems 1–9.

EXAMPLE

A soccer team drinks $5\frac{2}{3}$ liters of water during a game. Their opponents drink $4\frac{2}{3}$ liters of water. How much water do both teams drink?

Look at how you could show your work using pictures.

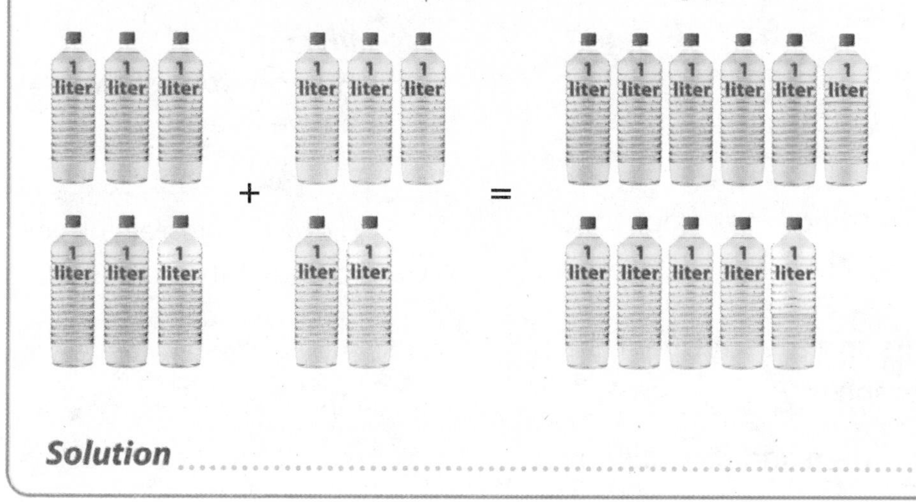

Solution ....

The student added the whole numbers and then combined the fractions!

PAIR/SHARE
How could you use a number line to help you solve this problem?

APPLY IT

1 Kelly buys $4\frac{7}{8}$ pounds of apples and $2\frac{3}{8}$ pounds of oranges. How many pounds of fruit does she buy altogether? Show your work.

Solution ....

What operation do you need to use?

PAIR/SHARE
Is there one way that works the best to solve this problem?

2 Kari reads a total of $20\frac{2}{4}$ pages in her science and social studies books combined. She reads $12\frac{3}{4}$ pages in her science book. How many pages does she read in her social studies book? Show your work.

Sometimes counting up or back can help you solve problems like this.

PAIR/SHARE
How can you tell if your answer is reasonable?

Solution ....

3 Which of the following describes the correct steps to take to find $15\frac{4}{5} - 9\frac{3}{5}$?

Ⓐ Subtract the whole numbers and then subtract the fractions. Subtract the differences.

Ⓑ Add the whole numbers and then add the fractions. Subtract the sums.

Ⓒ Subtract the whole numbers and then subtract the fractions. Add the differences.

Ⓓ Write the mixed numbers as fractions greater than one. Then add the fractions.

Marella chose Ⓐ as the correct answer. Did she choose the correct steps? Explain.

Solve the problem on your own and then check for your answer!

PAIR/SHARE
Draw a model to check your answer.

4 Ella orders 16 pizzas for a party. There are $3\frac{5}{8}$ pizzas left after the party. How many pizzas are eaten?

Ⓐ $12\frac{3}{8}$

Ⓑ $13\frac{3}{8}$

Ⓒ $13\frac{5}{8}$

Ⓓ $19\frac{5}{8}$

5 Shawn works in his yard for $3\frac{5}{6}$ hours on Saturday. He works another $4\frac{1}{6}$ hours in his yard on Sunday. How many hours does he work in the yard in all?

Ⓐ $\frac{2}{6}$ of an hour

Ⓑ 7 hours

Ⓒ $7\frac{5}{6}$ hours

Ⓓ 8 hours

6 Four friends share 3 orders of chicken wings.

- Alex eats $\frac{5}{8}$ of an order.
- Chase eats $\frac{7}{8}$ of an order.
- Ella eats $\frac{6}{8}$ of an order.

How much of an order of chicken wings is left for the fourth friend?

Solution ....

7 Marnel uses $4\frac{2}{3}$ cups of cereal and $3\frac{1}{3}$ cups of marshmallows to make cereal bars. How many more cups of cereal does Marnel use than marshmallows?
Show your work.

Solution ....

8 Kieran runs the first part of a relay in $4\frac{4}{6}$ minutes. David runs the next part in $3\frac{5}{6}$ minutes. How long do they take to run both parts of the relay?
Show your work.

Solution ....

9 MATH JOURNAL

Show two ways to add $2\frac{3}{8} + 3\frac{4}{8}$.

☑ SELF CHECK Go back to the Unit 4 Opener and see what you can check off.

Add and Subtract Fractions in Line Plots

Dear Family,

This week your child is learning to use line plots and to add and subtract fractions to solve problems.

A line plot is a way to organize a group of data, such as a set of measurements. A line plot gives a visual view of the data.

The line plot below shows the lengths of different pieces of yarn. Each **X** represents a piece of yarn. Since there are 9 **X**s, there are 9 pieces of yarn.

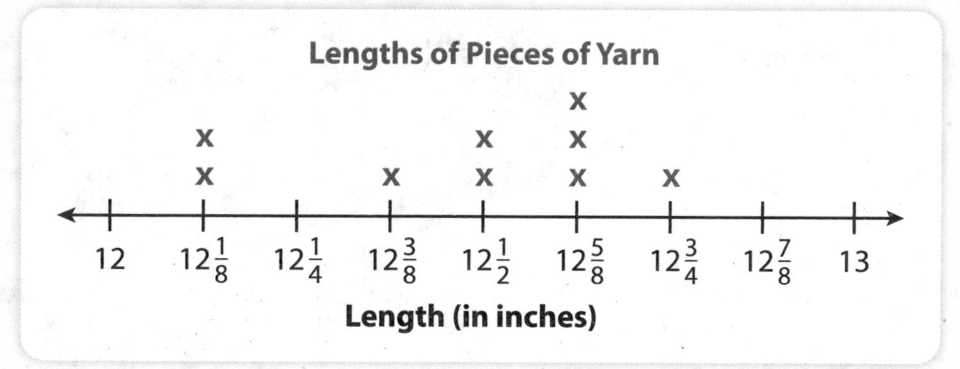

Xs that are one above another show pieces of yarn that have the same length. You can see at a glance that 2 pieces of yarn are $12\frac{1}{8}$ inches long and the longest piece of yarn is $12\frac{3}{4}$ inches.

To find the total length of all the pieces of yarn that are $12\frac{5}{8}$ inches long, add the individual lengths. There are 3 **X**s on the line plot above $12\frac{5}{8}$ inches, so find $12\frac{5}{8} + 12\frac{5}{8} + 12\frac{5}{8}$.

Add the whole numbers: $12 + 12 + 12 = 36$

Add the fractions: $\frac{5}{8} + \frac{5}{8} + \frac{5}{8} = \frac{15}{8}$

$\frac{15}{8} = \frac{8}{8} + \frac{7}{8}$, or $1\frac{7}{8}$

Add the two sums: $36 + 1\frac{7}{8} = 37\frac{7}{8}$

The total length of the three pieces of yarn is $37\frac{7}{8}$ inches.

Invite your child to share what he or she knows about using line plots to solve problems by doing the following activity together.

ACTIVITY ADD AND SUBTRACT FRACTIONS IN LINE PLOTS

Do this activity with your child to add and subtract fractions in line plots.

Steve takes 12 nails out of a toolbox. He measures the length of each nail. This is what he writes:

- 1 nail measures $\frac{1}{8}$ of an inch.
- 4 nails measure $\frac{3}{8}$ of an inch.
- 3 nails measure $\frac{1}{2}$ of an inch.
- 3 nails measure $\frac{5}{8}$ of an inch.
- 1 nail measures $\frac{7}{8}$ of an inch.

- Make a line plot to show the lengths of the nails. Use a blank number line. Label it with eighths fractions from 0 through 1.
- Write a title for the line plot, such as "Lengths of Nails from the Toolbox." Be sure to write a label below the number line, such as "Length (in inches)."
- Mark Xs on the line plot to show the data.
- Ask questions such as the ones below and have your child use the line plot to find the answers.

1. *Which length nail are there the most of?*
2. *What is the difference between the lengths of the longest nail and the shortest nail?*
3. *How would the line plot change if there were another nail that measures $1\frac{3}{8}$ inches?*

Answers: **1.** $\frac{3}{8}$ of an inch; **2.** $\frac{6}{8}$ of an inch; **3.** Extend the number line, add eighths labels through $1\frac{6}{8}$ and mark an X above $1\frac{3}{8}$.

Explore Adding and Subtracting Fractions in Line Plots

Learning Target

- Make a line plot to display a data set of measurements in fractions of a unit $\left(\frac{1}{2}, \frac{1}{4}, \frac{1}{8}\right)$. Solve problems involving addition and subtraction of fractions by using information presented in line plots.

SMP 1, 2, 3, 4, 5, 6, 7

You have learned how to add and subtract both fractions and mixed numbers and how to make line plots. Use what you know to try to solve the problem below.

Emma's class has a jar of earthworms. The class measures the length of each earthworm and records the data in a line plot. What is the difference between the lengths of the shortest and the longest earthworms?

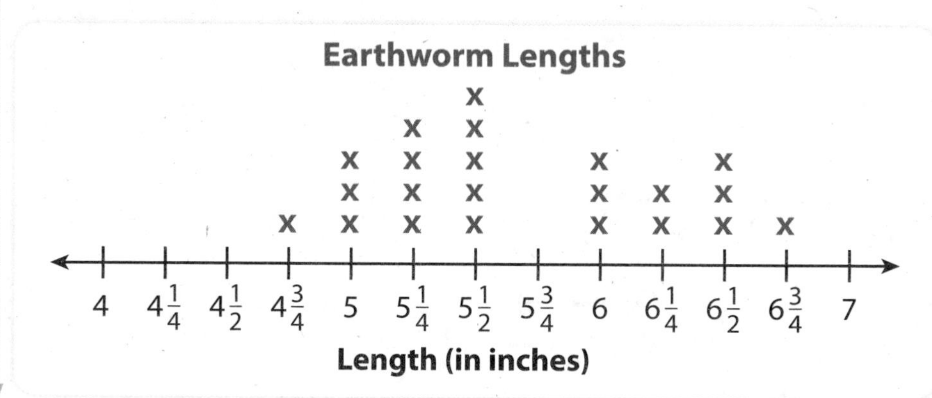

TRY IT

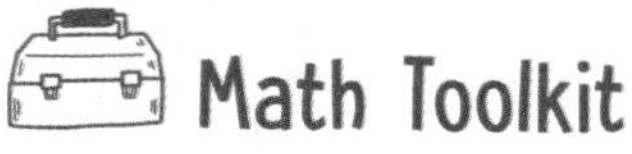

Math Toolkit

- fraction circles
- fraction tiles
- fraction bars
- number lines
- grid paper
- fraction models

DISCUSS IT

Ask your partner: Can you explain that again?

Tell your partner: I knew . . . so I . . .

CONNECT IT

LOOK BACK

Explain how to find the difference between the lengths of the shortest and longest earthworms.

LOOK AHEAD

A line plot is a data display that uses marks above a number line to show the number of times a data value occurs. Each data value is represented with an **X**.

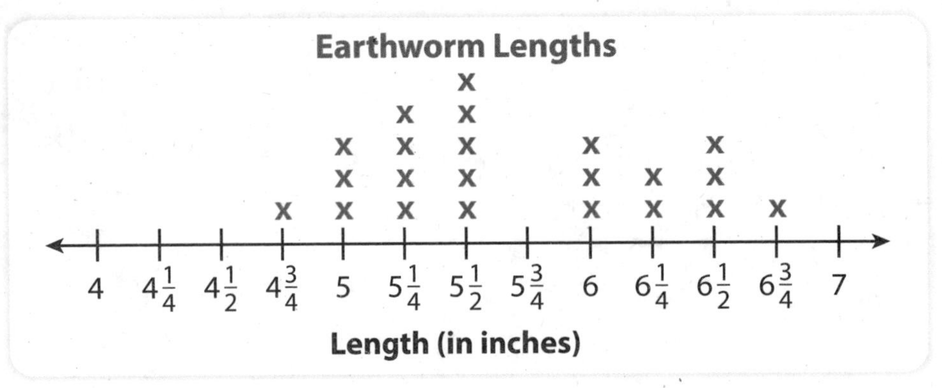

a. How many measurements are recorded on the line plot? Explain how you know.

b. What do the two Xs above $6\frac{1}{4}$ represent?

c. What length are the greatest number of earthworms? Explain.

d. Another earthworm has a length of $5\frac{3}{4}$ inches. Show this on the line plot.

3 REFLECT

If the number line is divided into fourths, why are numbers such as $4\frac{1}{2}$ and 5 used to label the number line in the line plot?

Name: ______________________________

Prepare for Adding and Subtracting Fractions in Line Plots

1 Think about what you know about line plots. Fill in each box. Use words, numbers, and pictures. Show as many ideas as you can.

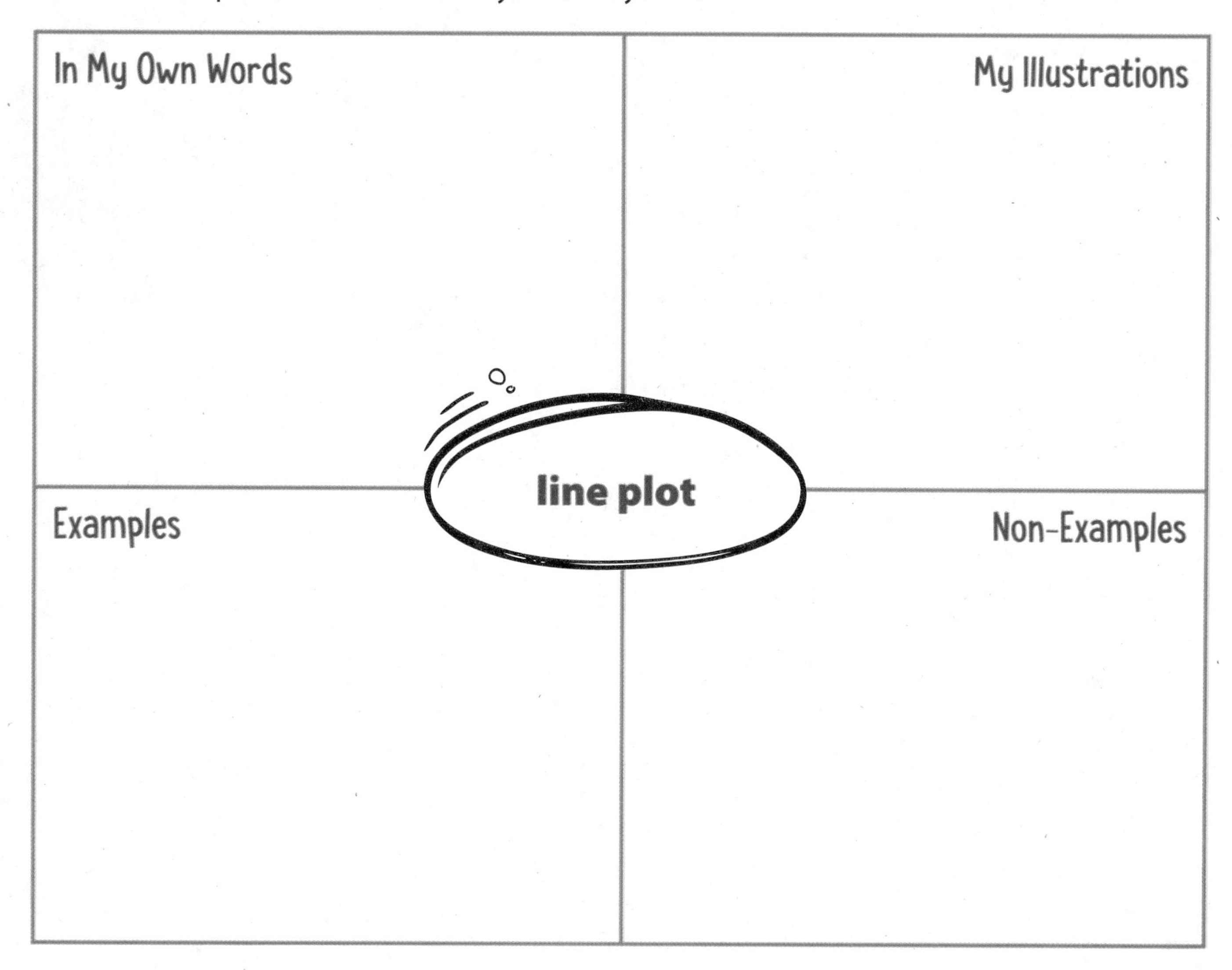

2 Use the line plot to answer the questions.

a. What length are the greatest number of ribbons? Explain.

b. Suppose there is another ribbon that is $9\frac{1}{2}$ inches. Show this on the line plot.

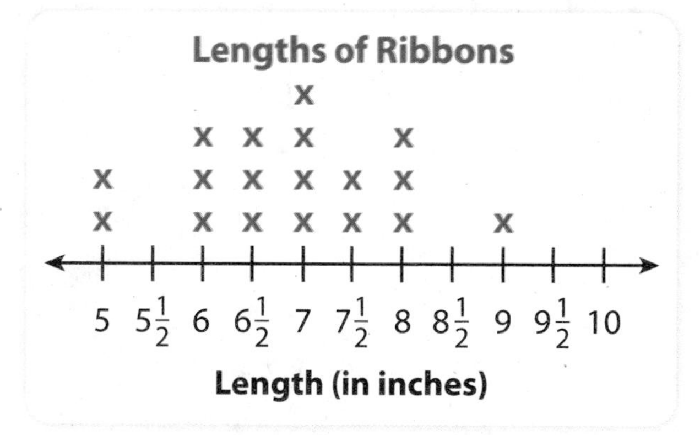

3 Solve the problem. Show your work.

Marlon measures the height of each flower in a vase. He records the data in a line plot. What is the difference between the heights of the shortest and tallest flowers?

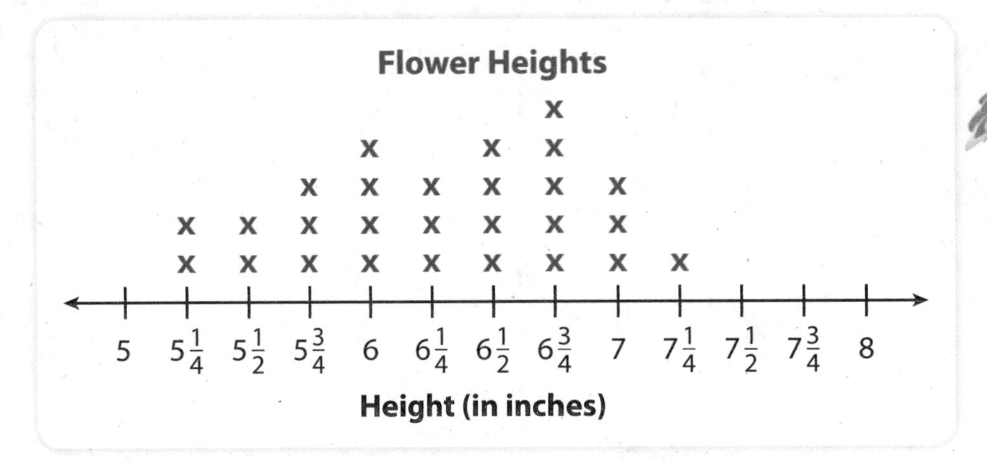

Solution ....

....

4 Check your answer. Show your work.

Develop Representing Data on a Line Plot

Read and try to solve the problem below.

Ten students in Mrs. Holbrook's class are growing plants. One day, they measure the heights of the plants in inches. The heights are shown below. Make a line plot to represent the data.

$2\frac{1}{2}$, $1\frac{7}{8}$, $1\frac{7}{8}$, $1\frac{1}{4}$, $2\frac{5}{8}$, $2\frac{1}{8}$, $1\frac{7}{8}$, $1\frac{1}{2}$, $1\frac{7}{8}$, $2\frac{1}{8}$

TRY IT

Math Toolkit
- number lines
- grid paper
- fraction models

DISCUSS IT

Ask your partner: Do you agree with me? Why or why not?

Tell your partner: I agree with you about . . . because . . .

Explore different ways to understand representing data on a line plot.

Ten students in Mrs. Holbrook's class are growing plants. One day, they measure the heights of the plants in inches. The heights are shown below. Make a line plot to represent the data.

$2\frac{1}{2}$, $1\frac{7}{8}$, $1\frac{7}{8}$, $1\frac{1}{4}$, $2\frac{5}{8}$, $2\frac{1}{8}$, $1\frac{7}{8}$, $1\frac{1}{2}$, $1\frac{7}{8}$, $2\frac{1}{8}$

MODEL IT

You can represent data values that are mixed numbers on a line plot.

The number line is divided into eighths from 1 to 3.

The first three data values of $2\frac{1}{2}$, $1\frac{7}{8}$, and $1\frac{7}{8}$ are represented with **X**s above the number line.

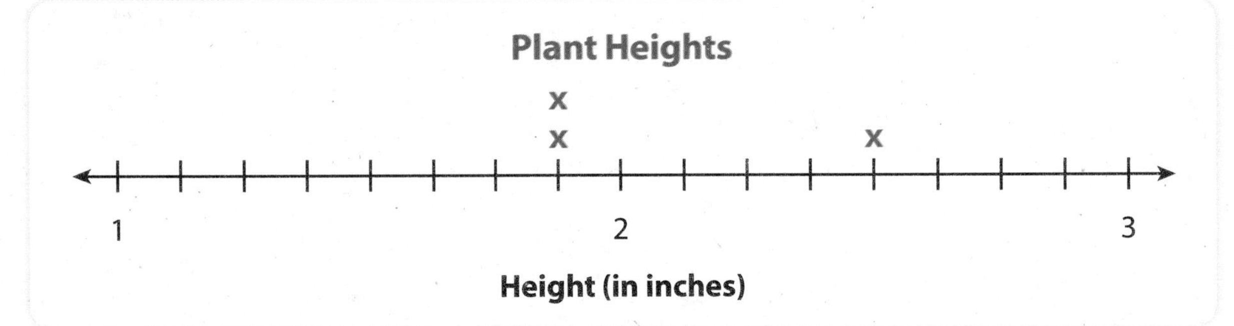

MODEL IT

You can represent data values that are mixed numbers on a line plot with a number line divided into eighths and labeled.

Each tick mark on the line plot is labeled. The labels help you locate where to put the **X**s for each data value. The first three data values of $2\frac{1}{2}$, $1\frac{7}{8}$, and $1\frac{7}{8}$ are shown.

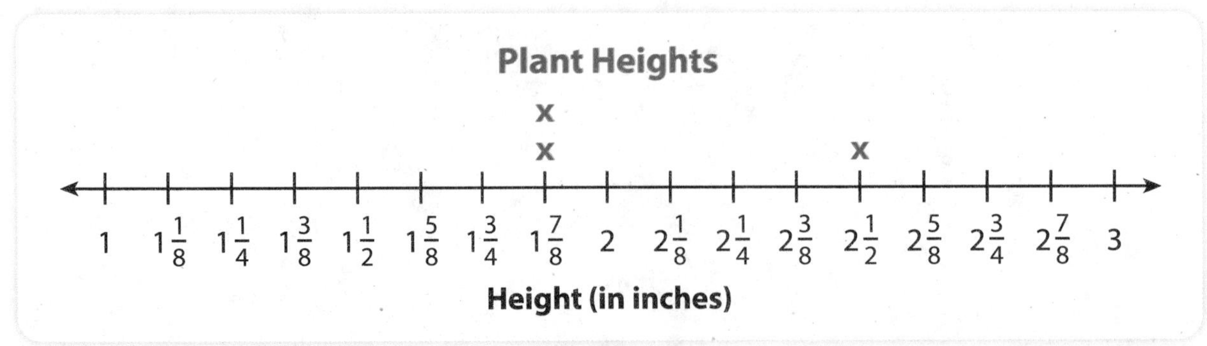

CONNECT IT

Now you will use the problem from the previous page to help you understand how to represent data on a line plot.

1 Look at the **Model Its**. Why do the number lines go from 1 to 3? Why are the number lines divided into eighths?

2 Why are there two Xs above one of the tick marks?

3 Plot the remaining data values to complete the Plant Heights line plot below.

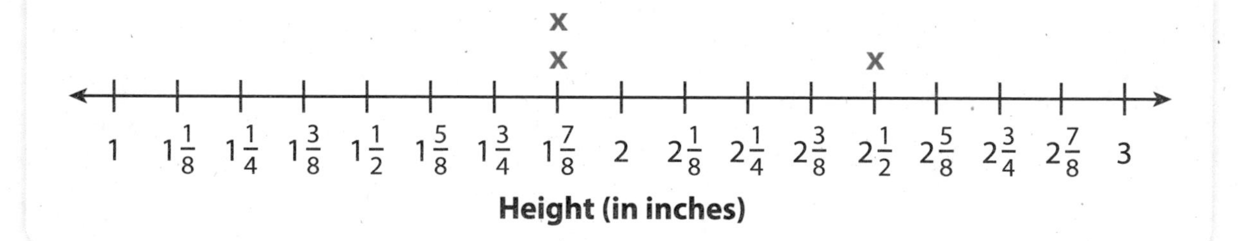

4 Describe how to make a line plot with data that include fractions.

5 **REFLECT**

Look back at your **Try It**, strategies by classmates, and **Model Its**. Which models or strategies do you like best for representing data on a line plot? Explain.

APPLY IT

Use what you just learned to solve these problems.

6 The data below show the length of leaves, in inches, that Jill collects. Complete the line plot to display the data.

$2\frac{1}{2}$, $2\frac{1}{4}$, $3\frac{1}{2}$, $2\frac{3}{4}$, 3, $2\frac{1}{2}$, $2\frac{1}{2}$, 3

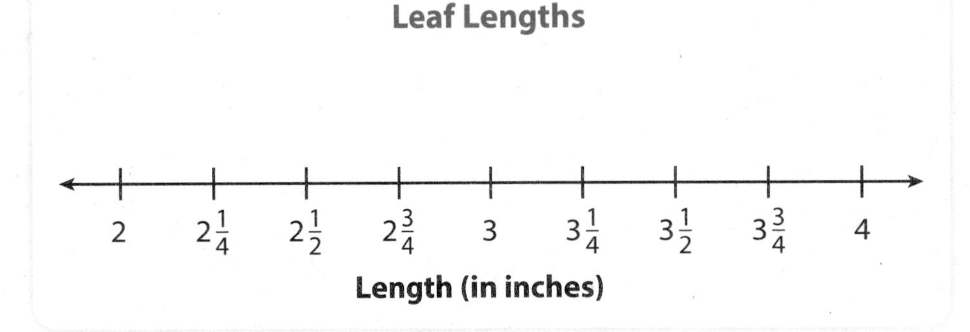

7 Al records the length of some fish, in inches: $9\frac{2}{8}$, $10\frac{4}{8}$, $10\frac{5}{8}$, $9\frac{6}{8}$, $9\frac{7}{8}$, 10, $10\frac{1}{8}$, $9\frac{6}{8}$, $10\frac{3}{8}$. Make a line plot of the data.

8 The lengths in feet of some pieces of wood are shown below. Fix the line plot at the right to correctly show the data.

1, $1\frac{1}{2}$, 2, $1\frac{3}{4}$, $1\frac{1}{2}$, 2

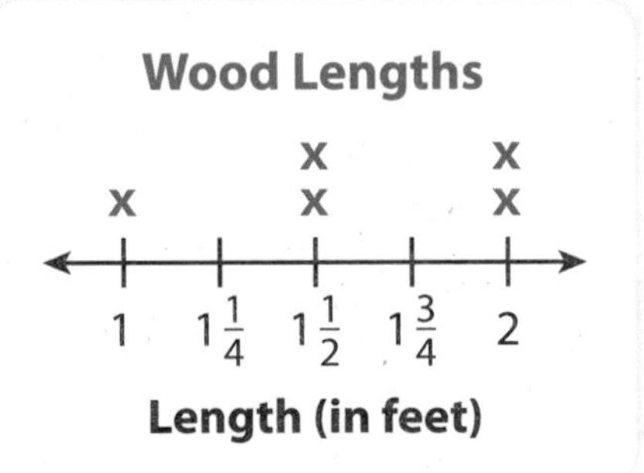

Name: ______________________________

Practice Representing Data on Line Plots

Study the Example showing how to make a line plot. Then solve problems 1–5.

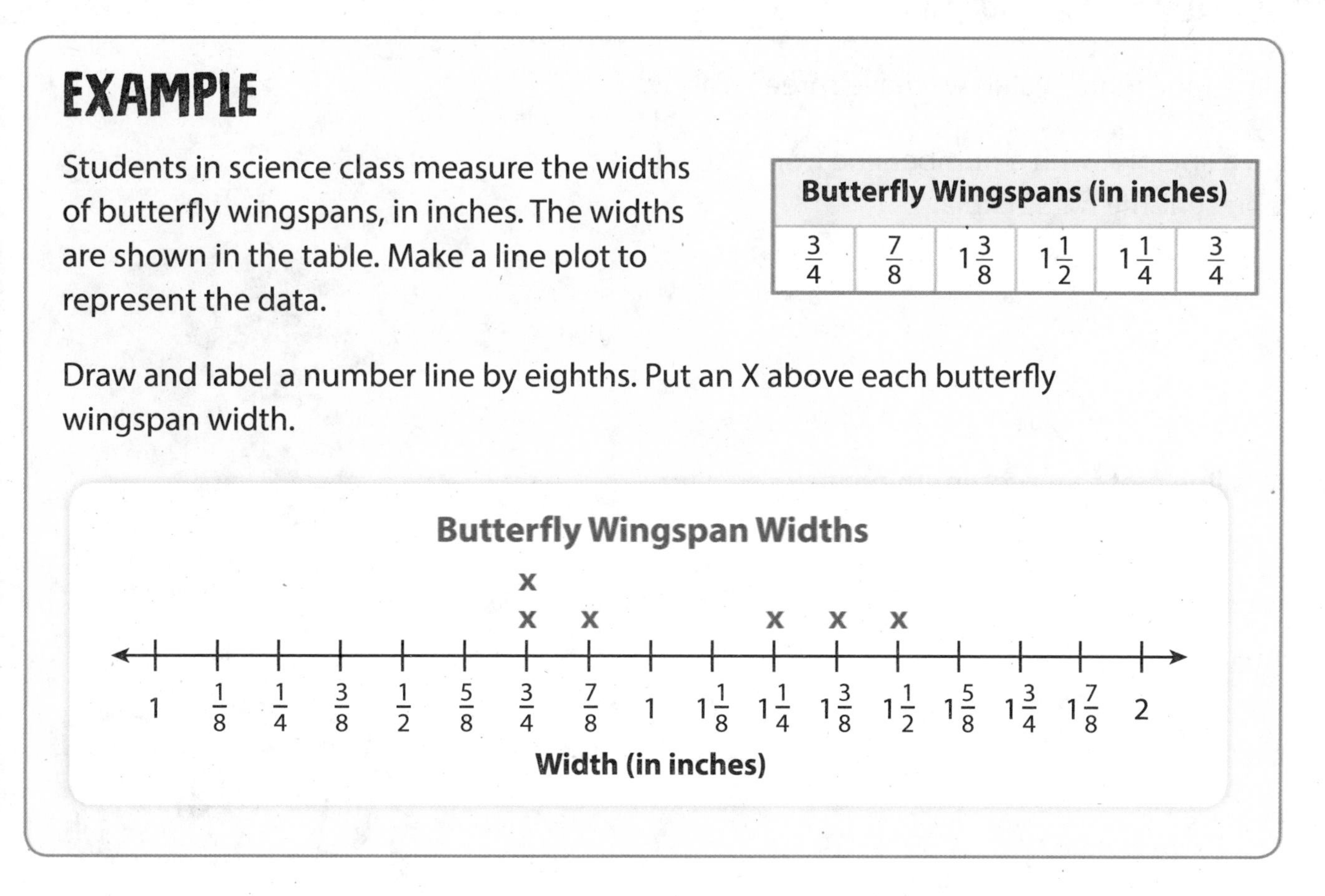

EXAMPLE

Students in science class measure the widths of butterfly wingspans, in inches. The widths are shown in the table. Make a line plot to represent the data.

Butterfly Wingspans (in inches)					
$\frac{3}{4}$	$\frac{7}{8}$	$1\frac{3}{8}$	$1\frac{1}{2}$	$1\frac{1}{4}$	$\frac{3}{4}$

Draw and label a number line by eighths. Put an X above each butterfly wingspan width.

The height of fourth graders is measured on the first day of school and on the last day of school. The growth, in inches, of some students is below.

3, $1\frac{6}{8}$, $2\frac{2}{8}$, $1\frac{4}{8}$, $2\frac{2}{8}$, $2\frac{7}{8}$

1. Complete the line plot below to show the data.

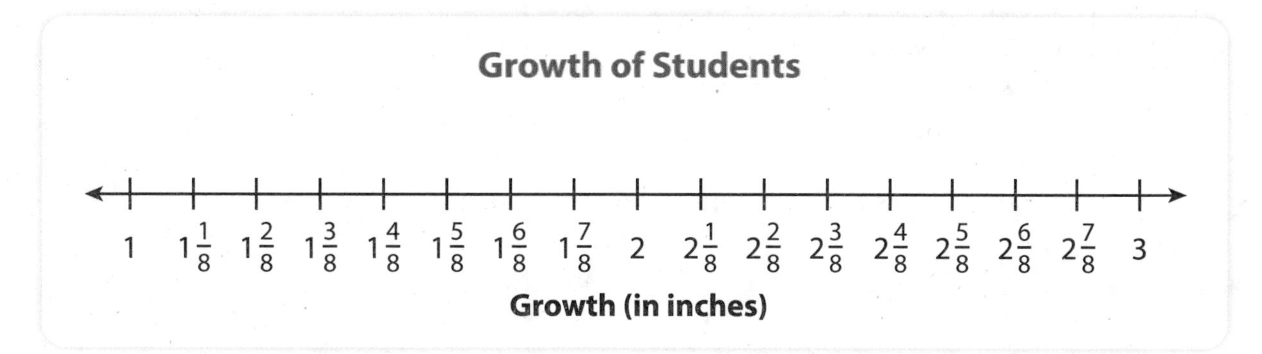

Micah's dog has 8 puppies. The length, in inches, of each puppy is listed below.

$4, 4\frac{3}{4}, 4\frac{1}{2}, 4\frac{1}{2}, 4\frac{1}{2}, 4\frac{3}{4}, 4\frac{1}{4}, 4$

 In a line plot, which value will have three Xs above it? ....

3 Could a line plot with a number line from 5 to 6 be used to represent the data? Explain.

 Draw a line plot to represent the data.

5 Use the line plot to answer the questions.

a. How many measurements are recorded? ....

b. What is the longest length of a puppy? ....

c. What is the shortest length of a puppy? ....

d. How many puppies are less than or equal to $4\frac{1}{2}$ inches in length? ....

e. How many puppies are greater than $4\frac{1}{2}$ inches in length? ....

Develop Adding Fractions in Line Plots

Read and try to solve the problem below.

Sophia is making a border for a quilt. She wants to use leftover strips of fabric. She measures the length of each strip and records the information in a line plot. Sophia puts together the five strips of fabric that are the same length. What is the total length of the five strips of fabric?

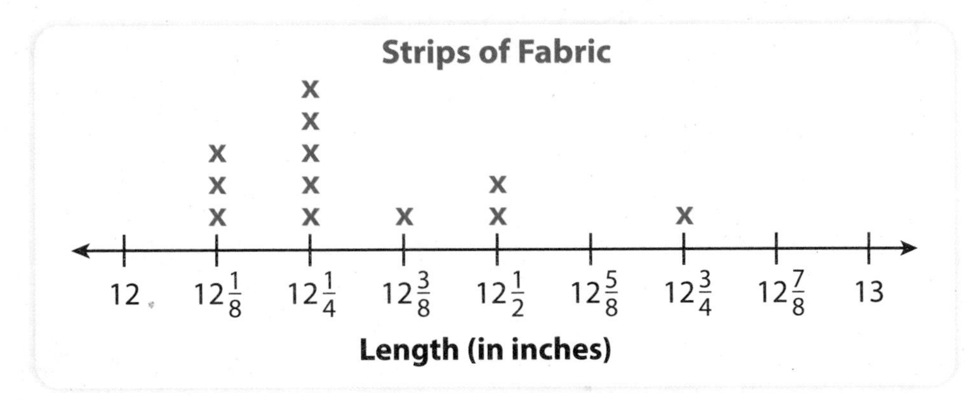

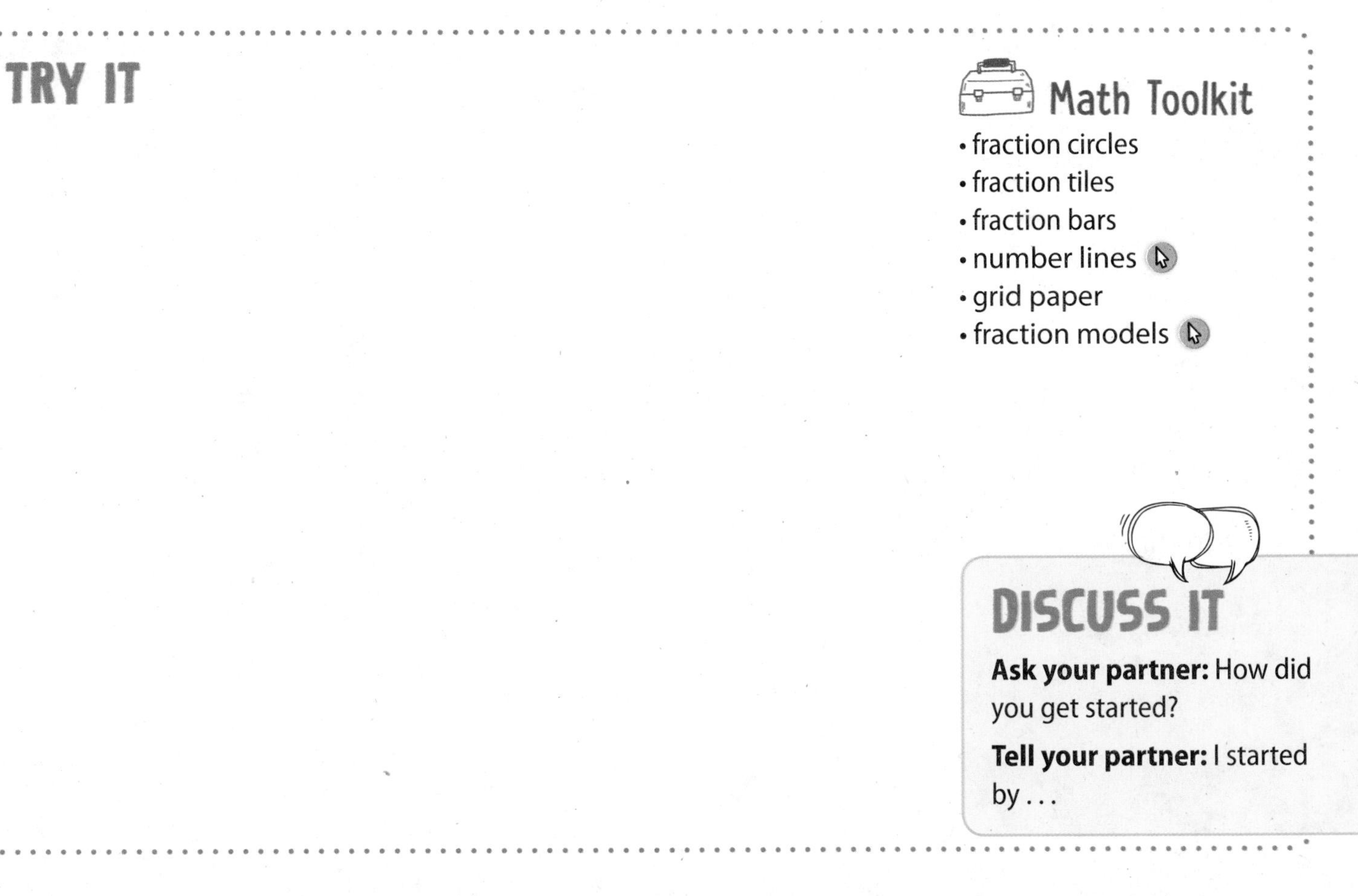

Explore different ways to understand addition of fractions in line plots.

Sophia is making a border for a quilt. She wants to use leftover strips of fabric. She measures the length of each strip and records the information in a line plot. Sophia puts together the five strips of fabric that are the same length. What is the total length of the five strips of fabric?

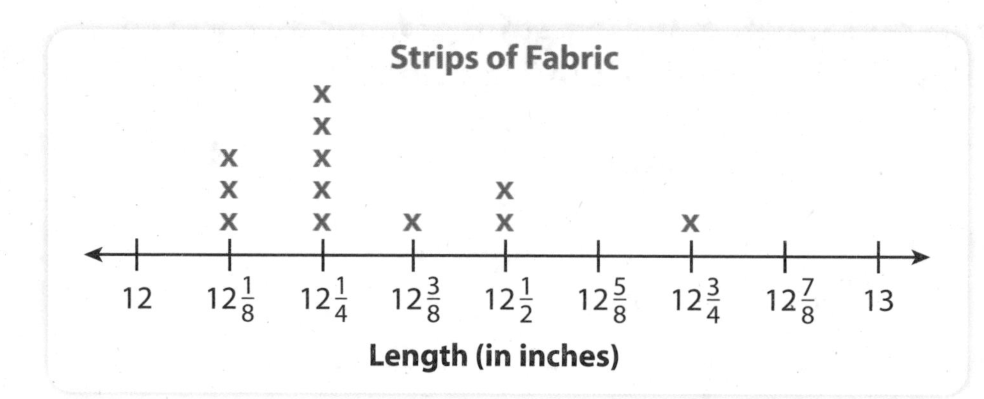

PICTURE IT

You can use a picture to help solve addition problems with line plots.

The picture shows the five strips of fabric placed next to one another to make one long strip.

$12\frac{1}{4}$	$12\frac{1}{4}$	$12\frac{1}{4}$	$12\frac{1}{4}$	$12\frac{1}{4}$

MODEL IT

You can break up the whole numbers and fractions to help you add the lengths.

Add the whole numbers first: $12 + 12 + 12 + 12 + 12$

Then add the fractions: $\frac{1}{4} + \frac{1}{4} + \frac{1}{4} + \frac{1}{4} + \frac{1}{4}$

CONNECT IT

Now you will use the problem from the previous page to help you understand how to solve problems involving the addition of fractions in line plots.

1 Write an expression to find the total length of the five strips of fabric that Sophia puts together.

2 What is the sum of the whole numbers? ....

What is the sum of the fractions? ....

Write the sum of the fractions as a mixed number. ....

What is the total length of the five strips? ....

3 How do you solve a problem about adding fractions or mixed numbers in a line plot?

4 REFLECT

Look back at your **Try It**, strategies by classmates, and **Picture It** and **Model It**. Which models or strategies do you like best for solving problems involving the addition of fractions in line plots? Explain.

....

....

....

....

APPLY IT

Use what you just learned to solve these problems.

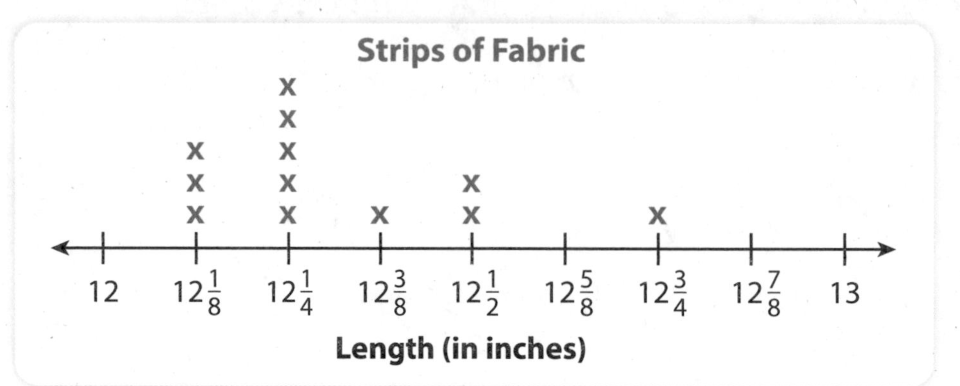

5 Use the line plot above. What is the length of all the $12\frac{1}{8}$-inch strips combined? Show your work.

Solution ....

6 Kay hikes on four days this week. The total distance she hikes is 10 miles. Mark Xs on the number line below to make a possible line plot for the data.

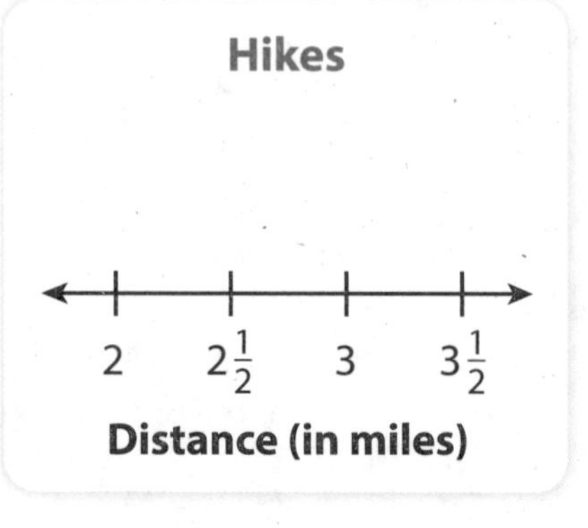

Name: ______________________________

Practice Adding Fractions in Line Plots

Study the Example showing how to solve an addition problem with a line plot. Then solve problems 1–5.

EXAMPLE

Ashley is decorating a frame with seashells. She wants to know if all the shells will fit along the edge of a 13-inch wide frame. She measures the width of each shell and records the information in a line plot. Suppose Ashley puts all the shells in a row. Will the total width of the shells fit on the frame?

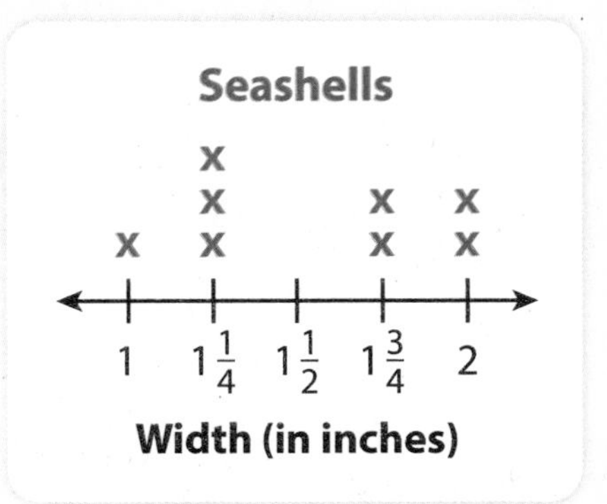

Write an addition expression. $1 + 1\frac{1}{4} + 1\frac{1}{4} + 1\frac{1}{4} + 1\frac{3}{4} + 1\frac{3}{4} + 2 + 2$

Then add. $10\frac{9}{4} = 10 + 2\frac{1}{4} = 12\frac{1}{4}$

The total width of the shells is $12\frac{1}{4}$ inches.

$12\frac{1}{4} < 13$, so the shells will fit on the frame.

1. Look at the line plot in the Example. Ashley decides to glue the four largest shells along the edge of another frame. The shells fit exactly. How wide is the other frame? Show your work.

Solution ....

2. Ashley puts the $1\frac{1}{4}$-inch shells in a row, touching without gaps. What is the total width of the row of shells? Show your work.

Solution ....

A standard-sized brick should be $7\frac{5}{8}$ inches long. The line plot shows the actual lengths of 12 different bricks.

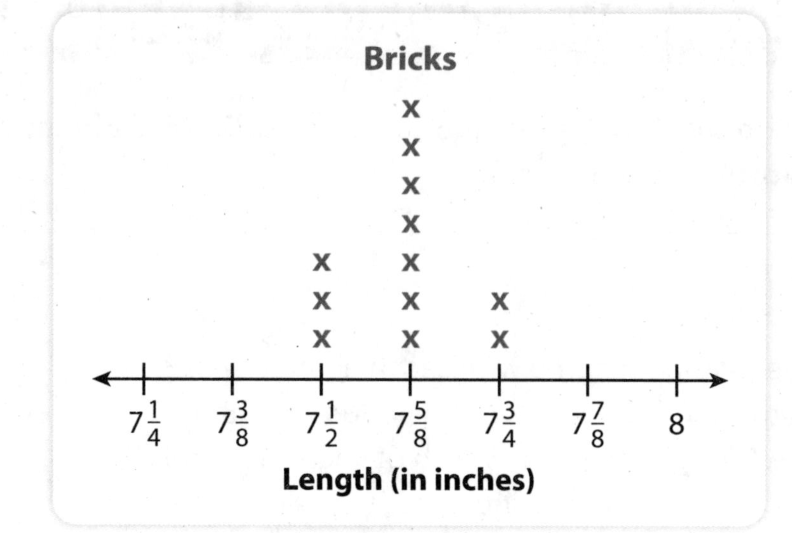

3. What is the sum of the lengths of all the bricks that are exactly $7\frac{5}{8}$ inches long? Show your work.

Solution ....

4. What is the sum of the lengths of all the bricks that are shorter than $7\frac{5}{8}$ inches long? Show your work.

Solution ....

5. What is the sum of the lengths of all the bricks that are longer than $7\frac{5}{8}$ inches long? Show your work.

Solution ....

Develop Subtracting Fractions in Line Plots

Read and try to solve the problem below.

There are many kinds of dragonflies that are different in length. A scientist measures the lengths of different dragonflies and makes a line plot to show the measurements. What is the difference between the lengths of the longest and the shortest dragonfly?

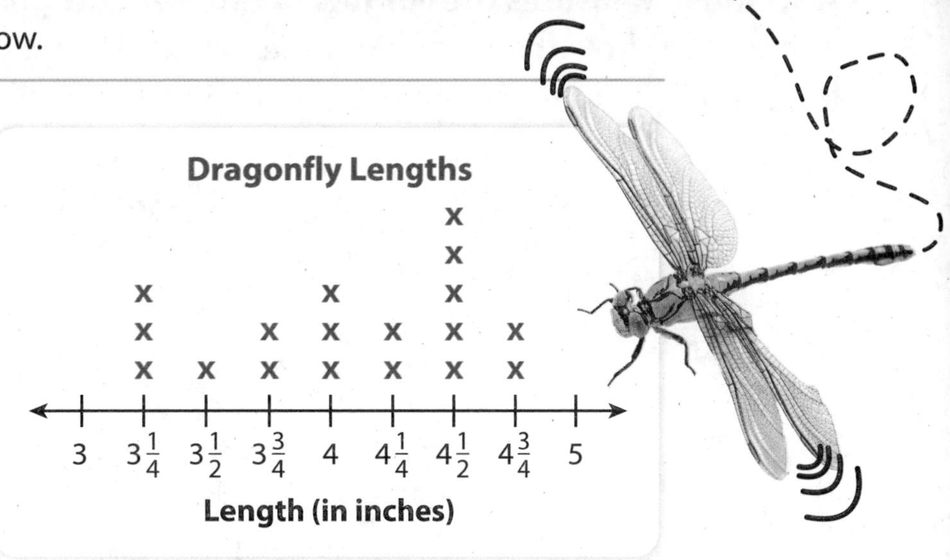

TRY IT

Math Toolkit
- fraction circles
- fraction tiles
- fraction bars
- number lines
- grid paper
- fraction models

DISCUSS IT

Ask your partner: Why did you choose that strategy?

Tell your partner: A model I used was . . . It helped me . . .

Explore different ways to understand subtraction of fractions in line plots.

There are many kinds of dragonflies that are different in length. A scientist measures the lengths of different dragonflies and makes a line plot to show the measurements. What is the difference between the lengths of the longest and the shortest dragonfly?

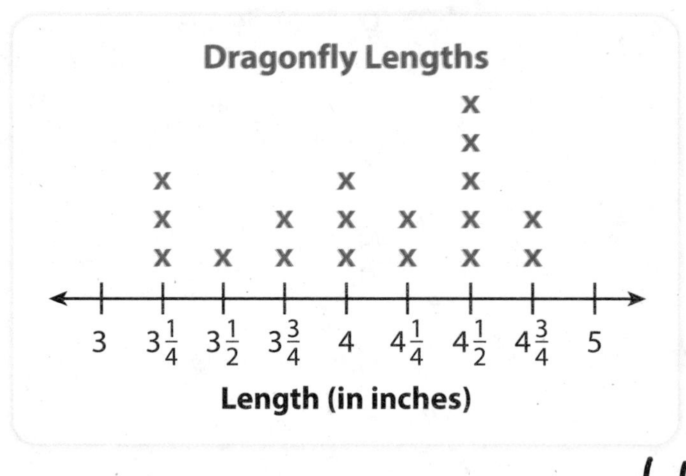

PICTURE IT

You can use a picture to help solve subtraction problems with line plots.

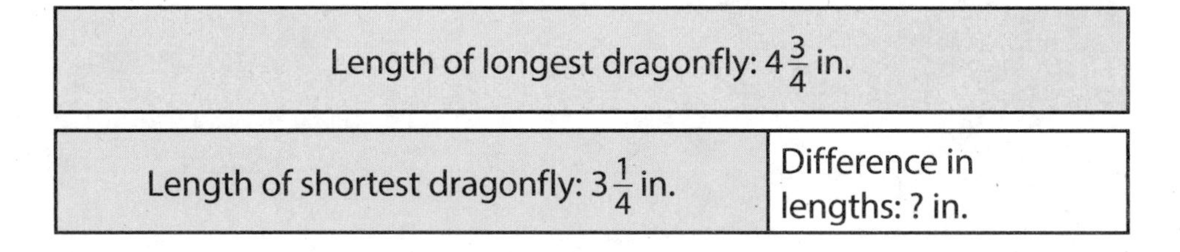

MODEL IT

You can use a number line to solve subtraction problems with line plots.

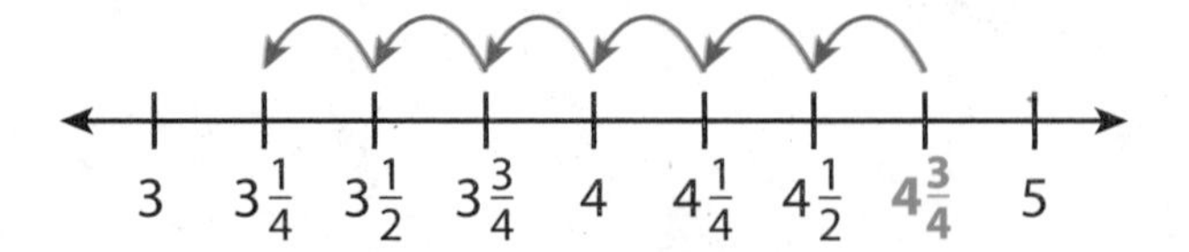

Start at $4\frac{3}{4}$. Jump back by fourths until you get to $3\frac{1}{4}$.

CONNECT IT

Now you will use the problem from the previous page to help you understand how to solve problems involving the subtraction of fractions in line plots.

1. Length of the longest dragonfly: ....

   Length of the shortest dragonfly: ....

2. Write an expression that can be used to find the difference between the two lengths. ....

3. Look at **Model It** on the previous page. Explain how you could use the number line with arrows to find the difference between the two lengths.

4. How can you check that the difference in lengths you found is correct?

5. ## REFLECT

   Look back at your **Try It**, strategies by classmates, and **Picture It** and **Model It**. Which models or strategies do you like best for solving problems involving the subtraction of fractions in line plots? Explain.

   ....

   ....

   ....

   ....

APPLY IT

Use what you just learned to solve these problems.

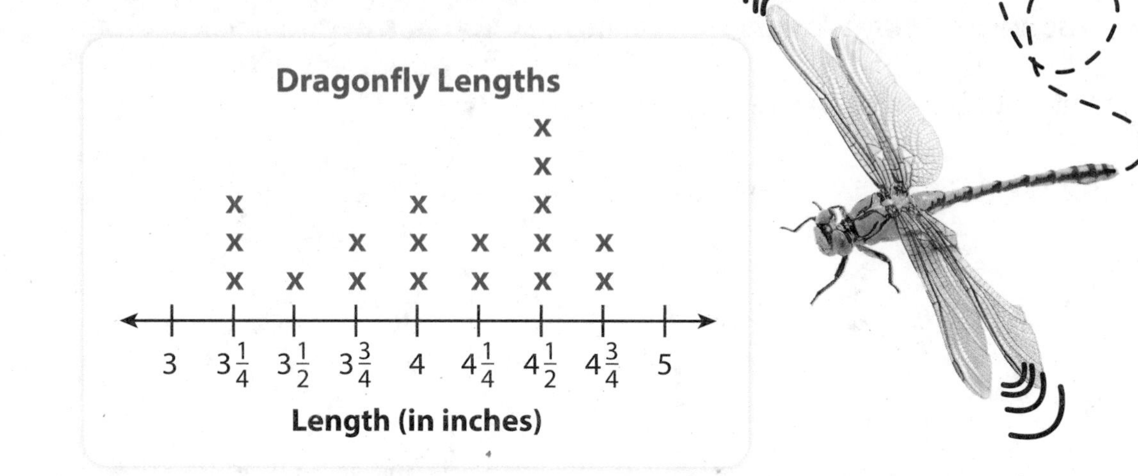

6 Use the line plot above. What length are the greatest number of dragonflies? What length are the least number of dragonflies? What is the difference between the two lengths?

7 The line plot below shows the lengths of pieces of ribbon.

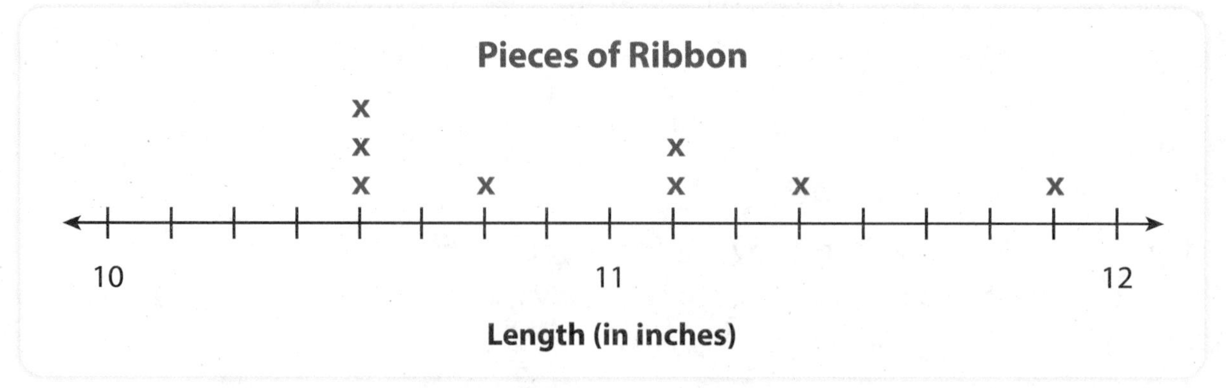

Terri's piece of ribbon is $1\frac{5}{8}$ inches shorter than the longest piece of ribbon. How long is Terri's piece of ribbon? Explain.

Name: ______________________________

Practice Subtracting Fractions in Line Plots

Study the Example showing how to solve a subtraction problem with a line plot. Then solve problems 1–4.

EXAMPLE

The monthly rainfall, in inches, for one city is shown in the line plot. What is the difference in inches of rain between the month with the greatest amount of rain and the month with the least amount of rain?

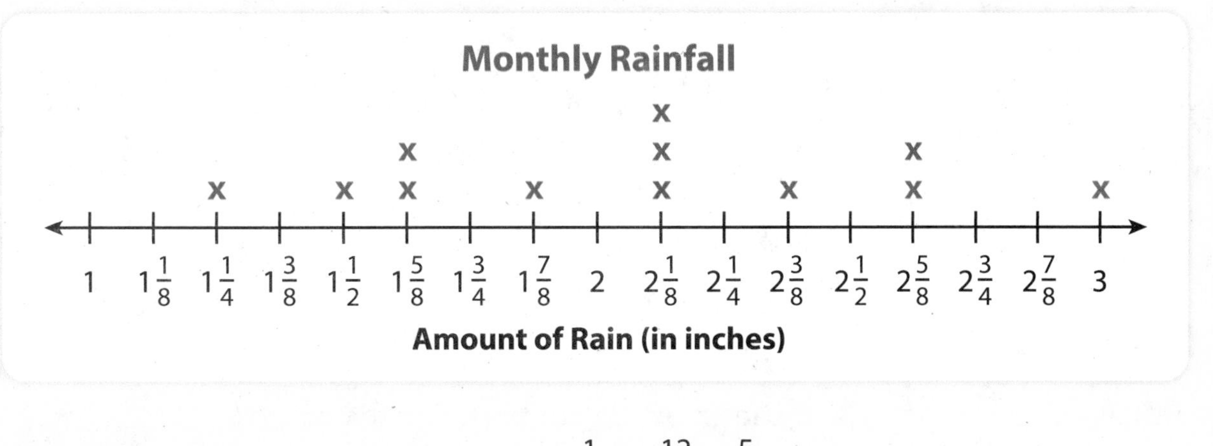

Write a subtraction expression. $3 - 1\frac{1}{4}$ or $\frac{12}{4} - \frac{5}{4}$

Find the difference. $\frac{12}{4} - \frac{5}{4} = \frac{7}{4}$ or $1\frac{3}{4}$

The difference is $1\frac{3}{4}$ inches.

1 Which questions below can be answered using the line plot in the Example above?

Ⓐ In 3 months, it rained the same amount. What is the difference between that amount and the amount in the month when it rained the most?

Ⓑ How much rain fell in the 3 months with the greatest amount of rainfall?

Ⓒ In how many months did it rain more than 2 inches?

Ⓓ How much rainfall occurred in January?

Ⓔ What is the sum of the amount of rainfall last month and this month?

Marine biologists catch fish for research. They measure the sea bass they catch and record the lengths in the line plot below.

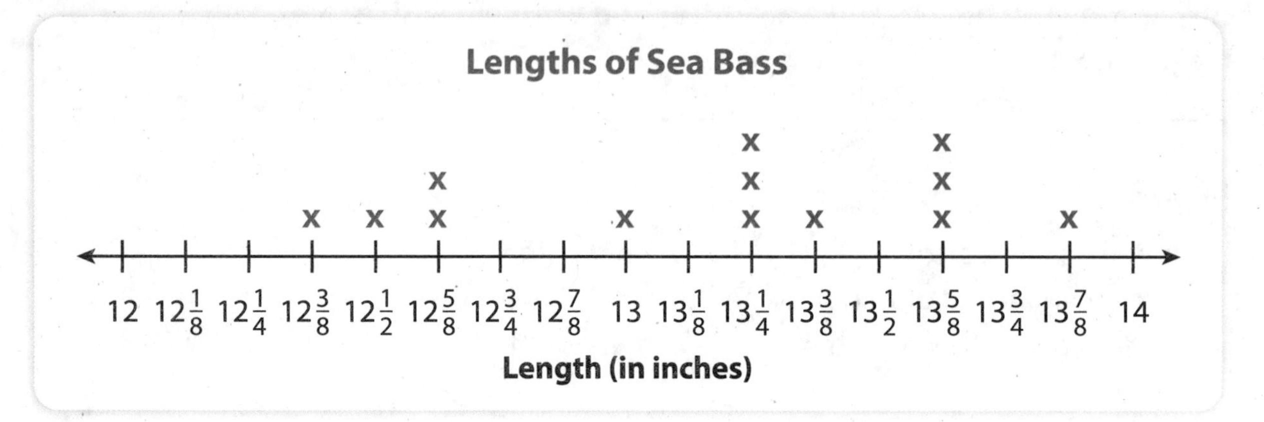

2 What is the difference in length between the longest and shortest sea bass that the biologists catch? Show your work.

Solution ....

3 Sea bass that are shorter than 13 inches must be put back into the ocean. How many more inches does the shortest fish need to grow to be 13 inches? Show your work.

Solution ....

4 Sea bass can grow to be 23 inches long. What is the difference between 23 inches and the length of the longest fish in this data? Show your work.

Solution ....

Refine Adding and Subtracting Fractions in Line Plots

Complete the Example below. Then solve problems 1–7.

EXAMPLE

Sue records the distances she runs in one week. How far does she run altogether?

Running Distances

Distance (in miles)	1	$1\frac{1}{8}$	$1\frac{1}{4}$	$1\frac{3}{8}$	$1\frac{1}{2}$	$1\frac{5}{8}$	$1\frac{3}{4}$	$1\frac{7}{8}$	2
	x	x		x x		x		x	

Look at how you could show your work using equations.

Add the whole numbers: $1 + 1 + 1 + 1 + 1 + 1 = 6$

Add the fractional parts of each mixed number:

$\frac{1}{8} + \frac{3}{8} + \frac{3}{8} + \frac{5}{8} + \frac{7}{8} = \frac{19}{8} = 2\frac{3}{8}$

Solution ....

The student adds the whole numbers and the fractions separately.

PAIR/SHARE
How else could you solve the problem?

APPLY IT

1 A marine biologist at an aquarium records the lengths of the dolphins in feet. Make a line plot of the data shown below.

$8\frac{3}{4}, 9\frac{1}{2}, 9\frac{1}{4}, 8\frac{1}{2}, 8\frac{7}{8}, 9\frac{1}{2}, 8\frac{1}{2}, 9\frac{1}{4}, 9\frac{5}{8}, 9\frac{1}{2}$

What length are the greatest number of dolphins?

PAIR/SHARE
Explain how you labeled the tick marks.

2 A park has several trails of different lengths. The lengths of the trails are shown in the line plot. Ellie's family hikes all the trails that are $1\frac{3}{8}$ miles long. How far do they hike? Show your work.

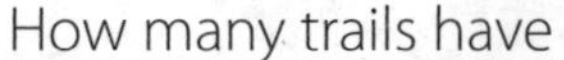

How many trails have a length of $1\frac{3}{8}$ miles?

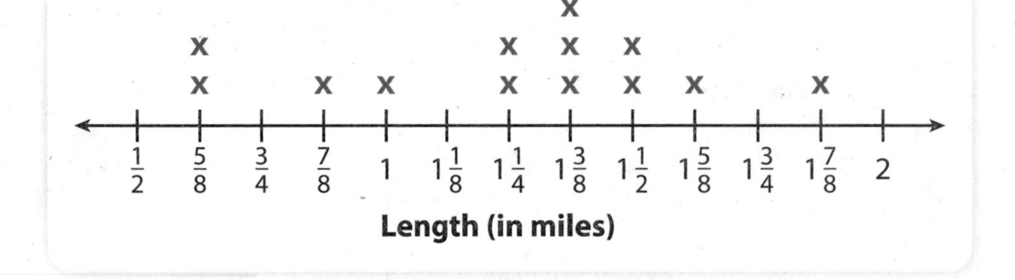

PAIR/SHARE
Describe all of the ways you can solve the problem. Which is your favorite? Why?

Solution ....

3 Use the line plot in problem 2.

What is the difference in length between the longest trail and the shortest trail?

Will you add or subtract to find the difference?

Ⓐ $\frac{6}{8}$ of a mile

Ⓑ 1 mile

Ⓒ $1\frac{2}{8}$ miles

Ⓓ $2\frac{4}{8}$ miles

Tom chose Ⓓ as the correct answer. How did he get that answer?

PAIR/SHARE
Does Tom's answer make sense?

4 The veterinarian at an animal shelter weighs the puppies every day. One day she records the weights in a line plot.

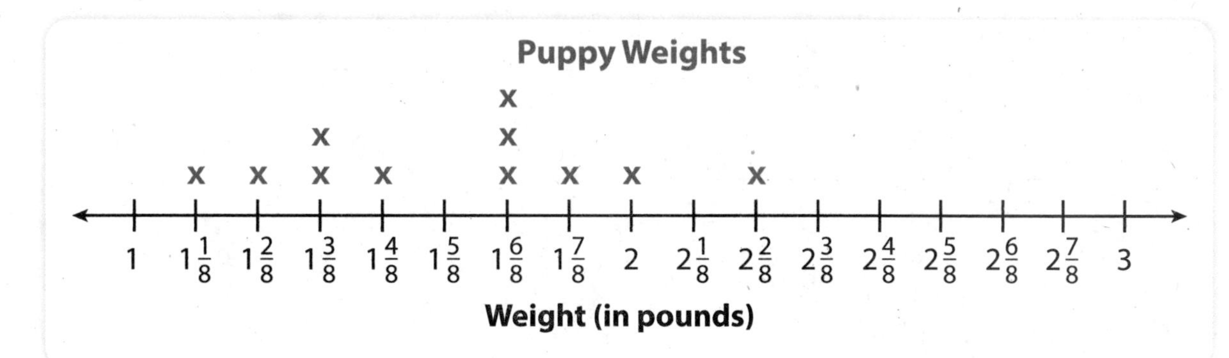

Use the line plot above to tell whether each sentence is *True* or *False*.

	True	False
The difference in weight between the two heaviest puppies is $\frac{1}{8}$ of a pound.	Ⓐ	Ⓑ
The combined weight of the two lightest puppies is $2\frac{2}{8}$ pounds.	Ⓒ	Ⓓ
The difference in weight between the heaviest puppy and the lightest puppy is $1\frac{1}{8}$ pounds.	Ⓔ	Ⓕ

5 In the line plot from problem 4, there are three puppies that weigh the same amount. What is the combined weight of those three puppies? Show your work.

Solution ....

6 Alexandra has a ribbon that is 50 inches long. She cuts off four pieces. The line plot below shows the lengths of the pieces she cuts off.

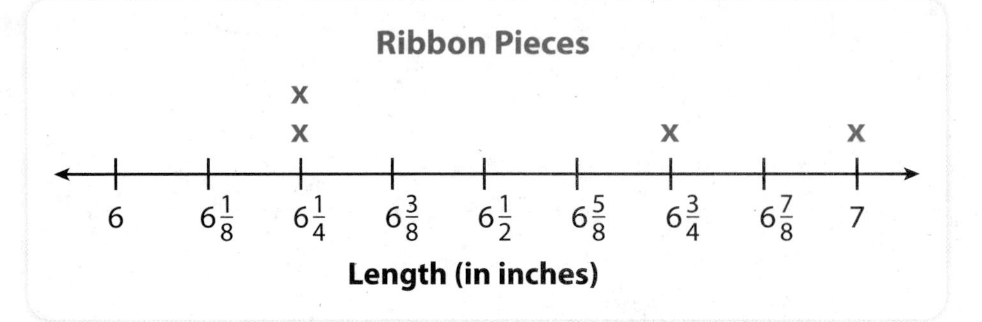

What is the total length of the four pieces? Show your work.

Solution ....

7 MATH JOURNAL

Write a different word problem for the line plot from problem 6 that you can solve by adding or subtracting mixed numbers. Explain how to find the answer.

SELF CHECK Go back to the Unit 4 Opener and see what you can check off.

Understand Fraction Multiplication

LESSON 23

Dear Family,

This week your child is exploring fraction multiplication.

Multiplying fractions is finding the total number of equal-sized parts in equal groups.

Your child can use a model to understand fraction multiplication.

This model shows $5 \times \frac{1}{3}$.

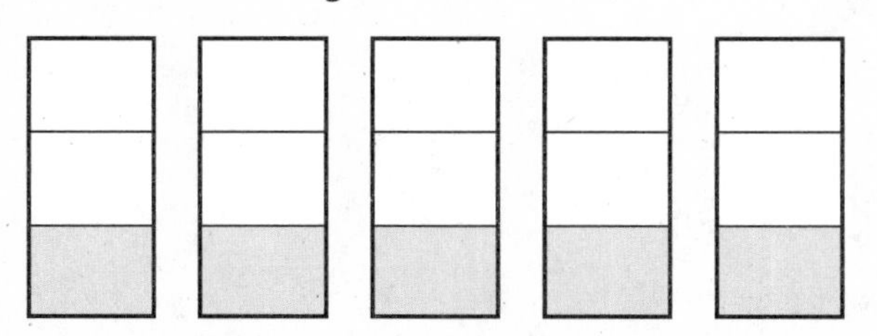

You can see that there are 5 groups of $\frac{1}{3}$.

There are $\frac{5}{3}$ in all.

The denominator tells the number of equal-sized parts in the whole.

There are 3 equal-sized parts in each whole.

Your child can also think about repeated addition to understand fraction multiplication.

Adding $\frac{1}{3}$ five times is the same as multiplying $\frac{1}{3}$ by 5.

$$\frac{1}{3} + \frac{1}{3} + \frac{1}{3} + \frac{1}{3} + \frac{1}{3} = \frac{5}{3}$$

Invite your child to share what he or she knows about fraction multiplication by doing the following activity together.

ACTIVITY FRACTION MULTIPLICATION

Do this activity with your child to explore fraction multiplication.

Materials bowl, measuring cup, ingredients shown in the recipe

- Look at the recipe below for snack mix.
- Rewrite the recipe so that you can make four times as much snack mix. Multiply the amount of each ingredient by 4.
- Make the recipe and enjoy!

Snack Mix

Ingredients

$\frac{1}{4}$ of a cup pretzels

$\frac{3}{4}$ of a cup nuts of your choice

$\frac{1}{2}$ of a cup raisins

$\frac{2}{3}$ of a cup cereal

$\frac{1}{3}$ of a cup chocolate chips (optional)

Directions

Mix all the ingredients together. Store in a container.

Answer: 1 cup pretzels, 3 cups nuts, 2 cups raisins, $\frac{8}{3}$ or $2\frac{2}{3}$ cups cereal, $\frac{4}{3}$ or $1\frac{1}{3}$ cups chocolate chips

Explore Fraction Multiplication

What is really going on when you multiply numbers?

Learning Targets

- Understand a fraction $\frac{a}{b}$ as a multiple of $\frac{1}{b}$.
- Understand a multiple of $\frac{a}{b}$ as a multiple of $\frac{1}{b}$, and use this understanding to multiply a fraction by a whole number.

SMP 1, 2, 3, 4, 5, 6, 7, 8

MODEL IT

Complete the problems below.

1 Look at the model. Write an addition equation to add the $\frac{1}{3}$s.

2 You can use multiplication with fractions to show repeated addition of fractions, just as you do with whole numbers. Complete the sentence and equation below.

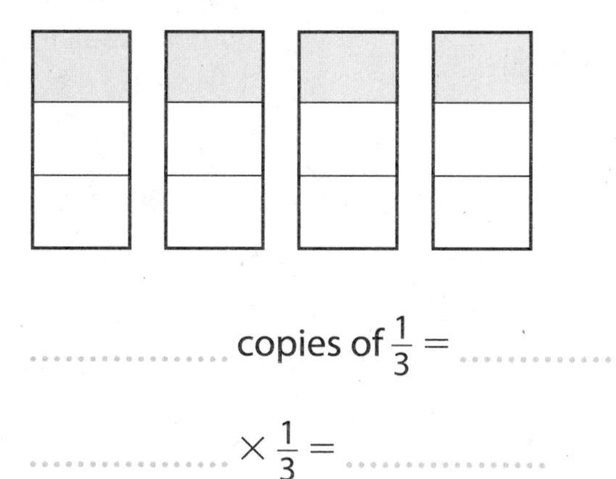

.... copies of $\frac{1}{3}$ = ...

.... $\times \frac{1}{3}$ = ...

DISCUSS IT

- Compare the equations you wrote in problems 1 and 2 to your partner's equations. Are they the same?
- I think multiplying fractions is like repeated addition of fractions because . . .

MODEL IT

Complete the problems below.

3 Look at the model below.

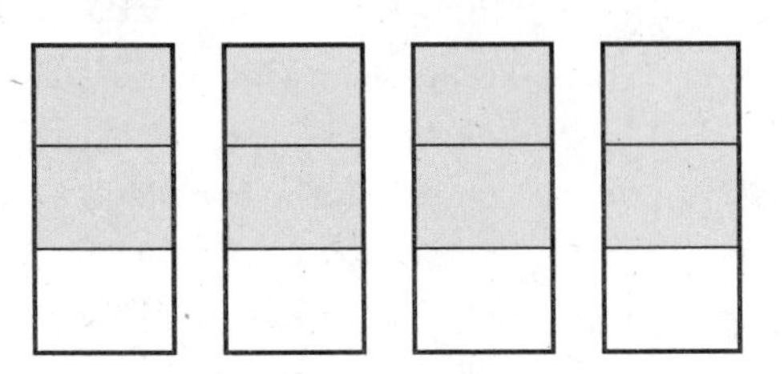

a. Write an addition equation to add the $\frac{2}{3}$s.

b. Complete the multiplication equation.

$\dots\dots \times \frac{2}{3} = \dots\dots$

4 Look at the model below.

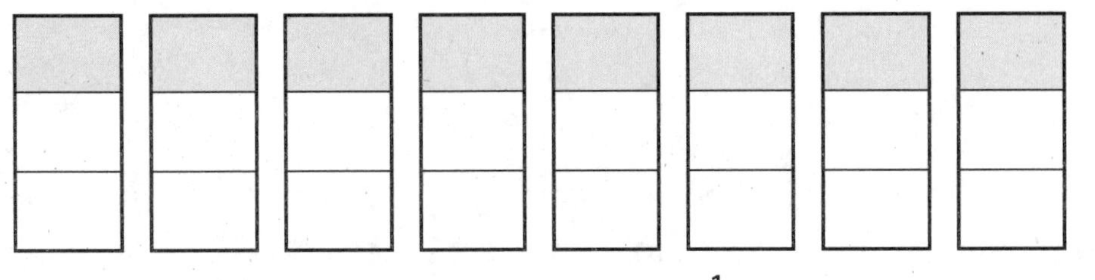

a. Write an addition equation to add the $\frac{1}{3}$s.

b. Complete the multiplication equation.

$\dots\dots \times \frac{1}{3} = \dots\dots$

DISCUSS IT

- Compare the models and equations in problems 3b and 4b. How are they alike? How are they different?
- How many copies of $\frac{1}{3}$ are in each model?

5 REFLECT

Look at your answers to problems 3 and 4. Why can you use addition or multiplication to describe each model?

....

....

Prepare for Fraction Multiplication

1 Think about what you know about fraction models. Fill in each box. Use words, numbers, and pictures. Show as many ideas as you can.

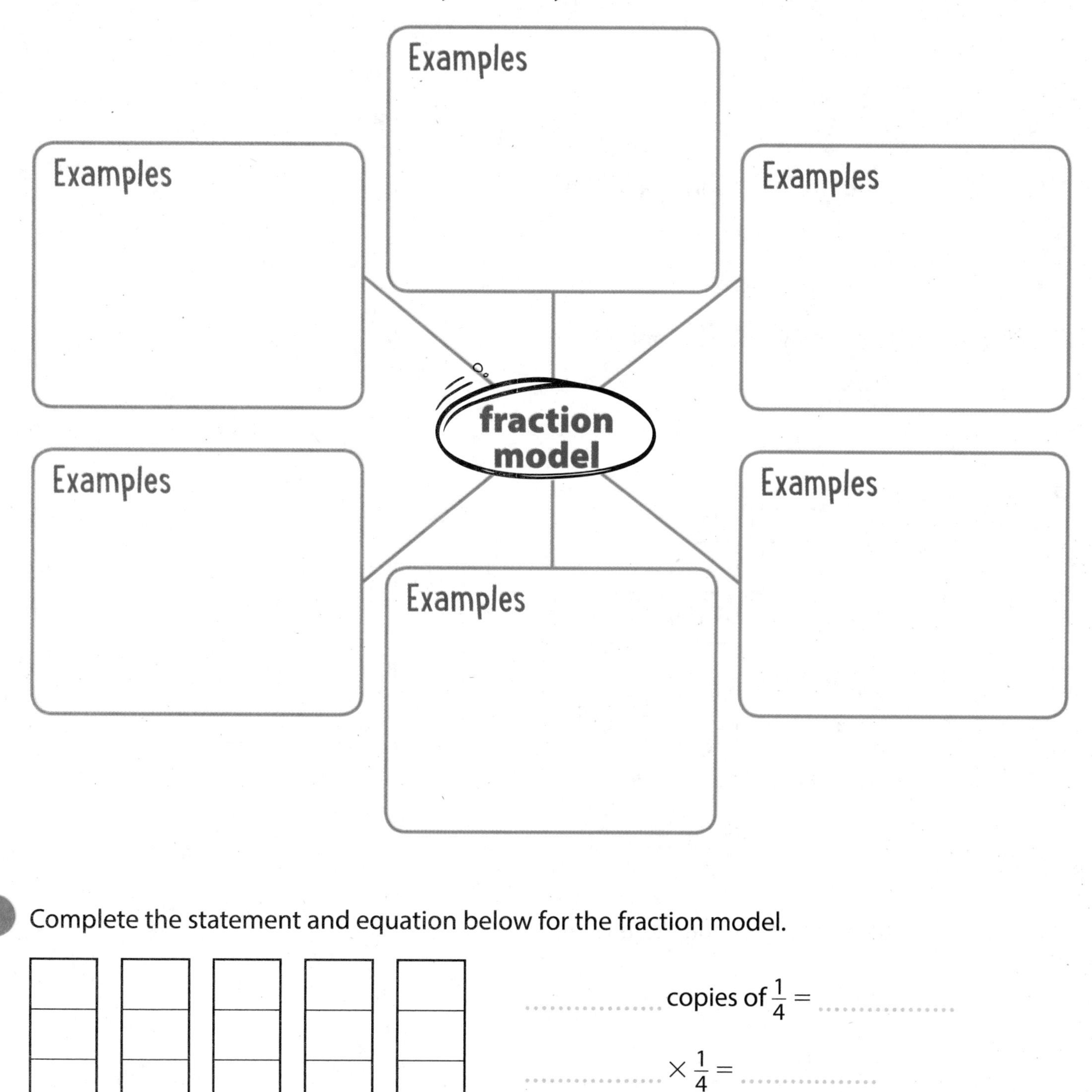

2 Complete the statement and equation below for the fraction model.

.... copies of $\frac{1}{4}$ = ...

.... $\times \frac{1}{4}$ = ...

Solve.

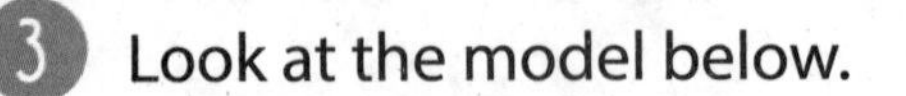

3 Look at the model below.

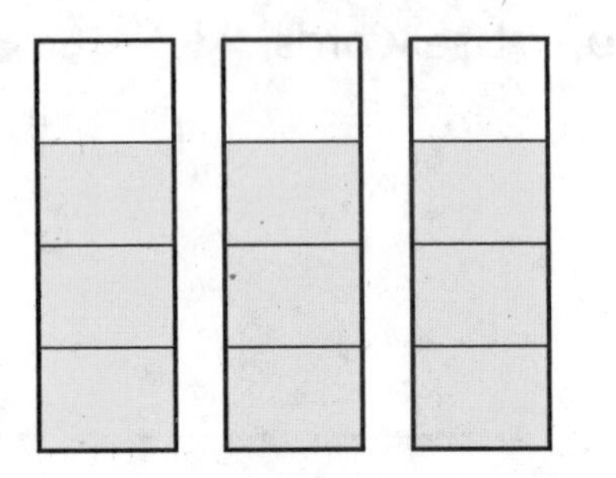

a. Write an addition equation to add the $\frac{3}{4}$s.

b. Complete the multiplication equation.

$\dotfill \times \frac{3}{4} = \dotfill$

4 Look at the model below.

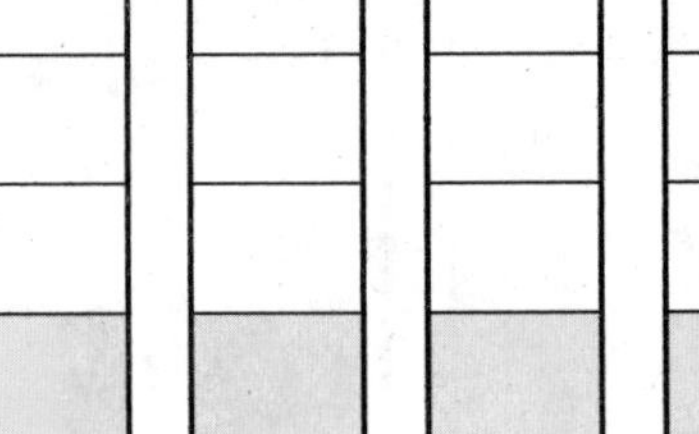

a. Write an addition equation to add the $\frac{1}{4}$s.

b. Complete the multiplication equation.

$\dotfill \times \frac{1}{4} = \dotfill$

Develop Understanding of Fraction Multiplication

MODEL IT: AREA MODELS

Try these two problems.

1. Draw an area model to show $3 \times \frac{2}{5}$. Then write the product.

$3 \times \frac{2}{5} =$ ....

2. Draw an area model to show $6 \times \frac{1}{5}$. Then write the product.

$6 \times \frac{1}{5} =$ ....

DISCUSS IT

- Compare your models in problems 1 and 2 to your partner's models. How are the models the same? How are the models different?
- I think area models show multiplying a fraction by a whole number because . . .

MODEL IT: NUMBER LINES

Use the number lines to show multiplying a fraction by a whole number.

3 Fill in the blanks on the number line to show $4 \times \frac{3}{5}$. Then write the product.

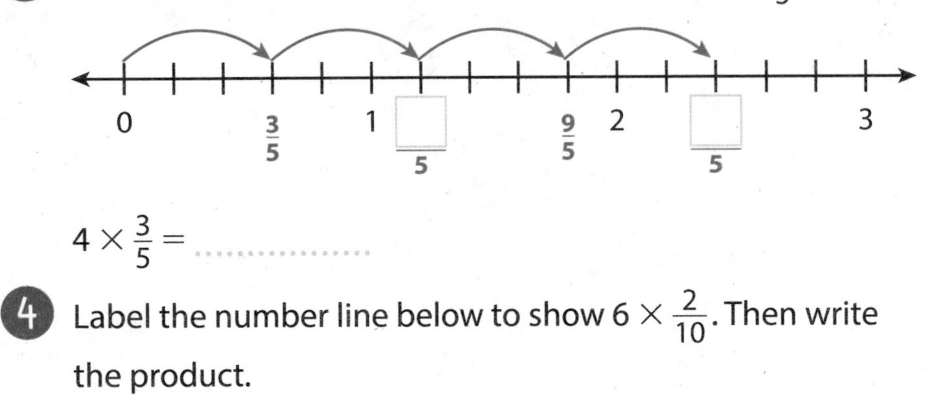

$4 \times \frac{3}{5} =$ ....

4 Label the number line below to show $6 \times \frac{2}{10}$. Then write the product.

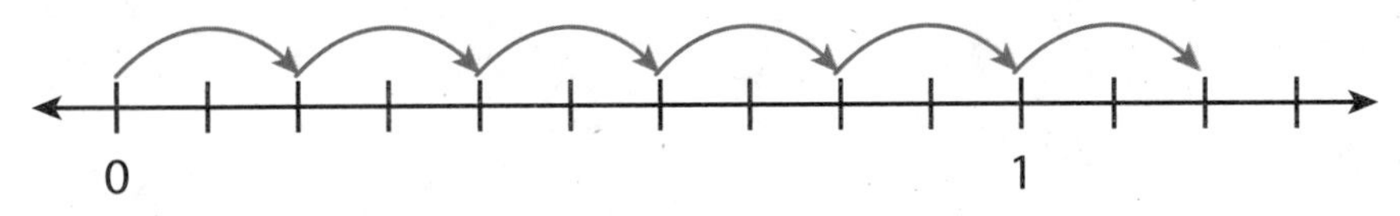

$6 \times \frac{2}{10} =$ ....

DISCUSS IT

- How did you know how to label the number lines in problems 3 and 4?
- I think using number lines can help me multiply a fraction by a whole number because . . .

CONNECT IT

Complete the problems below.

5 How are the area models and number line models alike and different in showing fraction multiplication?

6 Choose any model to show $3 \times \frac{2}{4}$. Then write the product.

$3 \times \frac{2}{4} =$ ....

Name: ______________________________

Practice Fraction Multiplication

Study how the Example shows how to multiply a fraction by a whole number. Then solve problems 1–7.

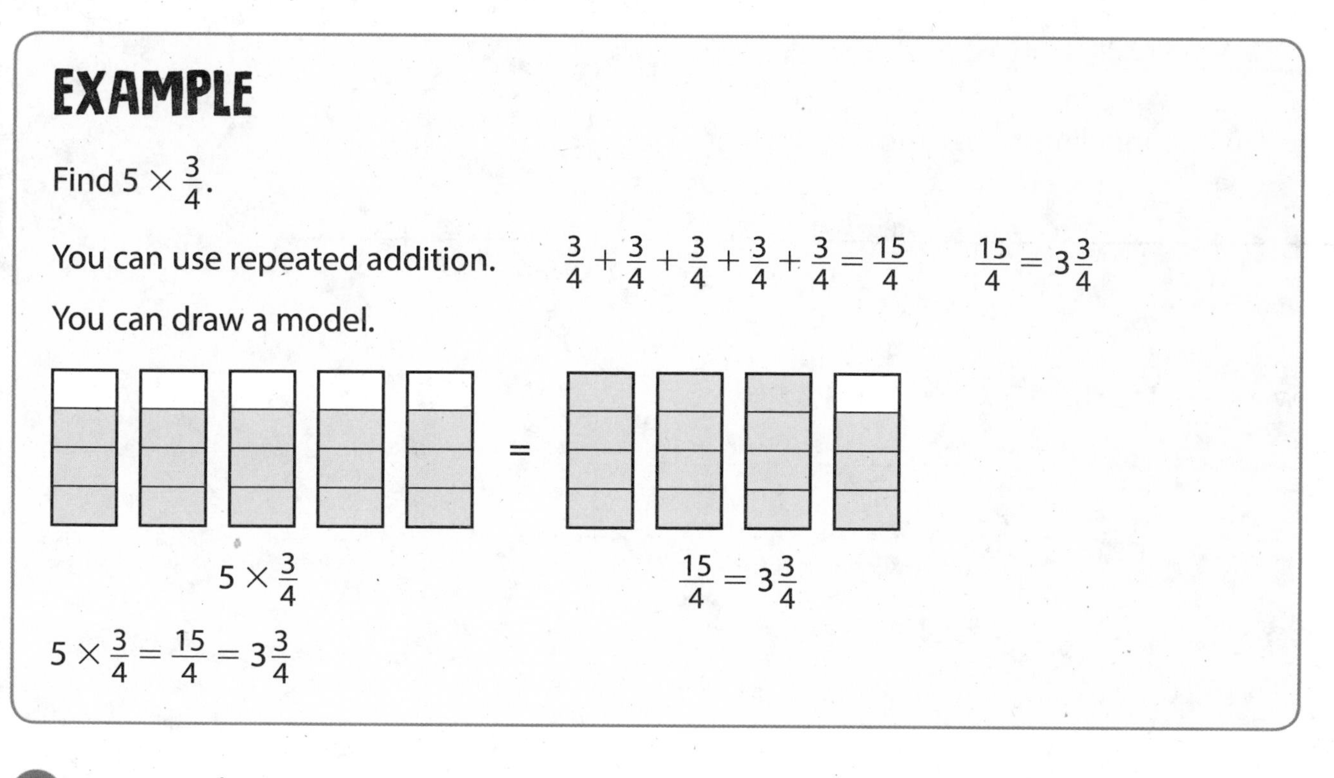

EXAMPLE

Find $5 \times \frac{3}{4}$.

You can use repeated addition. $\frac{3}{4} + \frac{3}{4} + \frac{3}{4} + \frac{3}{4} + \frac{3}{4} = \frac{15}{4}$ $\frac{15}{4} = 3\frac{3}{4}$

You can draw a model.

$5 \times \frac{3}{4}$ $\frac{15}{4} = 3\frac{3}{4}$

$5 \times \frac{3}{4} = \frac{15}{4} = 3\frac{3}{4}$

1 Find $6 \times \frac{1}{4}$ using repeated addition.

.... + ... + ... + ... + ... + ... = ...

2 Look at the model. Tell whether each expression shows the product of $3 \times \frac{5}{8}$.

	Yes	No
$5 \times \frac{3}{8}$	Ⓐ	Ⓑ
$\frac{5}{8} + \frac{5}{8} + \frac{5}{8}$	Ⓒ	Ⓓ
$24 \times \frac{1}{5}$	Ⓔ	Ⓕ
$15 \times \frac{1}{8}$	Ⓖ	Ⓗ

3 The number line below shows .... $\times$ $\frac{\square}{\square}$.

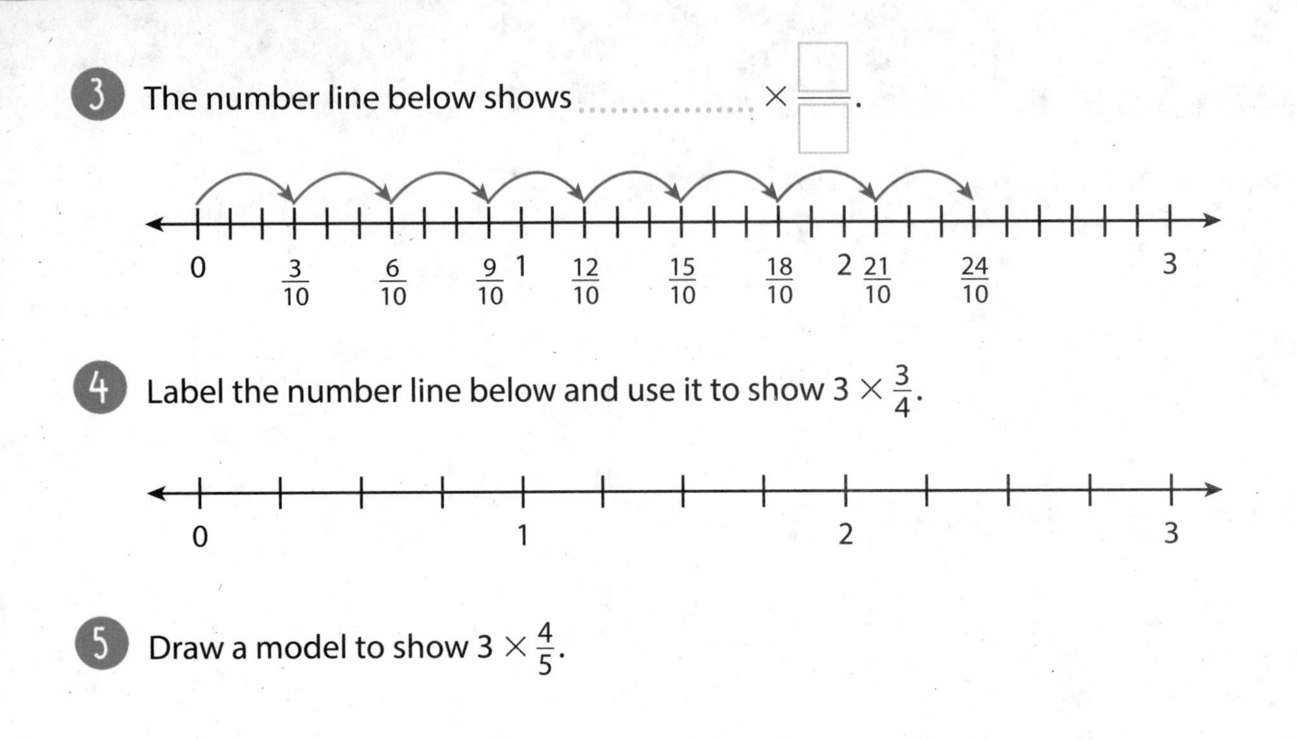

4 Label the number line below and use it to show $3 \times \frac{3}{4}$.

5 Draw a model to show $3 \times \frac{4}{5}$.

6 Look at the model you drew in problem 5. Use the digits 2, 3, 4, 5, and 6 to write two different multiplication problems with the same product as $3 \times \frac{4}{5}$. (Use a digit more than once.)

7 Lisa says that $3 \times \frac{1}{6}$ and $\frac{3}{6} + \frac{3}{6} + \frac{3}{6}$ have the same value. Is Lisa correct? Explain.

Refine Ideas About Fraction Multiplication

APPLY IT

Complete these problems on your own.

1 ANALYZE

How is $3 \times \frac{3}{6}$ the same as $9 \times \frac{1}{6}$?

2 EVALUATE

Violet solves $4 \times \frac{7}{10}$ as shown. What does she do wrong?

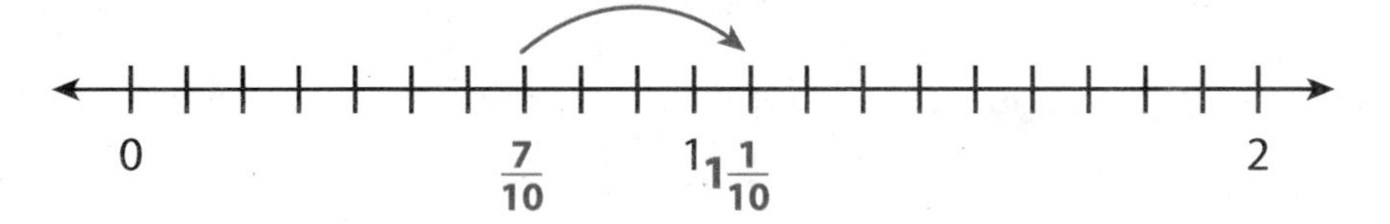

3 CONSTRUCT

Anders triples a recipe and needs $\frac{3}{2}$ cups of flour. He has a $\frac{1}{2}$-cup measuring cup. How many times does he fill the measuring cup with flour? Make a drawing and write a multiplication equation to model the situation.

Solution ....

PAIR/SHARE
Discuss your solutions for these three problems with a partner.

Use what you have learned to complete problem 4.

4 Joaquin runs $\frac{4}{5}$ of a mile each day on Monday, Wednesday, and Friday. How many miles does he run in all?

Part A Describe two methods you could use to solve the problem $3 \times \frac{4}{5}$.

i

ii

Part B Write a different multiplication problem with the same product as $3 \times \frac{4}{5}$. Use $\frac{1}{5}$ instead of $\frac{4}{5}$. ....

Part C Allison is starting to run each day. She runs $\frac{1}{5}$ of a mile on all 7 days this week. Joaquin and Allison each wanted to run at least 2 miles during the week. Do they? Use a drawing or words to explain how you know.

MATH JOURNAL

How are $4 \times \frac{2}{6}$ and $8 \times \frac{1}{6}$ the same? Use a model or words to show how you know.

Multiply Fractions by Whole Numbers

Dear Family,

This week your child is learning to multiply fractions by whole numbers to solve word problems.

Your child might see a problem such as the one below.

Randy practices guitar for $\frac{2}{3}$ of an hour on 4 days this week. How long does Randy practice guitar this week?

Using fraction models can help your child solve this word problem.

Each fraction model below is divided into thirds and shows $\frac{2}{3}$, the fractional amount of an hour that Randy practices guitar each day.

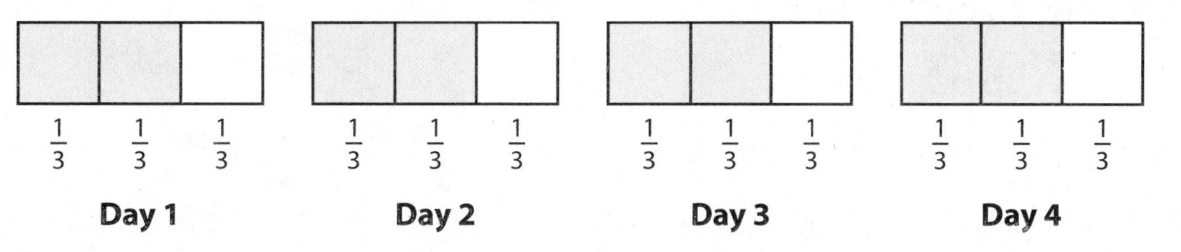

The fraction models show $4 \times \frac{2}{3}$. The fraction models show $\frac{8}{3}$.

Your child can also write an equation to find how long Randy practices guitar.

$$4 \times \frac{2}{3} = \frac{8}{3}$$

Then your child can check his or her answer by using repeated addition.

$$\frac{2}{3} + \frac{2}{3} + \frac{2}{3} + \frac{2}{3} = \frac{8}{3}$$

The answer is that Randy practices guitar $\frac{8}{3}$, or $2\frac{2}{3}$, hours this week.

Invite your child to share what he or she knows about multiplying fractions by whole numbers by doing the following activity together.

ACTIVITY MULTIPLYING FRACTIONS BY WHOLE NUMBERS

Do this activity with your child to multiply fractions by whole numbers.

Materials large pitcher, measuring cup, ingredients shown in the recipe

- Look at the recipe below for punch.
- Rewrite the recipe so that you can make three times as much punch. Multiply the amount of each ingredient by 3.
- Make the recipe and enjoy!

Cranberry Cooler Party Punch

Ingredients

3 cups cranberry juice

$\frac{1}{2}$ of a cup orange juice

2 cups grape juice

$\frac{1}{4}$ of a cup lemon juice

$\frac{1}{2}$ of a cup crushed pineapple

Directions

Stir all ingredients together.
Pour into serving glasses.

Answer: 9 cups cranberry juice, $\frac{3}{2}$ or $1\frac{1}{2}$ cups orange juice, 6 cups grape juice, $\frac{3}{4}$ of a cup lemon juice, $\frac{3}{2}$ or $1\frac{1}{2}$ cups crushed pineapple

Explore Multiplying Fractions by Whole Numbers

Previously, you learned about multiplying fractions by whole numbers. In this lesson, you will multiply fractions by whole numbers to solve word problems. Use what you know to try to solve the problem below.

Learning Target

- Solve word problems involving multiplication of a fraction by a whole number, e.g., by using visual fraction models and equations to represent the problem.

SMP 1, 2, 3, 4, 5, 6, 7

One serving of crackers is about $\frac{3}{10}$ of the whole box of crackers. Bella eats 3 servings this week. What fraction of the box of crackers does she eat?

TRY IT

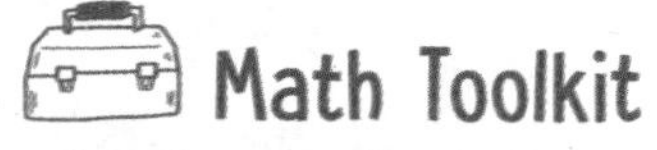

Math Toolkit

- fraction circles
- fraction tiles
- fraction bars
- number lines
- grid paper
- fraction models

DISCUSS IT

Ask your partner: Can you explain that again?

Tell your partner: A model I used was . . . It helped me . . .

CONNECT IT

1 LOOK BACK

Explain how you could find the fraction of the box of crackers that Bella eats.

2 LOOK AHEAD

You can multiply a fraction by a whole number to solve problems about combining equal-sized parts.

In the cracker problem, the equal-sized part is the serving size, or $\frac{3}{10}$ of the box of crackers. Bella eats 3 servings. The model at the right shows the fraction of the box of crackers that Bella eats.

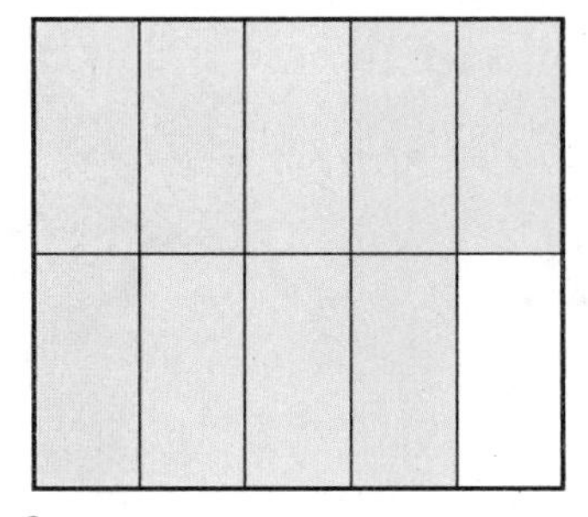

$\frac{3}{10}$ of the box = 1 serving

a. You can show three times the serving size as $3 \times \frac{3}{10}$, or $\frac{3 \times 3}{10}$.

Complete the equation. $3 \times \frac{3}{10} = \frac{\square}{\square}$

b. When you multiply a fraction by a whole number, the answer may be a fraction less than 1 or a fraction greater than 1. You can use what you know about fractions and mixed numbers to tell between which two whole numbers the answer lies. Is the fraction of the box of crackers that Bella eats less than 1 whole or more than 1 whole? ....

c. Between which two whole numbers is the fraction of the box of crackers that Bella eats? ....

3 REFLECT

Describe a real situation when you might want to multiply a fraction by a whole number.

....

....

Name: ______________________________

Prepare for Multiplying Fractions by Whole Numbers

1 Think about what you know about multiplying a fraction by a whole number. Fill in each box. Use words, numbers, and pictures. Show as many ideas as you can.

Word	In My Own Words	Example
multiply		
fraction		
whole number		

2 Complete the equation to tell how the model shows multiplying a fraction by a whole number.

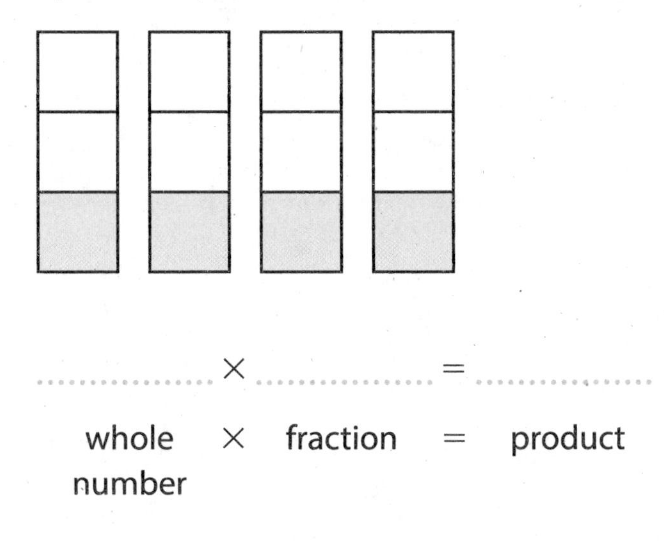

.... × .... = ...

whole number × fraction = product

3 Solve the problem. Show your work.

A family eats $\frac{3}{8}$ of a whole box of cereal each day. What fraction of the box of cereal does the family eat in 2 days?

Solution ....

4 Check your answer. Show your work.

Develop Multiplying Fractions by Whole Numbers

Read and try to solve the problem below.

James is baking cookies. One batch of cookies uses $\frac{2}{4}$ of a teaspoon of vanilla. James wants to make 3 batches of cookies. How much vanilla does James need?

TRY IT

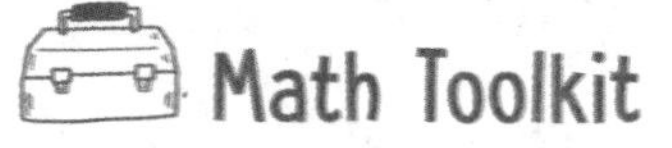

- fraction circles
- fraction tiles
- measuring spoons
- fraction bars
- number lines
- fraction models

DISCUSS IT

Ask your partner: How did you get started?

Tell your partner: I knew . . . so I . . .

Explore different ways to understand multiplying fractions by whole numbers to solve word problems.

James is baking cookies. One batch of cookies uses $\frac{2}{4}$ of a teaspoon of vanilla. James wants to make 3 batches of cookies. How much vanilla does James need?

PICTURE IT

You can use a picture to help solve the word problem.

The picture shows six $\frac{1}{4}$ teaspoons for 3 batches.

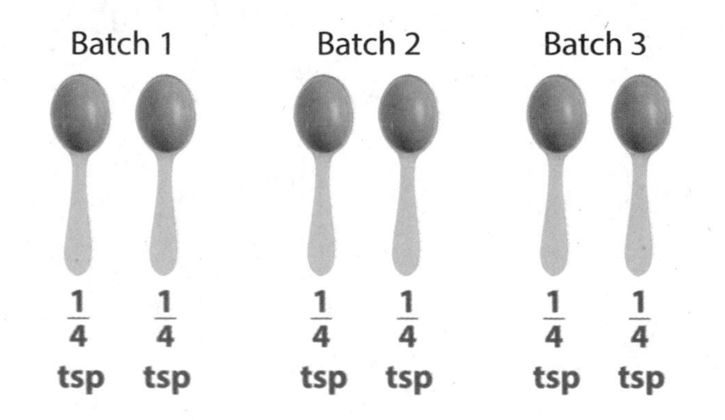

MODEL IT

You can also use fraction bars to solve the word problem.

The fraction bar below is divided into fourths and shows $\frac{2}{4}$, the amount of vanilla in each batch.

$\frac{1}{4}$	$\frac{1}{4}$	$\frac{1}{4}$	$\frac{1}{4}$

The model below shows the amount of vanilla needed for **3 batches.**

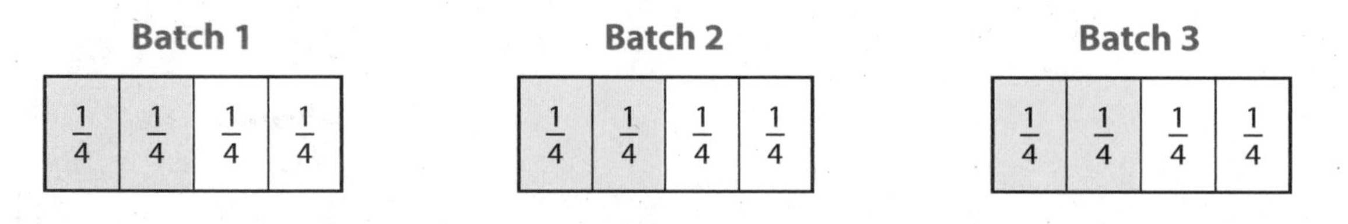

CONNECT IT

Now you will use the problem from the previous page to help you understand how to mutiply a fraction by a whole number to solve a word problem.

1. How much vanilla does James need for each batch? ....

2. How many batches does James want to make? ....

3. Write an equation to find how many teaspoons of vanilla James needs.

   .... × .... = ...

   number of batches | teaspoon for 1 batch | teaspoons needed

4. Explain how you can check your answer using repeated addition.

5. Write the fraction that shows how many teaspoons of vanilla James needs as a mixed number. ....

6. Between which two whole numbers of teaspoons is the amount of vanilla James needs?

7. How is the fraction bar model like the teaspoon model in showing how to multiply a fraction by a whole number?

8. **REFLECT**

   Look back at your **Try It**, strategies by classmates, and **Picture It** and **Model It**. Which models or strategies do you like best for multiplying a fraction by a whole number to solve a word problem? Explain.

APPLY IT

Use what you just learned to solve these problems.

9 Micah jogs $\frac{8}{10}$ of a mile. Sarah jogs this same distance 3 days in a row. How far does Sarah jog altogether?

Solution ....

10 On Monday, Sylvia spends $\frac{5}{12}$ of a day driving to her cousin's house. On Friday, she spends the same amount of time driving home. What fraction of a day does Sylvia spend driving to her cousin's house and back?

Solution ....

11 Isabella fills her fish tank using a water jug. The water jug holds $\frac{4}{5}$ of a gallon of water. Isabella uses 9 full jugs to fill her fish tank. How many gallons of water does the fish tank hold?

Ⓐ $\frac{36}{45}$ gallons

Ⓑ $2\frac{3}{5}$ gallons

Ⓒ $7\frac{1}{5}$ gallons

Ⓓ $36\frac{1}{5}$ gallons

Name: ______________________________

Practice Multiplying Fractions by Whole Numbers

Study the Example showing how to multiply a fraction by a whole number to solve a word problem. Then solve problems 1–7.

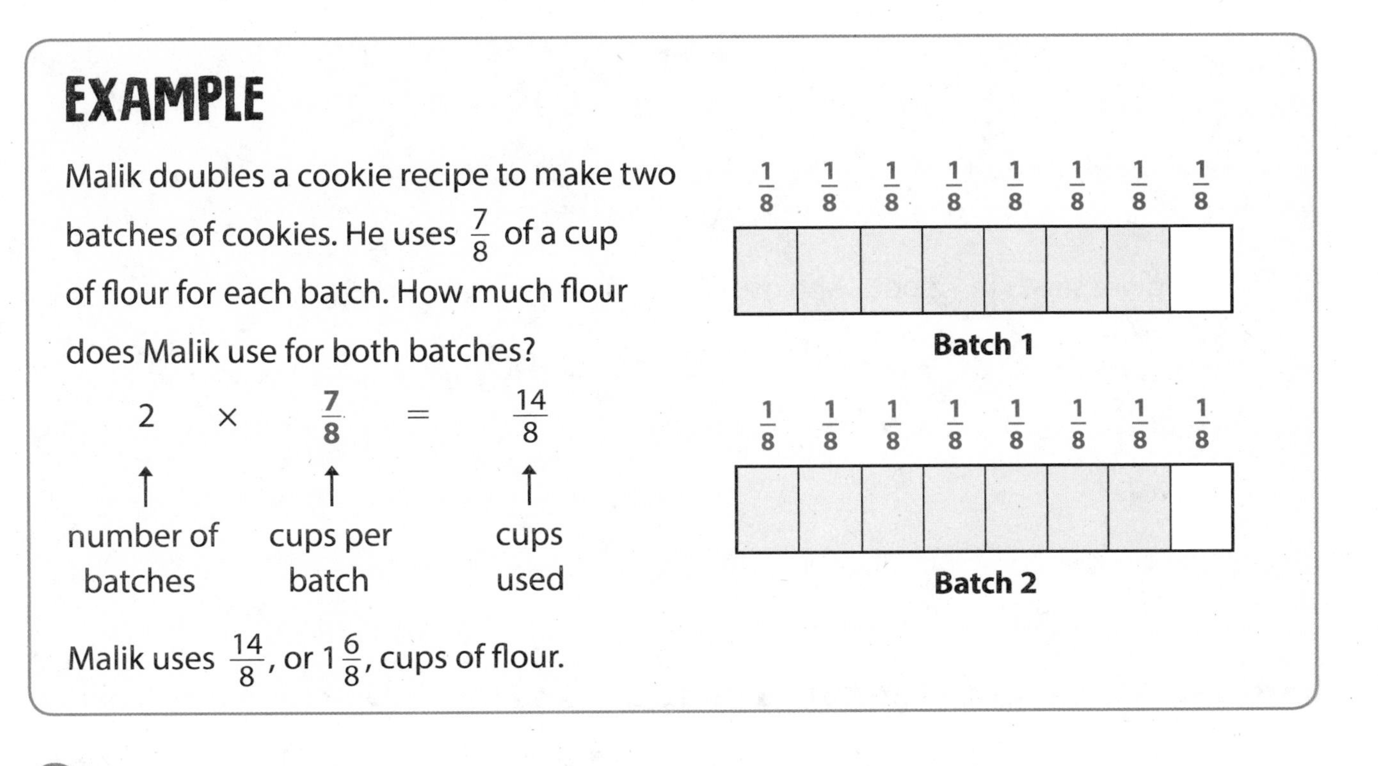

EXAMPLE

Malik doubles a cookie recipe to make two batches of cookies. He uses $\frac{7}{8}$ of a cup of flour for each batch. How much flour does Malik use for both batches?

$$2 \times \frac{7}{8} = \frac{14}{8}$$

number of batches → 2; cups per batch → $\frac{7}{8}$; cups used → $\frac{14}{8}$

Malik uses $\frac{14}{8}$, or $1\frac{6}{8}$, cups of flour.

1 Benson spends $\frac{5}{6}$ of an hour reading each day for 3 days. How long does Benson spend reading this week?

$3 \times \frac{5}{6} = \frac{\square}{\square} = \square\frac{\square}{\square}$

Benson spends .... hours reading.

2 Show how to use repeated addition to check your answer in problem 1.

3 Sabrina rides her bike $\frac{3}{4}$ of a mile. Katrin rides her bike this same distance on each of 4 days. How far does Katrin ride her bike altogether?

4. Jorge coaches soccer for $\frac{1}{12}$ of the day on Saturday. That day he also coaches tennis and swimming, each for the same amount of time as soccer. What fraction of the day does Jorge coach on Saturday? Show your work.

Solution ....

5. Greta plants flower seeds in 12 pots. She uses $\frac{2}{6}$ of a bag of flower seeds in each pot. How many bags of flower seeds does Greta use? Show your work.

Solution ....

Leslie practices the flute for $\frac{2}{6}$ of an hour 3 times this week. She practices piano for $\frac{2}{3}$ of an hour 2 times this week.

6. Which expressions can be used to show how much time Leslie practices both the flute and piano this week?

Ⓐ $\left(3 \times \frac{2}{6}\right) + \left(2 \times \frac{2}{3}\right)$

Ⓑ $5 \times \left(\frac{2}{6} + \frac{2}{3}\right)$

Ⓒ $\frac{2}{6} + \frac{2}{6} + \frac{2}{6} + \frac{2}{3} + \frac{2}{3}$

Ⓓ $\frac{(3 \times 2)}{6} + \frac{(2 \times 2)}{3}$

Ⓔ $\left(2 \times \frac{2}{6}\right) + \left(3 \times \frac{2}{3}\right)$

7. Which does Leslie practice for a longer amount of time, the flute or the piano? Show your work.

Solution ....

Refine Multiplying Fractions by Whole Numbers

Complete the Example below. Then solve problems 1–8.

EXAMPLE

Five friends share a pizza. Each friend eats $\frac{2}{12}$ of the pizza. How much pizza do they eat altogether?

Look at how you could show your work using a model.

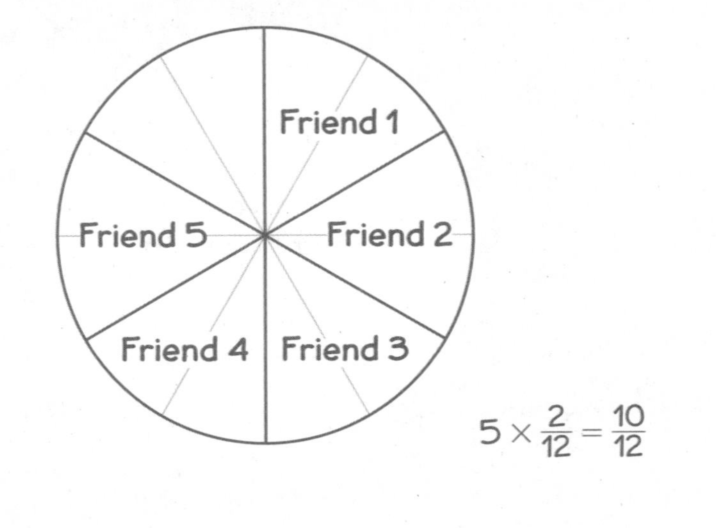

$5 \times \frac{2}{12} = \frac{10}{12}$

Solution ....

The student labeled the model to show each of the 5 friends!

PAIR/SHARE
How could you write the expression in a different way?

APPLY IT

1 Each of 4 tables at a party is set with a bowl of grapes. Each bowl contains $\frac{5}{8}$ of a pound of grapes. How many pounds of grapes are there altogether? Show your work.

Solution ....

Will the total weight be more or less than 1 whole pound?

PAIR/SHARE
Check your answer using repeated addition.

2. Leo paints for $\frac{2}{3}$ of an hour each day on Monday, Tuesday, Thursday, and Friday. How long does Leo paint this week? Show your work.

Does Leo paint for the same amount of time each day?

Solution ....

PAIR/SHARE
Draw a model to show the problem situation.

3. Karime walks $\frac{3}{4}$ of a mile each day for 5 days. The number of miles Karime walks altogether is between which two whole numbers?

Ⓐ 0 and 1

Ⓑ 1 and 2

Ⓒ 3 and 4

Ⓓ 4 and 5

Lacey chose Ⓐ as the correct answer. How did she get that answer?

Make sure your answer is reasonable!

PAIR/SHARE
How did you get the answer you chose?

4 A choir concert lasts for $\frac{5}{6}$ of an hour. The choir performs 3 concerts on the weekend. Find the number of hours the choir performs on the weekend. The answer is between which two whole numbers?

Ⓐ 0 and 1

Ⓑ 1 and 2

Ⓒ 2 and 3

Ⓓ 3 and 4

5 Find the products to complete the table.

	Product
$3 \times \frac{4}{6}$	
$2 \times \frac{4}{5}$	
$5 \times \frac{2}{3}$	
$2 \times \frac{3}{6}$	

6 Morgan buys 6 tomatoes that each weigh $\frac{1}{4}$ of a pound. Russ buys 14 tomatoes that each weigh $\frac{1}{8}$ of a pound. Who buys tomatoes that weigh more? Show your work.

.... buys tomatoes that weigh more.

Tell whether each expression has a value of $\frac{15}{4}$.

	Yes	No
$5 \times \frac{3}{4}$	Ⓐ	Ⓑ
$1 \times \frac{5}{4}$	Ⓒ	Ⓓ
$15 \times \frac{1}{4}$	Ⓔ	Ⓕ

8 MATH JOURNAL

Use words, equations, or pictures to explain how to find the answer to the problem below.

Brittany practices hitting softballs for $\frac{2}{3}$ of an hour each day for three days. For how many hours does she practice hitting softballs?

SELF CHECK Go back to the Unit 4 Opener and see what you can check off.

Fractions as Tenths and Hundredths

LESSON 25

Dear Family,

This week your child is learning about fractions as tenths and hundredths.

Your child might see a problem such as $\frac{2}{10} + \frac{30}{100}$. One fraction in the problem has a denominator of 10. The other fraction has a denominator of 100.

Your child is learning how to write **tenths** fractions as equivalent **hundredths** fractions. $\frac{1}{10} = \frac{10}{100}$

This model shows $\frac{2}{10}$.

This model shows $\frac{20}{100}$.

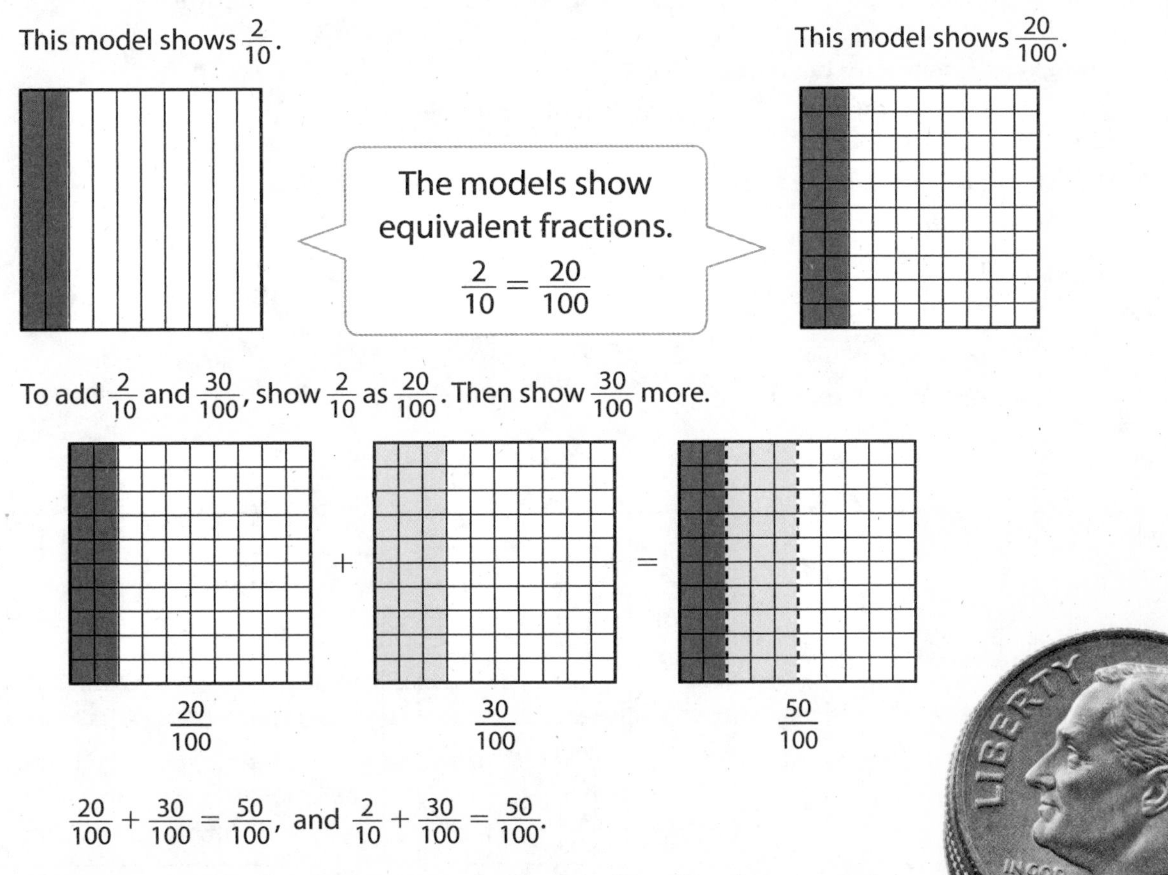

To add $\frac{2}{10}$ and $\frac{30}{100}$, show $\frac{2}{10}$ as $\frac{20}{100}$. Then show $\frac{30}{100}$ more.

$\frac{20}{100} + \frac{30}{100} = \frac{50}{100}$, and $\frac{2}{10} + \frac{30}{100} = \frac{50}{100}$.

Invite your child to share what he or she knows about fractions as tenths and hundredths by doing the following activity together.

ACTIVITY FRACTIONS AS TENTHS AND HUNDREDTHS

Do this activity with your child to explore fractions as tenths and hundredths.

- Use the tenths and hundredths models below or make your own models using lined paper and grid paper.
- Have your child choose a number between 1 and 5. Your child shades the tenths model to show that number of tenths.

  Example: Your child chooses 4.
  Your child shades 4 tenths $\left(\frac{4}{10}\right)$ of the tenths model.

- Then have another family member choose a two-digit number between 10 and 50. Your child shades the hundredths model to show that number of hundredths.

  Example: A family member chooses 28.
  Your child shades $\frac{28}{100}$ of the hundredths model.

- Next, have your child add the fractions. Your child shades the other hundredths model to show the sum.

  Example: $\frac{4}{10} + \frac{28}{100}$
  $\frac{40}{100} + \frac{28}{100} = \frac{68}{100}$
  Your child shades $\frac{68}{100}$ of the other hundredths model.

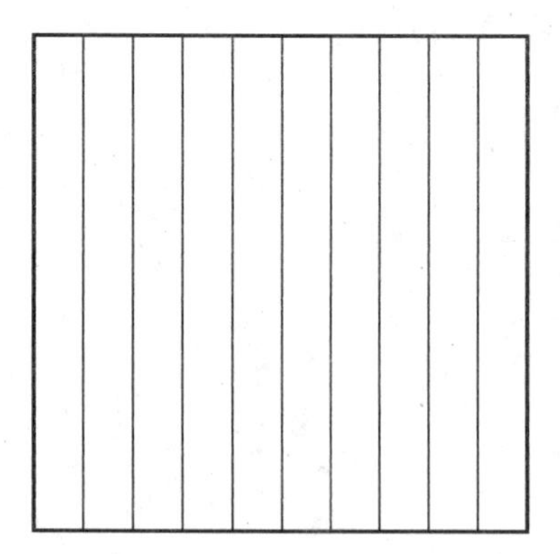

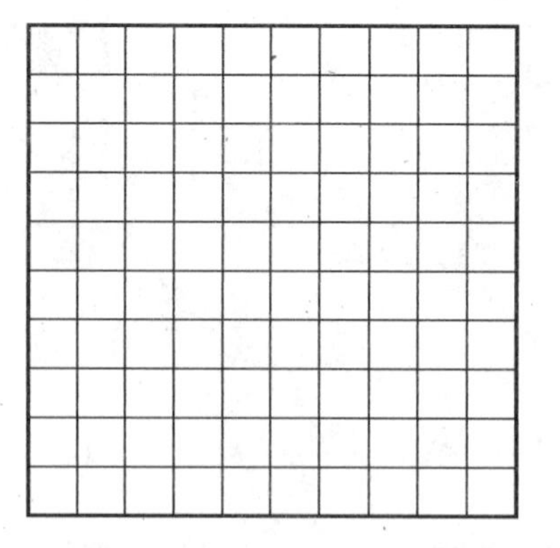

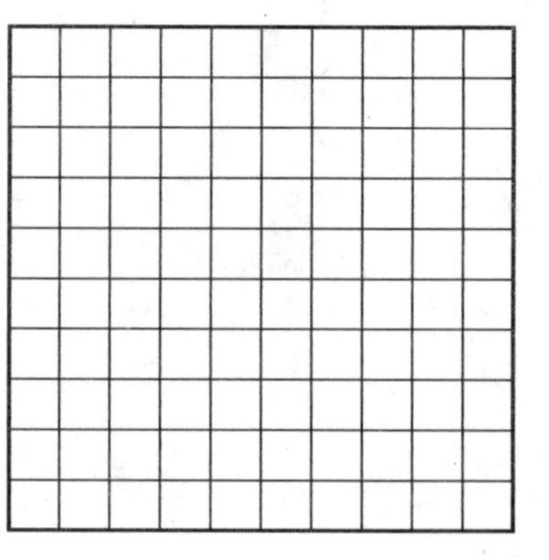

Explore Fractions as Tenths and Hundredths

Learning Target

- Express a fraction with denominator 10 as an equivalent fraction with denominator 100, and use this technique to add two fractions with respective denominators 10 and 100.

SMP 1, 2, 3, 4, 5, 6, 7

Previously, you worked with equivalent fractions. This lesson will focus on equivalent fractions with denominators of 10 and 100. Use what you know to try to solve the problem below.

Doss rides his bike home. He has seven tenths of a mile left to ride. Write an equivalent fraction to show how far Doss has left to ride in hundredths of a mile.

TRY IT

Math Toolkit

- base-ten blocks
- tenths grids
- hundredths grids
- number lines
- index cards

DISCUSS IT

Ask your partner: Why did you choose that strategy?

Tell your partner: I knew . . . so I . . .

CONNECT IT

LOOK BACK

Explain how you could use multiplication to find a fraction with a denominator of 100 that is equivalent to $\frac{7}{10}$.

LOOK AHEAD

Every fraction with a denominator of 10 can be written as a fraction with a denominator of 100.

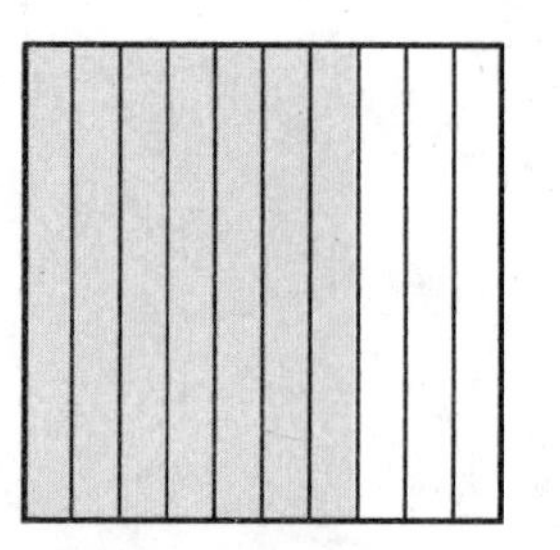

a. The model at the right is divided into 10 equal parts, or **tenths**. How many parts are shaded? ....

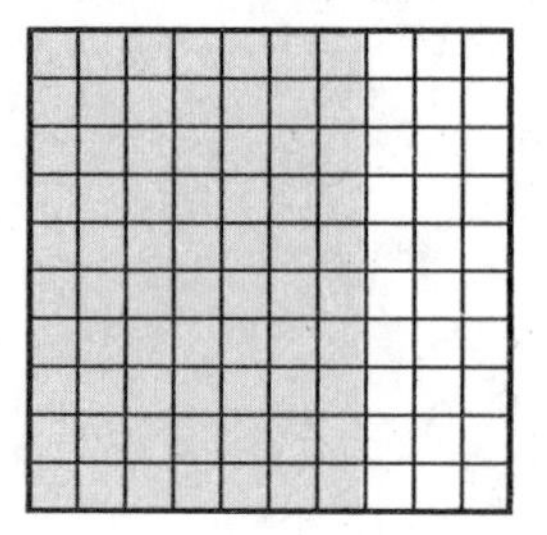

b. If you split each tenth into 10 equal parts, the whole is now divided into 100 equal parts, or **hundredths**.

How many hundredths parts are shaded? ....

c. Complete the equation to show a fraction with denominator 100 that is equivalent to $\frac{7}{10}$.

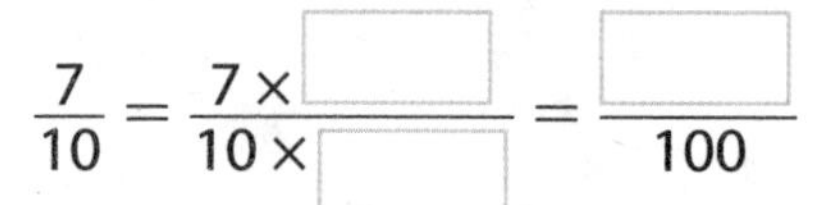

$$\frac{7}{10} = \frac{7 \times \square}{10 \times \square} = \frac{\square}{100}$$

d. You can also use money to think about equivalent fractions with denominators of 10 and 100. Think of 1 dollar, or 100 cents, as the whole. Fill in the blanks.

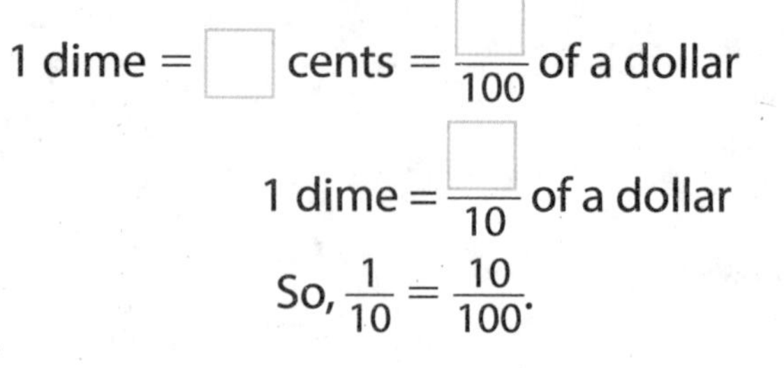

1 dime = $\square$ cents = $\frac{\square}{100}$ of a dollar

1 dime = $\frac{\square}{10}$ of a dollar

So, $\frac{1}{10} = \frac{10}{100}$.

3 REFLECT

How can you use equivalent fractions to write tenths as hundredths?

....

....

Name: ______________________________

Prepare for Fractions as Tenths and Hundredths

1. Think about what you know about fractions. Fill in each box. Use words, numbers, and pictures. Show as many ideas as you can.

Word	In My Own Words	Example
numerator		
denominator		
tenths		
hundredths		

2. Write seven tenths and seven hundredths as fractions. Tell how the two fractions are alike and how they are different.

3 Solve the problem. Show your work.

Akiko jogs to the park. She has six tenths of a mile left to jog. Write an equivalent fraction to show how far Akiko has left to jog in hundredths of a mile.

Solution ....

Check your answer. Show your work.

Develop Adding Tenths and Hundredths Fractions

Read and try to solve the problem below.

Carmen has $\frac{4}{10}$ of a dollar. Troy has $\frac{50}{100}$ of a dollar. Together, what fraction of a dollar do they have?

TRY IT

Math Toolkit
- base-ten blocks
- play money
- tenths grids
- hundredths grids
- number lines

DISCUSS IT

Ask your partner: How did you get started?

Tell your partner: At first, I thought . . .

Explore different ways to understand how to add fractions with denominators of 10 and 100.

Carmen has $\frac{4}{10}$ of a dollar. Troy has $\frac{50}{100}$ of a dollar. Together, what fraction of a dollar do they have?

PICTURE IT

You can use a picture to help you add fractions with denominators of 10 and 100.

You know that $\frac{4}{10}$ of a dollar is 4 dimes and $\frac{50}{100}$ of a dollar is 5 dimes.

Carmen's money

Troy's money

Together, Carmen and Troy have 9 dimes.

MODEL IT

You can use a model to help you add fractions with denominators of 10 and 100.

Carmen's money

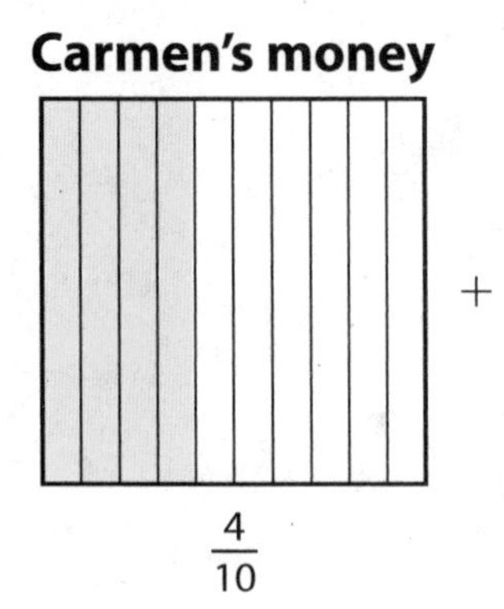

$\frac{4}{10}$

+

Troy's money

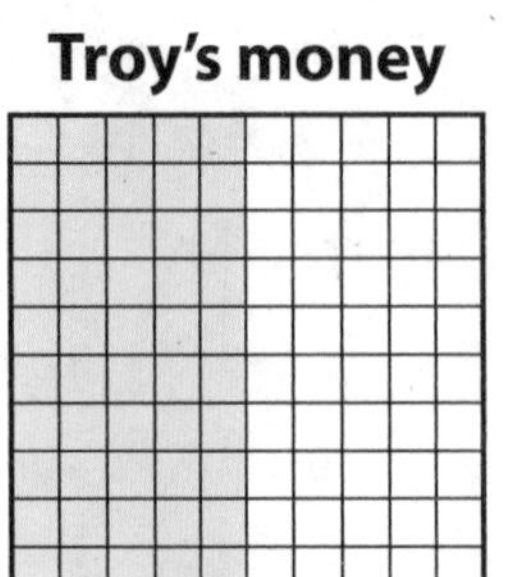

$\frac{50}{100}$

=

Total money

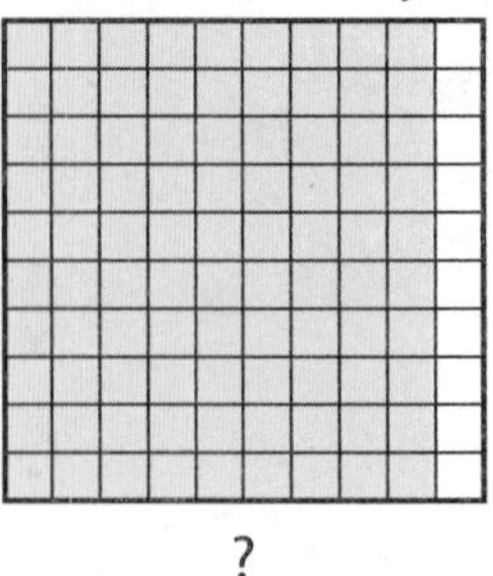

?

CONNECT IT

Now you will use the problem from the previous page to help you understand how to add fractions with denominators of 10 and 100.

1. What are the denominators of the fractions you are adding? Are they the same?

2. Complete the equation to use multiplication to find the fraction with denominator 100 that is equivalent to $\frac{4}{10}$.

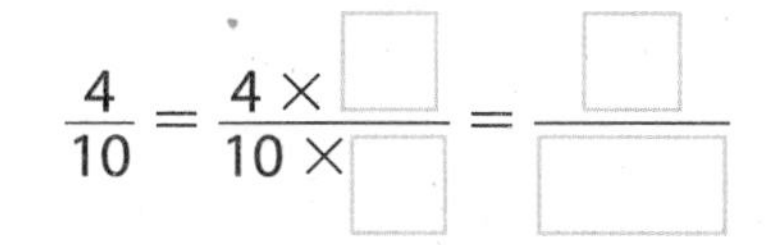

3. $\frac{40}{100} + \frac{50}{100} =$ ....

4. Together, Carmen and Troy have what fraction of a dollar? ....

5. Explain how you can use equivalent fractions to add a fraction with a denominator of 100 to a fraction with a denominator of 10.

REFLECT

Look back at your **Try It**, strategies by classmates, and **Picture It** and **Model It**. Which models or strategies do you like best for adding fractions with denominators of 10 and 100? Explain.

APPLY IT

Use what you just learned to solve these problems.

7 Giselle spends $\frac{7}{10}$ of her money on a book and $\frac{10}{100}$ of her money on food. What fraction of her money does she spend in all? Show your work.

Solution ....

8 Show how to add $\frac{4}{10}$ and $\frac{19}{100}$. Write the sum. Show your work.

Solution ....

9 Tucker is weeding his garden. The shaded model at the right represents the fraction of the garden that Tucker has already weeded.

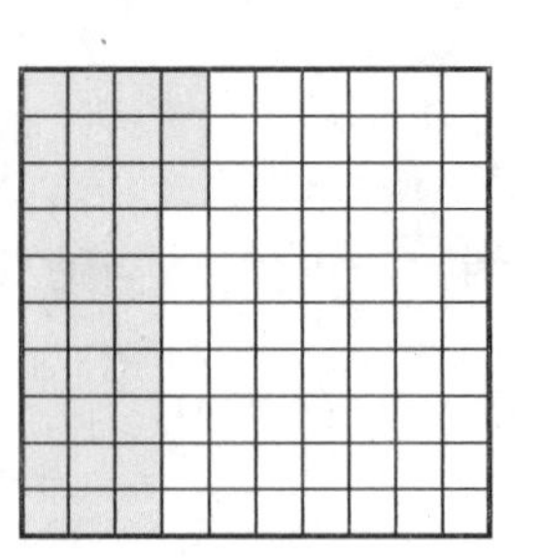

Tucker plans to weed $\frac{5}{10}$ more of the garden before lunch. What fraction of the garden will Tucker have weeded before lunch?

Ⓐ $\frac{38}{100}$

Ⓑ $\frac{83}{100}$

Ⓒ $\frac{38}{110}$

Ⓓ $\frac{83}{10}$

Practice Adding Tenths and Hundredths Fractions

Study the Example showing how to add fractions with denominators of 10 and 100. Then solve problems 1–7.

EXAMPLE

Jaden finds $\frac{8}{10}$ of a dollar in change in his backpack.
He finds $\frac{15}{100}$ of a dollar in change in his lunch bag.
What fraction of a dollar in change does he find altogether?

Multiply to find the fraction with denominator 100 that is equivalent to $\frac{8}{10}$.

$$\frac{8}{10} = \frac{8 \times 10}{10 \times 10} = \frac{80}{100}$$

Add the hundredths fractions.

$$\frac{80}{100} + \frac{15}{100} = \frac{95}{100}$$

Jaden finds $\frac{95}{100}$ of a dollar in change.

1 Write $\frac{2}{10}$ as an equivalent fraction with a denominator of 100.

$$\frac{2}{10} = \frac{2 \times 10}{10 \times 10} = \frac{\square}{\square}$$

2 Fill in the blanks to show how to find the sum of $\frac{2}{10}$ and $\frac{10}{100}$.

$$\frac{\square}{100} + \frac{10}{100} = \frac{\square}{\square}$$

3 What is the sum of $\frac{3}{10}$ and $\frac{50}{100}$? Show your work.

Solution ....

Mila has 100 math problems to finish this week. She finishes $\frac{2}{10}$ of the problems on Monday and $\frac{25}{100}$ of the problems on Tuesday.

4. Shade the models to show the fraction of math problems that Mila finishes on Monday and on Tuesday.

Monday

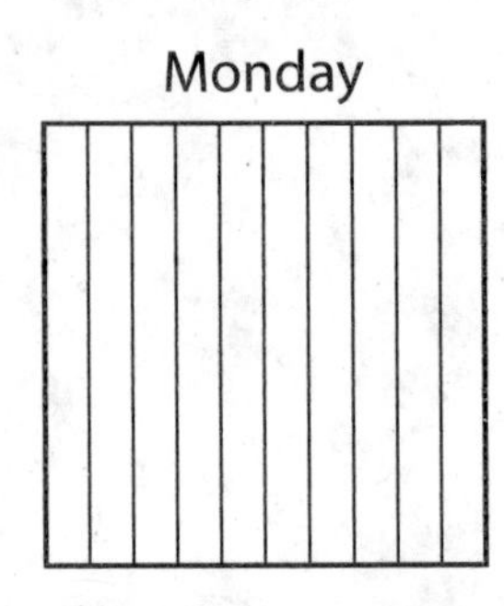

Tuesday

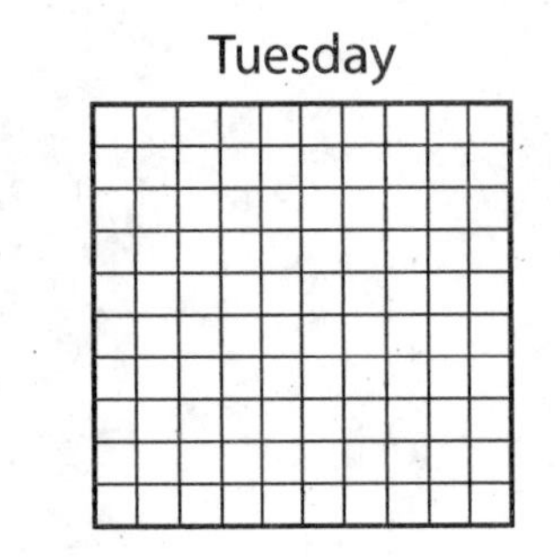

5. What fraction of the math problems for the week does Mila finish on Monday and Tuesday? Show your work.

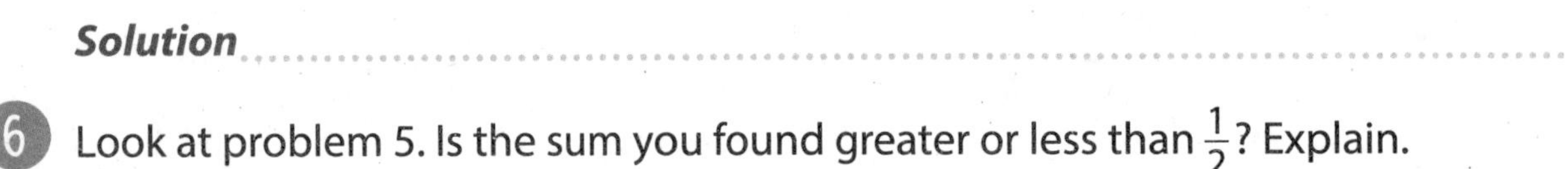

Solution

6. Look at problem 5. Is the sum you found greater or less than $\frac{1}{2}$? Explain.

7. Has Mila finished more than half of her math problems for the week? Explain.

Refine Fractions as Tenths and Hundredths

Complete the Example below. Then solve problems 1–10.

EXAMPLE

A farmer plants corn in $\frac{68}{100}$ of his field and beans in $\frac{3}{10}$ of the field. What fraction of his field does the farmer plant with corn and beans?

Look at how you could show your work using a model.

Solution ....

The student drew and shaded a model to show the sum of $\frac{68}{100}$ and $\frac{3}{10}$.

PAIR/SHARE
How can you solve the problem using equivalent fractions?

APPLY IT

1 What is the sum of $\frac{7}{100}$ and $\frac{1}{10}$? Show your work.

There is more than one way to solve this problem!

Solution ....

PAIR/SHARE
Can you explain the problem using dimes and pennies?

2 Jared, Consuela, and Reggie have an ant farm. Jared collected $\frac{25}{100}$ of the ants for the ant farm. Consuela collected $\frac{6}{10}$ of the ants. What fraction of the ants did Jared and Consuela collect altogether? Show your work.

What do you notice about the denominators of these fractions?

PAIR/SHARE
Draw a model to show the problem situation.

Solution ....

3 Heath has 100 trading cards. Space exploration cards make up $\frac{7}{100}$ of his card collection. Baseball cards make up $\frac{7}{10}$ of his card collection. Together, the space exploration and baseball cards make up what fraction of Heath's card collection?

Ⓐ $\frac{7}{110}$

Ⓑ $\frac{14}{100}$

Ⓒ $\frac{77}{200}$

Ⓓ $\frac{77}{100}$

Ezra chose Ⓒ as the correct answer. How did he get that answer?

To solve this problem without a model, what should you do first?

PAIR/SHARE
Chelsea chose Ⓓ. How did she get that answer?

4 Which equation is true?

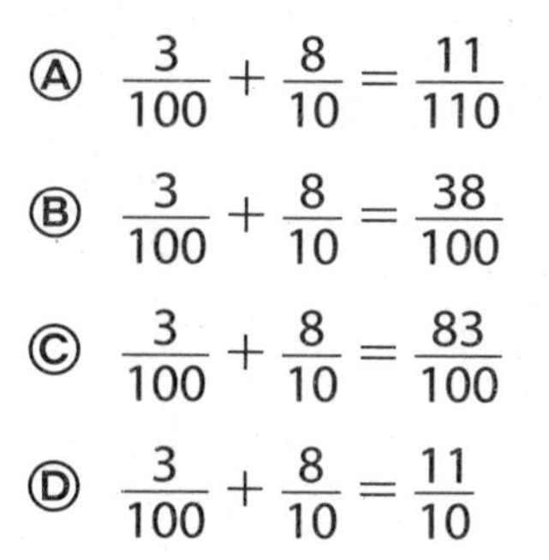

Ⓐ $\frac{3}{100} + \frac{8}{10} = \frac{11}{110}$

Ⓑ $\frac{3}{100} + \frac{8}{10} = \frac{38}{100}$

Ⓒ $\frac{3}{100} + \frac{8}{10} = \frac{83}{100}$

Ⓓ $\frac{3}{100} + \frac{8}{10} = \frac{11}{10}$

5 Noelle rides her bike $\frac{5}{10}$ of a kilometer to the library. Then she rides another $\frac{22}{100}$ of a kilometer to her friend's house. How far does Noelle ride her bike in all?

Ⓐ $\frac{27}{110}$ of a kilometer

Ⓑ $\frac{27}{100}$ of a kilometer

Ⓒ $\frac{72}{100}$ of a kilometer

Ⓓ $\frac{225}{100}$ kilometers

6 Fill in each box with either 10 or 100 to make the equation true.

$\frac{4}{\square} + \frac{20}{\square} = \frac{60}{100}$

7 What is the missing fraction in the equation below? Show your work.

$\frac{6}{10} + \square = \frac{82}{100}$

Solution ....

8 Tell whether each equation is *True* or *False*.

	True	False
$\frac{2}{10} + \frac{1}{100} = \frac{21}{110}$	Ⓐ	Ⓑ
$\frac{4}{10} + \frac{4}{100} = \frac{44}{100}$	Ⓒ	Ⓓ
$\frac{1}{100} + \frac{9}{10} = \frac{19}{100}$	Ⓔ	Ⓕ

9 Ramona has $100. She spends $\frac{60}{100}$ of her money on a pair of sneakers. She spends $\frac{3}{10}$ of her money on a tennis racket. What fraction of her money does Ramona spend? Show your work.

Ramona spends .... of her money.

10 MATH JOURNAL

Use words, equations, or pictures to explain how to solve the problem below.

Jasmine walks $\frac{6}{10}$ of a mile to school. Then she walks another $\frac{29}{100}$ of a mile to the library. How far does Jasmine walk in all?

☑ SELF CHECK Go back to the Unit 4 Opener and see what you can check off.

Relate Decimals and Fractions

LESSON 26

Dear Family,

This week your child is learning about relating decimals and fractions.

Tenths and hundredths can be written as decimal fractions.

You can use models to show the fraction $\frac{36}{100}$ as the **decimal** 0.36.

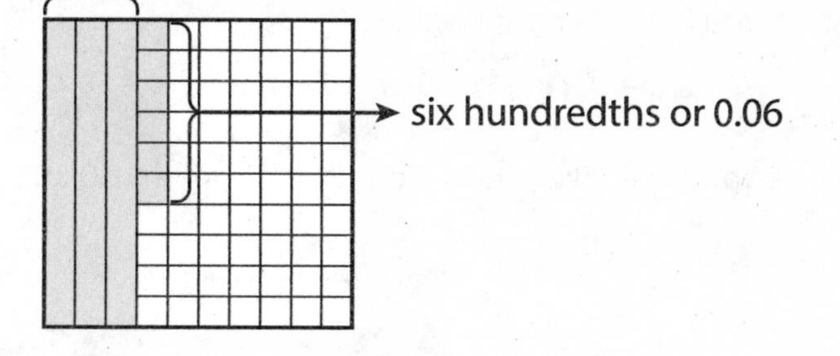

36 hundredths (0.36) is 3 tenths (0.3) and 6 hundredths (0.06).

You can use a place-value chart to write the mixed number $4\frac{36}{100}$ as a decimal.

decimal point

Ones	.	Tenths	Hundredths
4	.	3	6

whole number — number less than 1

Your child is learning to read the decimal 4.36:

1. Say the whole-number part, if there is one. *four*
2. Say *and* for the **decimal point**. *and*
3. Read the rest of the digits as a whole number. *thirty-six*
4. Say the place-value name of the last digit. *hundredths*

Say: *four and thirty-six hundredths.*

Invite your child to share what he or she knows about relating decimals and fractions by doing the following activity together.

ACTIVITY RELATING DECIMALS AND FRACTIONS

Do this activity with your child to relate decimals and fractions.

You can use money to relate decimals and fractions because money is counted in tenths and hundredths. There are 100 pennies in 1 dollar, so one penny is 0.01, or $\frac{1}{100}$, of a dollar. There are 10 dimes in 1 dollar, so one dime is 0.1 (or 0.10), or $\frac{1}{10}$, of a dollar.

- With your child, collect pennies from around your home. Have your child write the amount as a decimal and as a fraction.

  Example: You have 23 pennies.
  Write the decimal 0.23 and the fraction $\frac{23}{100}$.

  Example: You have 30 pennies. Write the decimal 0.30 and the fraction $\frac{30}{100}$.

- Next, collect dimes from around your home and have your child write the amount as a decimal and as a fraction.

Look for other real-life opportunities to relate decimals and fractions with your child.

Explore Relating Decimals and Fractions

Learning Target

- Use decimal notation for fractions with denominators 10 or 100.

SMP 1, 2, 3, 4, 5, 6, 7, 8

You know how to write equivalent fractions with denominators of 10 and 100. In this lesson, you will learn another way to write these fractions. Use what you know to try to solve the problem below.

Max has 248 pennies. How many whole dollars does Max have? What fraction of a dollar is left over?

TRY IT

Math Toolkit

- base-ten blocks
- play money
- hundredths grids
- index cards

DISCUSS IT

Ask your partner: Do you agree with me? Why or why not?

Tell your partner: I agree with you about . . . because . . .

CONNECT IT

1 LOOK BACK

Write the dollars and fraction of a dollar Max has as a mixed number. ....

2 LOOK AHEAD

a. Fractions with denominators 10 and 100 can be written as **decimals.** The models show the fraction $\frac{48}{100}$.

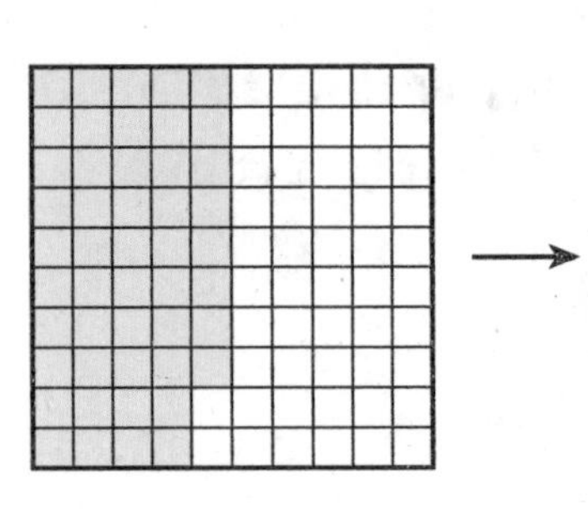

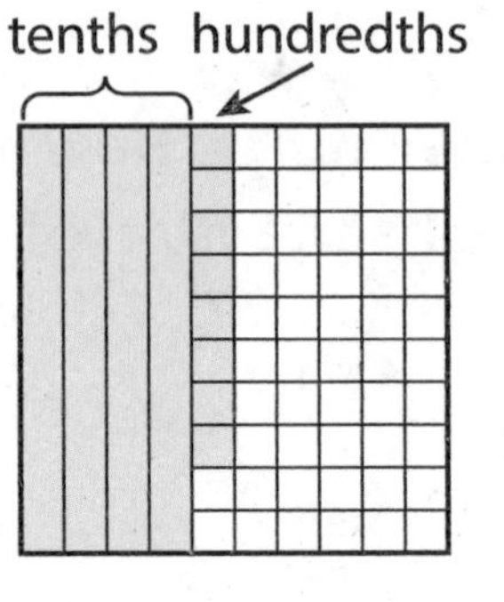

48 hundredths is .... tenths and .... hundredths.

b. Write the mixed number $2\frac{48}{100}$ as a decimal in the place-value chart below.

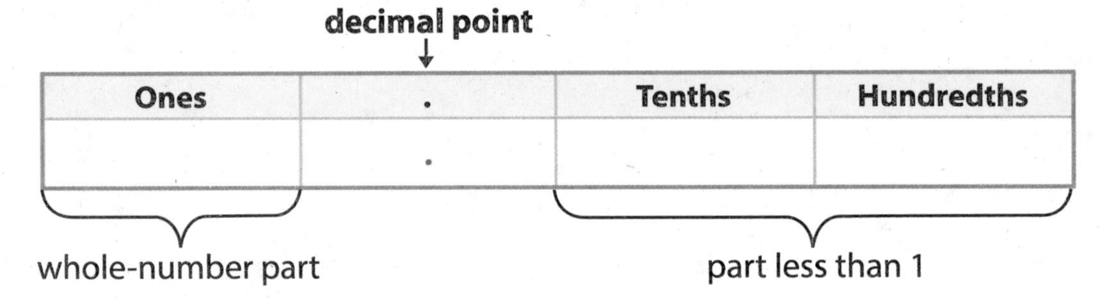

Ones	.	Tenths	Hundredths
	.		

c. Fill in the blanks to tell how to read the decimal.

whole-number part in word form	decimal point	part less than 1 in word form	place-value name of the last digit
↓	↓	↓	↓
....	*and*	....	....

3 REFLECT

Explain how thinking about money can help you understand decimals.

....

....

Name: ______________________

Prepare for Relating Decimals and Fractions

1 Think about what you know about decimals. Fill in each box. Use words, numbers, and pictures. Show as many ideas as you can.

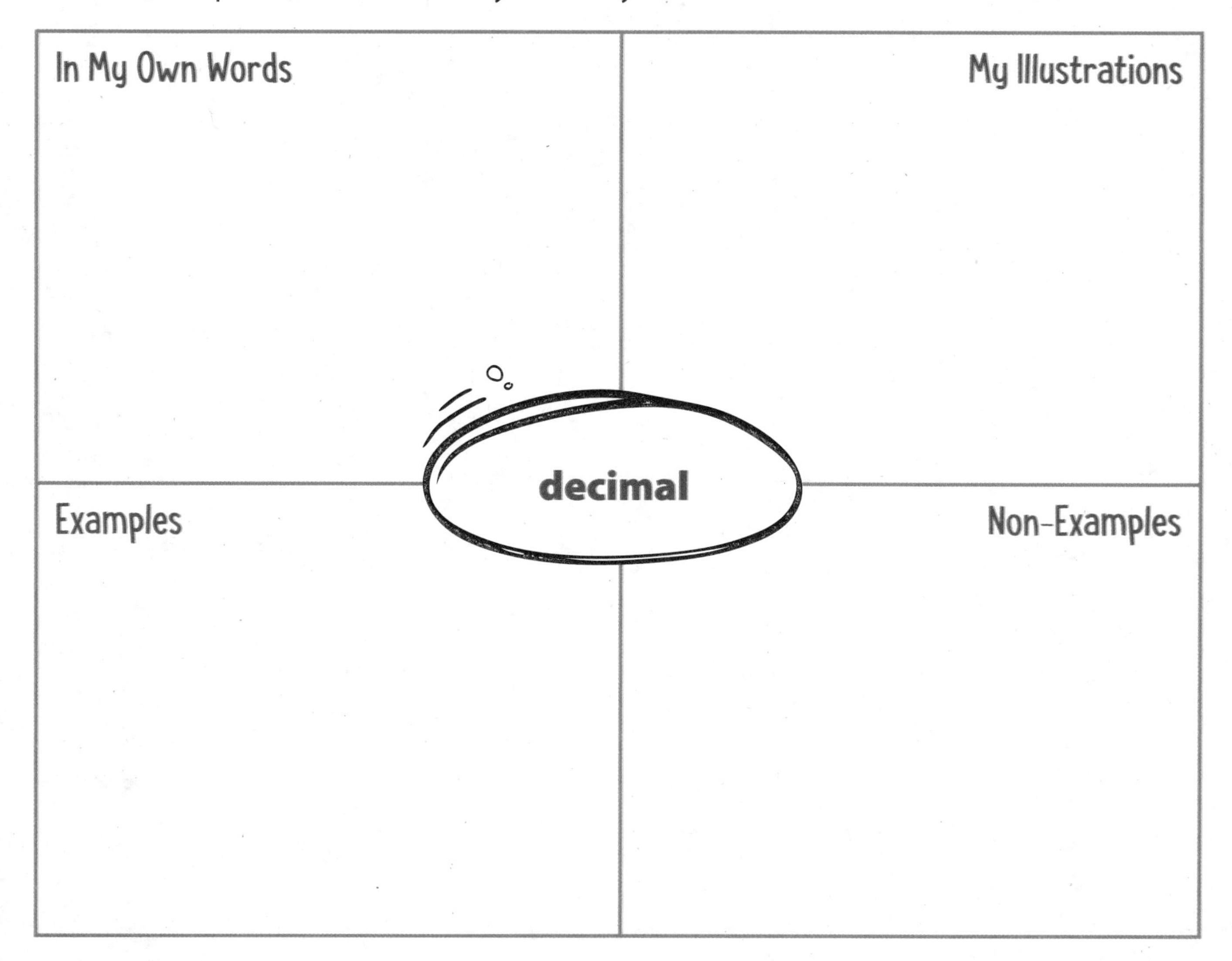

2 Fill in the blanks to tell how to read the decimal 1.32.

whole-number part in word form	decimal point	part less than 1 in word form	place-value name of the last digit
↓	↓	↓	↓
....	and	....	....

 Solve the problem. Show your work.

Lelia has 323 pennies. How many whole dollars does Lelia have? What fraction of a dollar is left over?

Solution ....

 Check your answer. Show your work.

Develop Decimals and Fractions

Read and try to solve the problem below.

A soccer camp has places for 100 students. So far, 60 of the places are filled. Write both a fraction and a decimal in both hundredths and tenths to show the part of the 100 places for students that are filled.

TRY IT

Math Toolkit

- base-ten blocks
- hundredths grids
- tenths grids
- hundredths decimal place-value charts
- number lines

DISCUSS IT

Ask your partner: Can you explain that again?

Tell your partner: I started by . . .

Explore different ways to understand how to use fractions and decimals to name the same amount.

A soccer camp has places for 100 students. So far, 60 of the places are filled. Write both a fraction and a decimal in both hundredths and tenths to show the part of the 100 places for students that are filled.

MODEL IT

You can use a model to understand how to write hundredths or tenths as a fraction and a decimal.

Each model represents the part of the 100 soccer camp places that are filled.

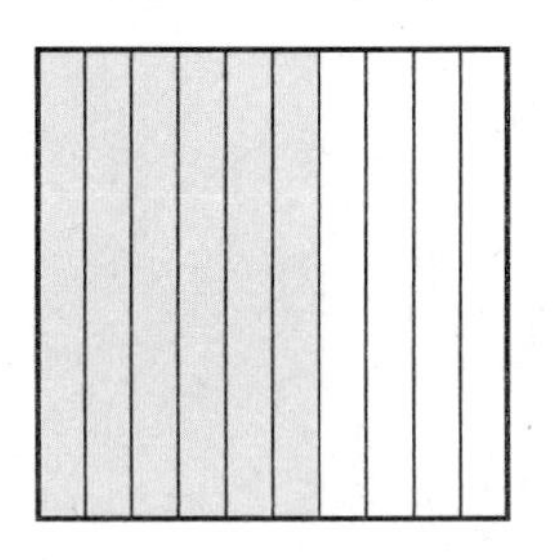

Each small square is $\frac{1}{100}$ of the whole.

Sixty small squares are shaded.

0.60 of the whole is shaded.

Each section is $\frac{1}{10}$ of the whole.

Six sections are shaded.

0.6 of the whole is shaded.

MODEL IT

You can use a place-value chart to understand how to write hundredths or tenths as a decimal.

The place-value chart shows the value of 0.60.

Ones	.	Tenths	Hundredths
0	.	6	0

CONNECT IT

Now you will use the problem from the previous page to help you understand how to write tenths and hundredths as fractions and decimals to name the same amount.

1. Look at the first **Model It**. The model on the left shows 60 squares shaded.

   Write a fraction for the model. .... The model on the right shows

   6 sections shaded. Write a fraction for the model. ....

2. How does the model on the right in the first **Model It** show the fraction you wrote for the model in problem 1?

3. Look at the place-value chart in the second **Model It**. Write a decimal in tenths and the equivalent decimal in hundredths. How are the two decimals different?

4. Write a number on each line below to describe how decimals relate to fractions with denominators of 10 and 100.

   If the denominator of a fraction is 10, the equivalent decimal has .... place after the decimal point.

   If the denominator of a fraction is 100, the equivalent decimal has .... places after the decimal point.

5. ## REFLECT

   Look back at your **Try It**, strategies by classmates, and **Model Its**. Which models or strategies do you like best for writing tenths and hundredths as fractions and decimals? Explain.

   ....

   ....

   ....

   ....

APPLY IT

Use what you just learned to solve these problems.

6 Write a decimal equivalent to $\frac{2}{10}$. Draw a model that shows the fraction and the decimal. Show your work.

7 Write a decimal equivalent to $\frac{83}{100}$. Show your work.

Solution

8 Write the mixed number $7\frac{9}{10}$ as a decimal. Show your work.

Solution

Name: ______________________________

Practice Decimals and Fractions

Study the Example showing ways to name the same amount as a fraction and a decimal. Then solve problems 1–7.

EXAMPLE

How do you write decimals equivalent to $\frac{7}{10}$ and $\frac{70}{100}$?

The model shows $\frac{7}{10}$. The model shows $\frac{70}{100}$.

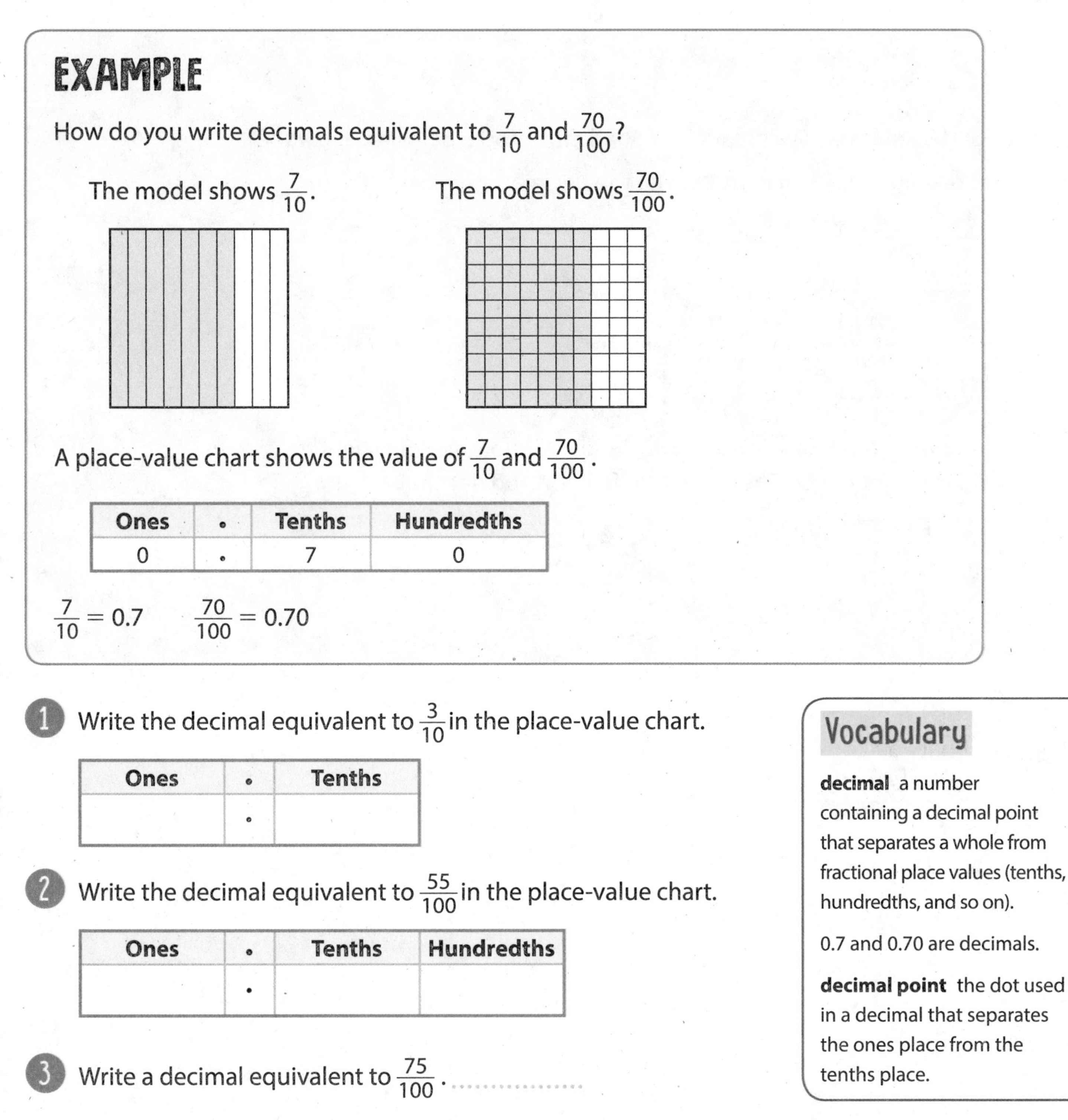

A place-value chart shows the value of $\frac{7}{10}$ and $\frac{70}{100}$.

Ones	•	Tenths	Hundredths
0	•	7	0

$\frac{7}{10} = 0.7$ $\frac{70}{100} = 0.70$

1 Write the decimal equivalent to $\frac{3}{10}$ in the place-value chart.

Ones	•	Tenths
	•	

2 Write the decimal equivalent to $\frac{55}{100}$ in the place-value chart.

Ones	•	Tenths	Hundredths
	•		

3 Write a decimal equivalent to $\frac{75}{100}$. ....

Vocabulary

decimal a number containing a decimal point that separates a whole from fractional place values (tenths, hundredths, and so on).

0.7 and 0.70 are decimals.

decimal point the dot used in a decimal that separates the ones place from the tenths place.

4 What is $2\frac{5}{10}$ written as a decimal?

Ⓐ 0.25

Ⓑ 2.05

Ⓒ 2.5

Ⓓ 5.2

5 What decimal is equivalent to $\frac{80}{100}$? Shade the model below to show the fraction and the decimal. Then write the decimal.

$\frac{80}{100}$ = ...

6 Look at problem 5. Shade the model below to show an equivalent fraction and decimal in tenths. Then write the fraction and decimal.

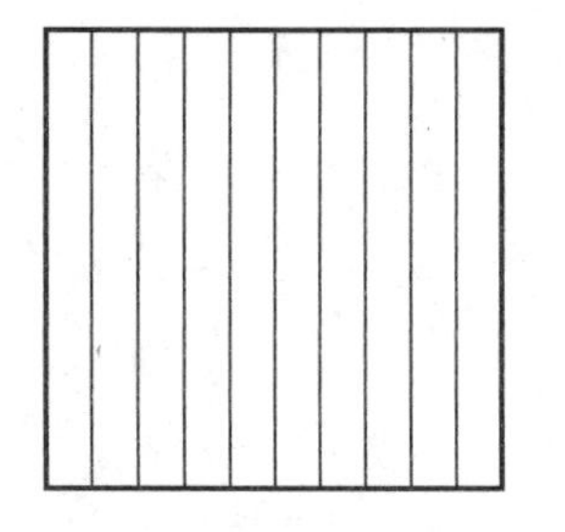

.... = ...

7 Use what you know about equivalent fractions to explain why 0.8 and 0.80 are equivalent.

Develop Writing Decimals as Equivalent Fractions

Read and try to solve the problem below.

Eli collects animal cards. He says that 0.05 of his cards are endangered animal cards. What fraction of his cards are endangered animal cards?

TRY IT

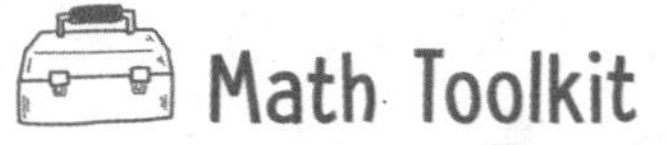

Math Toolkit

- base-ten blocks
- hundredths grids
- hundredths decimal place-value charts
- number lines

DISCUSS IT

Ask your partner: Why did you choose that strategy?

Tell your partner: A model I used was . . . It helped me . . .

Explore different ways to understand how to write a decimal as an equivalent fraction.

Eli collects animal cards. He says that 0.05 of his cards are endangered animal cards. What fraction of his cards are endangered animal cards?

MODEL IT

You can use a model to help write a decimal as an equivalent fraction.

The model shows 0.05.

MODEL IT

You can also use a place-value chart to help write a decimal as an equivalent fraction.

The place-value chart shows the value of 0.05.

Ones	.	Tenths	Hundredths
0	.	0	5

CONNECT IT

Now you will use the problem from the previous page to help you understand how to write a decimal as an equivalent fraction.

1. How can the model help you write a fraction equivalent to 0.05?

2. How can the place-value chart help you write a fraction equivalent to 0.05?

3. Use words to describe the fraction of Eli's cards that are endangered animal cards.

4. What fraction of Eli's cards are endangered animal cards? ....

5. Explain how you can write a decimal in hundredths as a fraction.

6. **REFLECT**

Look back at your **Try It**, strategies by classmates, and **Model Its**. Which models or strategies do you like best for writing a decimal in hundredths as an equivalent fraction? Explain.

....

....

....

....

APPLY IT

Use what you just learned to solve these problems.

7 Write 0.9 in words and as a fraction. Show your work.

Solution ....

8 Write 0.89 in words and as a fraction. Show your work.

Solution ....

9 Select all the fractions that are equivalent to 0.2.

Ⓐ $\frac{2}{100}$

Ⓑ $\frac{20}{100}$

Ⓒ $\frac{2}{10}$

Ⓓ $\frac{20}{10}$

Ⓔ $\frac{100}{2}$

Ⓕ $\frac{10}{2}$

Practice Writing Decimals as Equivalent Fractions

Study the Example showing how to write a decimal as an equivalent fraction. Then solve problems 1–8.

EXAMPLE

Alanna has an assortment of books in her bookcase. Comic books are 0.09 of the books. What fraction of the books are comic books?

Decimal: 0.09

Words: nine hundredths

Fraction: $\frac{9}{100}$

Ones	•	Tenths	Hundredths
0	•	0	9

$\frac{9}{100}$ of the books are comic books.

1. Shade the model below to show 0.34.

2. Show 0.34 in the place-value chart.

Ones	•	Tenths	Hundredths
	•		

3. Write 0.34 in words. ....

4. Write 0.34 as a fraction. ....

5 Tell whether each statement is *True* or *False*.

	True	False
$0.3 = \frac{3}{100}$	Ⓐ	Ⓑ
$0.03 = \frac{3}{100}$	Ⓒ	Ⓓ
$0.3 = \frac{30}{100}$	Ⓔ	Ⓕ
$0.3 = \frac{3}{10}$	Ⓖ	Ⓗ

6 Write two fractions equivalent to 0.4.

7 Which words or fractions name the same number as 0.62?

Ⓐ sixty-two hundredths

Ⓑ six and two hundredths

Ⓒ six tenths and two hundredths

Ⓓ $\frac{62}{10}$

Ⓔ $\frac{62}{100}$

8 The number line below shows 1 whole divided into tenths. Write numbers in the boxes to label the missing fractions and decimal. Explain how you know what numbers to write.

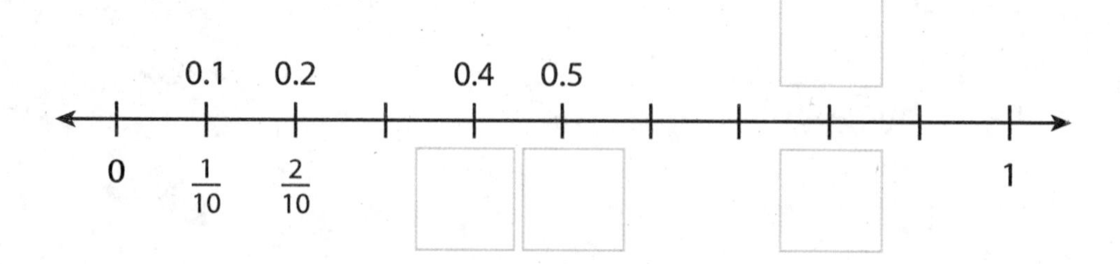

Refine Relating Decimals and Fractions

Complete the Example below. Then solve problems 1–8.

EXAMPLE

The length of a ribbon is 0.33 of a meter. How can you locate 0.33 on a number line?

Look at how you could show your work using a number line.

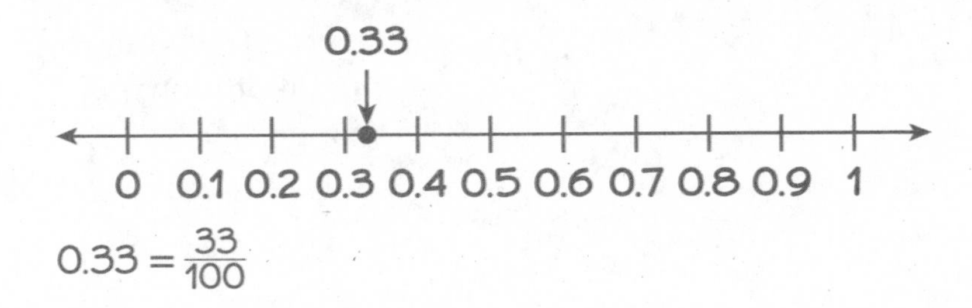

$0.33 = \frac{33}{100}$

Solution ....

....

The student used a number line with tenths marks and placed 0.33 between 0.3 and 0.4.

PAIR/SHARE
How many hundredths are there between each of the tenths marks on the number line?

APPLY IT

1 What is 0.7 written as a fraction? Show your work.

How could drawing a model help you?

Solution ....

PAIR/SHARE
How do you know if the decimal represents tenths or hundredths?

2 The number line below shows 1 whole divided into tenths. Write numbers in the boxes to label the missing fractions and decimals. Explain how you know what numbers to write.

Could saying each number aloud help?

0, $\frac{1}{10}$, ☐, $\frac{6}{10}$, ☐

0, 0.1, 0.3, ☐, ☐, 1

PAIR/SHARE
How could you show hundredths on this number line?

3 Which decimal names the same amount as $\frac{50}{100}$?

Ⓐ 0.50

Ⓑ 0.05

Ⓒ 50.0

Ⓓ 50.10

Abby chose Ⓑ as the correct answer. How did she get that answer?

What does the denominator of the fraction tell you?

PAIR/SHARE
What is a decimal in tenths that is equivalent to $\frac{50}{100}$?

What is 0.75 written as a fraction?

Ⓐ $\frac{.75}{100}$

Ⓑ $\frac{0}{75}$

Ⓒ $\frac{75}{100}$

Ⓓ $\frac{75}{10}$

5 Which fractions and decimals are equivalent?

Ⓐ $\frac{4}{10}$ and 0.04

Ⓑ $\frac{6}{100}$ and 0.60

Ⓒ $\frac{3}{10}$ and 0.3

Ⓓ $\frac{9}{100}$ and 0.09

Ⓔ $\frac{7}{10}$ and 7.10

6 Model *A* is shaded to represent a value that is less than 1 whole.

Tell whether each fraction or decimal correctly represents the shaded part of Model *A*.

	Yes	No
$\frac{8}{10}$	Ⓐ	Ⓑ
$\frac{80}{100}$	Ⓒ	Ⓓ
0.08	Ⓔ	Ⓕ

Model *A*

7 A test has 100 questions. Cora gets 85 questions correct. What decimal shows the part of the test she gets correct? What decimal shows the part of the test she gets incorrect? Model the decimals below. Show your work.

Solution ....

8 MATH JOURNAL

Show how to plot $\frac{4}{10}$, 0.8, $\frac{2}{10}$, and 0.4 on the number line below. Explain how you know your answer is correct.

SELF CHECK Go back to the Unit 4 Opener and see what you can check off.

Compare Decimals

LESSON 27

Dear Family,

This week your child is learning to compare decimals.

A model can help your child compare decimals when one decimal is in tenths and the other decimal is in hundredths.

The models show 0.65 and 0.7.

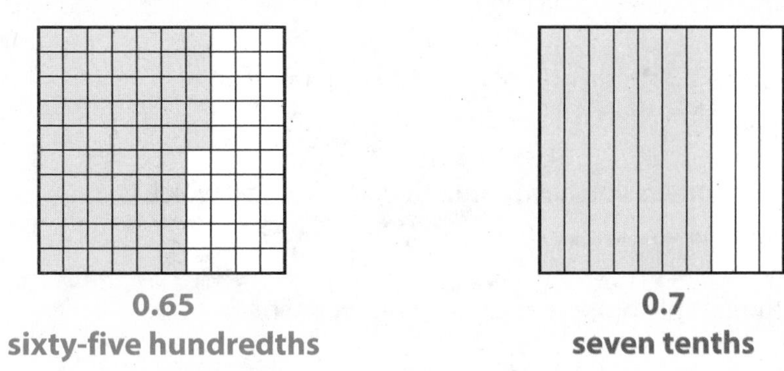

A greater area is shaded for 0.7 than for 0.65, so 0.7 is greater than 0.65.

Your child can also use a place-value chart to compare decimals in tenths and hundredths.

7 tenths equals 70 hundredths. $\frac{7}{10} = \frac{70}{100}$

Ones	.	Tenths	Hundredths
0	.	6	5
0	.	7	0

The place-value chart shows that seventy hundredths, or seven tenths, is greater than sixty-five hundredths. Compare the digits in the tenths place: $7 > 6$.

$0.70 > 0.65$ and $0.7 > 0.65$

Invite your child to share what he or she knows about comparing decimals by doing the following activity together.

ACTIVITY COMPARING DECIMALS

Do this activity with your child to compare decimals.

Materials fliers for grocery, drug, or hardware stores (optional)

- Look for items around the house or look through the fliers to find at least six decimal numbers. Make a list of the numbers as you find them; do not include the units that are shown with the numbers.

  Example: You have a box of crackers that is 6.75 ounces.
  Write the decimal 6.75 on your list.

- Take turns. One person marks two decimal numbers for the other person to compare. Make and use place-value charts, if needed.

- Challenge! Of all the decimal numbers you have compared, can you tell which is the greatest of all? Talk about how you know.

Look for other real-life opportunities to compare decimals with your child.

Explore Comparing Decimals

Learning Target

- Compare two decimals to hundredths by reasoning about their size. Recognize that comparisons are valid only when the two decimals refer to the same whole. Record the results of comparisons with the symbols >, =, or <, and justify the conclusions, e.g., by using a visual model.

SMP 1, 2, 3, 4, 5, 6, 7, 8

You know how to compare whole numbers and fractions. In this lesson, you will compare decimals. Use what you know to try to solve the problem below.

Kele and Kaci each buy equal-sized bottles of water. They each drink some of their water. Kele now has 0.5 of his bottle left. Kaci has 0.4 of her bottle left. Who has more water left?

TRY IT

Math Toolkit

- base-ten blocks
- tenths grids
- hundredths decimal place-value charts
- number lines
- index cards

DISCUSS IT

Ask your partner: Do you agree with me? Why or why not?

Tell your partner: I disagree with this part because . . .

CONNECT IT

LOOK BACK

Does Kele or Kaci have more water left? Explain how you know.

2 LOOK AHEAD

You compare the decimals 0.5 and 0.4 to decide who has more water left.

a. Suppose you have two more same-sized bottles of water. One bottle is 0.8 full of water, and the other bottle is 0.9 full of water.

Compare the decimals 0.8 and 0.9 to tell which bottle has more water. Write both decimals in the place-value chart.

Ones	.	Tenths

b. Compare the places from left to right, just as you do with whole numbers. Write $>$, $<$, or $=$ to compare.

9 ◯ 8, so 0.9 ◯ 0.8.

c. Which has more water, the bottle that is 0.8 full of water or the bottle that is 0.9 full of water?

REFLECT

Suppose the water bottles were different sizes. Could you compare the bottle that is 0.8 full and the bottle that is 0.9 full in the same way as in problem 2? Explain.

Name: ______________________________

Prepare for Comparing Decimals

1 Think about what you know about comparing decimals. Fill in each box. Use words, numbers, and pictures. Show as many ideas as you can.

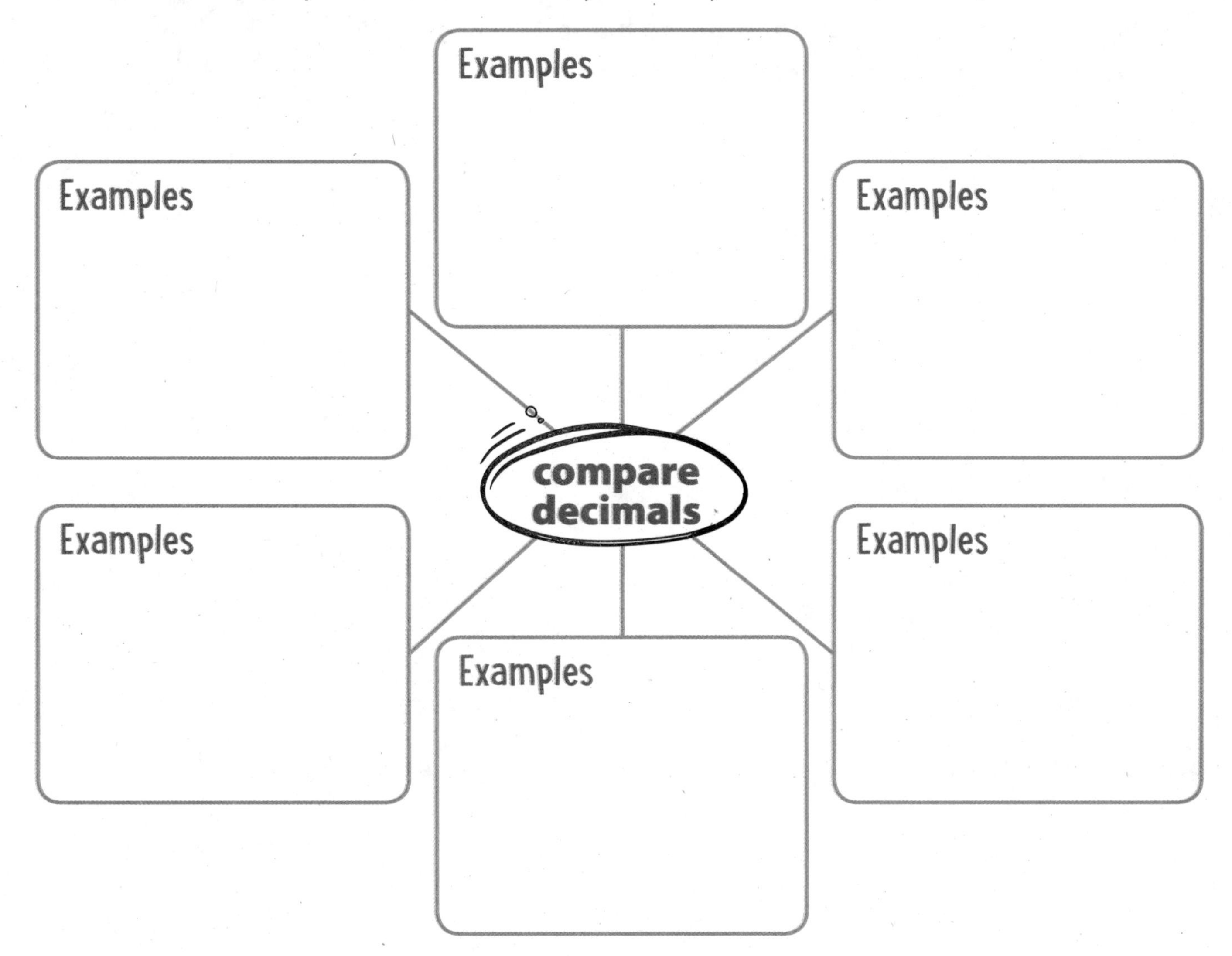

2 Compare the decimals 0.4 and 0.5. Write both decimals in the place-value chart. Then write >, <, or = to compare.

4 ◯ 5, so 0.4 ◯ 0.5.

Ones	.	Tenths

3 Solve the problem. Show your work.

Rafael and Zina each buy equal-sized granola bars. They each eat some of their granola bar. Rafael now has 0.6 of his granola bar left. Zina has 0.7 of her granola bar left. Who has more of their granola bar left?

Solution ....

4 Check your answer. Show your work.

Develop Comparing Decimals in Hundredths

Read and try to solve the problem below.

Dora lives 0.35 of a mile from school. Katrina lives 0.53 of a mile from school. Who lives a greater distance from school?

TRY IT

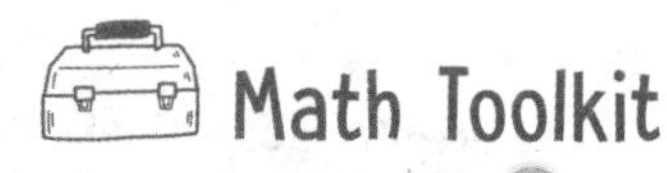

Math Toolkit

- base-ten blocks
- hundredths grids
- hundredths decimal place-value charts
- number lines
- index cards

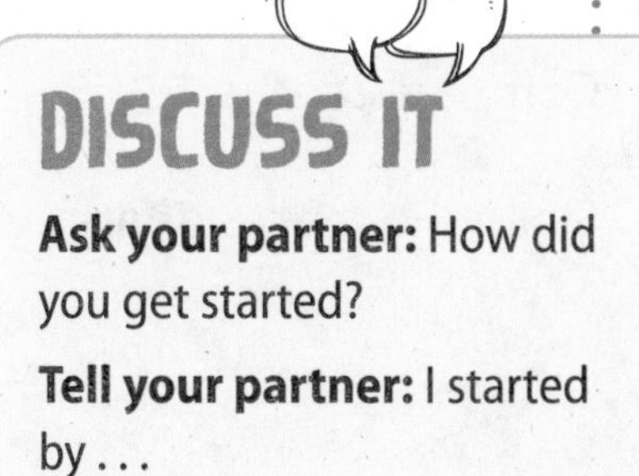

DISCUSS IT

Ask your partner: How did you get started?

Tell your partner: I started by . . .

Explore different ways to understand how to compare two decimals when both are in hundredths.

Dora lives 0.35 of a mile from school. Katrina lives 0.53 of a mile from school. Who lives a greater distance from school?

MODEL IT

You can use a model to help compare decimals in hundredths.

Each large square is one whole. The shaded areas show 0.35 and 0.53.

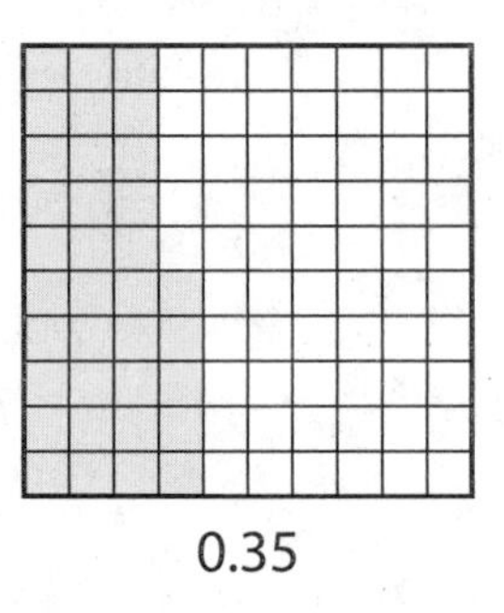

0.35

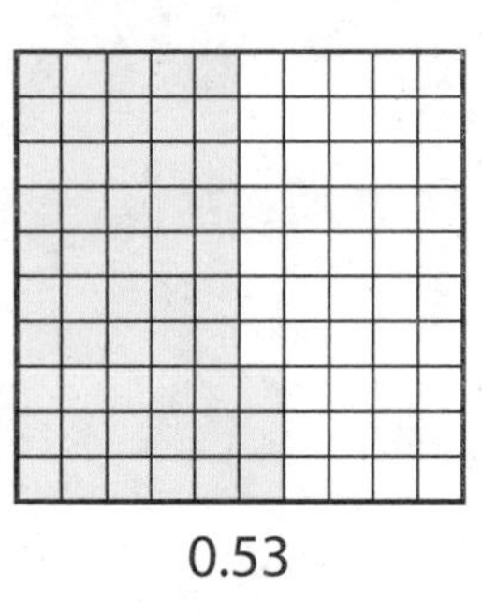

0.53

0.35 is thirty-five hundredths. 0.53 is fifty-three hundredths.

MODEL IT

You can also use a place-value chart to help compare decimals in hundredths.

The place-value chart shows 0.35 and 0.53.

Ones	.	Tenths	Hundredths
0	.	3	5
0	.	5	3

Compare ones: The digits are the same.

Compare tenths: **5** > **3**.

Since the tenths digits are different, you do not need to compare hundredths digits.

CONNECT IT

Now you will use the problem from the previous page to help you understand how to compare two decimals when both are in hundredths.

1. Look at the models on the previous page.

   Write a fraction equivalent to 0.35: ....; to 0.53: ....

2. Which fraction is greater? Explain how you know.

3. Write >, <, or = in the circle to make a true statement: 0.35 ◯ 0.53.

   Who lives a greater distance from school? ....

   Do the model and place-value chart support your answer? Explain.

4. Explain how you can use fractions to compare two decimals when both are in hundredths.

5. **REFLECT**

   Look back at your **Try It**, strategies by classmates, and **Model Its**. Which models or strategies do you like best for comparing two decimals when both are in hundredths? Explain.

   ....

   ....

   ....

   ....

APPLY IT

Use what you just learned to solve these problems.

6 Compare 4.21 and 4.12 using >, <, or =. Explain how you got your answer. Show your work.

Solution ....

....

....

7 Kord writes a decimal number that is greater than 0.39 but less than 0.44. What number could Kord have written? Show your work.

Solution ....

8 Which is less: 0.97 or 0.79? Show your work.

Solution ....

Name: ______________________________

Practice Comparing Decimals in Hundredths

Study the Example showing how to compare decimals to solve a word problem when both decimals are in hundredths. Then solve problems 1–5.

EXAMPLE

Jacob buys an apple and a pear. The apple weighs 0.33 of a pound. The pear weighs 0.35 of a pound. Which piece of fruit weighs less?

Write equivalent fractions.
The denominators are the same.
Compare the numerators: 33 < 35.

$0.33 = \frac{33}{100}$ $0.35 = \frac{35}{100}$

same denominator

So, 0.33 < 0.35.
The apple weighs less than the pear.

1 Shade and label the models to show 0.33 and 0.35. Then explain how the models show which decimal is less.

....

2 Complete the place-value chart to show 0.33 and 0.35. Then explain how the chart shows which decimal is less.

Ones	.	Tenths	Hundredths
	.		
	.		

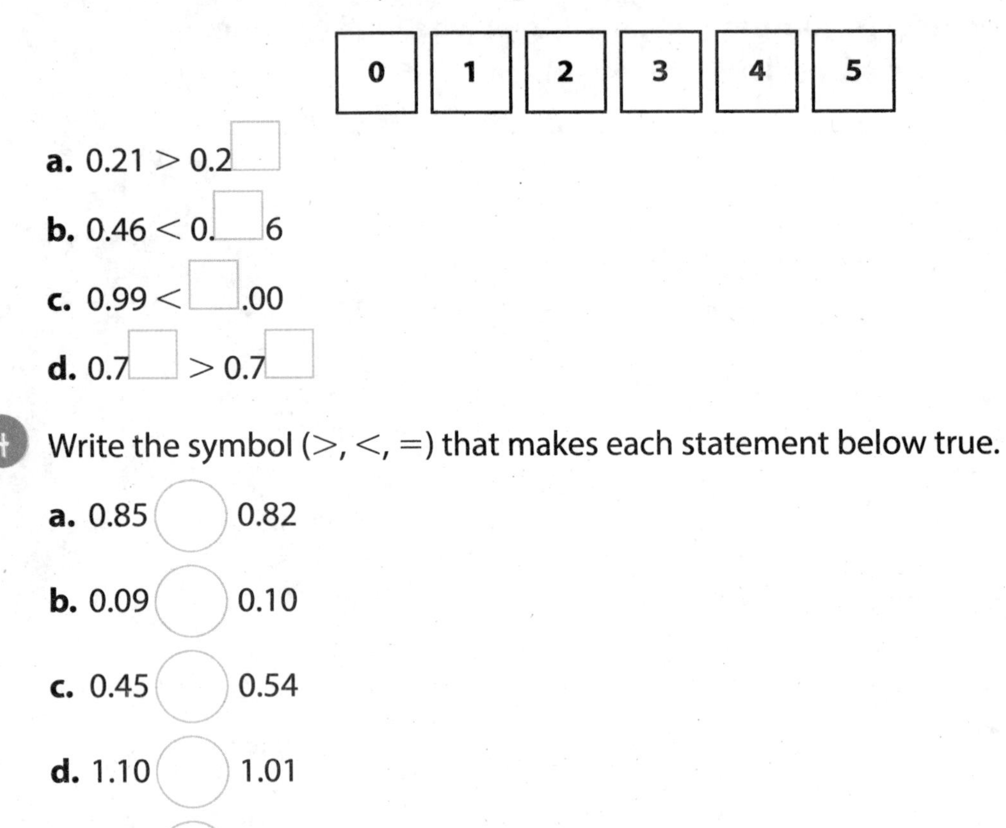

3 Use the digits in the tiles below to write decimals that make each statement true. You may use a digit more than once.

0	1	2	3	4	5

a. $0.21 > 0.2\square$

b. $0.46 < 0.\square 6$

c. $0.99 < \square.00$

d. $0.7\square > 0.7\square$

4 Write the symbol ($>$, $<$, $=$) that makes each statement below true.

a. 0.85 ◯ 0.82

b. 0.09 ◯ 0.10

c. 0.45 ◯ 0.54

d. 1.10 ◯ 1.01

e. 0.30 ◯ 0.3

5 Ryder buys 0.75 of a pound of turkey and 0.57 of a pound of cheese. Does he buy more turkey or more cheese? Show your work.

Solution ....

Develop Comparing Decimals in Tenths and in Hundredths

Read and try to solve the problem below.

Matt measures two insects. The bumblebee is 0.75 of an inch long. The hornet is 0.8 of an inch long. Which insect is longer?

TRY IT

Math Toolkit
- base-ten blocks
- hundredths grids
- tenths grids
- hundredths decimal place-value charts
- number lines

DISCUSS IT

Ask your partner: Can you explain that again?

Tell your partner: A model I used was . . . It helped me . . .

Explore different ways to understand how to compare decimals in tenths and hundredths.

Matt measures two insects. The bumblebee is 0.75 of an inch long. The hornet is 0.8 of an inch long. Which insect is longer?

MODEL IT

You can use a model to help compare decimals in tenths and hundredths.

Each large square is one whole. The models show 0.75 and 0.8.

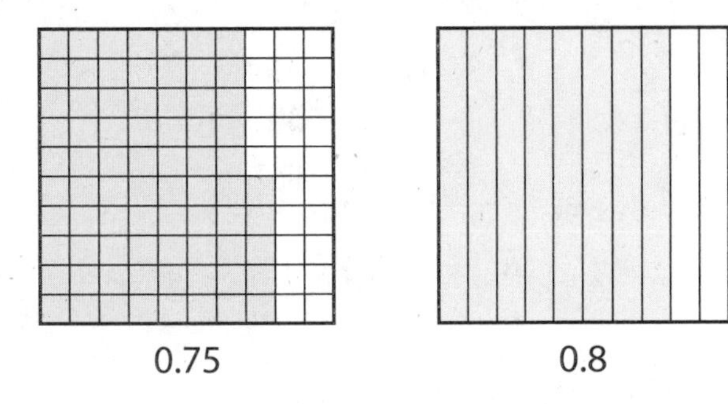

MODEL IT

You can also use a place-value chart to compare decimals in tenths and hundredths.

Notice that 0.8 has a 0 in the hundredths place in the chart. Remember that 8 tenths is equivalent to 80 hundredths.

Ones	.	Tenths	Hundredths
0	.	7	5
0	.	8	0

Compare ones: The digits are the same.

Compare tenths: **8** $>$ **7**.

Since the tenths digits are different, you do not have to compare hundredths.

CONNECT IT

Now you will use the problem from the previous page to help you understand how to compare decimals in tenths and hundredths.

1 Write fractions equivalent to 0.75 and 0.8.

2 How can you compare fractions with denominators of 100 and 10?

3 What fraction with a denominator of 100 is equivalent to $\frac{8}{10}$? ....

4 Compare the fractions. Then compare 0.75 and 0.8 using >, <, or =.

Which insect is longer? ....

5 Explain how you can compare decimals when one is in tenths and the other is in hundredths.

6 REFLECT

Look back at your **Try It**, strategies by classmates, and **Model Its**. Which models or strategies do you like best for comparing two decimals when one is in tenths and the other is in hundredths? Explain.

....

....

....

....

APPLY IT

Use what you just learned to solve these problems.

7 Which is greater: 0.9 or 0.92? Show how you can use fractions to solve the problem. Show your work.

Solution ....

8 The locations of points *B* and *C* on the number line represent decimal numbers. Explain why the value of point *C* is greater than the value of point *B*.

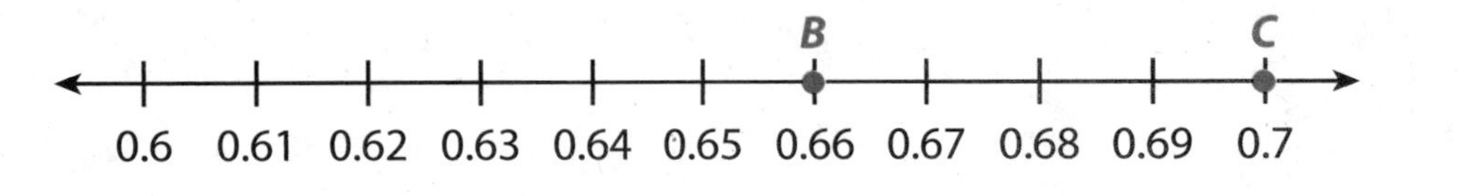

Solution ....

....

....

9 Compare 0.37 and 0.4 using >, <, or =. Explain how you got your answer. Show your work.

Solution ....

....

....

Name: ______________________________

Practice Comparing Decimals in Tenths and in Hundredths

Study the Example showing how to compare decimals in tenths and hundredths. Then solve problems 1–6.

EXAMPLE

Colin lives 0.6 of a mile from school and 0.65 of a mile from the park. Which place is closer to his home?

Write each decimal as an equivalent fraction. $0.6 = \frac{6}{10}$ $0.65 = \frac{65}{100}$

Write the tenths fraction as a hundredths fraction. $\frac{6}{10} = \frac{60}{100}$

Compare hundredths fractions. $\frac{60}{100} < \frac{65}{100}$

$0.6 < 0.65$

The school is closer to his home.

Lucas buys 0.6 of a pound of fish and 0.85 of a pound of shrimp to make a stew.

1. Shade the models below to compare 0.6 and 0.85.

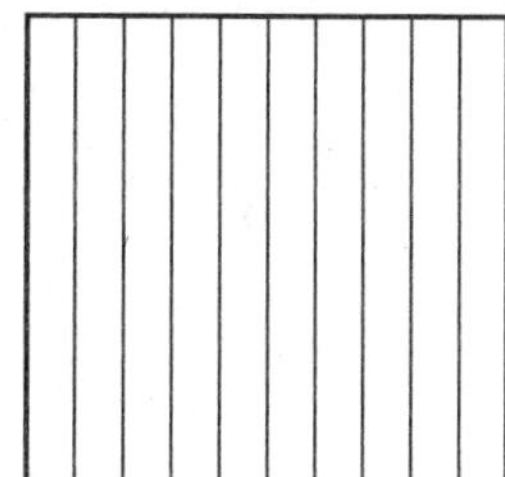

2. Write a symbol to compare the decimals. 0.6 ◯ 0.85

3. Does Lucas buy more fish or more shrimp? Use equivalent fractions to explain your answer.

4 Compare 0.2 and 0.25 using $>$, $<$, or $=$. Use equivalent fractions to explain your answer.

Solution ....

....

5 Compare 0.09 and 0.1 using $>$, $<$, or $=$. Use a place-value chart to explain your answer.

Ones	.	Tenths	Hundredths
	.		
	.		

Solution ....

....

....

6 Write the decimals 1.00, 0.20, and 0.03 in the place-value chart below. Which number is the greatest? Which number is the least? Use equivalent fractions to explain.

Ones	.	Tenths	Hundredths
	.		
	.		
	.		

Solution ....

....

....

Refine Comparing Decimals

Complete the Example below. Then solve problems 1–9.

EXAMPLE

Show the numbers 0.59 and 0.8 in their correct locations on the number line. Then write >, <, or = to compare the numbers.

Look at how you could show your work using a number line.

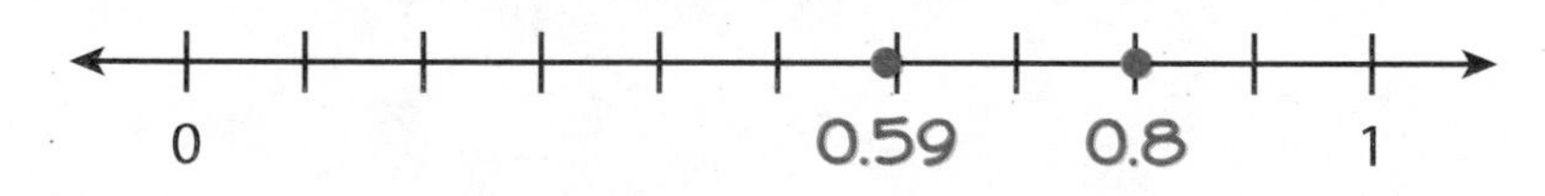

0.59 is less than 0.8, and 0.8 is greater than 0.59.

Solution ....

The student placed 0.59 on the number line between the tenths marks for 0.5 and 0.6 but closer to 0.6.

PAIR/SHARE
What does its position on a number line tell you about the value of a number?

APPLY IT

1 Compare 0.3 and 0.8 using >, <, or =. Draw a model or number line to support your solution. Show your work.

Solution ....

What models can you use to support your solution?

PAIR/SHARE
Compare the models that you and your partner used.

2 Mika runs the 50-yard dash in 7.39 seconds. Felix runs it in 7.6 seconds. Who runs faster? Show your work.

Does the greater number mean a faster or slower time?

Solution ....

PAIR/SHARE
How did you and your partner decide what method to use to solve the problem?

3 Which statement and reasoning is true about the decimals 0.45 and 0.5?

Ⓐ $0.45 < 0.5$ because hundredths are greater than tenths.

Ⓑ $0.45 < 0.5$ because $\frac{45}{100} < \frac{50}{100}$.

Ⓒ $0.45 > 0.5$ because $45 > 5$.

Ⓓ $0.45 > 0.5$ because hundredths are greater than tenths.

Sarah chose Ⓒ as the correct answer. How did she get that answer?

Make sure that the reasoning makes sense, too—not just the comparison.

PAIR/SHARE
Explain how you chose your answer.

4 Which change would make the following a true statement?

$0.5 < 0.43$

Ⓐ Put a 3 in the hundredths place to change 0.5 to 0.53.

Ⓑ Change the hundredths digit in 0.43 to 0.

Ⓒ Put a 0 in the tenths place to change 0.5 to 0.05.

Ⓓ Put a 0 in the hundredths place to change 0.5 to 0.50.

5 Which decimal is less than 3.75?

Ⓐ 3.9

Ⓑ 3.94

Ⓒ 3.80

Ⓓ 3.7

6 Tell whether each statement is *True* or *False*.

	True	**False**
$0.5 < 0.6$ because $\frac{5}{10}$ is less than $\frac{6}{10}$.	Ⓐ	Ⓑ
$0.25 > 0.3$ because 25 is greater than 3.	Ⓒ	Ⓓ
$0.89 > 0.8$ because $\frac{89}{100}$ is greater than $\frac{80}{100}$.	Ⓔ	Ⓕ
$0.06 = 0.6$ because 6 equals 6.	Ⓖ	Ⓗ
$0.4 < 0.14$ because 4 is less than 14.	Ⓘ	Ⓙ

7 Which decimals are greater than 0.07 but less than 0.3?

Ⓐ 0.02

Ⓑ 0.34

Ⓒ 0.27

Ⓓ 0.73

Ⓔ 0.1

8 Jana writes two numbers that are between 0.4 and 0.45 on the board. What numbers could Jana write?

Solution ....

9 MATH JOURNAL

Troy says that $0.9 > 0.90$ because tenths are greater than hundredths. Keith says that $0.9 < 0.90$ because 90 is greater than 9. Is either Troy or Keith correct? How would you compare 0.9 and 0.90? Explain.

☑ SELF CHECK Go back to the Unit 4 Opener and see what you can check off.

Problems About Time and Money

LESSON 28

Dear Family,

This week your child is learning how to solve multi-step problems about time and money.

Your child is learning different ways to solve multi-step problems that involve converting larger units of measurement to smaller units for time and money. Here is a time problem that your child might see.

Penny has 2 hours to complete her chores. She spends 10 minutes putting away her clean clothes. She spends 45 minutes cleaning her closet. It takes her 35 minutes to clean the bathroom. How much time does Penny have left to give her dog a bath?

The problem has information in both minutes and hours, so the first step is to convert the hours to minutes. There are 60 minutes in 1 hour, so multiply 60 by 2 to convert 2 hours to minutes: $2 \times 60 = 120$.

Then one way to solve the problem is to show the information using a bar model.

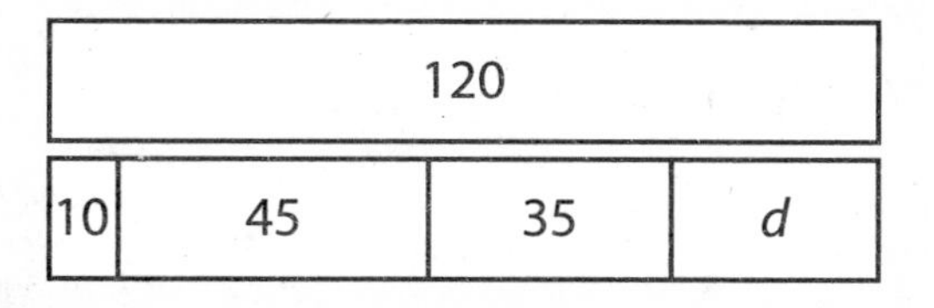

Solve the problem by using the bar model to write an equation such as $d = 120 - 10 - 45 - 35$, where d is the time, in minutes, left for the dog bath. Ask your child to compare the equation and the bar model to see how they are similar. Then solve the equation to find $d = 30$. There are 30 minutes left for the dog bath.

Invite your child to share what he or she knows about converting units to solve multi-step problems about time and money by doing the following activity together.

ACTIVITY SOLVING PROBLEMS ABOUT TIME AND MONEY

Do this activity with your child to solve multi-step problems about time and money.

Make up multi-step problems about time and money that might occur in everyday life. Here are some examples you might use:

1. Pete bought 4 rolls of tape and 2 packages of markers. The tape cost $0.75 a roll, and the markers cost $1.25 for each package. Pete gave the clerk a $10 bill. How much change did Pete receive?

2. Marta wanted to spend 1 hour gardening. She spent 30 minutes planting flowers, 10 minutes watering flowers, and 15 minutes pruning roses. Did Marta spend more or less time than she wanted to spend gardening?

3. Nico has $10 in quarters to spend on games at the fair. Each game cost 75¢. How many games can he play? How much money will he have left over?

Look for other real-life opportunities to practice solving multi-step problems about time and money with your child.

Answers: **1.** $4.50; **2.** She spent less time. There are 60 minutes in an hour, and she spent 55 minutes; **3.** He can play 13 games and he will have 25¢ left over.

Explore Problems About Time and Money

You have learned how to solve multi-step problems. Now you will solve multi-step problems involving time and money. Use what you know to try to solve the problem below.

Shing does chores for 1 hour 15 minutes on Wednesday and 25 minutes on Thursday. Shing spends a total of 115 minutes doing chores on Wednesday, Thursday, and Friday. How many minutes does he spend doing chores on Friday?

Learning Target

- Use the four operations to solve word problems involving distances, intervals of time, liquid volumes, masses of objects, and money, including problems involving simple fractions or decimals, and problems that require expressing measurements given in a larger unit in terms of a smaller unit. Represent measurement quantities using diagrams such as number line diagrams that feature a measurement scale.

SMP 1, 2, 3, 4, 5, 6, 7

TRY IT

Math Toolkit

- clocks
- math reference sheet
- number lines
- index cards

DISCUSS IT

Ask your partner: How did you get started?

Tell your partner: I started by . . .

CONNECT IT

LOOK BACK

Explain how to find how many minutes Shing spends doing chores on Friday.

LOOK AHEAD

You can use a visual model, such as a bar model, to solve multi-step problems. You can also write and solve an equation. Suppose you want to solve the problem below.

Lucy has **2 hours to do errands**. She spends **15 minutes at the post office**, **45 minutes at the grocery store**, and **40 minutes getting a haircut**. How much time does Lucy have left to get her **car washed**?

The bar model at the right shows the information in the problem. Remember that **2 hours** is the same as **120 minutes**.

120			
15	45	40	w

a. Use the bar model to write an expression to represent the time Lucy spends on errands so far. ....

b. Write and solve an equation to find the amount of time Lucy has left to get her car washed.

c. How much time does Lucy have left to get her car washed? ....

3 REFLECT

How does the bar model help you solve the problem?

....

....

....

Prepare for Problems About Time and Money

1. Think about what you know about modeling and solving problems. Fill in each box. Use words, numbers, and pictures. Show as many ideas as you can.

What Is It?	What I Know About It

multi-step problem

Examples	Examples	Examples

2. Draw a bar model and write an equation for the multi-step problem below.

Sam buys a table and 2 chairs. The table costs $300, and each chair costs $50. Sam has $500. How much money does Sam have left after he buys the table and 2 chairs?

3 Solve the problem. Show your work.

Angela exercises for 1 hour 45 minutes on Wednesday and 35 minutes on Thursday. She spends a total of 165 minutes exercising on Wednesday, Thursday, and Friday. How many minutes does she spend exercising on Friday?

Solution ....

4 Check your answer. Show your work.

Develop Solving Problems About Time

Read and try to solve the problem below.

Sadie spends $1\frac{1}{2}$ hours doing homework. She plays outside for 20 minutes and practices the piano for a quarter of an hour. How many more minutes does Sadie spend doing homework than practicing the piano and playing outside?

TRY IT

Math Toolkit

- clocks
- math reference sheet
- number lines
- index cards

DISCUSS IT

Ask your partner: Why did you choose that strategy?

Tell your partner: At first, I thought . . .

Explore different ways to understand how to solve problems about time.

Sadie spends $1\frac{1}{2}$ hours doing homework. She plays outside for 20 minutes and practices the piano for a quarter of an hour. How many more minutes does Sadie spend doing homework than practicing the piano and playing outside?

MODEL IT

You can use a bar model to solve time comparison problems.

Draw one bar to show the amount of time that Sadie spends **doing homework**. Draw two bars next to each other to show the amount of time she spends **playing outside** and **practicing the piano**. Draw a bar from the end of those two bars to the end of the homework bar to represent **how much more time** she spends **on homework**. Show all the times in minutes.

90		
20	15	*h*

MODEL IT

You can use the bar model to write an equation to solve the problem.

homework minutes = (playing + practicing) minutes + how many more homework minutes

The number of minutes Sadie spends on homework, playing outside, and practicing piano are known. How much more time Sadie spends on homework, *h*, is unknown.

$90 = (20 + 15) + h$

CONNECT IT

Now you will use the problem from the previous page to help you understand how to solve problems about time by converting units of time and using equations. Use the Math Reference Sheet as necessary.

1. Look at the bar model in the first **Model It**. Why do you think the amount of time Sadie does her homework and practices piano changed to a number of minutes?

2. How much time does Sadie spend doing homework? ....

3. How much time does Sadie spend playing outside and practicing the piano?

4. Write and solve another equation to model the situation. Use the time Sadie spends doing homework and the total time Sadie spends practicing the piano and playing outside that you found in problems 2 and 3.

5. Look back at the equation at the bottom of the previous page. How is that equation similar to or different from the equation you wrote in problem 4?

6. ## REFLECT

   Look back at your **Try It**, strategies by classmates, and **Model Its**. Which models or strategies do you like best for solving multi-step problems about time? Explain.

   ....

   ....

   ....

APPLY IT

Use what you just learned to solve these problems.

7 Coach Douglas has a soccer practice from 4:00 PM to 5:15 PM. The team spends 10 minutes stretching and $\frac{1}{2}$ of an hour passing the ball. The team spends the rest of the time on skill drills. How many minutes does the team spend on skill drills? Use the number line to help solve the problem. Show your work.
(1 hour = 60 minutes)

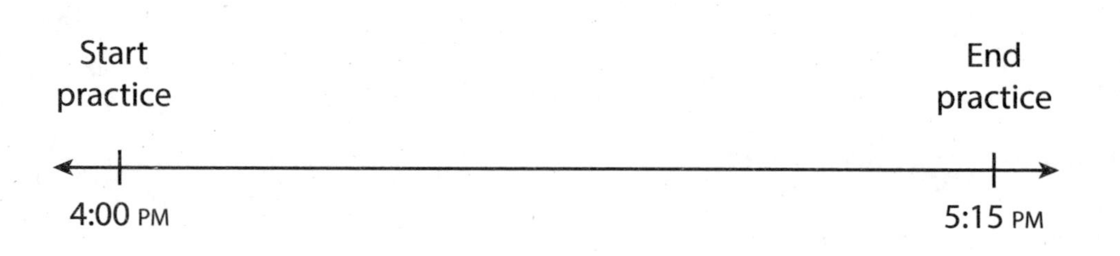

Solution ....

8 Trevor has 1 hour 15 minutes to practice for the school play. This is 3 times as long as it takes him to finish his homework. How long does it take Trevor to finish his homework? Show your work. (1 hour = 60 minutes)

Solution ....

9 Kwame spends $\frac{3}{4}$ of an hour riding his bike in all. He spends $\frac{1}{4}$ of an hour biking to the lake, 10 minutes biking around the lake, and the rest of the time biking home. How many minutes does he spend biking home? Show your work.
(1 hour = 60 minutes)

Solution ....

Name: ______________________________

Practice Solving Problems About Time

Study the Example showing how to solve a multi-step problem about time. Then solve problems 1–6.

EXAMPLE

Amy has 1 hour to do activities. She talks on the phone for 5 minutes. She rides her bike for 15 minutes. She plays a game with her brother for 25 minutes. How much time does Amy have left to spend painting a picture?

Amy has 60 minutes to do activities.	1 hour = 60 minutes
Add the minutes for the known activities.	$5 + 15 + 25 = 45$ minutes
Write an equation to find how much time Amy has left to paint a picture.	$45 + p = 60$ or $p = 60 - 45$ $p = 15$ $\quad$ $p = 15$

Amy has 15 minutes left to paint a picture.

1 Complete the labels on the bar model to represent the Example.

60			
			p

2 Look at the bar model in problem 1. What does p represent?

3 Milo visits an amusement park for 3 hours. He goes on rides for 50 minutes, plays carnival games for 40 minutes, and eats food for 30 minutes. He spends the rest of the time waiting in lines. How much time does Milo spend waiting in lines? Write and solve an equation to find the answer.

3 hours = ... minutes

Known activities = ... + ... + ... = ... minutes

Equation: ....

Milo spends .... minutes waiting in lines.

4 Suki watches a movie and eats a snack afterward. The movie starts at 7:15 PM and is $1\frac{1}{2}$ hours long. Suki finishes her snack at 9:10 PM. How long does Suki spend eating a snack? Use the number line to help solve the problem. Show your work.

Movie starts — 7:15 PM

Finishes snack — 9:10 PM

Solution ....

5 One of the fastest times for a 1,500-meter race is 3 minutes and 34 seconds. How many seconds is this time? Show your work. (1 minute = 60 seconds)

Solution ....

6 Bennett spends 4 hours at school today. He attends three 70-minute classes. There is a 5-minute break between classes. Then he eats lunch before going home. How long does Bennett spend eating lunch? Show your work.

Solution ....

Develop Solving Problems About Money

Read and try to solve the problem below.

Prim buys 3 muffins at the school bake sale. Each muffin costs $0.75. She also buys a cookie for $0.50. Prim gives Mr. Hall a $5.00 bill. How much change does she get?

TRY IT

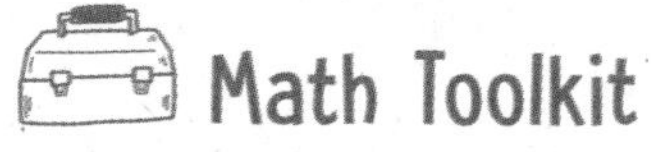

Math Toolkit

- play money
- number lines
- sticky notes

DISCUSS IT

Ask your partner: Do you agree with me? Why or why not?

Tell your partner: I disagree with this part because . . .

Explore different ways to understand how to solve problems about money.

Prim buys 3 muffins at the school bake sale. Each muffin costs $0.75. She also buys a cookie for $0.50. Prim gives Mr. Hall a $5.00 bill. How much change does she get?

PICTURE IT

You can use bills and coins to help solve money problems.

Show the amount Prim spends using quarters. 1 quarter = $0.25

Show the amount Prim gives Mr. Hall using bills and quarters. There are 4 quarters in 1 dollar. Prim spends **11 quarters**.

The amount that is not crossed out is the change that Prim gets.

CONNECT IT

Now you will use the problem from the previous page to help you understand how to solve problems about money by using money conversions and equations.

1. The money Prim uses to pay is in dollars. The prices are in cents. Which is the larger unit of money? ....

2. Explain how you can convert $5.00 to cents.

   How many cents are in $5.00? ....

3. Each muffin costs $0.75, or 75 cents. The cookie costs $0.50, or 50 cents. Fill in the blanks to find how many cents Prim spends on 3 muffins and 1 cookie.

   3 × .... cents + ... cents = ... cents

4. Show how to find how many cents Prim gets for change. ....

5. You have found Prim's change in cents. Explain how to find this amount in dollars and cents.

6. **REFLECT**

   Look back at your **Try It**, strategies by classmates, and **Picture It**. Which models or strategies do you like best for solving multi-step problems about money? Explain.

   ....

   ....

   ....

   ....

APPLY IT

Use what you just learned to solve these problems.

7 Aaron buys $1\frac{1}{2}$ pounds of cheese and four bottles of water. One pound of cheese costs \$10.00. Each bottle of water costs a half dollar. Aaron gives the clerk a \$20.00 bill. How much change does he get? Show your work.

Solution ....

8 Keisha has \$3,600. She uses \$1,900 to pay rent. She uses half of the money that is left to pay bills. Then she puts the rest of the money in her savings account. How much money does Keisha put in her savings account? Show your work.

Solution ....

9 Knox has three \$10.00 bills. He spends \$7.50 on a book and \$9.25 on a pizza. How much money does Knox have left?

Ⓐ \$12.25

Ⓑ \$13.25

Ⓒ \$16.75

Ⓓ \$23.25

Practice Solving Problems About Money

Study the Example showing how to solve a multi-step problem about money. Then solve problems 1–7.

EXAMPLE

Rita buys milk for \$0.50, a sandwich for \$2.50, and a fruit salad for \$1.25. She pays for her lunch with a \$5.00 bill. How much change does Rita get?

Rita spends: $50 + 250 + 125 = 425$ cents

500 cents − 425 cents = 75 cents

Rita gets 75 cents, or \$0.75, in change.

1. The picture below shows that \$5.00 is the same as \$3.00 in bills plus 8 quarters. Cross out the bills and coins to show the amount that Rita spends on lunch in the Example above.

2. How can you find the change Rita gets by looking at the picture above?

3. Josh buys 4 movie tickets and 2 large popcorns. Each movie ticket is \$8. Each popcorn is \$5. How much money does Josh spend?

Tickets: .... Popcorn: ....

Tickets and popcorn: ....

Josh spends ....

4 Mandy has \$84.00 in the bank. She also has 20 half-dollar coins and a \$20.00 bill at home. How much money does she have in all?

Ⓐ \$104.00

Ⓑ \$114.00

Ⓒ \$119.00

Ⓓ \$124.00

5 A pound of apples costs \$1.30. Sawyer buys $2\frac{1}{2}$ pounds of apples. How much does Sawyer spend on apples? Show your work.

Solution ....

6 Brie earns \$3,000 a month. She spends \$1,400 on rent and bills, \$700 on groceries, \$200 on a car payment, and \$100 on gas each month. She saves the rest of her money. How much money does Brie save? Show your work.

Solution ....

7 Regular bananas cost \$0.20 each at the supermarket. Organic bananas cost \$0.30 each. Suppose you have \$3.00. How many more regular bananas than organic bananas can you buy? Show your work.

Solution ....

Refine Problems About Time and Money

Complete the Example below. Then solve problems 1–9, using the Math Reference Sheet as necessary.

EXAMPLE

Vivian has $6.00. She buys 4 pens for $0.75 each and a pad of paper for $2.25. How much money does she have left?

Look at how you could show your work using a number line.

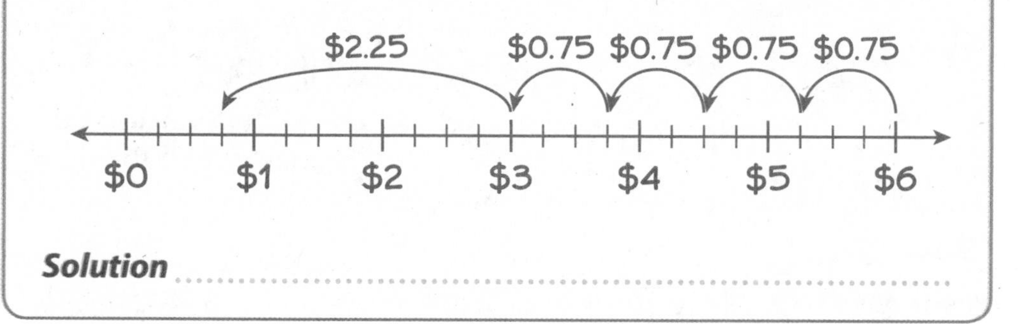

Solution ....

Vivian can use a number line divided into dollars and quarters as a tool to subtract the cost of the pens and pad of paper from $6.00.

PAIR/SHARE
How else could you solve the problem?

APPLY IT

1 The price of peaches is $1.80 for each pound. Frank buys $3\frac{1}{2}$ pounds of peaches. How much does Frank pay for the peaches? Show your work.

Solution ....

How can you find the price of a half pound of peaches?

PAIR/SHARE
How did you solve the problem? Why did you choose that method?

2 Steve sweeps the kitchen floor after he washes the dishes. Then he takes out the trash. He spends 18 minutes washing the dishes. This is 3 times as long as it takes him to sweep the floor. It takes him 3 minutes to take out the trash. How long does it take Steve to complete his chores? Show your work.

How can you use the time spent washing the dishes to find the time spent sweeping the floor?

PAIR/SHARE
How could you use a bar model to solve this problem?

Solution ....

3 Victoria has two $20.00 bills in her wallet. She spends $12.25 on a gift and $5.25 on a card. How much money does Victoria have left?

Ⓐ $2.50

Ⓑ $17.50

Ⓒ $22.50

Ⓓ $27.75

Amir chose Ⓐ as the correct answer. How did he get that answer?

How much does Victoria have in her wallet before she buys the gift and the card?

PAIR/SHARE
How can you estimate to see if Amir's answer is reasonable?

4 Bena buys a bottle of water for $1.20 and a pack of gum for $1.80. How much money does Bena give the clerk if she gets $7.00 in change?

Ⓐ $4.00

Ⓑ $9.00

Ⓒ $10.00

Ⓓ $20.00

5 Lena does chores for neighbors to earn money during the summer.

The table below shows how much money Lena earns for each chore.

Chore	Lawn Mowing	Dog Walking	Car Washing
Money Earned for Each Chore	$8.50	$4.00	$7.50

Lena does all the chores shown above for 3 neighbors.
Write two different expressions that can be used to find the total amount of money Lena earns.

6 A TV movie is 1 hour 45 minutes long with commercial breaks. There are 6 commercial breaks, each 4 minutes long. Which choices show how long the movie is without commercial breaks?

Ⓐ 81 minutes

Ⓑ 95 minutes

Ⓒ 105 minutes

Ⓓ 1 hour 21 minutes

Ⓔ 1 hour 35 minutes

7 Kyana wants to paint each wall of her bedroom a different color. She needs two quarts of paint for each wall. Each quart costs $11. She also needs to buy two paintbrushes for $3 each. She pays with a $100 bill. How much change does Kyana get? Show your work.

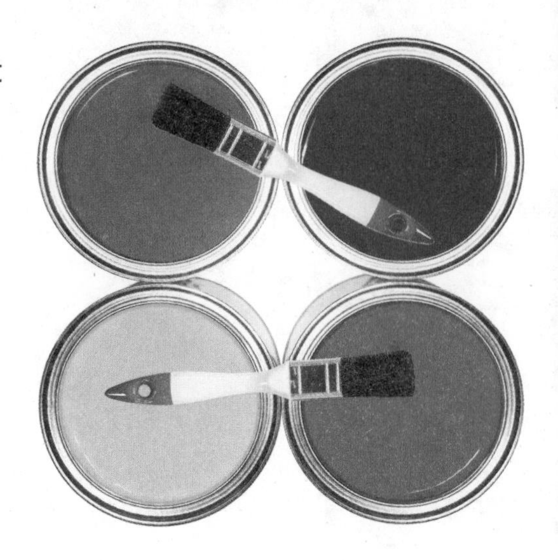

Solution ....

8 Johnny can walk 5 kilometers in 60 minutes. That is 3 times as long as it takes Donovan to run the same distance. How many more minutes does it take Johnny to walk 5 kilometers than it takes Donovan to run the same distance? Show your work.

Solution ....

9 MATH JOURNAL

Michael has three $5.00 bills. He buys a soda for $1.75 and a basketball for $12.50. How much money does Michael have left? Explain how to find the answer.

☑ SELF CHECK Go back to the Unit 4 Opener and see what you can check off.

Problems About Length, Liquid Volume, Mass, and Weight

Dear Family,

This week your child is learning to solve problems about length, liquid volume, mass, and weight.

Your child is learning different ways to solve multi-step problems that involve converting larger units to smaller units for measurements of length, liquid volume, mass, and weight. Here is a liquid volume problem your child might see.

Robert makes punch for a party. He combines 1 liter of lemonade, a 2-liter bottle of sparkling water, and 750 milliliters of fruit juice. How many milliliters of punch does Robert make for the party?

One way to help solve the problem is to use a table to think about the measurements and units given in the problem. Since the problem is in liters and milliliters, the first step is to convert liters to milliliters. Then combine the milliliters to find the total. You can organize the measurements in a table like the one below.

Given Volume	Volume in Milliliters
1 liter	1,000 milliliters
2 liters	2,000 milliliters
750 milliliters	750 milliliters

There are 1,000 milliliters in 1 liter. Multiply 1,000 by 2 to convert 2 liters to milliliters: $2 \times 1{,}000 = 2{,}000$. Add all the milliliter measurements to find the total: $1{,}000 + 2{,}000 + 750 = 3{,}750$ milliliters.

Invite your child to share what he or she knows about converting units to solve multi-step problems about length, liquid volume, mass, and weight by doing the following activity together.

ACTIVITY SOLVING PROBLEMS ABOUT LENGTH, LIQUID VOLUME, MASS, AND WEIGHT

Do this activity with your child to solve multi-step problems about length, liquid volume, mass, and weight.

Make up multi-step problems about length, liquid volume, mass, and weight that might occur in everyday life. Here are some examples you might use:

1. Josh wants to put in a new washing machine. The machine is 27 inches wide. Josh measured the width of his doorway. The doorway is 2 feet 8 inches wide. Will the new washing machine fit through the doorway? Remember that there are 12 inches in 1 foot.

2. Morgan wants to find out how much paint she has. She has two cans with 1 gallon of paint each, one can with 1 quart of paint, and one can with $\frac{1}{2}$ of a gallon of paint. How many quarts of paint does she have in all? Remember that there are 4 quarts in 1 gallon.

3. Aki has 3 pounds of cheese. He uses 4 ounces of cheese on each serving of pasta. How many servings of pasta can Aki put cheese on using the cheese he has? Remember that there are 16 ounces in 1 pound.

Look for other real-life opportunities to practice converting units to solve multi-step problems about length, liquid volume, mass, and weight with your child.

Answers: **1.** Yes, because 2 feet 8 inches is the same as 32 inches, and 27 inches is less than 32 inches; **2.** 11 quarts of paint: $4 + 4 + 1 + 2 = 11$; **3.** 12 servings, because 3 pounds is $3 \times 16 = 48$ ounces, and $48 \div 4 = 12$.

Explore Problems About Length, Liquid Volume, Mass, and Weight

You have learned how to solve multi-step problems. Now you will solve multi-step problems involving length, liquid volume, mass, and weight. Use what you know to try to solve the problem below.

Julia buys a spool with 12 yards of wire. The students in her jewelry-making class use 4 yards 2 feet of the wire for one project and 7 feet of the wire for another project. How many feet of wire does Julia have left?

Learning Target

- Use the four operations to solve word problems involving distances, intervals of time, liquid volumes, masses of objects, and money, including problems involving simple fractions or decimals, and problems that require expressing measurements given in a larger unit in terms of a smaller unit. Represent measurement quantities using diagrams such as number line diagrams that feature a measurement scale.

SMP 1, 2, 3, 4, 5, 6, 7, 8

TRY IT

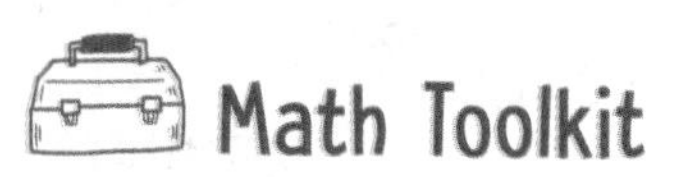

Math Toolkit

- counters
- rulers
- math reference sheet
- number lines

DISCUSS IT

Ask your partner: Why did you choose that strategy?

Tell your partner: I do not understand how . . .

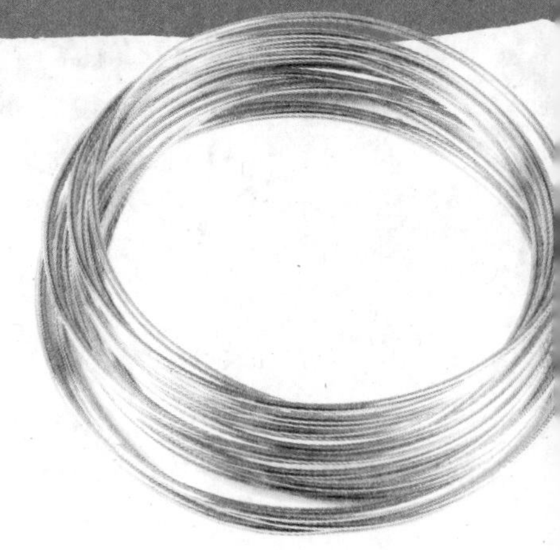

CONNECT IT

1 LOOK BACK

Explain how to find how many feet of wire Julia has left.

2 LOOK AHEAD

You can use a visual model or equation to solve a multi-step problem that involves converting units of length. Suppose you have the problem below.

Martin has **8 yards of twine**. He uses **2 yards 1 foot for one project** and **4 feet for another project**. How many **feet of twine does Martin have left**?

a. The bar model shows the information in the problem. Convert yards to feet and complete the bar model. 8 yards is the same as .... **feet** and **2 yards 1 foot** is the same as .... **feet.**

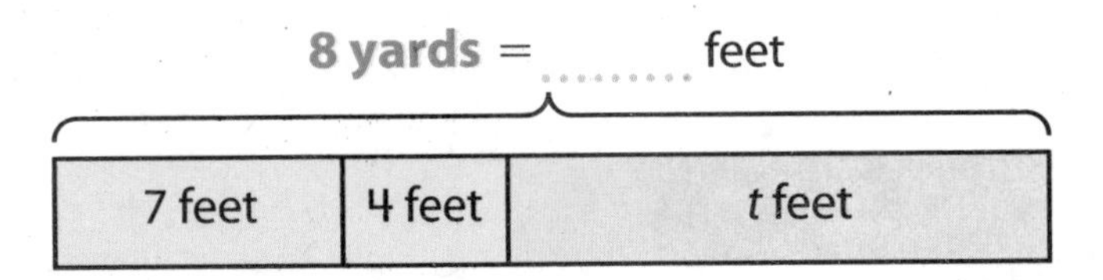

b. Use the bar model to write an expression to represent the number of feet of twine Martin uses for both projects. ....

c. Write and solve an equation to find the number of feet of twine Martin has left.

d. How many feet of twine does Martin have left? ....

3 REFLECT

How does the bar model show what operation(s) to use to solve the problem?

....

....

Name: ____________________

Prepare for Problems About Length, Liquid Volume, Mass, and Weight

1 Think about what you know about measurement. Fill in each box. Use words, numbers, and pictures. Show as many ideas as you can.

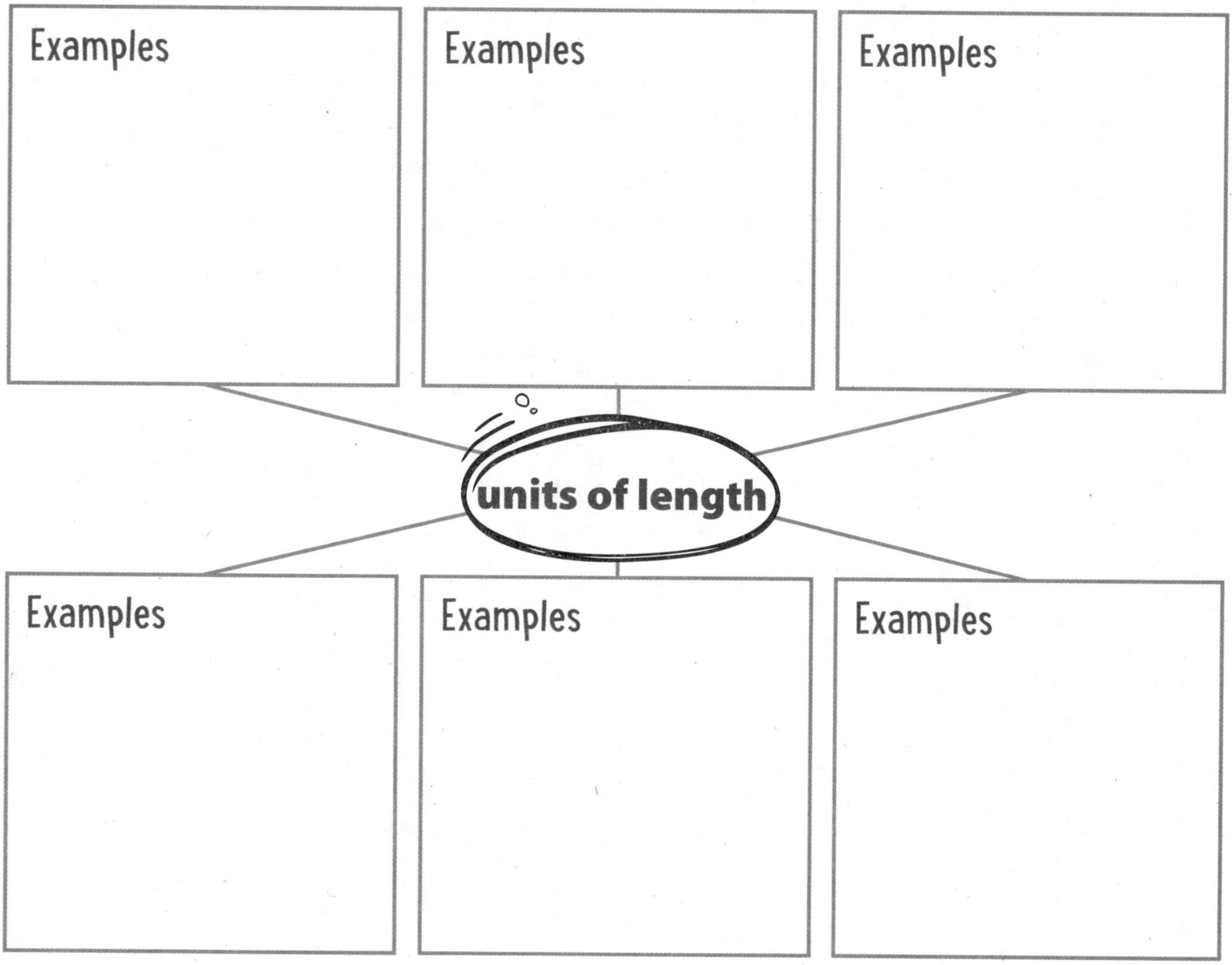

Examples	Examples	Examples

units of length

Examples	Examples	Examples

2 Write two different units you could use to measure the following.

your finger: ....

your desk: ....

the length of your classroom: ....

3 Maya has 7 yards of ribbon. She uses 4 yards to make bows and 1 yard 2 feet for a wreath. How many feet of ribbon does Maya have left?

Solution ....

4 Check your answer. Show your work.

Develop Solving Problems About Length

Read and try to solve the problem below.

Cindy buys a party sandwich that is 5 feet long. Her brother cuts off a piece of the sandwich that is $\frac{3}{4}$ of a foot long. Cindy cuts the remaining sandwich into 3-inch pieces to share with guests. How many 3-inch pieces does she make?

TRY IT

Math Toolkit
- counters
- rulers
- math reference sheet
- number lines

DISCUSS IT

Ask your partner: Can you explain that again?

Tell your partner: The strategy I used to find the answer was . . .

Explore different ways to understand how to solve problems about length.

Cindy buys a party sandwich that is 5 feet long. Her brother cuts off a piece of the sandwich that is $\frac{3}{4}$ of a foot long. Cindy cuts the remaining sandwich into 3-inch pieces to share with guests. How many 3-inch pieces does she make?

MODEL IT

You can use a model to help solve length problems.

The top bar of the model shows the length of the full sandwich. The bottom bar shows the amount of sandwich that is cut off, **$\frac{3}{4}$ of a foot**, and the part of the sandwich that will be **cut into 3-inch pieces.**

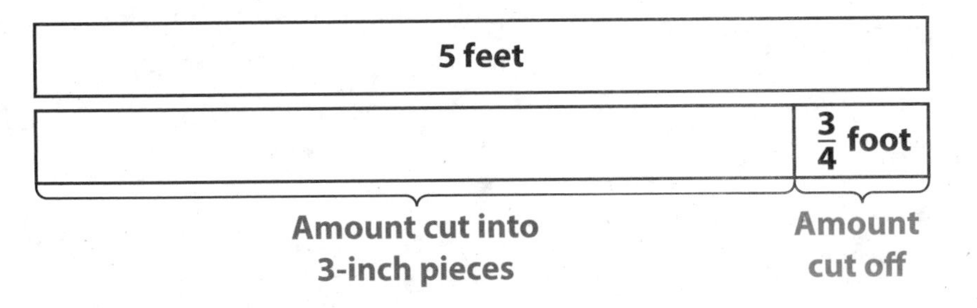

MODEL IT

You can use a number line to solve length problems.

The number line shows the length of the sandwich, 5 feet.
Each foot is divided into four 3-inch sections.

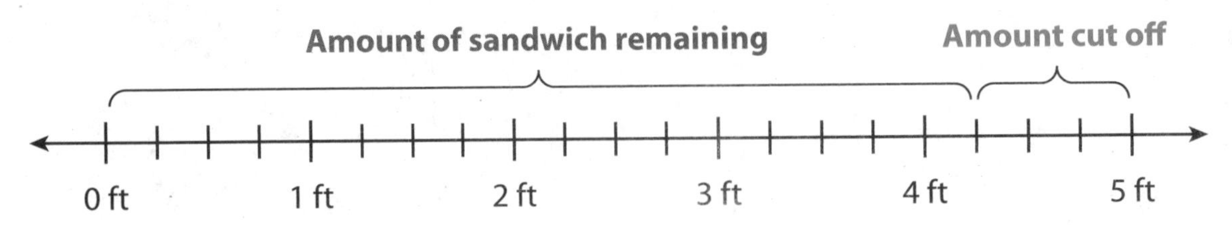

CONNECT IT

Now you will use the problem from the previous page to help you understand how to solve problems about length.

1. How are the bar model and the number line similar? How are they different?

2. What part of a foot does each tick mark on the number line model stand for?

   ....

   How many inches does each tick mark stand for? ....

3. Use the number line to find the length of the sandwich that is left, in feet.

   ....

4. How many 3-inch pieces are there in the remaining sandwich? Explain.

5. Explain how a number line helps you see both inches and fractional parts of a foot at the same time.

6. **REFLECT**

   Look back at your **Try It**, strategies by classmates, and **Model Its**. Which models or strategies do you like best for solving multi-step problems about length? Explain.

APPLY IT

Use what you just learned to solve these problems.

 Lulu has 10 feet of ribbon. She uses $1\frac{1}{3}$ feet of ribbon for a project. She uses the rest of the ribbon to make bows. She uses 8 inches of ribbon for each bow. How many bows does Lulu make? Show your work.

Solution ....

8 Raquel and Bernie drive a total of 1,836 kilometers in 4 days. They drive 630 kilometers on the first day. They drive an equal number of kilometers of the remaining distance on each of the next 3 days. How many kilometers do they drive on each of these 3 days? Show your work.

Solution ....

9 Tom and Paul enter the long jump contest at Field Day. Tom jumps a distance of 2 yards 9 inches. Paul jumps a distance of 4 yards. How many inches farther does Paul jump than Tom?

Solution ....

Name: ______________________________

Practice Solving Problems About Length

Study the Example showing how to solve a multi-step problem about length. Then solve problems 1–5.

EXAMPLE

Wendy has a fence that is 10 feet long. Vines cover a section of fence that is $\frac{1}{2}$ of a foot long. Wendy and 2 friends each paint an equal length of the rest of the fence. How long, in inches, is the section of the fence each friend paints? (1 foot = 12 inches)

Length of fence

Length with vines

Each length to paint

Length of fence: 10 feet = 120 inches

Length covered with vines: $\frac{1}{2}$ of a foot = 6 inches

Length painted: 120 – 6 = 114 inches

Length of each section: 114 ÷ 3 = 38 inches

The section of fence that each friend paints is 38 inches long.

1 Nestor needs 750 centimeters of rope. Rope comes in lengths of $4\frac{1}{2}$ meters and 9 meters at the hardware store. Which length of rope should Nestor buy? (1 meter = 100 centimeters)

$4\frac{1}{2}$ meters = ... centimeters 9 meters = ... centimeters

a. Which length is greater than 750 centimeters? .... centimeters

b. Nestor should buy rope with a length of .... meters.

2 Which length is greater, $\frac{1}{2}$ of a meter or 240 centimeters? Explain.

3 Jorge carries a football forward $5\frac{2}{3}$ yards on one play. He carries the football backward 1 foot on the next play. How far forward is the ball, in feet, from the place where Jorge started to carry the ball? Show your work. (1 yard = 3 feet)

Solution ....

4 Marion is $3\frac{1}{2}$ feet tall. She is 4 inches taller than her brother Elijah. She is $1\frac{1}{4}$ feet shorter than her sister Lorie. How tall are Elijah and Lorie, in inches? Show your work. (1 foot = 12 inches)

Elijah: .... Lorie: ....

5 Tracy needs 31.5 meters of wood for a porch railing. She has three pieces of wood that are each 8 meters long and one piece that is 7 meters long. Does Tracy have enough wood for the porch railing? Show your work.

Solution ....

Develop Solving Problems About Liquid Volume

Marco, Javier, and Jim go to a party. Marco brings $1\frac{1}{2}$ liters of lemonade, Javier brings a 2-liter bottle of lemonade, and Jim brings 450 milliliters of lemonade. How many milliliters of lemonade do the boys bring to the party in all? (1 liter = 1,000 milliliters)

TRY IT

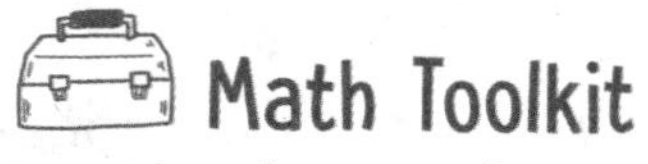

- math reference sheet
- number lines
- grid paper

DISCUSS IT

Ask your partner: How did you get started?

Tell your partner: I started by . . .

Explore different ways to understand how to solve problems about liquid volume.

Marco, Javier, and Jim go to a party. Marco brings $1\frac{1}{2}$ liters of lemonade, Javier brings a 2-liter bottle of lemonade, and Jim brings 450 milliliters of lemonade. How many milliliters of lemonade do the boys bring to the party in all? (1 liter = 1,000 milliliters)

PICTURE IT

You can use a picture to help solve liquid volume problems.

Think about the units for each amount of lemonade.

MODEL IT

You can use a table to help solve liquid volume problems.

Make a table to show the volumes of the three containers in the given units in one column and the volumes in milliliters in the other column.

1 liter = 1,000 milliliters and $\frac{1}{2}$ of a liter = 500 milliliters

Given Volume	Volume in Milliliters
$1\frac{1}{2}$ liters	1,500 milliliters
2 liters	2,000 milliliters
450 milliliters	450 milliliters

CONNECT IT

Now you will use the problem from the previous page to help you understand how to solve problems about liquid volume.

1. Use the amounts of lemonade given in the problem to write an equation that shows the total amount of lemonade, *t*, the boys bring to the party.

2. What units are included in the equation? ....

3. Look at the table in **Model It**. Explain how to convert $1\frac{1}{2}$ liters to milliliters.

   How many milliliters are in 2 liters? ....

4. What is the total amount of lemonade the three boys bring to the party? Explain.

5. Explain how to solve a problem about liquid volume when measurements are given in different units.

6 REFLECT

Look back at your **Try It**, strategies by classmates, and **Picture It** and **Model It**. Which models or strategies do you like best for solving multi-step problems about liquid volume? Explain.

....

....

....

APPLY IT

Use what you just learned to solve these problems.

7 Joanne is making punch. She uses $\frac{1}{2}$ of a gallon of orange juice, 3 quarts of lemonade, and $1\frac{1}{4}$ gallons of apple cider. How many quarts of punch does Joanne have in all? How many 1-cup servings are there in all? Show your work. (1 gallon = 4 quarts and 1 quart = 4 cups)

Solution ....

8 Matt has $4\frac{3}{4}$ cups of milk. He drinks 10 fluid ounces of the milk. How many fluid ounces of milk does Matt have left? Show your work. (1 cup = 8 fluid ounces)

Solution ....

9 Carlos makes 3 liters of horchata. His sister drinks 300 milliliters. His brother drinks 550 milliliters. How many milliliters of horchata does Carlos have left? Show your work. (1 liter = 1,000 milliliters)

Solution ....

Practice Solving Problems About Liquid Volume

Study the example showing how to solve a multi-step problem about liquid volume. Then solve problems 1–5.

EXAMPLE

Naomi has a container of water. She uses 4 liters to water her vegetable garden. She uses $3\frac{1}{2}$ liters to water flowers. She uses the remaining 500 milliliters in the container to fill up a bird bath. How many milliliters of water did Naomi have in the container? (1 liter = 1,000 milliliters)

Write an equation to find the total amount of water.	$w = 4\text{ L} + 3\frac{1}{2}\text{ L} + 500\text{ mL}$
Convert liters to milliliters.	$4 \times 1{,}000\text{ mL} = 4{,}000\text{ mL}$ $3 \times 1{,}000\text{ mL} = 3{,}000\text{ mL}$ and $\frac{1}{2}$ of $1{,}000\text{ mL}$ is 500 mL
Write the equation using milliliters and solve.	$w = 4{,}000\text{ mL} + 3{,}500\text{ mL} + 500\text{ mL}$ $w = 8{,}000\text{ mL}$

Naomi had 8,000 milliliters of water in the container.

Benny has two small fish tanks with one fish in each tank. One tank has $3\frac{1}{2}$ quarts of water. The other tank has 12 cups of water. Benny combines the water into one large fish tank with both fish in the large tank.

1. How many cups of water are in the large tank? (1 quart = 4 cups)

   $3\frac{1}{2}$ quarts: 3×4 cups = ______ cups and $\frac{1}{2}$ of 4 cups is ______ cups

   $3\frac{1}{2}$ quarts = ______ cups; ______ cups + ______ cups = ______ cups

   There are __________ of water in the large tank.

2. At least 5 cups of water are needed for each fish in a tank. How many more fish would Benny be able to put in the large tank? Explain.

   Solution ....

   ....

3 Ms. Tam has three containers to use in an experiment. The first container has 600 milliliters of water, the second has 2 liters, and the third has 1.5 liters. How many milliliters of water does Ms. Tam have in all? Show your work. (1 liter = 1,000 milliliters)

Solution ....

4 Sharon and her cousin make smoothies at a family reunion. Sharon brings $2\frac{1}{2}$ gallons of milk. Her cousin brings 2 quarts of milk. The girls use 8 quarts of milk for the smoothies. How much milk is left? (1 gallon = 4 quarts)

Ⓐ 4 quarts

Ⓑ 6 quarts

Ⓒ 4 gallons

Ⓓ 6 gallons

5 Rob has 6 quarts of apple cider for the fall fair. He pours all the cider into glasses to set on picnic tables. He pours 6 fluid ounces of cider into each glass. How many glasses of cider does Rob set on the tables? Show your work. (1 quart = 4 cups; 1 cup = 8 fluid ounces)

Solution ....

Develop Solving Problems About Mass and Weight

Kyle has a jar filled with quarters. The empty jar has a mass of 400 grams. The same jar filled with quarters has a mass of 1.5 kilograms. If each quarter has a mass of about 5 grams, about how many quarters are in the jar? (1 kilogram = 1,000 grams)

TRY IT

Math Toolkit

- math reference sheet
- number lines

DISCUSS IT

Ask your partner: Do you agree with me? Why or why not?

Tell your partner: I agree with you about . . . because . . .

Explore different ways to understand how to solve problems about mass and weight.

Kyle has a jar filled with quarters. The empty jar has a mass of 400 grams. The same jar filled with quarters has a mass of 1.5 kilograms. If each quarter has a mass of about 5 grams, about how many quarters are in the jar? (1 kilogram = 1,000 grams)

PICTURE IT

You can use a picture to help understand the problem.

Think about the relationship between the mass of each quarter, the mass of the empty jar, and the mass of the jar filled with quarters.

5 grams

400 grams

1.5 kilograms

MODEL IT

You can use a bar model to help solve problems about mass and weight.

Use n to represent the number of quarters.

The mass of 1 quarter is 5 grams, so the expression $5 \times n$ represents the mass of the quarters in the jar, in grams.

total mass: 1.5 kilograms

mass of quarters $(5 \times n)$ grams	mass of empty jar 400 grams

CONNECT IT

Now you will use the problem from the previous page to help you understand how to solve problems about mass and weight.

1. The mass of the empty jar is .... grams.

   The total mass of the jar filled with quarters is .... kilograms or .... grams.

2. Write and solve an equation to find the mass of the quarters in grams.

3. Write and solve an equation to find about how many quarters are in the jar.

4. How does using a bar model to write an equation help you solve a word problem about mass?

5. ## REFLECT

   Look back at your **Try It**, strategies by classmates, and **Picture It** and **Model It**. Which models or strategies do you like best for solving multi-step problems about mass or weight? Explain.

   ....

   ....

   ....

   ....

   ....

APPLY IT

Use what you just learned to solve these problems.

6 A baker has one recipe for dinner rolls that uses 1 kilogram of flour. The baker has another recipe that uses 700 grams of flour. How many grams of flour does the baker use to make two batches of each recipe? Show your work. (1 kilogram = 1,000 grams)

Solution ....

....

7 A can of nuts weighs 1 pound, 1 ounce. The empty can weighs 3 ounces. Suppose you pour half the nuts from the can into a bowl. How many ounces of nuts are in the bowl? Show your work. (1 pound = 16 ounces)

Solution ....

8 Tia picks 2 kilograms of strawberries. Her brother picks 850 grams of strawberries. Her sister picks $2\frac{1}{2}$ kilograms of strawberries. How many grams of strawberries do they pick in all? Show your work. (1 kilogram = 1,000 grams)

Solution ....

Name: ____________________

Practice Solving Problems About Mass and Weight

Study the example problem showing how to solve a multi-step problem about weight. Then solve problems 1–5.

EXAMPLE

The softball coach has a box filled with softballs. The weight of the empty box is 3 pounds. When it is filled with softballs, the box weighs 12 pounds. Each softball has a weight of 6 ounces. How many softballs are in the box? (1 pound = 16 ounces)

Find the weight of the softballs in ounces.

$s = 12 \text{ pounds} - 3 \text{ pounds} = 9 \text{ pounds}$

$s = 9 \times 16 \text{ ounces} = 144 \text{ ounces}$

Find the number of softballs.

$s = 6 \times n$

$144 = 6 \times n$

$24 = n$

There are 24 softballs in the box.

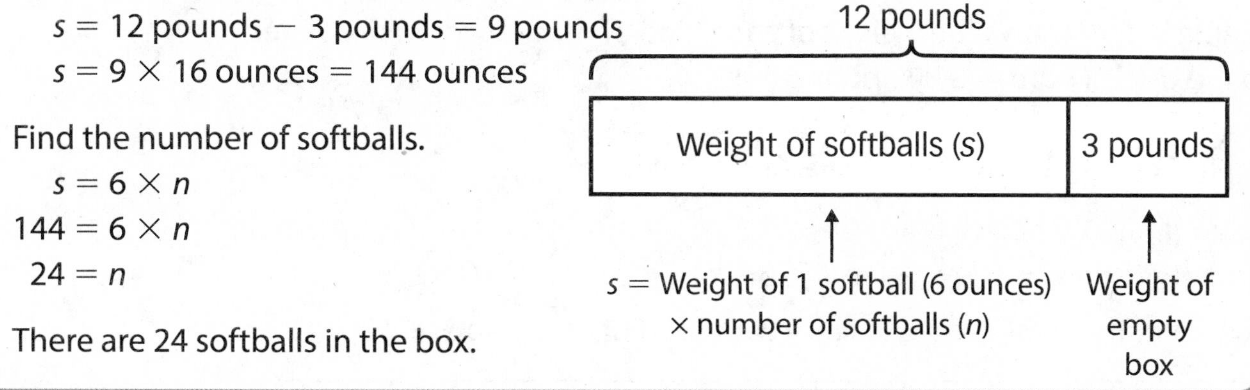

1 Look at the example above. Explain why you need to find the weight of the softballs in the box in ounces.

2 Tyson's baby brother weighed 7 pounds, 3 ounces when he was born. The baby lost 9 ounces after a few days, and then gained 1 pound, 6 ounces by the end of the second week. How many ounces did the baby weigh at the end of the second week? Show your work. (1 pound = 16 ounces)

Solution ....

3 Melinda makes 5 pounds of trail mix. She puts 4 ounces in each bag. She has 20 ounces of trail mix left over. How many bags of trail mix does Melinda make? Show your work. (1 pound = 16 ounces)

Solution ....

4 A large truck that moves cars can carry a maximum load of 15,720 pounds. The table below shows the weight of each kind of car that could be loaded onto the truck. (1 ton = 2,000 pounds)

Kind of Car	Compact	Mid-size	Full-size
Weight (in tons)	$1\frac{1}{2}$	$2\frac{1}{4}$	3

Tell whether the truck is able to carry each load of cars below.

	Yes	No
2 full-size cars, 1 compact car	Ⓐ	Ⓑ
2 compact cars, 2 full-size cars	Ⓒ	Ⓓ
2 mid-size cars, 2 compact cars	Ⓔ	Ⓕ
4 mid-size cars	Ⓖ	Ⓗ

5 A paper clip has a mass of 1 gram. A box of paper clips has 100 paper clips. Which equations below can be used to find the number of boxes of paper clips that have a mass of 1 kilogram? Let n be the number of boxes. (1 kilogram = 1,000 grams)

Ⓐ $100 = 1{,}000 \div n$

Ⓑ $n = 1{,}000 \times 100$

Ⓒ $n = 1{,}000 \div 100$

Ⓓ $1{,}000 = n \times 100$

Ⓔ $n = 1{,}000 - 100$

Refine Problems About Length, Liquid Volume, Mass, and Weight

Complete the Example below. Then solve problems 1–9, using the Math Reference Sheet as necessary.

EXAMPLE

Vera has a piece of ribbon. She cuts off a 40-centimeter length for a project. She cuts the remaining length of ribbon into 7 pieces that are each 30 centimeters long. How long was the original piece of ribbon?

Look at how you could show your work using a bar model.

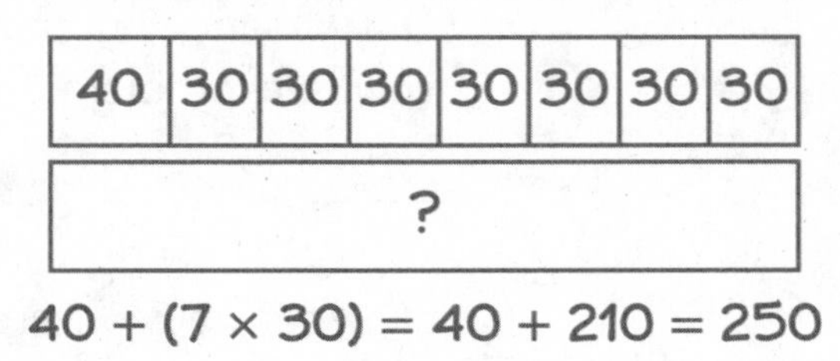

$40 + (7 \times 30) = 40 + 210 = 250$

Solution ....

Vera can multiply to find the length of the 7 equal-sized pieces and then add the length of the cut-off piece to find the original length.

PAIR/SHARE
How else could you solve the problem?

APPLY IT

1 Mary has a board that is 7 feet long. She cuts off $\frac{1}{4}$ of a foot of the board to make an even edge. Then Mary cuts the remaining board into 3 pieces that are the same length. How long, in feet, is each piece? Show your work.

Solution ....

Will Mary add, subtract, multiply, or divide to get 3 equal lengths?

PAIR/SHARE
How did you solve the problem? Why did you choose that method?

2 A wildlife sanctuary has two elephants. One has a weight of 11,028 pounds and the other has a weight of $5\frac{1}{2}$ tons. A platform can hold 22,000 pounds. Can the platform hold both elephants? Explain your reasoning. Show your work.

Will the combined weight be measured in pounds or tons?

Solution ....

....

PAIR/SHARE
Did you and your partner solve the problem the same way?

3 Jessica is making punch. She mixes 132 fluid ounces of juice and 15 cups of seltzer. How many 6-ounce glasses can she fill with punch?

Ⓐ 20 glasses

Ⓑ 22 glasses

Ⓒ 24 glasses with 3 ounces left over

Ⓓ 42 glasses

Jason chose Ⓒ as the correct answer. How did he get that answer?

How can you convert 15 cups to fluid ounces?

PAIR/SHARE
Does Jason's answer make sense?

4 John is mixing paint for an art project. He combines 4 quarts of white paint with $3\frac{1}{2}$ gallons of blue paint. He uses 2 quarts of the paint. How much paint does he have left?

Ⓐ 4 quarts

Ⓑ $9\frac{1}{2}$ quarts

Ⓒ 16 quarts

Ⓓ 20 quarts

5 Four friends pick small pumpkins at a pumpkin patch. The table below shows the weight of each pumpkin.

Friend	Kelly	Neelam	Jackson	Raul
Weight of Pumpkin	2 pounds 9 ounces	30 ounces	$2\frac{1}{2}$ pounds	38 ounces

Order the weights of the pumpkins, in ounces, from least to greatest.

................, ..., ..., ...

6 Tara has a 5-liter container of water. She pours 3 liters of the water into a pitcher. She pours the rest of the water into 8 glasses so that each glass has an equal amount of water. How many milliliters of water does Tara pour into each glass?

Ⓐ 25 milliliters

Ⓑ 250 milliliters

Ⓒ 500 milliliters

Ⓓ 1,000 milliliters

7 A parking lot is 316 feet long. Workers paint lines to make one row of parking spaces. They do not paint lines on a 28-foot length at one end of the row in order to allow cars room to turn. The workers paint lines along the rest of the row to make 9-foot-wide parking spaces. How many parking spaces does the parking lot have? Show your work.

Solution ....

8 Tony is making potato salad for a school picnic. He needs a total of 3 kilograms of potatoes. He has a 1.5- kilogram bag and an 850-gram bag. How many more grams of potatoes does Tony need? Show your work.

Solution ....

9 MATH JOURNAL

Frida has 14 yards of yarn. She gives 5 feet of the yarn to a friend. Then she uses 8 yards, 1 foot of the yarn to finish a project. How many feet of yarn does Frida have left? Explain how to find the answer.

☑ SELF CHECK Go back to the Unit 4 Opener and see what you can check off.

Self Reflection

In this unit you learned to . . .

Skill	Lesson
Compare fractions with unlike denominators, for example: $\frac{2}{5} > \frac{3}{10}$.	17, 18
Add and subtract fractions and mixed numbers.	19, 20, 21, 25
Add and subtract fractions in line plots.	22
Multiply a fraction by a whole number, for example: $3 \times \frac{1}{2} = \frac{3}{2}$.	23, 24
Write decimals as fractions and write fractions as decimals, for example: $0.75 = \frac{3}{4}$.	26
Compare decimals, for example: $0.65 < 0.7$.	27
Solve problems about time and money.	28
Solve problems about length, liquid volume, and mass.	29

Think about what you learned.

Use words, numbers, and drawings.

1. The most important math I learned was .... because . . .

2. The hardest thing I learned to do is .... because . . .

3. One thing I still need to work on is . . .

Use Fractions and Decimals

Study an Example Problem and Solution

SMP 1 Make sense of problems and persevere in solving them.

Read this problem involving fractions and decimals. Then look at Luna's solution to this problem.

Sand Jars

Luna made these notes after she made a sand art design in a 2-cup jar.

- I used a glass jar that holds 2 cups.
- I used less than 1 cup of yellow sand.
- I filled less than 0.4 of the jar with pink sand.
- I filled more than 0.2 of the jar with purple sand.

Luna wants to write specific instructions for making the same kind of design that would work for a jar of any size.

- Find fractions or decimals to tell exactly what part of each jar to fill with pink, purple, and yellow sand.
- Write instructions using those numbers.

Read the sample solution on the next page. Then look at the checklist below. Find and mark parts of the solution that match the checklist.

PROBLEM-SOLVING CHECKLIST

- ☐ Tell what is known.
- ☐ Tell what the problem is asking.
- ☐ Show all your work.
- ☐ Show that the solution works.

a. **Circle** something that is known.

b. **Underline** something that you need to find.

c. **Draw a box around** what you do to solve the problem.

d. **Put a checkmark** next to the part that shows the solution works.

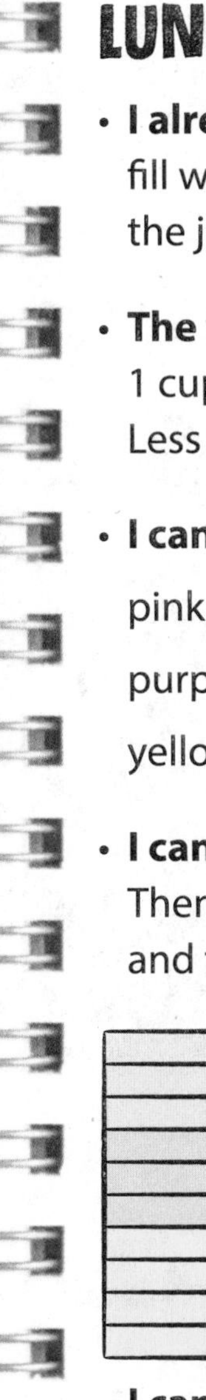

LUNA'S SOLUTION

Hi, I'm Luna. Here's how I solved this problem.

- **I already know** the decimals for what part of the jar to fill with purple and pink. I need to find what part of the jar should be yellow.

- **The whole jar was 2 cups and yellow was less than 1 cup.**
  1 cup is half of the jar.
  Less than 1 cup means less than $\frac{1}{2}$ of the jar is yellow.

- **I can list all the information with fractions.**
  pink: less than 0.4, so less than $\frac{4}{10}$ of the jar.
  purple: more than 0.2, so more than $\frac{2}{10}$ of the jar.
  yellow: less than $\frac{1}{2}$, so less than $\frac{5}{10}$ of the jar.

I had to choose either fractions or decimals. I chose fractions because I like them!

- **I can make a diagram with 10 equal parts.**
  Then color it to find 3 fractions that are the right size and total $\frac{10}{10}$.

pink: $\frac{3}{10} < \frac{4}{10}$

purple: $\frac{3}{10} > \frac{2}{10}$

yellow: $\frac{4}{10} < \frac{5}{10}$

I drew a diagram to show all the parts and organize my thinking.

- **I can write an equation to show the sum is equivalent to 1.**

$$\frac{3}{10} + \frac{3}{10} + \frac{4}{10} = \frac{10}{10}$$

$\frac{10}{10} = 1$, so my fractions work.

- **So, here are instructions for any size jar.**
  Fill any jar $\frac{3}{10}$ with pink sand, $\frac{3}{10}$ with purple sand, and $\frac{4}{10}$ with yellow sand.

Try Another Approach

There are many ways to solve problems. Think about how you might solve the Sand Jars problem in a different way.

Sand Jars

Luna made these notes after she made a sand art design in a 2-cup jar.

- I used a glass jar that holds 2 cups.
- I used less than 1 cup of yellow sand.
- I filled less than 0.4 of the jar with pink sand.
- I filled more than 0.2 of the jar with purple sand.

Luna wants to write specific instructions for making the same kind of design that would work for a jar of any size.

- Find fractions or decimals to tell exactly what part of each jar to fill with pink, purple, and yellow sand.
- Write instructions using those numbers.

PLAN IT

Answer these questions to help you start thinking about a plan.

A. Luna's solution showed how to write all the amounts as fractions. How could you write all of the amounts as decimals? Explain and show.

B. There is more than one possible solution for this task. Look back at the problem. How can you tell that a different solution is possible? Explain.

SOLVE IT

Find a different solution for the Sand Jars problem. Show all your work on a separate sheet of paper.

You may want to use the Problem-Solving Tips to get started.

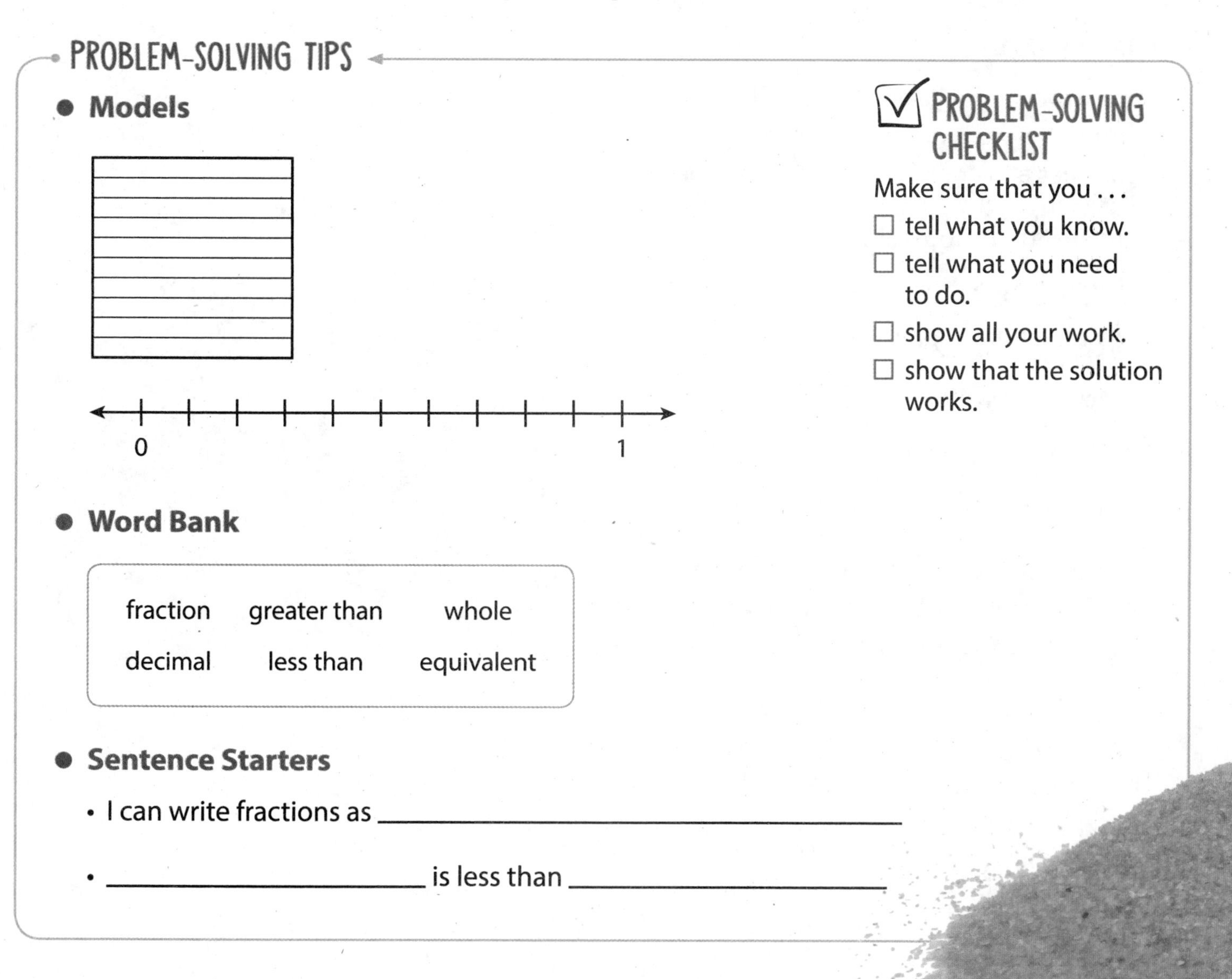

PROBLEM-SOLVING TIPS

- **Models**

- **Word Bank**

fraction	greater than	whole
decimal	less than	equivalent

- **Sentence Starters**
  - I can write fractions as ______________________
  - ______________ is less than ______________

PROBLEM-SOLVING CHECKLIST

Make sure that you . . .

- ☐ tell what you know.
- ☐ tell what you need to do.
- ☐ show all your work.
- ☐ show that the solution works.

REFLECT

Use Mathematical Practices As you work through the problem, discuss these questions with a partner.

- **Use Structure** How can you use the relationship between fractions and decimals?
- **Use Repeated Reasoning** Can you think of problems that you have solved before that could help you solve this problem? Explain.

Discuss Models and Strategies

Read the problem. Write a solution on a separate sheet of paper. Remember, there are lots of ways to solve a problem!

Coin Purses

Luna wants to make and sell small coin purses with gold braid around the perimeter. She will show a sample of each of the two styles at a craft fair. If people like them, she will make more.

Here are Luna's notes about the two styles.

Square style:

- all sides are $2\frac{1}{2}$ inches long

Rectangle style:

- sides are $3\frac{1}{4}$ inches and $2\frac{1}{4}$ inches long

Note: I will have to cut pieces of braid to fit, but I won't put together two small pieces for one side.

Luna needs to buy enough gold braid to make one sample purse for each design. She wants to spend as little as possible.

How can Luna use this price chart to decide what lengths of gold braid to buy?

Length (inches)	2	4	6	8	10	12	20
Cost	\$2	\$4	\$6	\$8	\$10	\$11	\$17

PLAN IT AND SOLVE IT

Find a solution for the Coin Purses problem.

Write a detailed plan and support your answer. Be sure to include:

- a diagram.
- the lengths of gold braid Luna should buy.
- how you used the cost to help make your decision.

You may want to use the Problem-Solving Tips to get started.

PROBLEM-SOLVING TIPS

- **Questions**
  - What are some steps that I might take to solve the problem?
  - What step should I do first? Why?
- **Word Bank**

length	rectangle	whole
cost	square	perimeter

- **Sentence Starters**
  - The length of gold braid needed for each design is ______________
  - The total length of gold braid is ______________
  - The perimeter of the square is ______________
  - I can add ______________

☑ PROBLEM-SOLVING CHECKLIST

Make sure that you . . .

- ☐ tell what you know.
- ☐ tell what you need to do.
- ☐ show all your work.
- ☐ show that the solution works.

REFLECT

Use Mathematical Practices As you work through the problem, discuss these questions with a partner.

- **Make Sense of Problems** How can you decide what to do first?
- **Make an Argument** What can you do to support your plan to show that it makes sense?

Persevere On Your Own

Read the problem. Write a solution on a separate sheet of paper.

Hair Ribbons

Luna is teaching 3 friends how to make hair ribbons. She plans to use leftover ribbons from another project. She will share the ribbon among the 3 friends so they all get the same total length of ribbon. Luna's notes and the lengths of the pieces of ribbon she has are shown below.

- Cut the ribbons so each friend gets the same total length.
- Cut the pieces to be as long as possible.
- It does not matter how many pieces of ribbon each friend receives.
- It does not matter what color ribbon each friend receives.
- There are $4\frac{3}{4}$ feet of the blue ribbon, $6\frac{1}{4}$ feet of the purple ribbon, and 10 feet of the green ribbon.

How should Luna cut the ribbons?

SOLVE IT

Suggest a way that Luna could cut the ribbons so that each friend gets the same total length.

Tell the number of pieces of ribbon each friend gets and the length of each piece. Explain how you got your answer, and how you made your decision.

REFLECT

Use Mathematical Practices After you complete the task, choose one of these questions to discuss with a partner.

- **Persevere** Did you try approaching the task in different ways before deciding on a plan? Explain.
- **Real-Life Problems** Did you think about a real-life situation that is like this problem? Describe it.

Picture Frame

Luna is designing a picture frame made out of craft sticks. Below are her instructions.

- Paint 6 craft sticks. Each stick is $\frac{3}{4}$ of an inch wide and $5\frac{3}{4}$ inches long.
- Glue the craft sticks side-by-side on a piece of cardboard.
- Glue a photograph $2\frac{1}{4}$ inches wide and $2\frac{1}{4}$ inches tall on the frame.
- Leave a space at least $2\frac{2}{4}$ inches wide to the right of the photo. You can put your decorations here.
- There needs to be at least $\frac{2}{4}$ of an inch of space above and below the photo.

Explain if Luna's plan works.

SOLVE IT

Help Luna design the picture frame.

- Copy the outline of the frame at the right and fill in all the measurements.
- Show and explain why your measurements work.

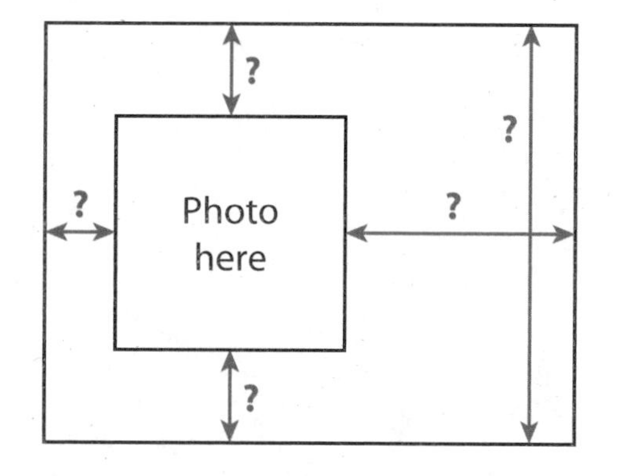

REFLECT

Use Mathematical Practices After you complete the task, choose one of these questions to discuss with a partner.

- **Use a Model** How did the frame outline help you solve the problem?
- **Make an Argument** How did you show that your measurements work?

Unit Review

1 In a community garden, Alex paints $\frac{1}{12}$ of the fence and Bobby paints $\frac{3}{12}$ of the fence. Charles paints the rest of the fence. What fraction of the fence does Charles paint?

Ⓐ $\frac{1}{12}$

Ⓑ $\frac{3}{12}$

Ⓒ $\frac{4}{12}$

Ⓓ $\frac{8}{12}$

2 Which equations are true? Choose all the correct answers.

Ⓐ $5\frac{4}{5} - 2\frac{3}{5} = 3\frac{1}{5}$

Ⓑ $2\frac{7}{8} + 2\frac{2}{8} = 4\frac{9}{16}$

Ⓒ $6\frac{6}{12} - 3\frac{5}{12} = 3\frac{11}{12}$

Ⓓ $9\frac{2}{10} + 2\frac{1}{10} = 11\frac{3}{10}$

Ⓔ $10\frac{5}{6} - 5\frac{3}{6} = 5\frac{1}{6}$

Ⓕ $2\frac{1}{3} + 1\frac{1}{3} = 3\frac{2}{3}$

3 Fill in the missing numbers to find a fraction that is equivalent to $\frac{3}{5}$.

Write the answers in the boxes.

$$\frac{3}{5} = \frac{3 \times 2}{5 \times \square} = \frac{\square}{\square}$$

4 Zorana measures $\frac{1}{2}$ of a foot of string for a science activity. She needs 7 pieces of string with that same length.

Write and solve a multiplication equation that Zorana can use to find the total length of string that she needs.

Solution Zorana needs .... feet of string.

5 Emilio cuts 12 pieces of string for a craft project. He measures each piece and records the information in a line plot.

Emilio attaches the 4 pieces of string that are the same length. What is the total length, in inches, of those 4 pieces of string? Show your work.

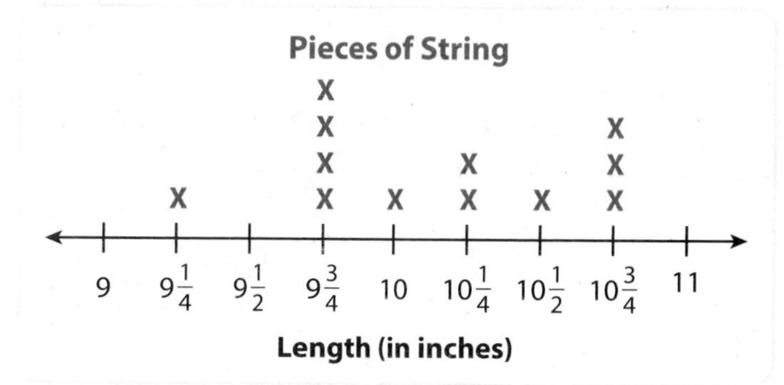

Solution ....

6 The number line below shows one whole divided into tenths.

Write numbers in the boxes to label the missing fractions and decimals.

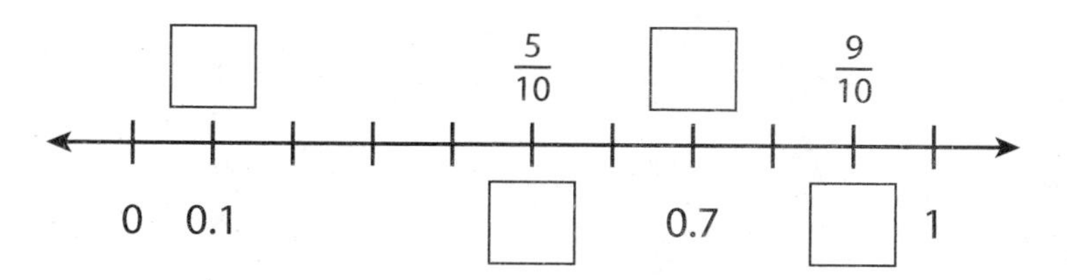

7 Laura rows her boat 1.3 kilometers. Daniel rows his boat 1.25 kilometers. Annabelle rows farther than Daniel, but not as far as Laura. How many kilometers could Annabelle have rowed? Show your work.

.... kilometers

Performance Task

Answer the questions and show all your work on separate paper. Use the Math Reference Sheet, as necessary.

Ciara is using the recipe below to make 6 dozen cupcakes for a family party. She needs to buy flour, milk, and vanilla. Ciara also needs to buy boxes to carry the cupcakes to the party. Each box holds one layer of cupcakes. Ciara has \$25 to spend. Does she have enough money to buy everything she needs to make the cupcakes and bring them to the party? Explain how you know.

Checklist

Did you . . .

- ☐ organize the information?
- ☐ draw a diagram?
- ☐ use words and numbers in your explanation?

RECIPE Ciara's Vanilla Cupcakes
makes 1 dozen cupcakes 3 inches across

256 grams flour	200 grams sugar
1 teaspoon baking soda	4 eggs
5 tablespoons butter	5 milliliters vanilla
$\frac{1}{2}$ cup milk	

Below are the products Ciara needs to buy and their prices.

1 foot

\$2.50 \$2.00 \$8.50 \$1.00

REFLECT

Use Mathematical Practices After you complete the task, choose one of the following questions to answer.

- **Model** What equations did you use to help you solve this problem?
- **Be Precise** Why is it important to use labels for all of the amounts while you are solving this problem?

UNIT 4

Vocabulary

Draw or write to show examples for each term.

benchmark fraction a common fraction that you might compare other fractions to. For example, $\frac{1}{4}$, $\frac{1}{2}$, $\frac{2}{3}$, and $\frac{3}{4}$ are often used as benchmark fractions.

My Example

common denominator a number that is a common multiple of the denominators of two or more fractions.

My Example

decimal a number containing a decimal point that separates a whole from fractional place values (tenths, hundredths, thousandths, and so on).

My Example

decimal point the dot used in a decimal that separates the ones place from the tenths place.

My Example

hundredths the parts formed when a whole is divided into 100 equal parts.

My Example

tenths the parts formed when a whole is divided into 10 equal parts.

My Example

weight the measurement that tells how heavy an object is. Units of weight include ounces and pounds.

My Example

My Word: ____________

____

____

My Example

My Word: ____________

____

____

My Example

My Word: ____________

____

____

My Example

My Word: ____________

____

____

My Example

My Word: ____________

____

____

My Example

UNIT

5

Geometry and Measurement

Figures, Classification, and Symmetry

SELF CHECK

Before starting this unit, check off the skills you know below. As you complete each lesson, see how many more skills you can check off!

I can . . .	Before	After
Identify points, lines, line segments, rays, and perpendicular and parallel lines, for example: a plus sign has perpendicular lines.	☐	☐
Measure angles using a protractor, for example: an angle on a stop sign is 135°.	☐	☐
Add and subtract angle measures to solve problems.	☐	☐
Classify two-dimensional figures based on sides and angles, for example: squares and rectangles have parallel sides.	☐	☐
Draw and identify lines of symmetry in shapes, for example: a square has 4 lines of symmetry.	☐	☐

UNIT 5

Build Your Vocabulary

REVIEW

triangle
trapezoid
quadrilateral
parallelogram

Math Vocabulary

Complete the table using the review words to name the shape. Then explain what you know about the shape that helped you identify it.

Shape	Name	Description

Academic Vocabulary

Put a check next to the academic words you know. Then use the words to complete the sentences.

☐ characteristic ☐ critical ☐ assumption ☐ brief

1. When a fact is .... for solving a problem, it is very important.
2. If an explanation is ...., it is not very long.
3. When you make an ...., you use what you know to make a best guess.
4. A .... of a triangle is that it has three angles.

Points, Lines, Rays, and Angles

LESSON 30

Dear Family,

This week your child is learning about points, lines, rays, and angles.

Here are some vocabulary words that tell about the geometry concepts that your child is learning.

A **point** is a single location in space. Point *A* is shown at the right.

A **line segment** is a straight row of points that starts at one point and ends at another point. Line segment *AB* is written as $\overline{AB}$.

A **line** is a straight row of points that goes on forever in both directions. Line *AB* is written as $\overleftrightarrow{AB}$.

A **ray** is a straight row of points that starts at one point and goes on forever in one direction. Ray *AB* is written as $\overrightarrow{AB}$.

An **angle** is formed by two rays, lines, or line segments that meet at a common point called the **vertex**. The angle shown at the right can be named $\angle A$, $\angle CAB$, or $\angle BAC$.

Parallel lines are always the same distance apart and never cross.

Perpendicular lines cross to form a right angle.

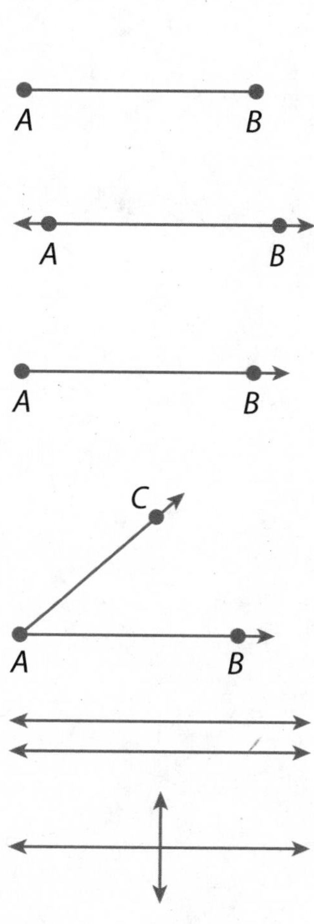

Invite your child to share what he or she knows about points, lines, rays, and angles by doing the following activity together.

ACTIVITY POINTS, LINES, RAYS, AND ANGLES

Do this activity with your child to identify lines, rays, and angles.

Together with your child, find examples of real-life objects that have parts that look like lines, rays, and angles.

- Give clues to describe the objects to each other without naming the objects. Use some of the geometry vocabulary words that your child is learning about.
- Try to guess each object from the other person's description of it.
- Here are some real-life examples you might use:

Guitar strings
(parallel line segments)

Brick wall (perpendicular and parallel line segments)

Ceiling fan (angles and line segments)

Fence (angles, parallel and perpendicular line segments)

Explore Points, Lines, Rays, and Angles

Learning Targets

- Draw points, lines, line segments, rays, angles (right, acute, obtuse), and perpendicular and parallel lines. Identify these in two-dimensional figures.
- Recognize angles as geometric shapes that are formed wherever two rays share a common endpoint, and understand concepts of angle measurement.

SMP 1, 2, 3, 4, 5, 6

Previously, you have learned about shapes such as squares, rectangles, and triangles. Now you will learn more about what makes up these shapes. Use what you know to try to solve the problem below.

Traci tries to teach her younger sister how to draw a rectangle. Traci tells her, "Draw a shape with four straight sides." Traci's sister draws the shape shown.

The drawing of the shape includes 4 straight sides, but it is not a rectangle. How can Traci make her directions more clear?

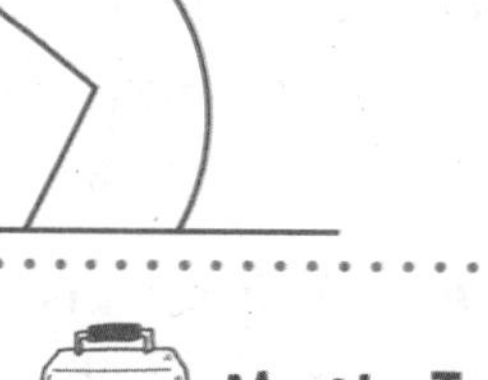

TRY IT

Math Toolkit

- geoboards
- chenille stems
- rulers
- grid paper

DISCUSS IT

Ask your partner: Do you agree with me? Why or why not?

Tell your partner: I agree with you about . . . because . . .

CONNECT IT

1 LOOK BACK

Explain how Traci can make her directions more clear.

2 LOOK AHEAD

Certain words in geometry are used to describe shapes in detail. Read each description and use it to label the point or points in the figure at the right.

a. A **point** is a single location in space. A dot can show a point. You can name a point with a capital letter, such as point *A*.

b. A **line segment** is a straight row of points that starts at one point and ends at another point. You can write "line segment *AB*" as $\overline{AB}$.

c. A **line** is a straight row of points that goes on forever in both directions. You can write "line *AB*" as $\overleftrightarrow{AB}$.

d. A **ray** is a straight row of points that starts at one point and goes on forever in one direction. You can write "ray *AB*" as $\overrightarrow{AB}$. When you name a ray, you always start with the endpoint.

e. Rays, lines, or line segments that meet at a common point, or **vertex**, form an **angle**. You can write "angle *A*" as $\angle A$ or $\angle CAB$ or $\angle BAC$. The vertex is always the middle letter.

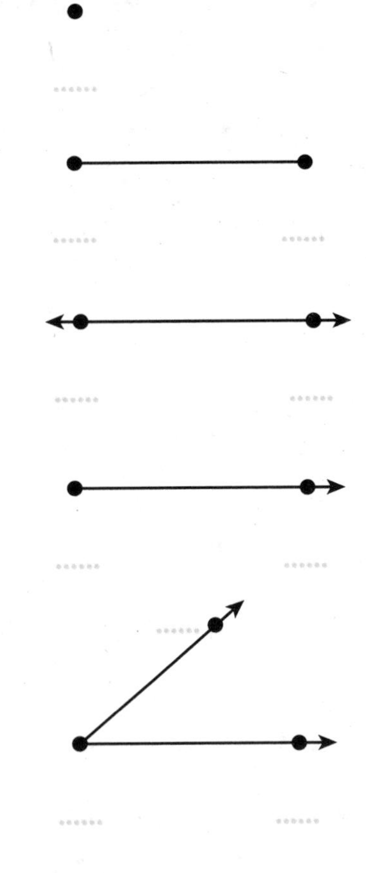

3 REFLECT

Does a rectangle contain lines or line segments? Explain.

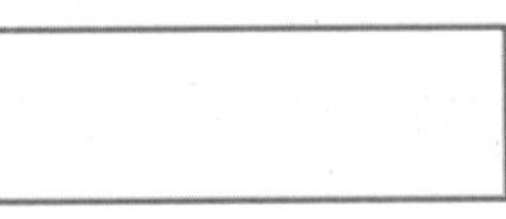

Name: ________________________________

Prepare for Points, Lines, Rays, and Angles

1 Think about what you know about geometric figures. Fill in each box. Use words, numbers, and pictures. Show as many ideas as you can.

Word	In My Own Words	Example
point		
line segment		
line		
ray		
angle		

2 Label each figure as a *point, line segment, line, ray,* or *angle*.

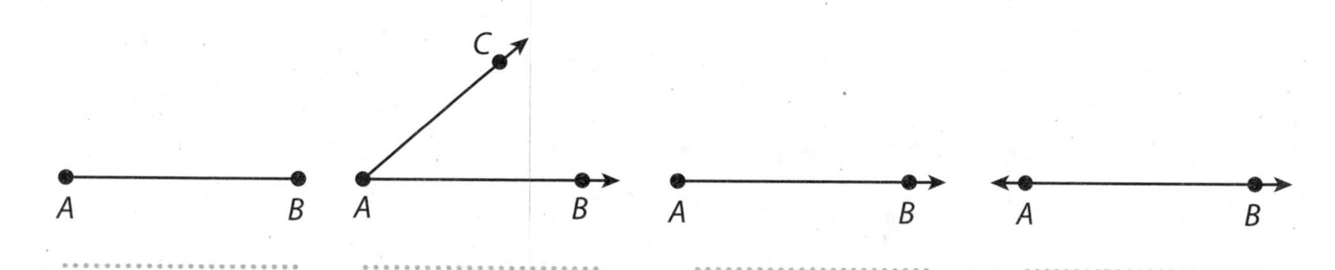

3 Solve the problem. Show your work.

Marshall tries to teach his younger sister how to draw a square. Marshall tells her, "Draw a shape with four straight sides." Marshall's sister draws the shape shown.

The drawing of the shape includes 4 straight sides, but it is not a square. How can Marshall make his directions more clear?

Solution ....

....

....

4 Check your answer. Show your work.

Develop Points, Lines, Line Segments, and Rays

Read and try to solve the problem below.

Kent draws a shape using three different geometric figures. Describe the three geometric figures that Kent uses in his shape.

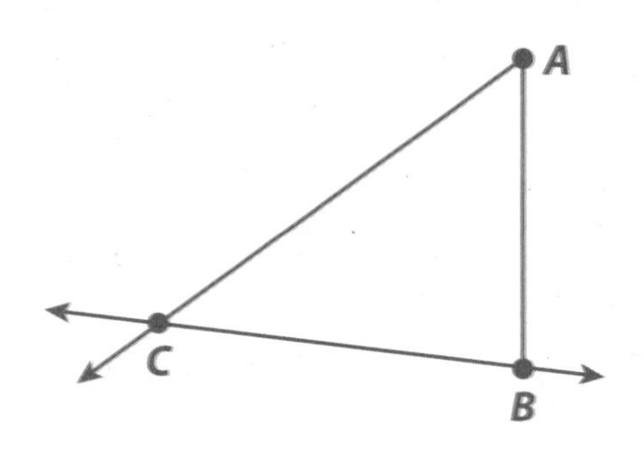

TRY IT

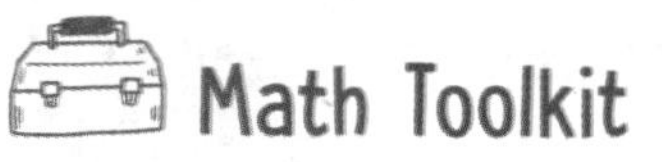

Math Toolkit

- chenille stems
- rulers
- tracing paper

DISCUSS IT

Ask your partner: How did you get started?

Tell your partner: I started by . . .

Explore different ways to understand points, lines, line segments, and rays.

Kent draws a shape using three different geometric figures. Describe the three geometric figures that Kent uses in his shape.

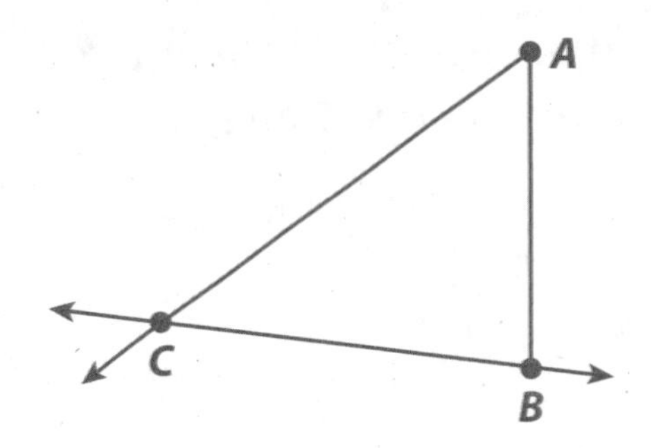

PICTURE IT

You can make some drawings to help describe the figures used in the shape.

Each figure is straight. Draw the different kinds of straight rows of points that you know.

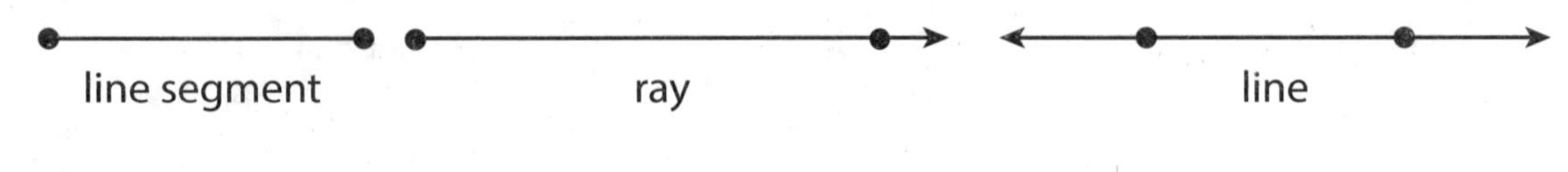

MODEL IT

You can also use words to help describe the figures used in the shape.

Label the line segment, ray, and line that are drawn as the figures in Kent's shape. Look for endpoints and arrowheads.

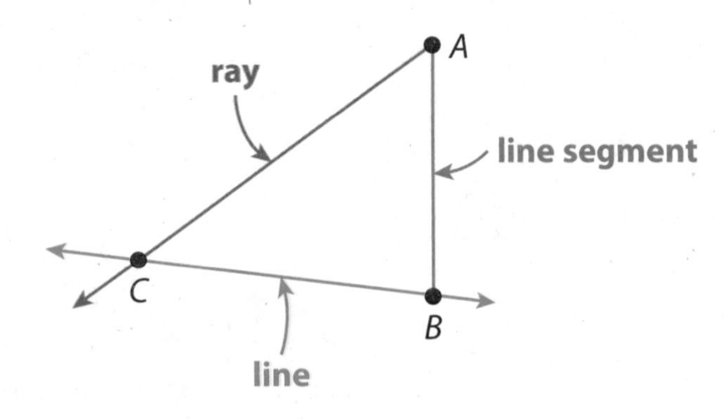

CONNECT IT

Now you will use the problem from the previous page to help you understand how to identify line segments, angles, and rays and to help you solve a similar problem.

1 Name a real-world example of a line segment.

2 When two line segments, lines, or rays meet at a point, they form an angle. Name a real-world example of an angle.

3 Is a beam of light from a flashlight more like a line or a ray? Explain.

4 The drawing below represents one line, three line segments, four rays, and one angle. Name each of these figures.

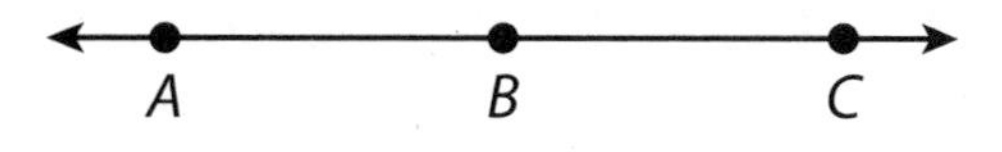

Look back at your **Try It**, strategies by classmates, and **Picture It** and **Model It**. Which models or strategies do you like best for understanding and describing points, lines, line segments, angles, and rays? Explain.

APPLY IT

Use what you just learned to solve these problems.

 How many lines are in this shape? How many rays? Explain how you know.

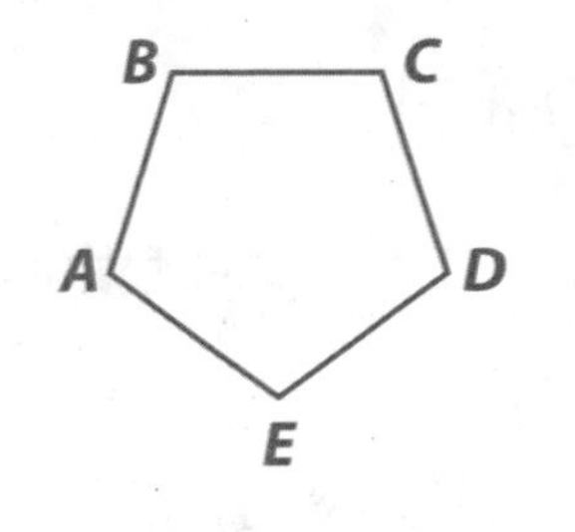

 How many line segments are in this shape? Explain how you know.

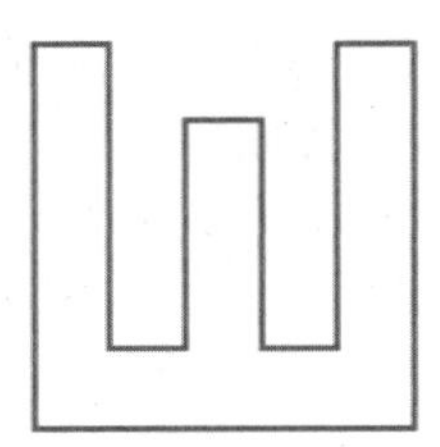

 Draw and label a point, line, line segment, and ray.

Name: ______________________________

Practice Points, Lines, Line Segments, and Rays

Study the Example showing a drawing with points, lines, line segments, and rays. Then solve problems 1–9.

EXAMPLE

Amy makes a drawing of a letter "A" in her math notebook. Use geometry words to describe the drawing.

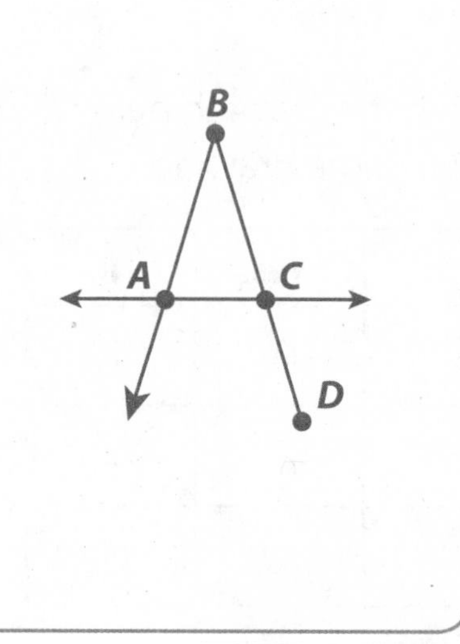

There are 4 points on the drawing:
point *A*, point *B*, point *C*, and point *D*.

There is a line segment from point *B* to point *D*. $\overline{BD}$

There is a line through points *A* and *C*. $\overleftrightarrow{AC}$

There is a ray from point *B* through point *A*. $\overrightarrow{BA}$

Use the drawing below to solve problems 1–4.

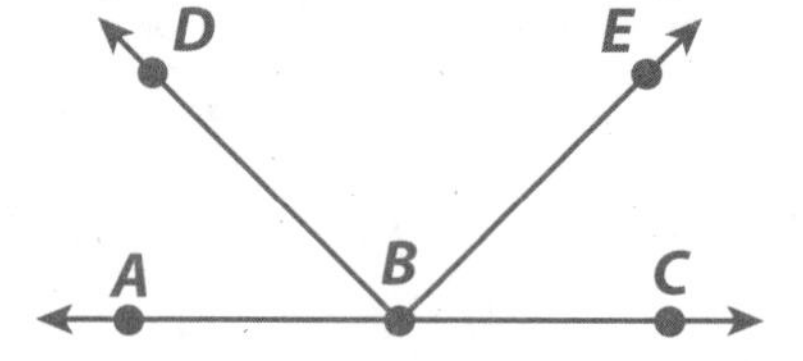

1. How many lines are in the drawing? ....

2. How many rays are in the drawing? ....

3. Write the name of the line in the drawing.

4. Write the names of the rays in the drawing.

5. Look at the shape at the right. How many line segments are in the shape? ....

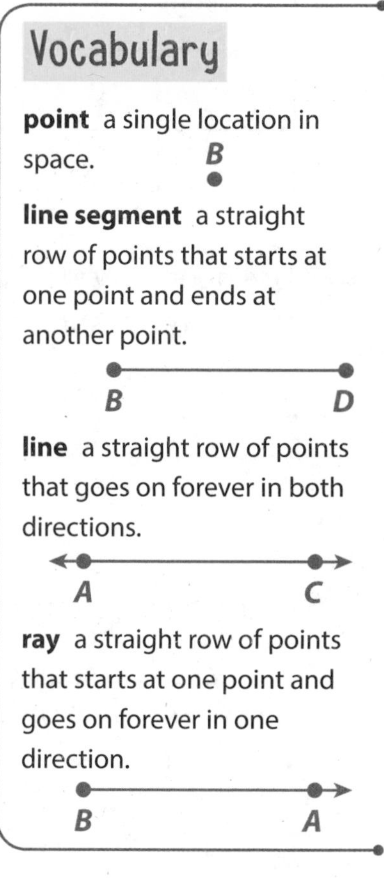

Label each sign below. Write *line(s)*, *line segment(s)*, or *ray(s)*.

....

7 Look at the drawing below. Tell whether each line, line segment, ray, or angle is shown in the drawing.

	Yes	No
$\overleftrightarrow{XY}$	Ⓐ	Ⓑ
$\overleftrightarrow{XZ}$	Ⓒ	Ⓓ
$\overrightarrow{WX}$	Ⓔ	Ⓕ
$\overrightarrow{YX}$	Ⓖ	Ⓗ
$\overline{ZY}$	Ⓘ	Ⓙ
$\angle XYZ$	Ⓚ	Ⓛ

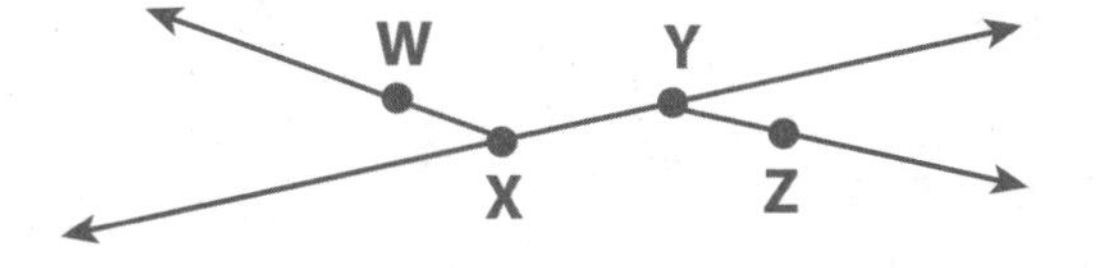

8 Use geometry words and symbols to describe the rhombus shown.

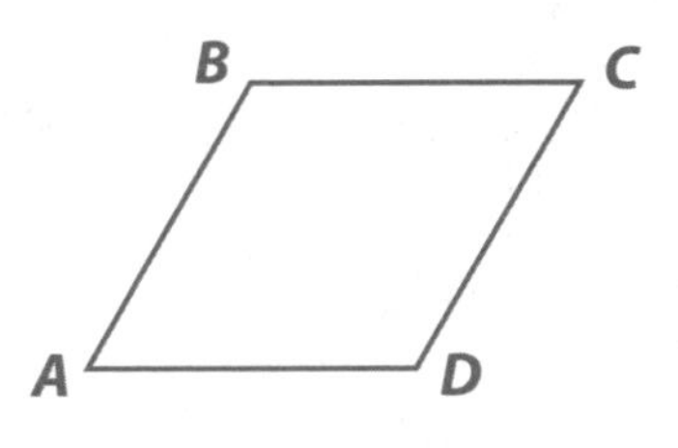

9 Read the description of a shape below. Then draw the shape.

- It has 3 line segments, $\overline{RS}$, $\overline{ST}$, $\overline{TR}$.
- Line segments $\overline{RS}$ and $\overline{TR}$ are the same length.
- It has 3 angles, $\angle R$, $\angle S$, and $\angle T$.

Develop Identifying Angles

Read and try to solve the problem below.

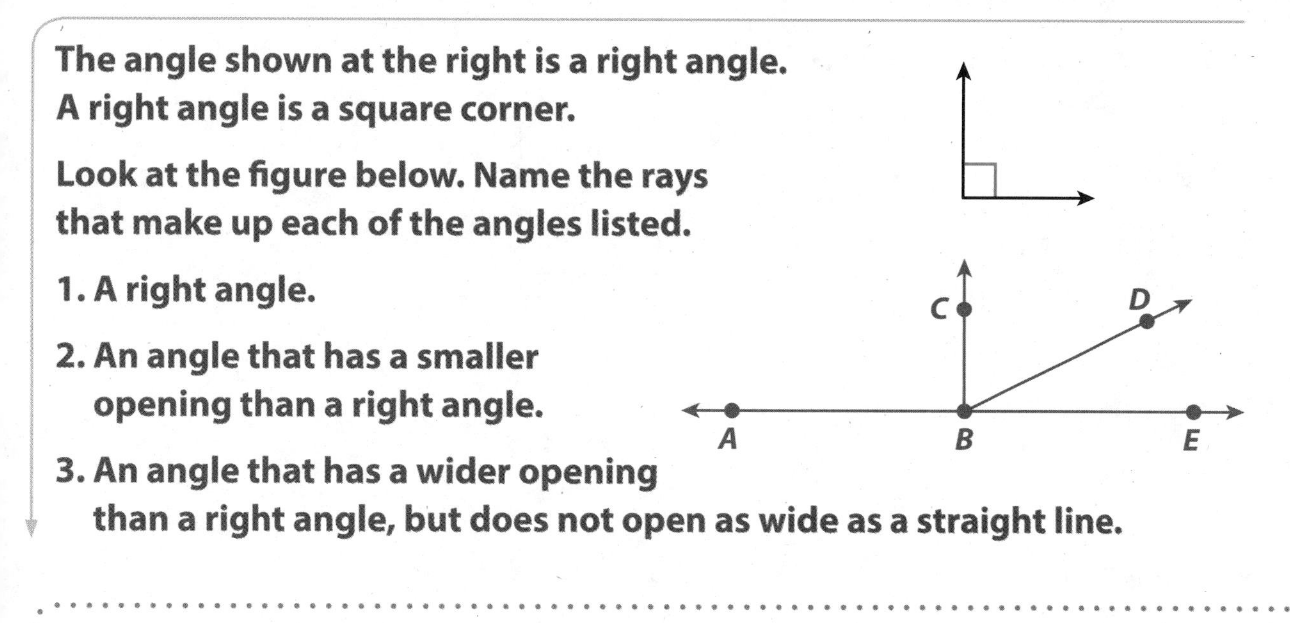

The angle shown at the right is a right angle. A right angle is a square corner.

Look at the figure below. Name the rays that make up each of the angles listed.

1. A right angle.

2. An angle that has a smaller opening than a right angle.

3. An angle that has a wider opening than a right angle, but does not open as wide as a straight line.

TRY IT

Math Toolkit

- chenille stems
- rulers
- tracing paper

Explore different ways to understand how to identify angles.

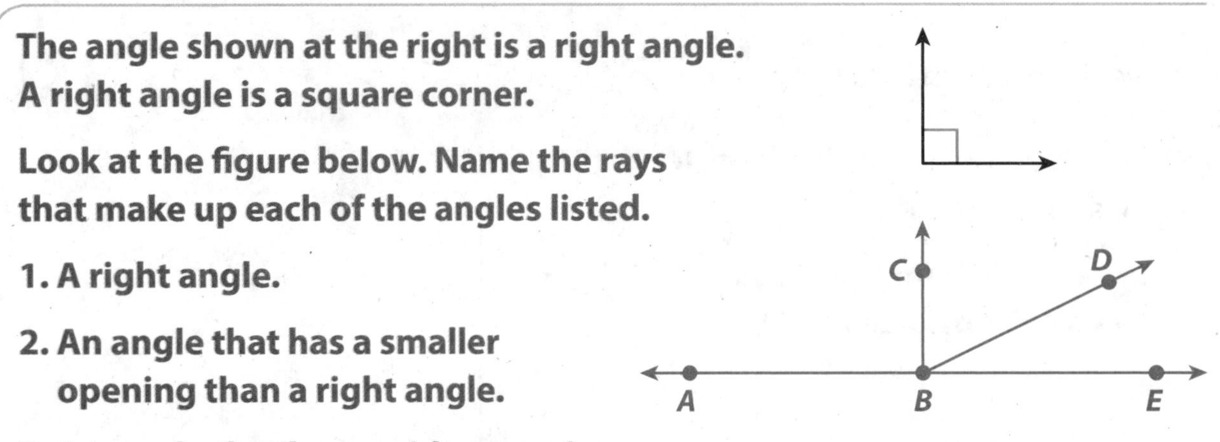

The angle shown at the right is a right angle.
A right angle is a square corner.

Look at the figure below. Name the rays that make up each of the angles listed.

1. **A right angle.**
2. **An angle that has a smaller opening than a right angle.**
3. **An angle that has a wider opening than a right angle, but does not open as wide as a straight line.**

PICTURE IT

You can make a drawing to help identify different types of angles.

Use shading to find the rays that make each angle.

A right angle is shaded. Look at the rays along the edges of the shaded area.

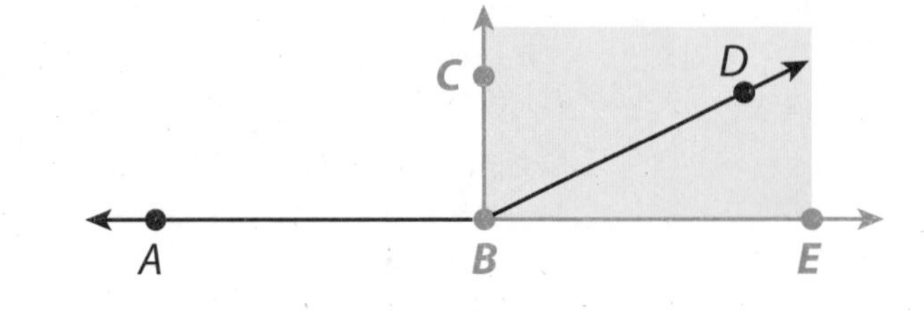

MODEL IT

You can also use a model to help identify different types of angles.

Compare the opening of an angle to a right angle by holding the corner of a sheet of paper next to the angle. The angle below opens as wide as a right angle.

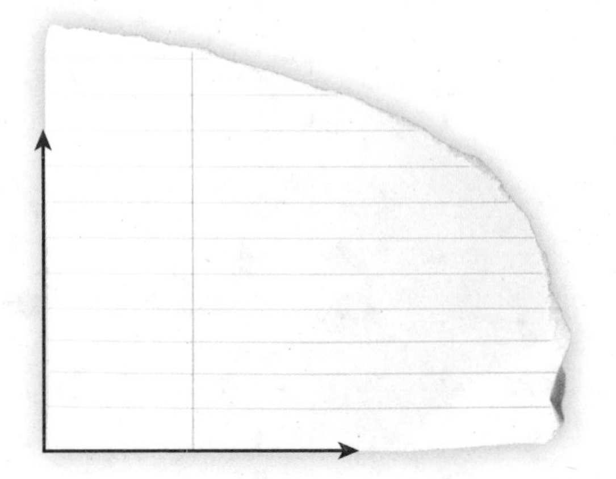

CONNECT IT

Now you will use the problem from the previous page to help you understand how to identify angles in figures.

1 **Model It** shows a right angle. Draw a right angle. Then use 3 points to name a right angle in the figure on the previous page. ....

2 An angle that has a smaller opening than a right angle is called an **acute angle**.

Name an acute angle in the figure on the previous page. ....
Draw an acute angle.

3 An angle that has a wider opening than a right angle, but does not open as wide as a straight line, is called an **obtuse angle**. Name an obtuse angle in the figure on the previous page. .... Draw an obtuse angle.

4 Explain how you can decide whether any angle is acute, right, or obtuse.

5 REFLECT

Look back at your **Try It**, strategies by classmates, and **Picture It** and **Model It**. Which models or strategies do you like best for identifying angles? Explain.

....

....

APPLY IT

Use what you just learned to solve these problems.

 How many acute angles are in the shape below? Explain how you know.

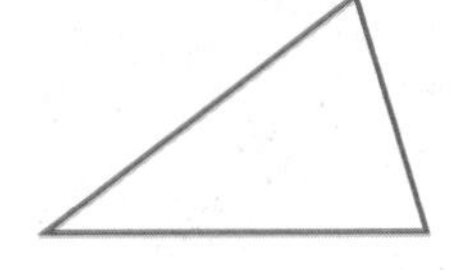

 Look at the shape below. How many obtuse angles are in the shape? Explain how you know.

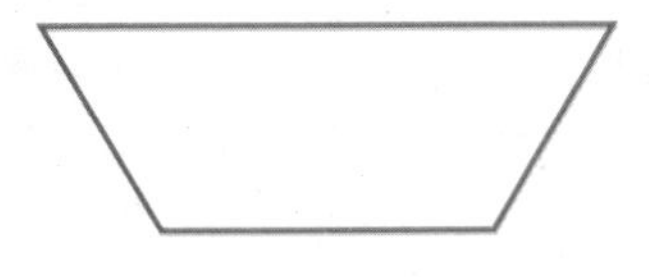

 Which angle is obtuse?

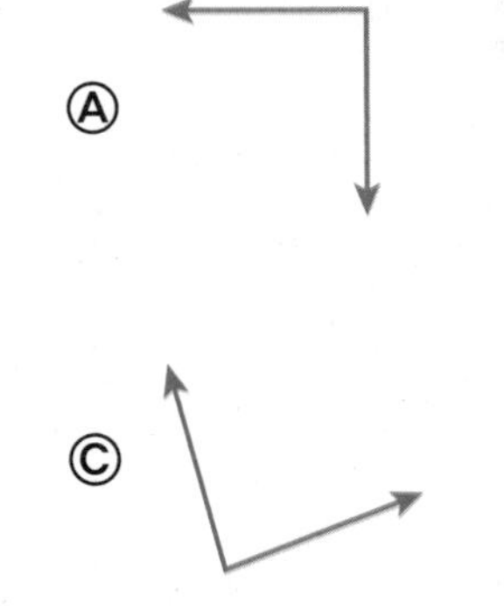

Ⓐ

Ⓒ

Ⓑ 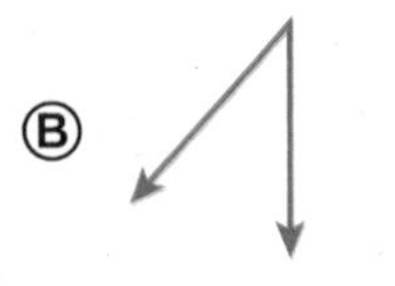

Ⓓ 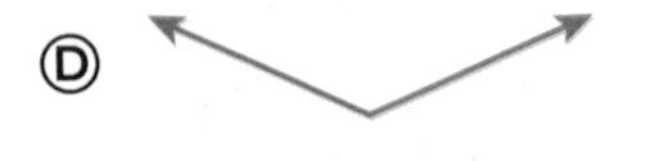

Name: ______________________________

Practice Identifying Angles

Study the Example showing how to identify angles in a shape. Then solve problems 1–10.

EXAMPLE

Name and describe the angles in the shape shown.

B C A D

$\angle A$ is a right angle. It has a shape like a square corner.

$\angle B$ is also a right angle.

$\angle C$ is an obtuse angle. It has a wider opening than a right angle.

$\angle D$ is an acute angle. It has a smaller opening than a right angle.

The shape has 2 right angles, 1 acute angle, and 1 obtuse angle.

Use the shape at the right to solve problems 1–5.

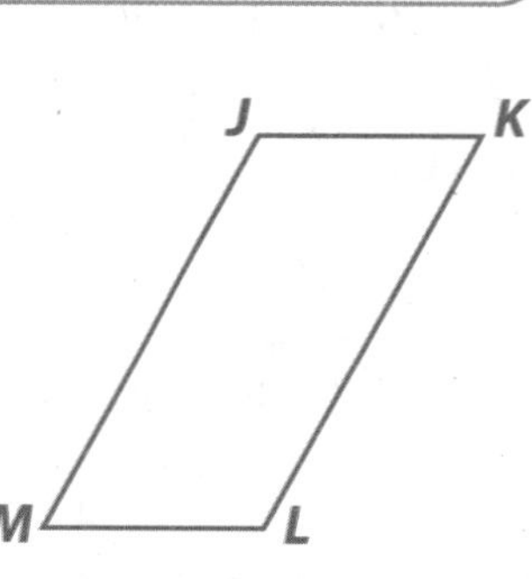

1. How many right angles are in this shape? ....

2. How many acute angles are in this shape? ....

3. How many obtuse angles are in this shape? ....

4. Name the acute angles in the shape.

5. Name the obtuse angles in the shape.

6. Look at the shape of the sign at the right. Describe the number and kind of angles the shape has.

STOP

Jasmine draws the pentagon shown at the right. She says that all pentagons have 5 sides of equal length and 5 obtuse angles.

7 Draw a pentagon that is different from the one Jasmine drew. Describe the sides and angles of your pentagon.

8 In what way is Jasmine's thinking correct?

9 In what way is Jasmine's thinking incorrect?

10 Which statements correctly describe the shape below?

Ⓐ The shape has acute angles.

Ⓑ The shape has right angles.

Ⓒ The shapes has obtuse angles.

Ⓓ The shape has 6 angles.

Ⓔ The shape has more acute angles than obtuse angles.

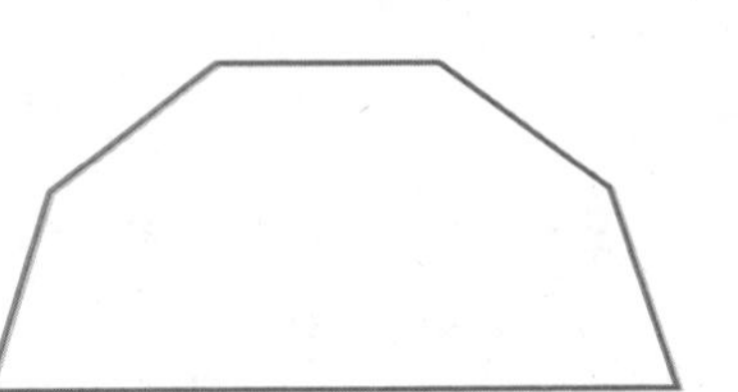

Develop Parallel and Perpendicular Lines

Read and try to solve the problem below.

Jordan looks at the street map below.

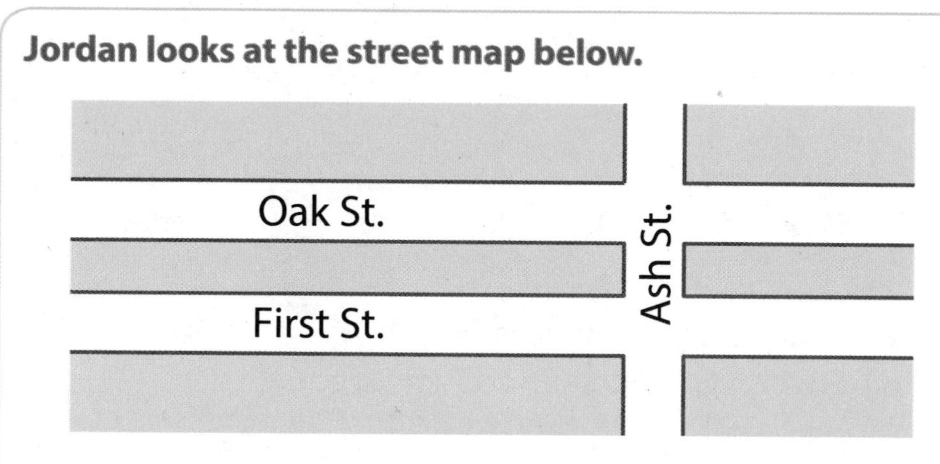

Describe the relationship between Oak Street and First Street. Then describe the relationship between Oak Street and Ash Street.

TRY IT

Math Toolkit

- geoboard
- straws
- tracing paper
- grid paper

DISCUSS IT

Ask your partner: Why did you choose that strategy?

Tell your partner: At first, I thought . . .

Explore different ways to understand parallel and perpendicular lines and line segments.

Jordan looks at the street map below.

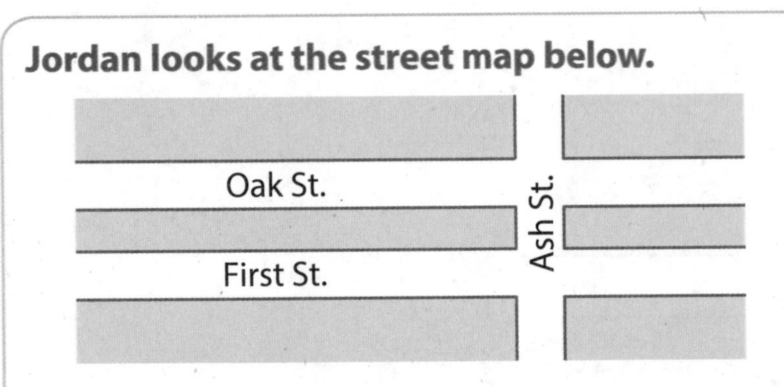

Describe the relationship between Oak Street and First Street. Then describe the relationship between Oak Street and Ash Street.

PICTURE IT

You can use a sketch to help understand the problem.

Sketch a picture of Oak Street and First Street. Shade the streets.

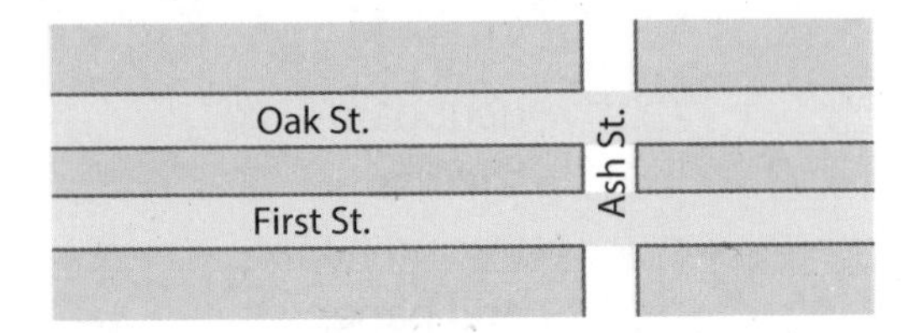

Notice that the streets do not cross.

MODEL IT

You can also use a model to help understand the problem.

Look at Oak Street and Ash Street. Think of each street as a line. When the two lines cross, they form four angles.

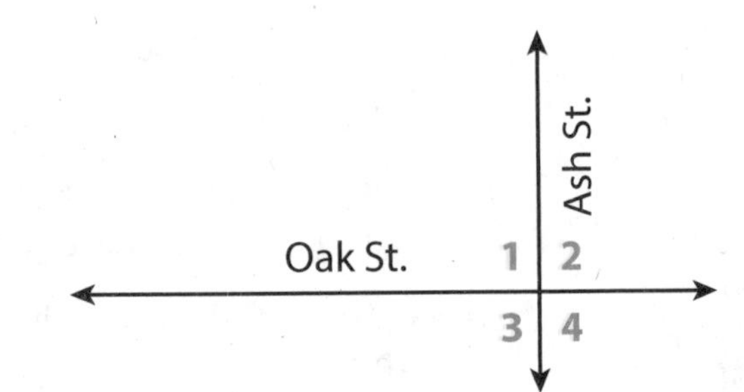

CONNECT IT

Now you will use the problem from the previous page to help you understand how to identify parallel and perpendicular lines.

1. Lines that are always the same distance apart and never cross are called **parallel lines**. Name a real-world example of parallel lines.

2. Suppose each street keeps going in a straight line. If Jordan travels on Oak Street and makes no turns, can he ever get to First Street? Explain.

3. Describe the angles that Oak Street and Ash Street make when they cross.

4. Lines that cross and form a right angle are called **perpendicular lines**. Name a real-world example of perpendicular lines.

5. Explain why 3 separate lines can all be parallel to each other, but cannot all be perpendicular to each other. Use a drawing to show your answer.

6. ## REFLECT

Look back at your **Try It**, strategies by classmates, and **Picture It** and **Model It**. Which models or strategies do you like best for identifying parallel and perpendicular lines? Explain.

APPLY IT

Use what you just learned to solve these problems.

 How many pairs of parallel sides does the shape below have? Explain how you know.

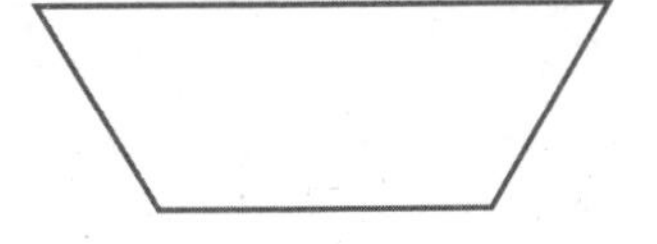

 How many pairs of parallel sides does the shape below have? Explain how you know.

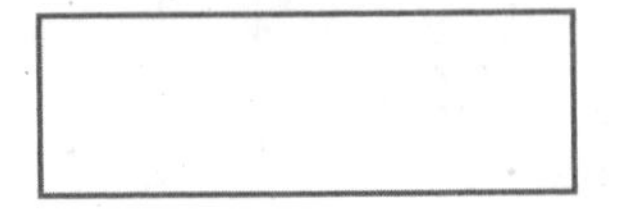

9 Which pair of lines are perpendicular?

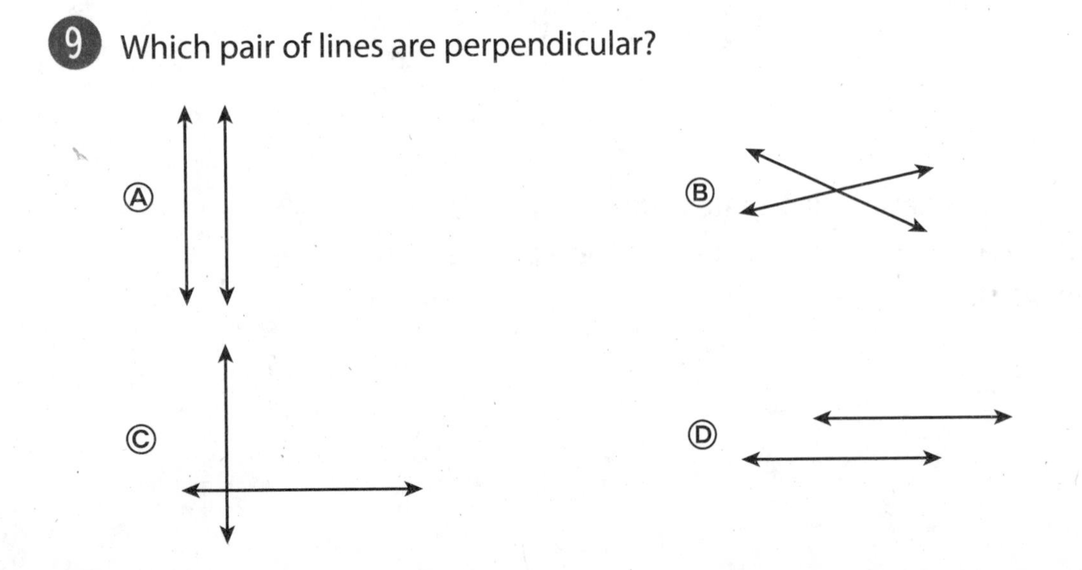

Name: ______________________

Practice Parallel and Perpendicular Lines

Study the Example showing how to identify parallel and perpendicular lines and line segments. Then solve problems 1–6.

EXAMPLE

Colby draws parallel and perpendicular lines to place the bases and pitcher's mound on a drawing of a baseball field.

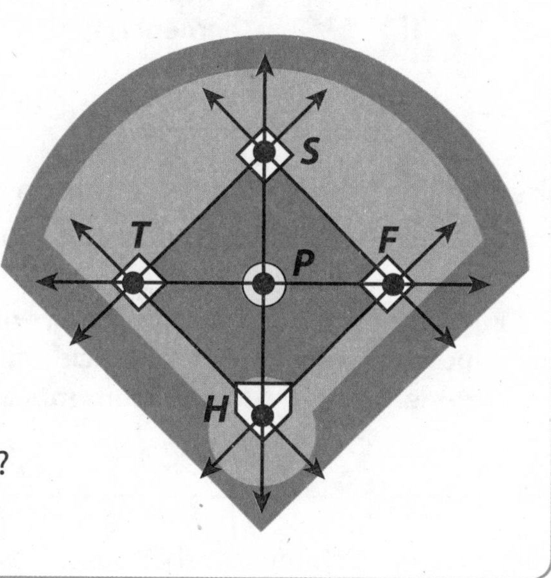

$\overleftrightarrow{SF}$ and $\overleftrightarrow{TH}$ are parallel lines.
$\overleftrightarrow{ST}$ and $\overleftrightarrow{FH}$ are parallel lines.

The pitcher's mound is one place where perpendicular lines cross. At what point do perpendicular lines cross at the pitcher's mound?

They cross at point P, where $\overleftrightarrow{TF}$ crosses $\overleftrightarrow{SH}$.

For problems 1 and 2, use the shape at the right.

1. How many pairs of parallel sides does the square have? ....

2. Put Xs on the square where each pair of perpendicular line segments meet.

3. Look at the drawing of a window at the right. Circle 3 parallel line segments in the drawing.

4 Look at the line segments in the letters on the tiles at the right. Fill in the table with each letter to identify parallel line segments. The first one is done for you.

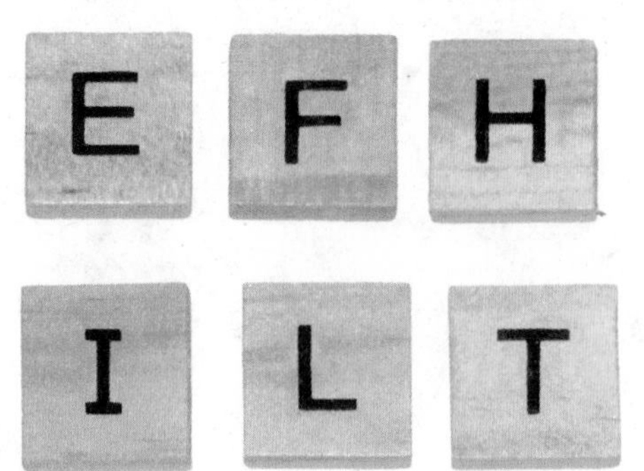

No parallel line segments	Only 1 pair of parallel line segments	More than 1 pair of parallel line segments
L		

5 Look at the line segments in the letters on the tiles again. Fill in the table to identify perpendicular line segments.

Only 1 pair of perpendicular line segments	Only 2 pairs of perpendicular line segments	3 pairs of perpendicular line segments

6 Tell whether each statement that describes the streets shown on the map below is *True* or *False*.

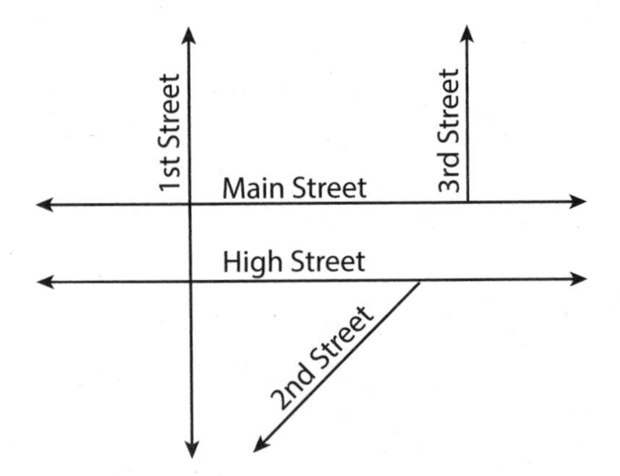

	True	False
1st and 3rd Street are perpendicular.	Ⓐ	Ⓑ
Main and High Street are parallel.	Ⓒ	Ⓓ
2nd Street is perpendicular to Main St.	Ⓔ	Ⓕ
1st Street is perpendicular to High St.	Ⓖ	Ⓗ

Refine Points, Lines, Rays, and Angles

Complete the Example below. Then solve problems 1–9.

EXAMPLE

In the shape below, list each pair of parallel sides and circle the letter marking each obtuse angle.

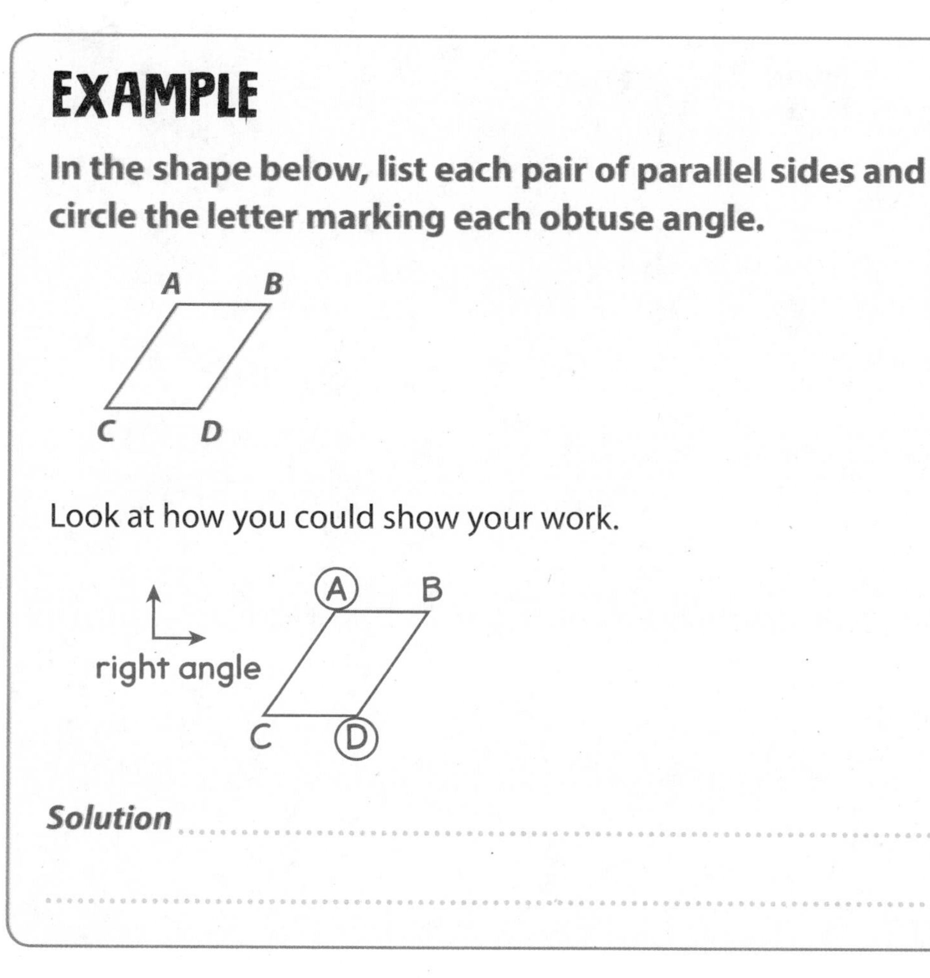

Look at how you could show your work.

Solution ....

....

Even if the sides of the shape went on forever, the opposite sides would never cross each other.

PAIR/SHARE
What kind of angles are $\angle B$ and $\angle C$? How do you know?

APPLY IT

1 Put an X where each pair of perpendicular line segments meet in the shape below.

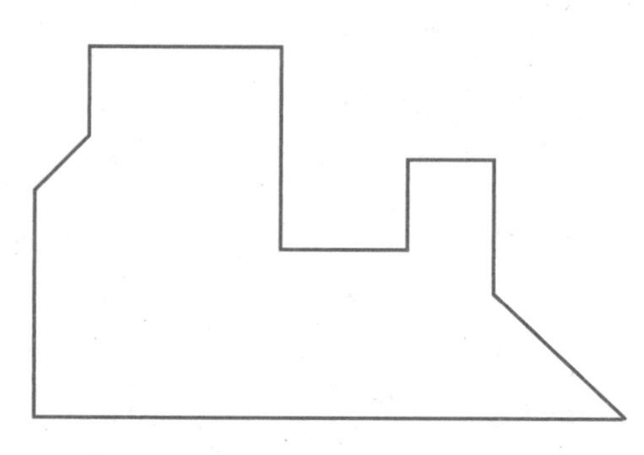

Perpendicular line segments meet to form right angles.

PAIR/SHARE
Describe the angles that are NOT marked with an X.

2 A crosswalk is marked with a pair of parallel line segments that extend from one side of the street to the other. The distance between the two line segments from point *A* to point *B* is 6 feet. What is the distance from point *C* to point *D*?

What facts do I know about parallel lines?

Solution

PAIR/SHARE
Can the lines still be parallel if the distance from *C* to *D* is 3 feet?

3 Toshi cuts one fourth of a circle out of paper. How many angles does this shape have?

I know that it takes two rays to make an angle.

Ⓐ 0

Ⓑ 1

Ⓒ 2

Ⓓ 3

Esme chose Ⓓ as the correct answer. How did she get that answer?

PAIR/SHARE
Does Esme's answer make sense?

4 Think about a real-world example of where a wall meets the floor and where the same wall meets the ceiling. Which term best describes what it looks like where these surfaces meet?

Ⓐ parallel line segments

Ⓑ perpendicular line segments

Ⓒ right angle

Ⓓ acute angle

5 Which drawing shows 3 lines?

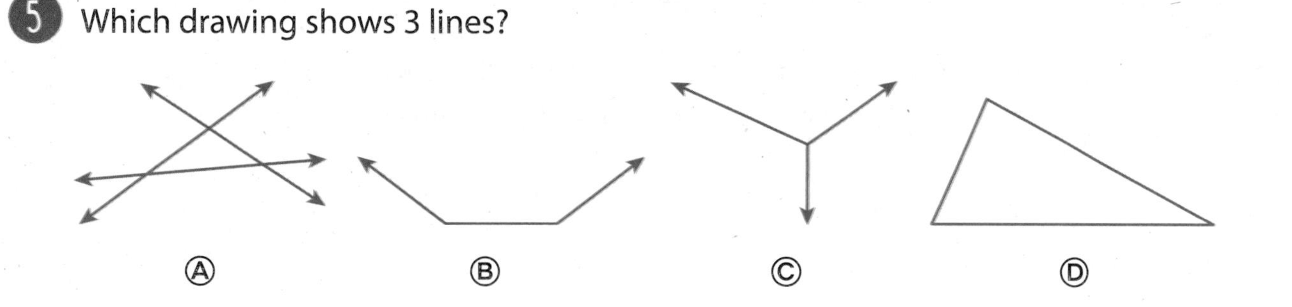

6 Look at the shape below. For which terms is an example shown in the shape?

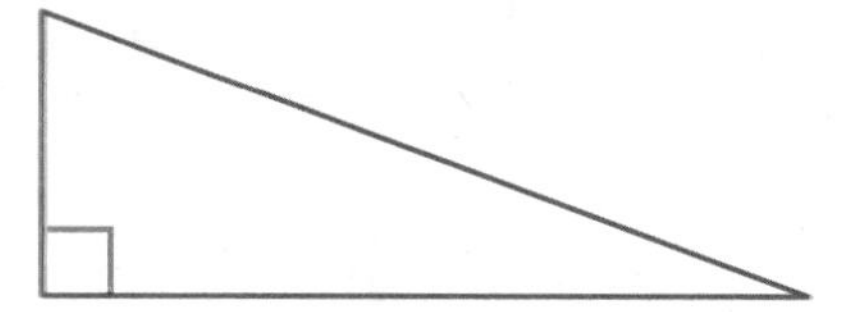

Ⓐ parallel line segments

Ⓑ perpendicular line segments

Ⓒ right angle

Ⓓ acute angle

Ⓔ obtuse angle

Tell whether each sentence is *True* or *False*.

	True	False
A ray goes on forever in two directions.	Ⓐ	Ⓑ
A line segment has exactly two endpoints.	Ⓒ	Ⓓ
An obtuse angle has a wider opening than a right angle.	Ⓔ	Ⓕ
Parallel lines meet to form an acute angle.	Ⓖ	Ⓗ

8 Liz draws the two shapes below. Use words you have learned in this lesson to describe what the shapes have in common. How are they different?

9 MATH JOURNAL

A triangle can have one pair of perpendicular sides. Can a triangle have one pair of parallel sides? Use drawings and words to explain your answer.

SELF CHECK Go back to the Unit 5 Opener and see what you can check off.

Angles

Dear Family,

This week your child is learning to measure and draw angles.

Your child is learning how to find an angle's exact measure.

Before measuring an angle, it is helpful to estimate the measure by using benchmarks, such as a right angle and a straight angle. For example, to estimate the measure of the blue angle below, compare it to a right angle and to a straight angle.

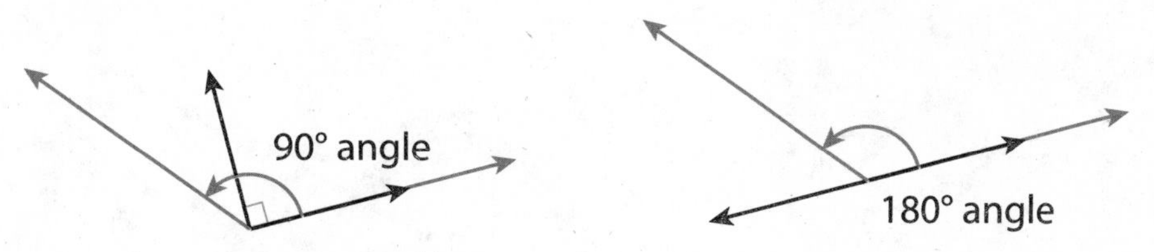

A right angle has a measure of 90 **degrees**. A straight angle has a measure of 180 degrees. The measure of the blue angle is between 90 degrees and 180 degrees.

To find the exact measure of the angle, your child is learning to use a tool called a **protractor**.

- Line up the center point of the protractor with the vertex of the angle.
- Then line up one ray with the 0° mark.
- Read the mark on the protractor that the other ray passes through.

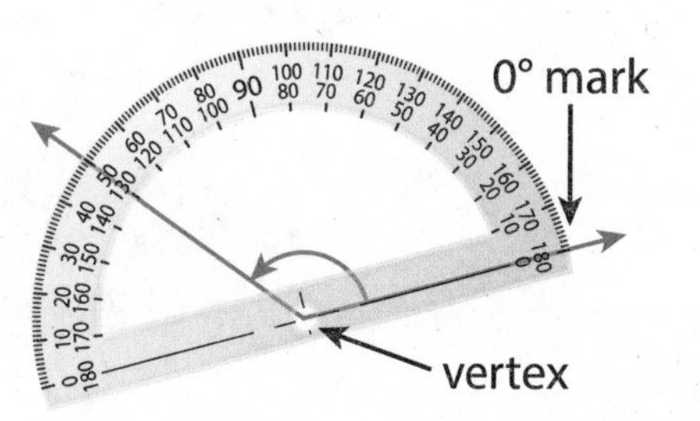

The angle measures 130°. (The ray also passes through the 50° mark, but since the angle is bigger than a 90° angle, the measure is not 50°.)

Invite your child to share what he or she knows about measuring and drawing angles by doing the following activity together.

ACTIVITY MEASURING ANGLES

Do this activity with your child to estimate the measure of angles.

- Identify angles in and around your home or outside in the yard or neighborhood. You can also look through magazines or newspapers for pictures that show angles.

  Here are some examples of angles you might find (or make):

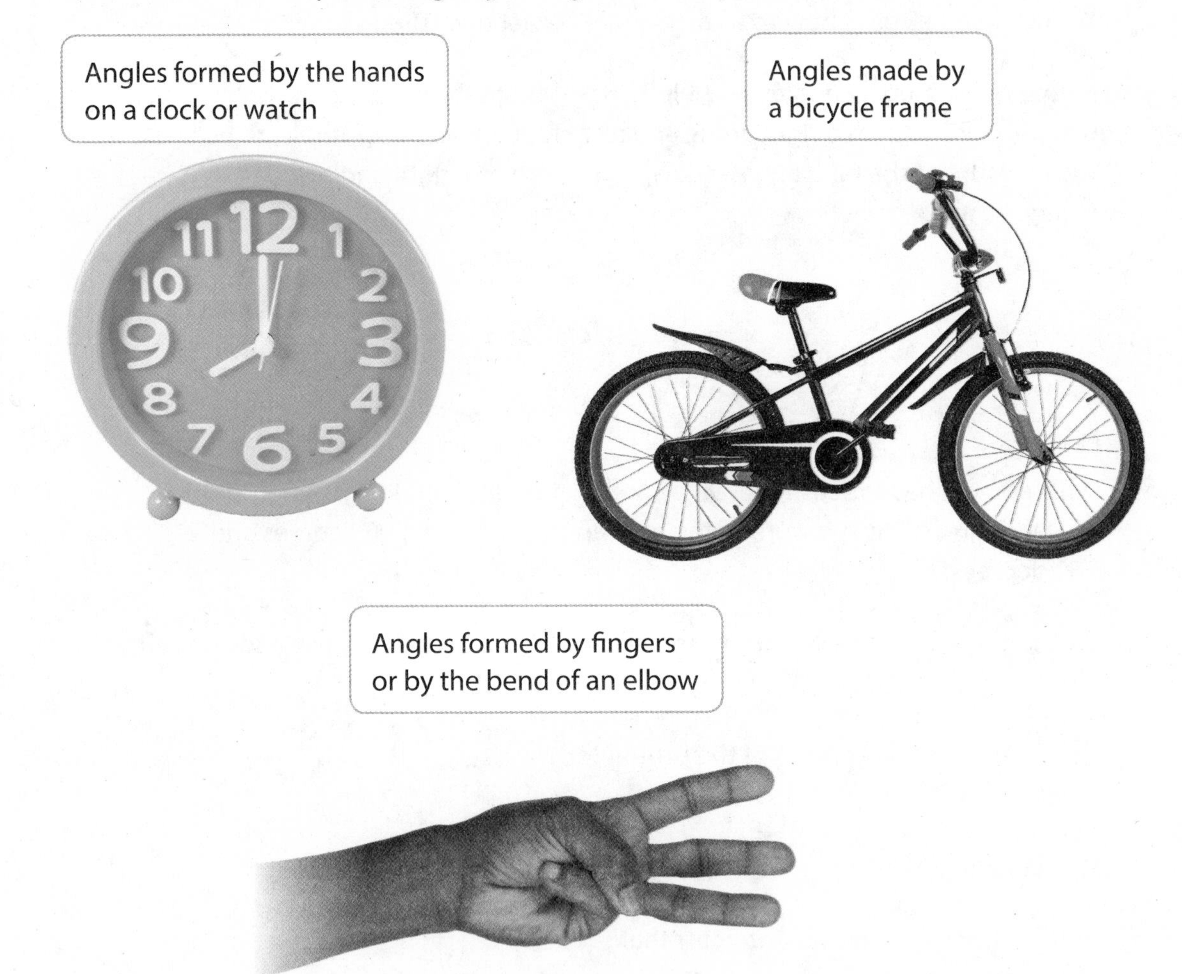

- Estimate the measure of each angle by using right angles (such as the corner of a sheet of paper) and straight angles (such as the side of a sheet of paper) as benchmarks.

Look for other real-world opportunities to estimate angle measures with your child.

Explore Angles

Learning Targets

- An angle that turns through n one-degree angles is said to have an angle measure of n degrees.
- Measure angles in whole-number degrees using a protractor. Sketch angles of specified measure.

SMP 1, 2, 3, 4, 5, 6, 7

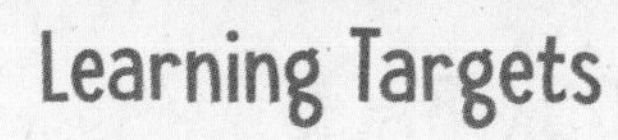

Previously, you learned to identify angles. Now you will learn more about angles and angle measurement. Use what you know to try to solve the problem below.

Lily and Dora each turn the hour hand on a clock face. They make different angles by turning the hour hand. Who makes the greater angle? Explain how you know.

Lily's angle

Dora's angle

TRY IT

Math Toolkit

- clocks
- clock face
- index cards
- sticky notes

DISCUSS IT

Ask your partner: How did you get started?

Tell your partner: I started by . . .

CONNECT IT

1 LOOK BACK

Explain how you know who makes the greater angle, Lily or Dora.

2 LOOK AHEAD

You can measure angles to compare them. A **degree** is a unit of measure for angles. Show degrees with the symbol °. The angle made by a full turn of a ray in a circle measures 360 degrees, or 360°.

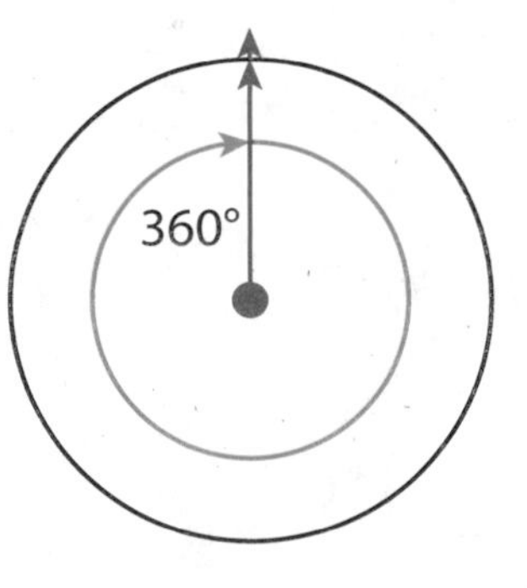

a. Look at the diagram below. An angle that turns through $\frac{1}{360}$ of a circle is called a 1° angle. How many 1° angles are in a circle? ....

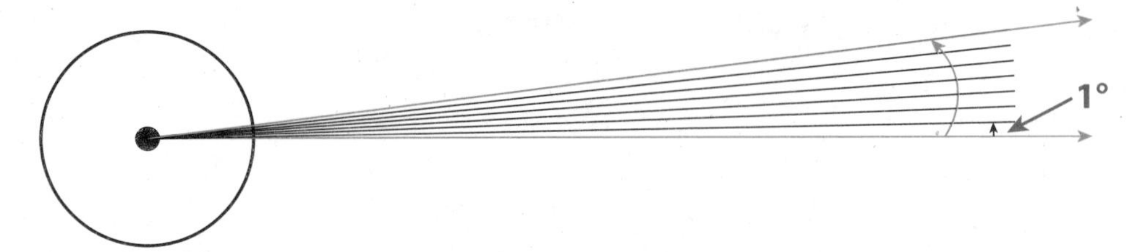

b. The red angle in the diagram turns through part of the circle. Count to find the measure of the red angle. Write the measure of the red angle. ....

c. A ray turns to form a right angle in the circle at the right. What is the measure, in degrees, of a right angle? Explain.

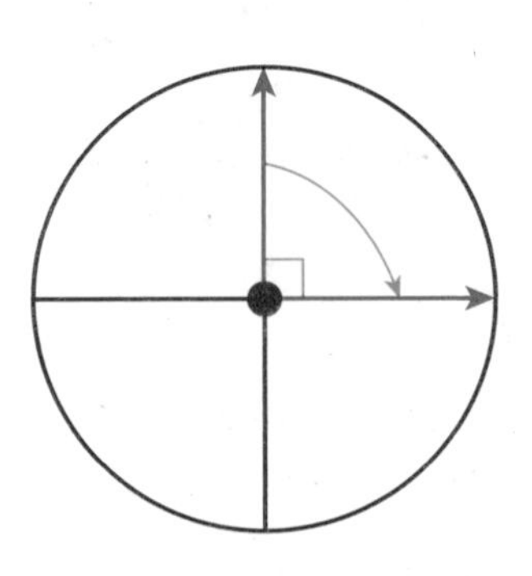

3 REFLECT

How does the way a ray turns through a circle help you think about the measure of an angle?

....

....

Name: ______________________

Prepare for Angles

1. Think about what you know about angles. Fill in each box. Use words, numbers, and pictures. Show as many ideas as you can.

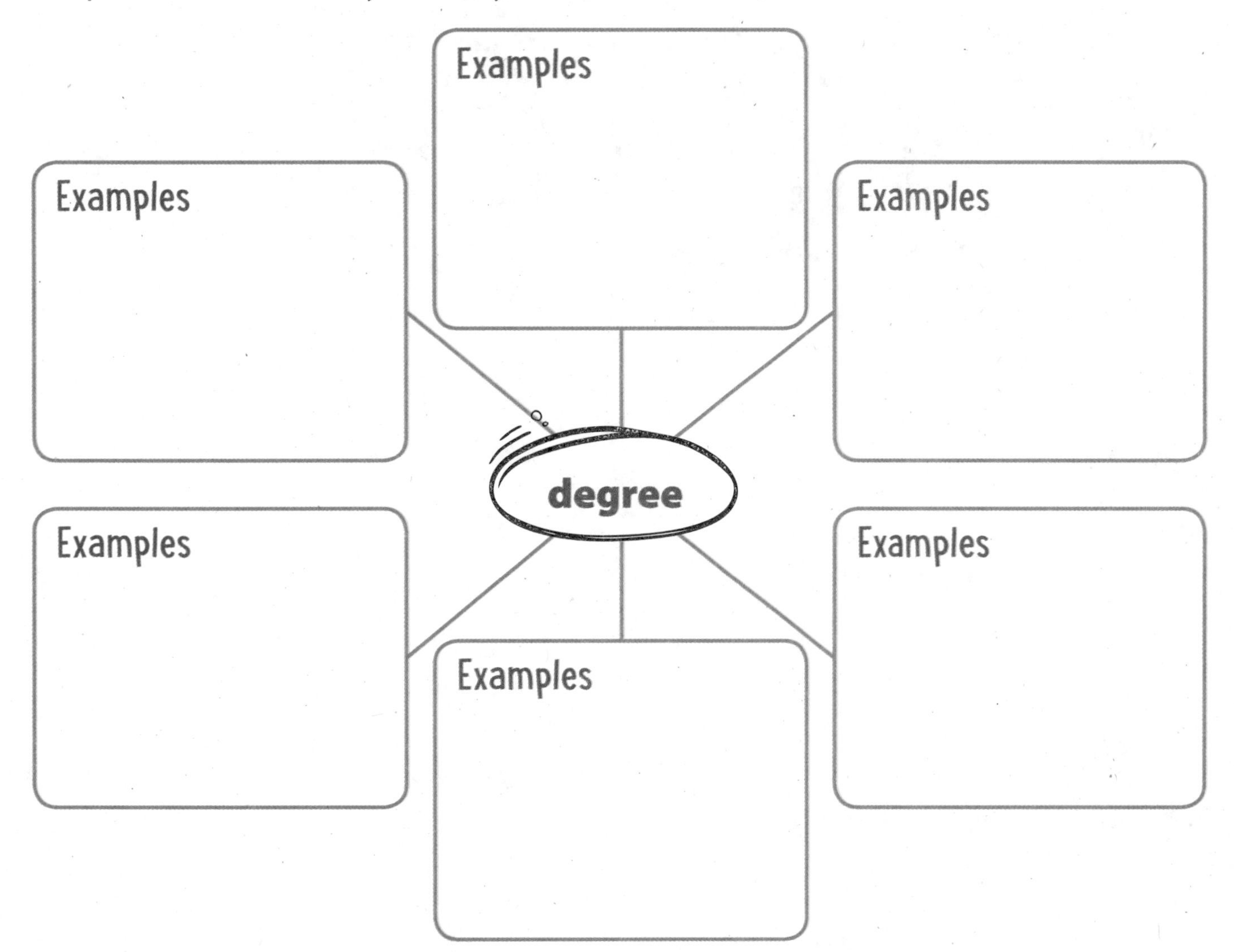

2. The red angle below turns through part of the circle. Count to find the measure of the red angle. Write the measure of the angle in degrees. ....

1°

Solve the problem. Show your work.

Beau and Kong each turn the hour hand on a clock face. They make different angles by turning the hour hand. Who makes the greater angle? Explain how you know.

Beau's angle

Kong's angle

Solution ....

4 Check your answer. Show your work.

Develop Using a Protractor

Read and try to solve the problem below.

A protractor is a tool used to measure angles. The protractor below shows that the measure of a right angle is 90°. Kara draws the other angle below. What is the measure of Kara's angle? How can you find out?

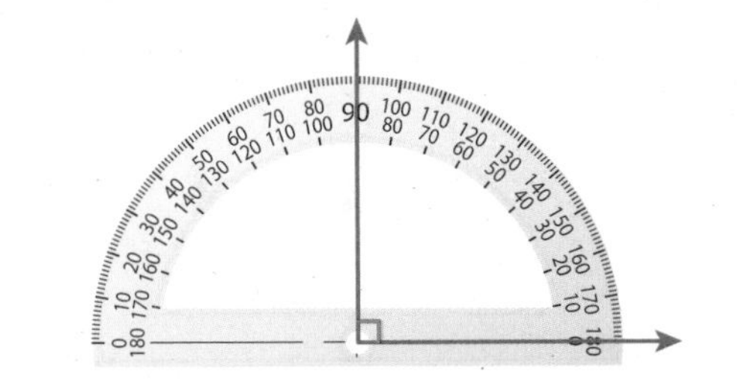

TRY IT

Math Toolkit

- protractors
- rulers
- index cards
- sticky notes

DISCUSS IT

Ask your partner: Can you explain that again?

Tell your partner: I knew . . . so I . . .

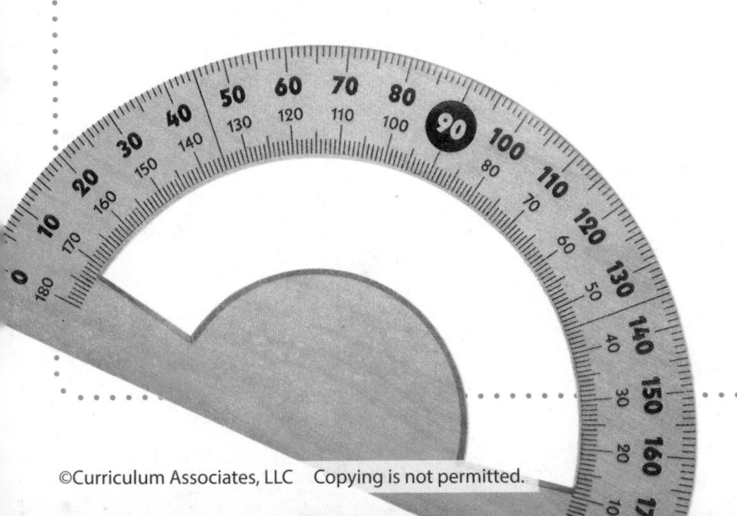

Explore different ways to understand how to use benchmarks and a protractor to measure an angle.

A protractor is a tool used to measure angles. The protractor below shows that the measure of a right angle is 90°. Kara draws the other angle below. What is the measure of Kara's angle? How can you find out?

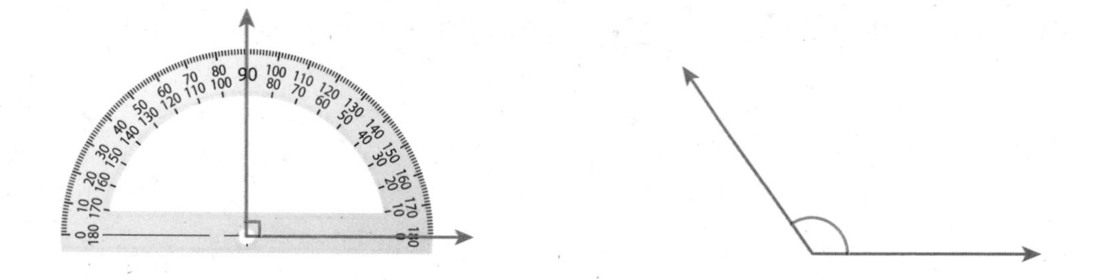

PICTURE IT

You can use benchmarks to estimate the measure.

Kara's angle seems to be between 90° and 180°. It is obtuse.

MODEL IT

You can use a protractor to measure the angle.

- First, line up either mark showing 0° on the protractor with one ray of the angle.

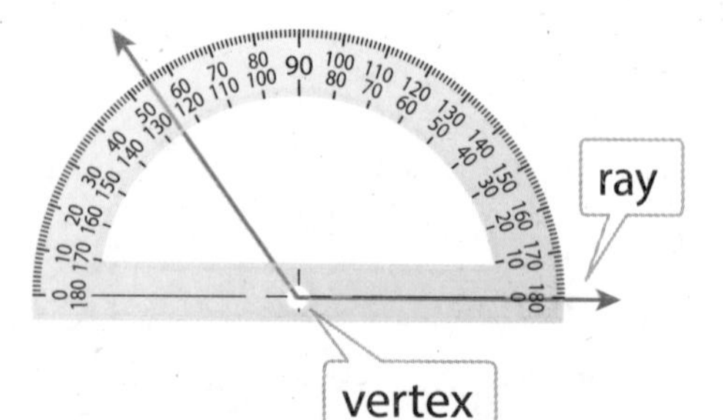

- Next, line up the center point of the protractor with the vertex of the angle. Remember that the vertex is the point where two rays meet to form an angle.
- Then look at the other ray to read the number of degrees.

CONNECT IT

Now you will use the problem from the previous page to help you understand how to use a protractor to measure an angle.

1. Estimate the angle measure of Kara's angle.

2. Why must you line up the protractor's center point with the vertex of the angle?

3. Suppose you line up one ray with either mark showing 10° or 170° instead of either mark showing 0° or 180°. How would it change which mark the other ray points to?

4. Line up either mark showing 0° or 180° with one ray. Which mark does the other ray point to?

5. Which number of degrees is the measure of the angle? Explain how you know.

6. ### REFLECT

Look back at your **Try It**, strategies by classmates, and **Picture It** and **Model It**. Which models or strategies do you like best for measuring an angle? Explain.

APPLY IT

Use what you just learned to solve these problems.

7 What is the measure, in degrees, of the angle shown? ....

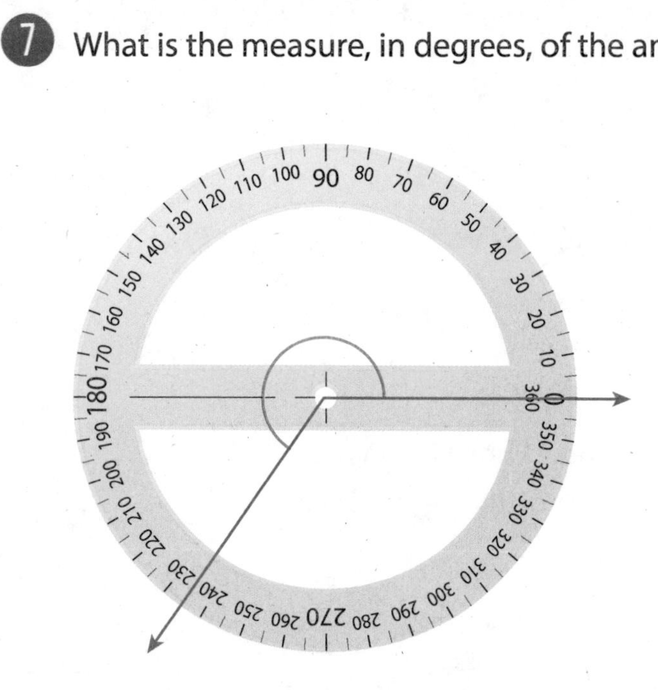

 What is the measure of the angle shown? ....

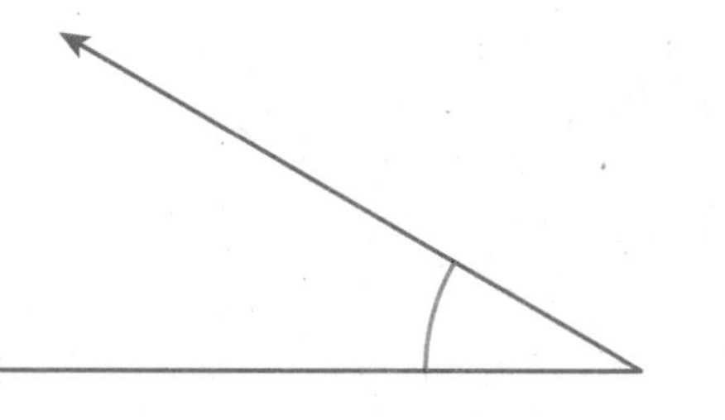

9 What is the measure of the angle shown? ....

Name: ______________________________

Practice Using a Protractor

Study the Example showing how to use a protractor to measure an angle. Then solve problems 1–5.

EXAMPLE

Omar draws the angle at the right. What is the measure of the angle?

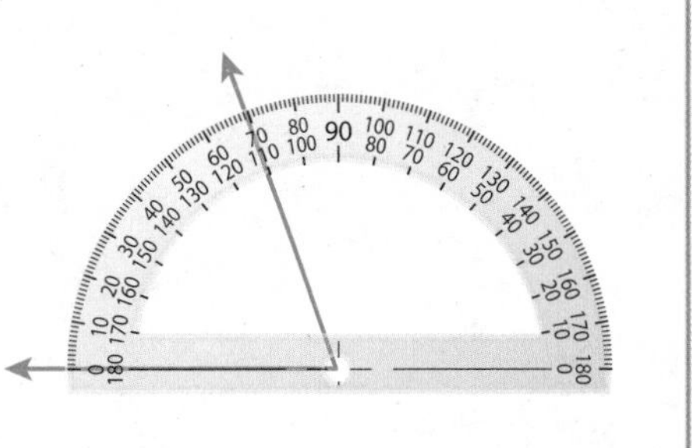

Line up the 0° or the 180° mark on a protractor with one ray of the angle.

Line up the center point of the protractor with the vertex of the angle.

Look at the other ray. Read the number of degrees on the protractor. Read the number that is less than 90, since the angle is less than 90°.

The angle measures 70°.

 Read the number of degrees on the protractor to find the measure of the angle.

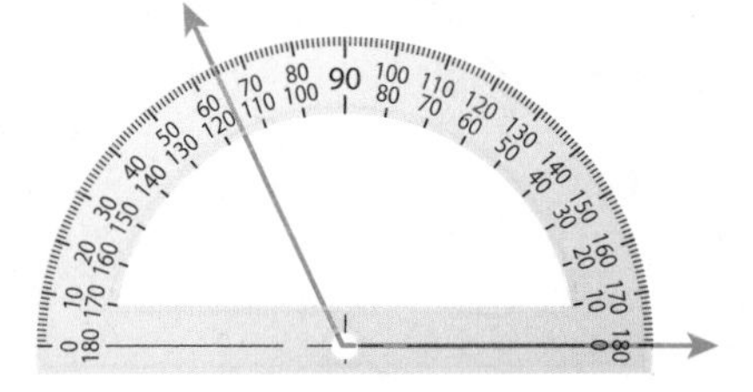

The angle measures .... degrees.

2 Use a protractor to measure the angle below.

The angle measures .... degrees.

Vocabulary

degree (°) a unit of measure for angles.

protractor a tool used to measure angles.

vertex the point where two rays, lines, or line segments meet to form an angle.

For problems 3–5, use a protractor to measure the angles. Write each measure.

3 Measure the angle at the right.

The angle measures .... degrees.

4 Measure one angle of the polygon at the right.

The angle measures .... degrees.

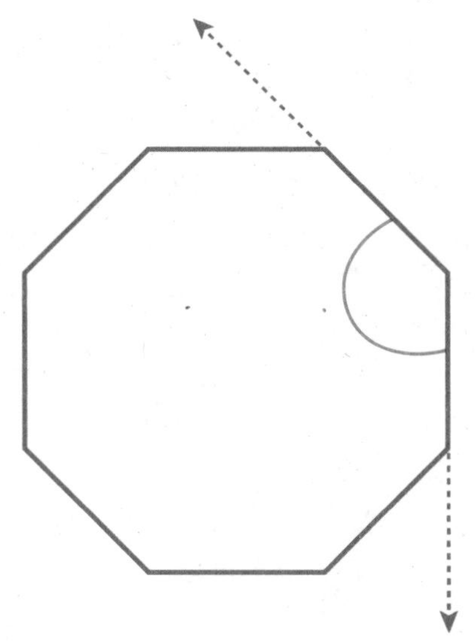

5 Measure the angles of the triangle at the right.

Angle A measures .... degrees.

Angle B measures .... degrees.

Angle C measures .... degrees.

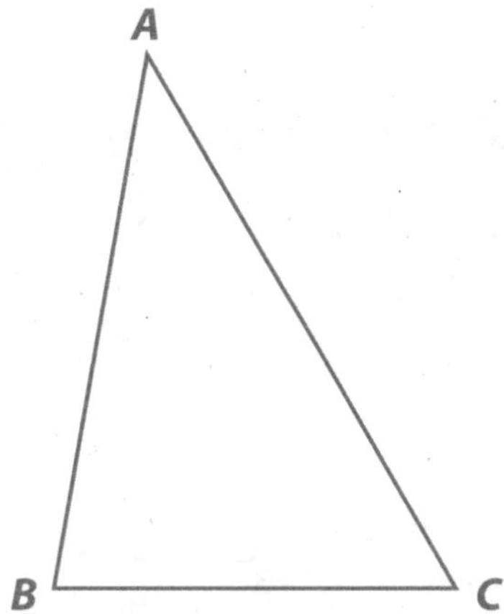

Develop Drawing Angles

Read and try to solve the problem below.

Draw a 30° angle. Think about using two pencils to make an angle.

TRY IT

Math Toolkit

- protractors
- rulers
- index cards
- sticky notes

DISCUSS IT

Ask your partner: Do you agree with me? Why or why not?

Tell your partner: I agree with you about . . . because . . .

Explore different ways to understand how to draw angles.

Draw a 30° angle. Think about using two pencils to make an angle.

PICTURE IT

You know an angle is made up of two rays with a common endpoint, called the vertex.

You can use two pencils to make an angle.

MODEL IT

You can use a benchmark angle to get an idea of what your drawing should look like.

Think about a right angle. A right angle measures 90°.

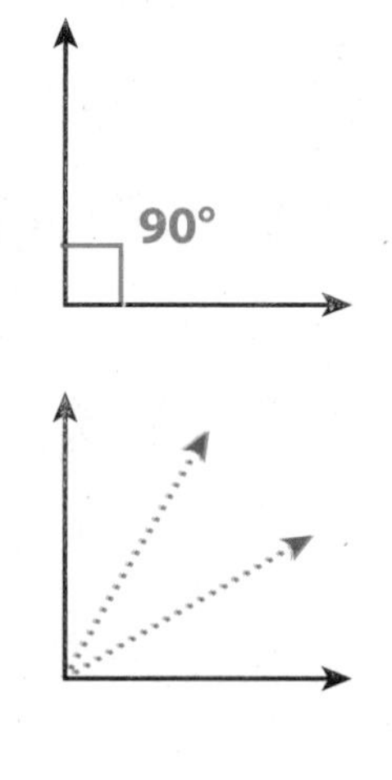

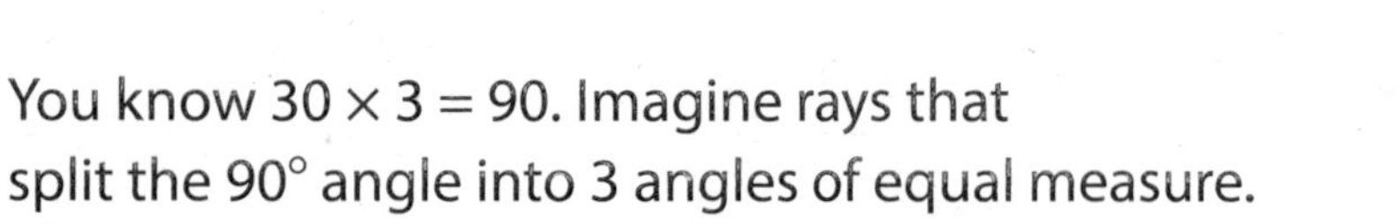

You know $30 \times 3 = 90$. Imagine rays that split the 90° angle into 3 angles of equal measure.

A 30° angle opens about the same amount as the angle shown at the right.

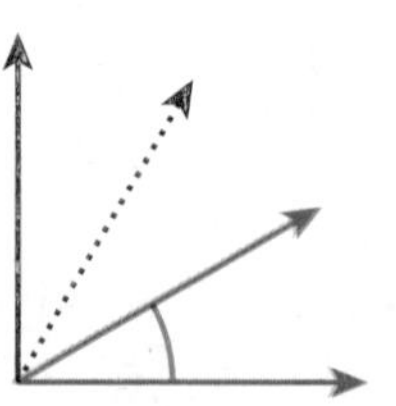

CONNECT IT

Now you will use the problem from the previous page to help you understand how to draw angles.

 Draw a ray on a sheet of paper. Then place the protractor's center point on the endpoint of your ray. What part of the angle is that point? ....

 Keeping the protractor's center point on the endpoint of your ray, draw a point on your ray at 0°.

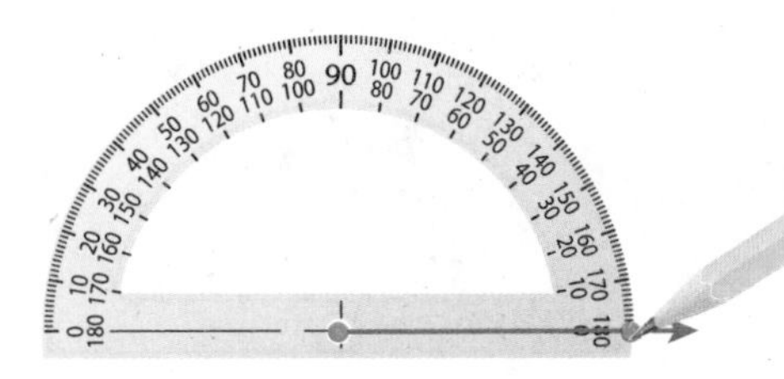

3 There are two marks on the protractor labeled "30." Choose the one that is 30° from your 0° mark. Draw a point at this mark.

4 Use the straight edge of the protractor to draw a ray from the vertex through the point you drew at 30°.

5 Suppose you choose the other "30" mark and draw a point at that mark. What would be the measure of your angle? ....

6 Think about a right angle. Compare it to the angle you drew. How wide does your angle open compared to a right angle? ....

7 ## REFLECT

Look back at your **Try It**, strategies by classmates, and **Picture It** and **Model It**. Which models or strategies do you like best for drawing angles? Explain.

....

....

....

....

APPLY IT

Use what you just learned to solve these problems.

8 Angle *D* measures 80°. One ray of angle *D* is shown. Draw another ray to make angle *D*.

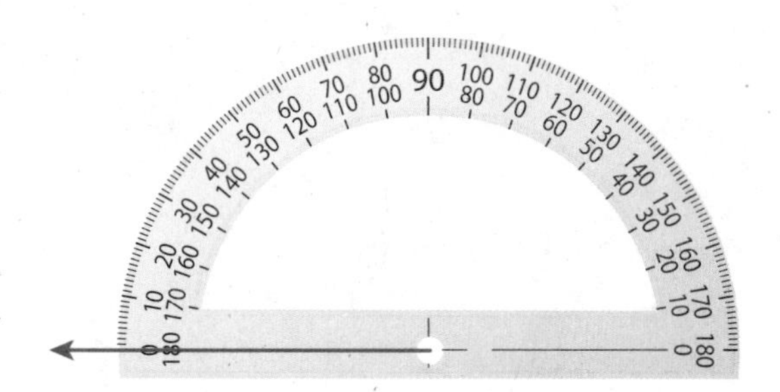

9 Draw a 75° angle.

10 Draw a 100° angle.

Practice Drawing Angles

Study the Example showing how to draw an angle. Then solve problems 1–6.

EXAMPLE

Stephanie wants to draw a 60° angle. She draws a ray and positions the endpoint of the ray on a protractor's center point. Then she lines up the protractor so the ray passes through the 0° mark on the protractor. How does she draw the other ray to form a 60° angle?

Find 60° on the protractor.

Choose the mark that is 60° from the first ray.
Draw a point at this 60° mark.

Draw a ray from the vertex through this point.

1 Draw a ray to show a 70° angle.

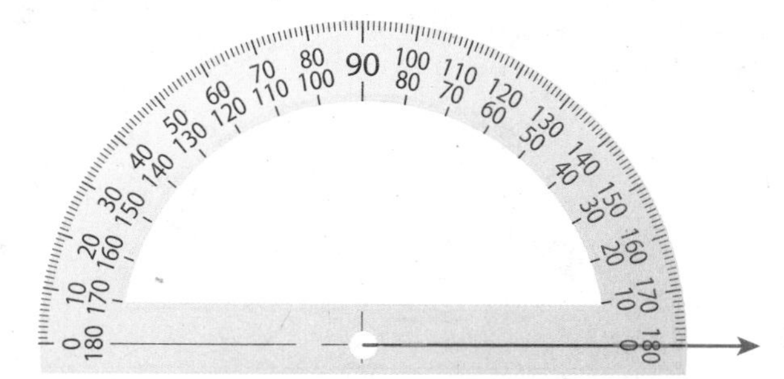

2 Draw a ray to show a 110° angle.

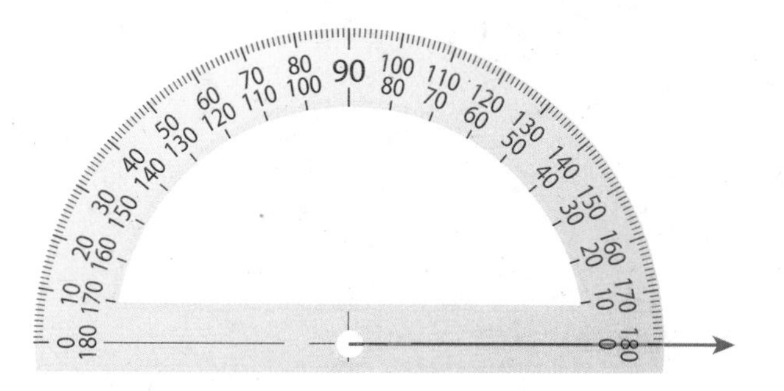

3 Draw a 160° angle.

 Draw a 20° angle.

 Draw a 45° angle.

 Draw a 135° angle.

Refine Angles

Complete the Example below. Then solve problems 1–8.

EXAMPLE

What is the measure of the angle below?

Look at how you could use a protractor to measure the angle.

Solution ....

The center point lines up with the vertex of the angle, and the 0° mark lines up with one ray of the angle. The other ray points to the measure of the angle.

PAIR/SHARE
Does it matter which ray you choose to line up with the 0° mark?

APPLY IT

1 What is the measure of the angle below?

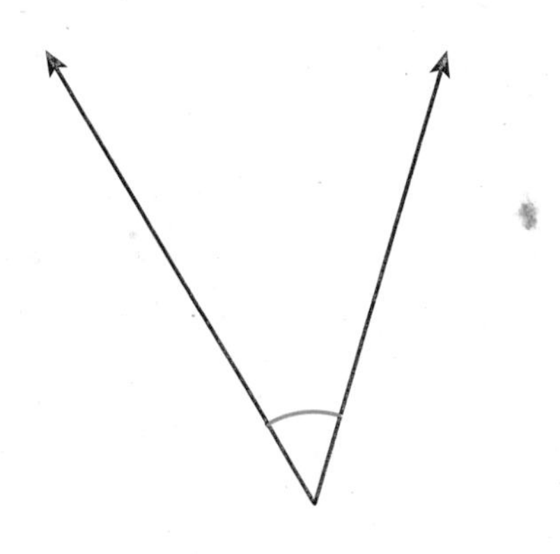

Solution ....

The angle looks like it opens less than a right angle. The measure will be less than 90°.

PAIR/SHARE
How did you and your partner decide where the vertex is?

 Draw a 145° angle.

I'll need to draw two rays to make an angle.

If you had drawn a point at the other 0° mark, how would it change your angle?

3 Which set of points can be used to draw a 105° angle?

Will a 105° angle be wider or narrower than a right angle?

Ⓐ 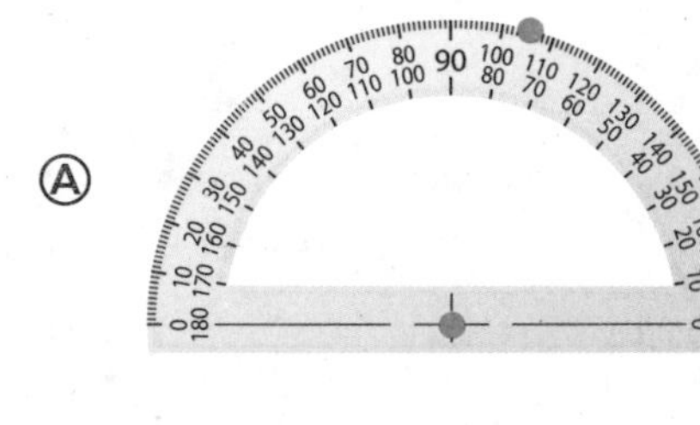

Ⓑ 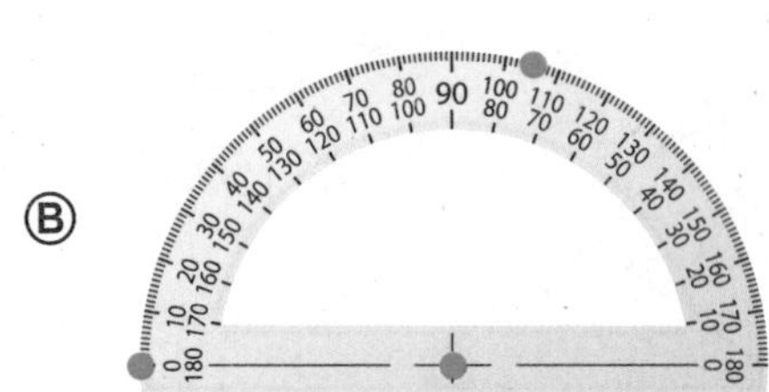

Ⓒ 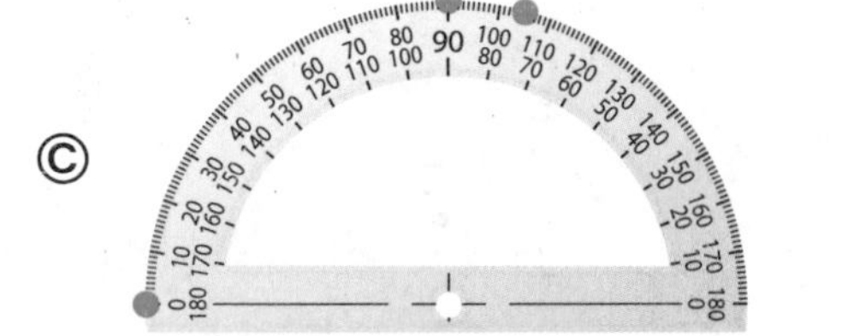

Ⓓ 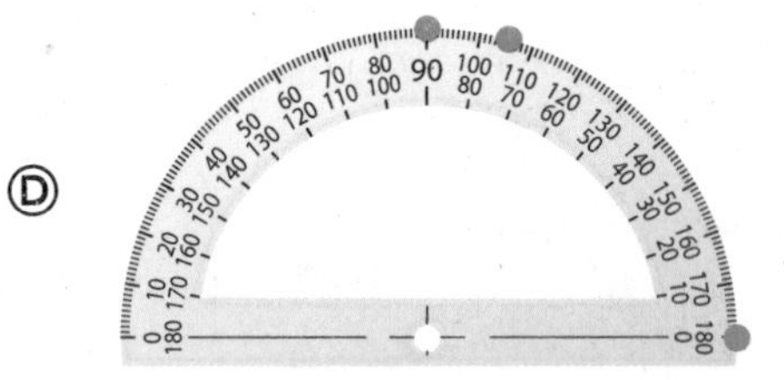

Mia chose Ⓒ as the correct answer. How did she get that answer?

PAIR/SHARE
Does Mia's answer make sense?

4 Which point could be the vertex of an 80° angle that you could measure without moving the protractor?

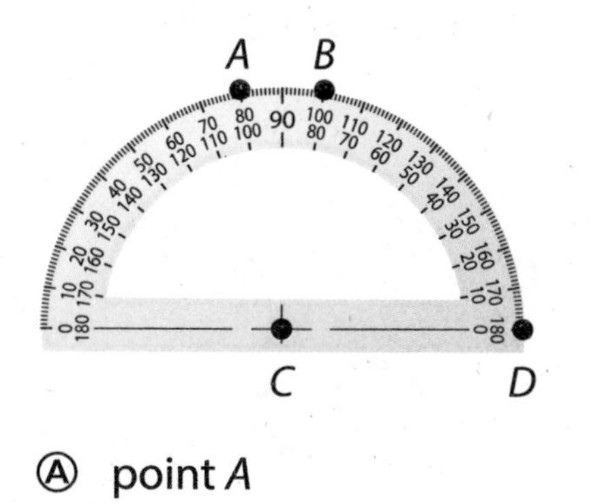

Ⓐ point *A*

Ⓑ point *B*

Ⓒ point *C*

Ⓓ point *D*

5 Which diagrams show a 25° angle?

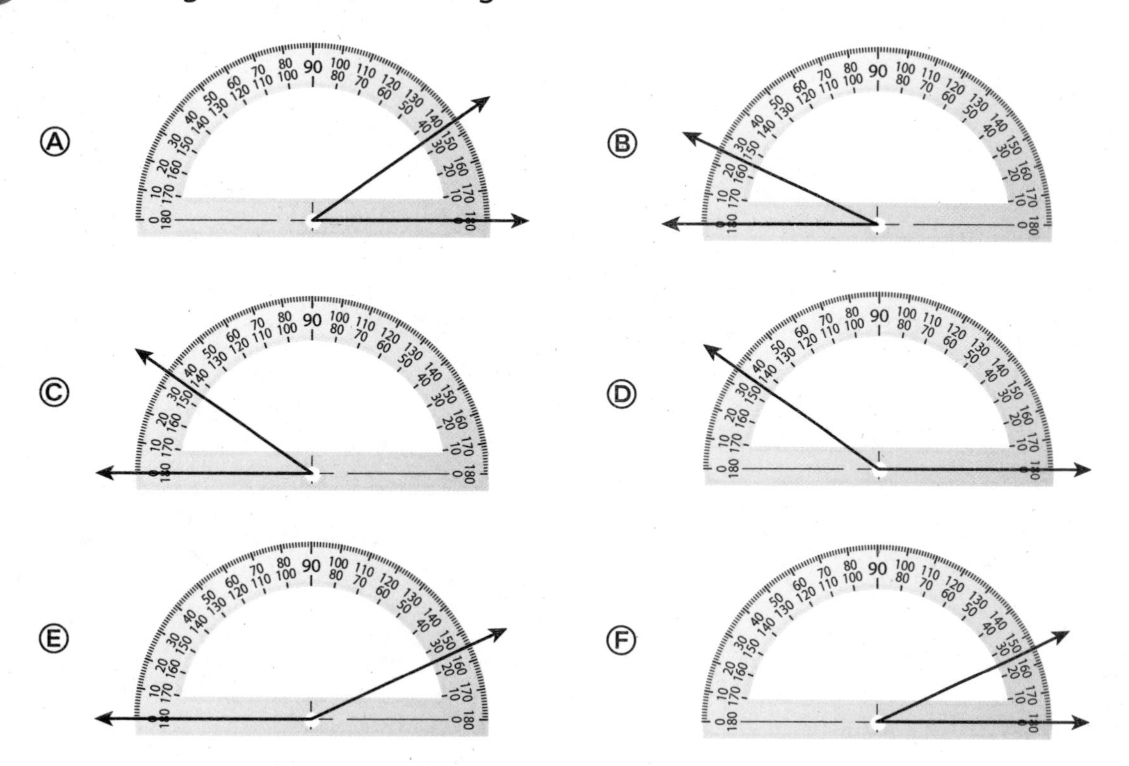

 What is the measure of the angle below?

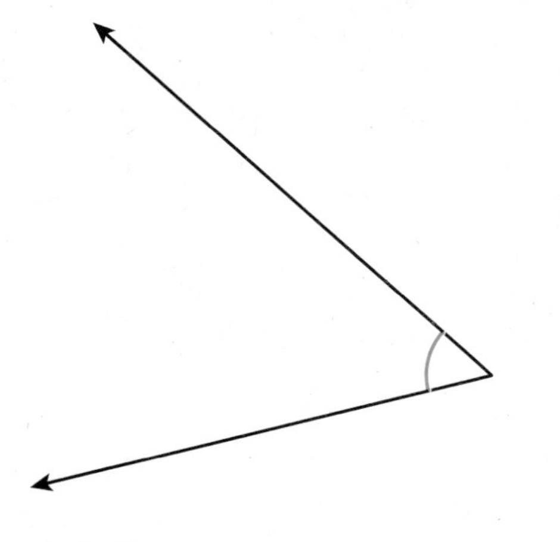

Solution ....

7 Draw a 40° angle.

 MATH JOURNAL

Explain how you can use a protractor to measure the angle below.

SELF CHECK Go back to the Unit 5 Opener and see what you can check off.

Add and Subtract with Angles

LESSON 32

Dear Family,

This week your child is learning to add and subtract with angles.

The two shapes at the right are placed together as shown. Two angle measures are given: 108° and 55°.

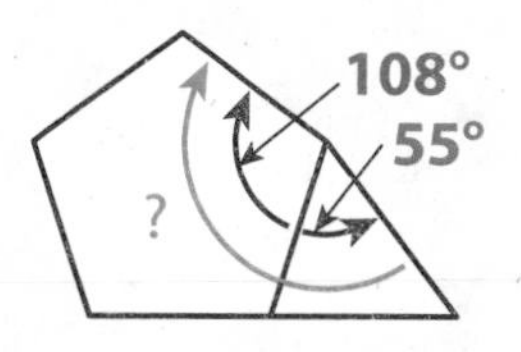

Since there are no gaps and no overlaps between the shapes, you can add the two angle measures together to find the measure of the larger angle formed by the two angles in the shapes.

108° + 55° = 163°

The larger combined angle measures 163°.

Your child is also learning to use subtraction to find angle measures. In the example above, if the measure of the larger angle was given and the measure of one of the other angles was unmarked, your child could subtract to find the measure of the unmarked angle.

For example, **163° − 108° = 55°**.

Invite your child to share what he or she knows about adding and subtracting angles by doing the following activity together.

ACTIVITY ADDING WITH ANGLES

Do this activity with your child to add angles.

Materials sheet of paper, scissors

- Cut out a piece from a rectangular sheet of paper. Cut at an angle.

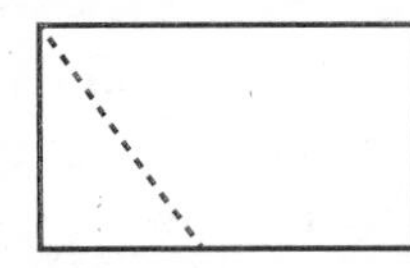

- Estimate the measure of the angle at the bottom of the piece you cut. For example, estimate that the angle measures about 50 degrees.

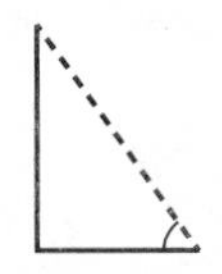

- Then estimate the measure of the angle at the bottom corner where you cut the sheet of paper. For example, estimate that the angle measures about 130 degrees.

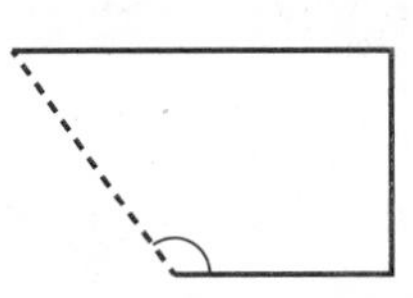

- Now put the two pieces of paper back together. Add the estimates of the angle measures in order to find the measure of the angle formed by combining both angles. For example, $50° + 130° = 180°$.

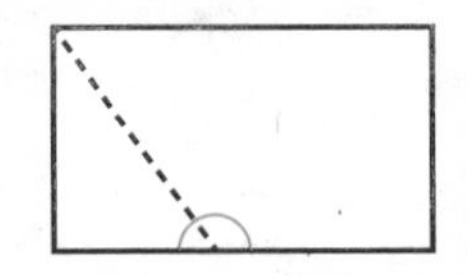

- Ask your child to explain how you know the measure of the combined angle is 180 degrees. (Both angles combine to form a straight angle, which has a measure of 180°.)

Explore Adding and Subtracting with Angles

Learning Target

- Recognize angle measure as additive. When an angle is decomposed into non-overlapping parts, the angle measure of the whole is the sum of the angle measures of the parts. Solve addition and subtraction problems to find unknown angles on a diagram in real world and mathematical problems, e.g., by using an equation with a symbol for the unknown angle measure.

SMP 1, 2, 3, 4, 5, 6, 7

Previously, you learned how to use a protractor to measure and draw angles. Now you will learn about adding and subtracting angle measures. Use what you know to try to solve the problem below.

Flora cuts a rectangular sheet of paper into two pieces on the dotted line.

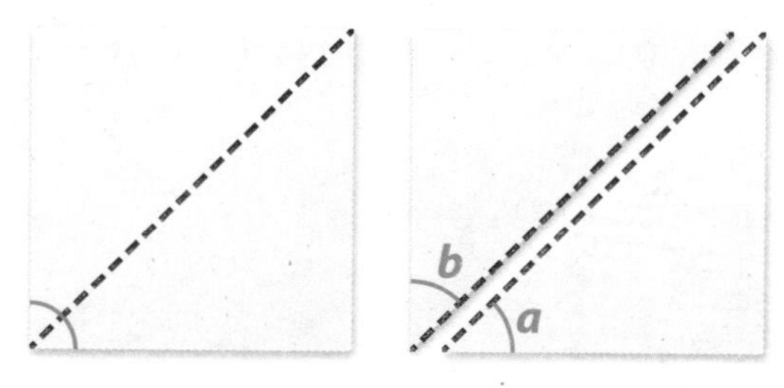

What is the sum of the measures of angle *a* and angle *b*?

TRY IT

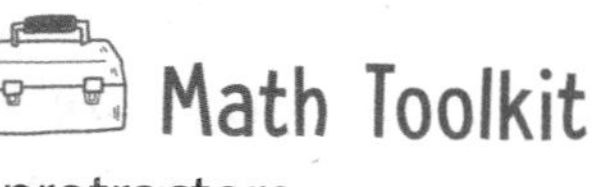

- protractors
- rulers
- index cards
- sticky notes

DISCUSS IT

Ask your partner: How did you get started?

Tell your partner: At first, I thought . . .

CONNECT IT

LOOK BACK

Explain how to find the sum of the measures of angle *a* and angle *b*.

LOOK AHEAD

You can decompose, or break apart, any angle into smaller angles that do not overlap. Look at the 10° angle below.

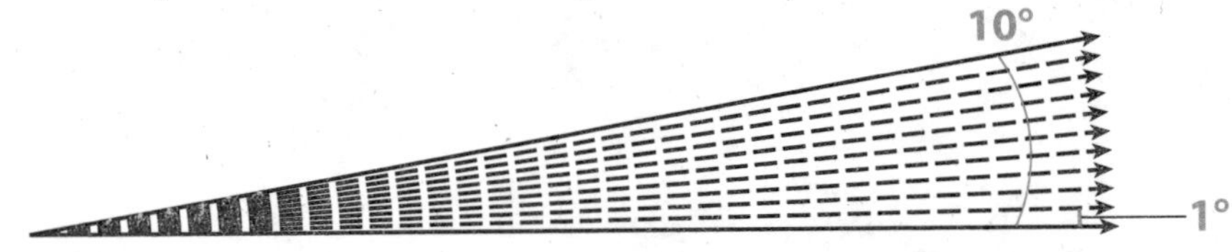

a. How many 1° angles make up the 10° angle? ....

b. Look below at one way to decompose a 10° angle. You can write an equation to show that the measure of the 10° angle is the sum of the angle measures of the two smaller angles. Fill in the blanks in the equation.

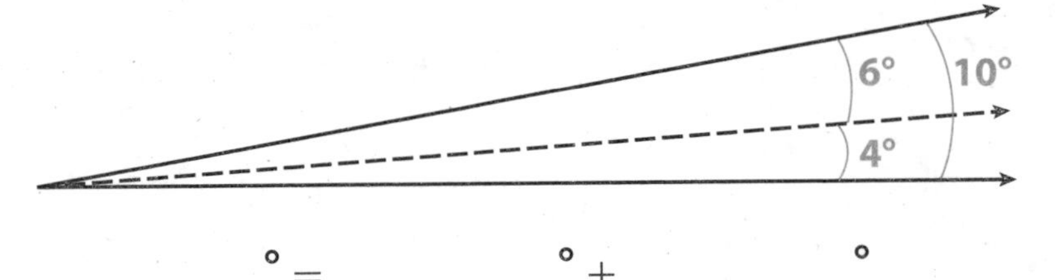

..............° = ...° + ...°

c. Below is another way to decompose a 10° angle. Write an equation to represent the angle measures that combine to form the 10° angle.

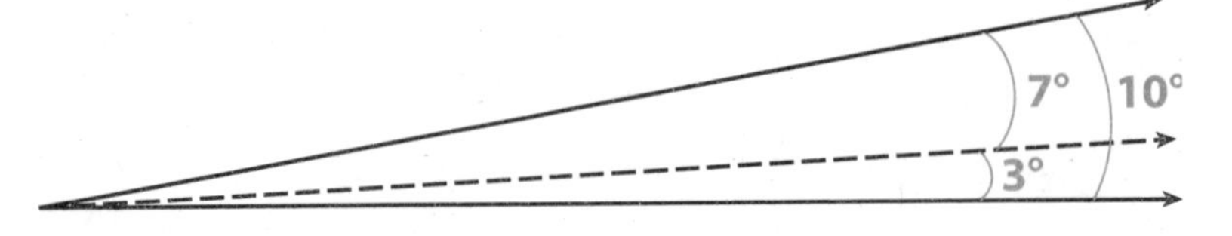

....

3 REFLECT

What are two other ways you can decompose a 10° angle? Write two equations.

....

Name: ______________________________

Prepare for Adding and Subtracting with Angles

1 Think about what you know about angles. Fill in each box. Use words, numbers, and pictures. Show as many ideas as you can.

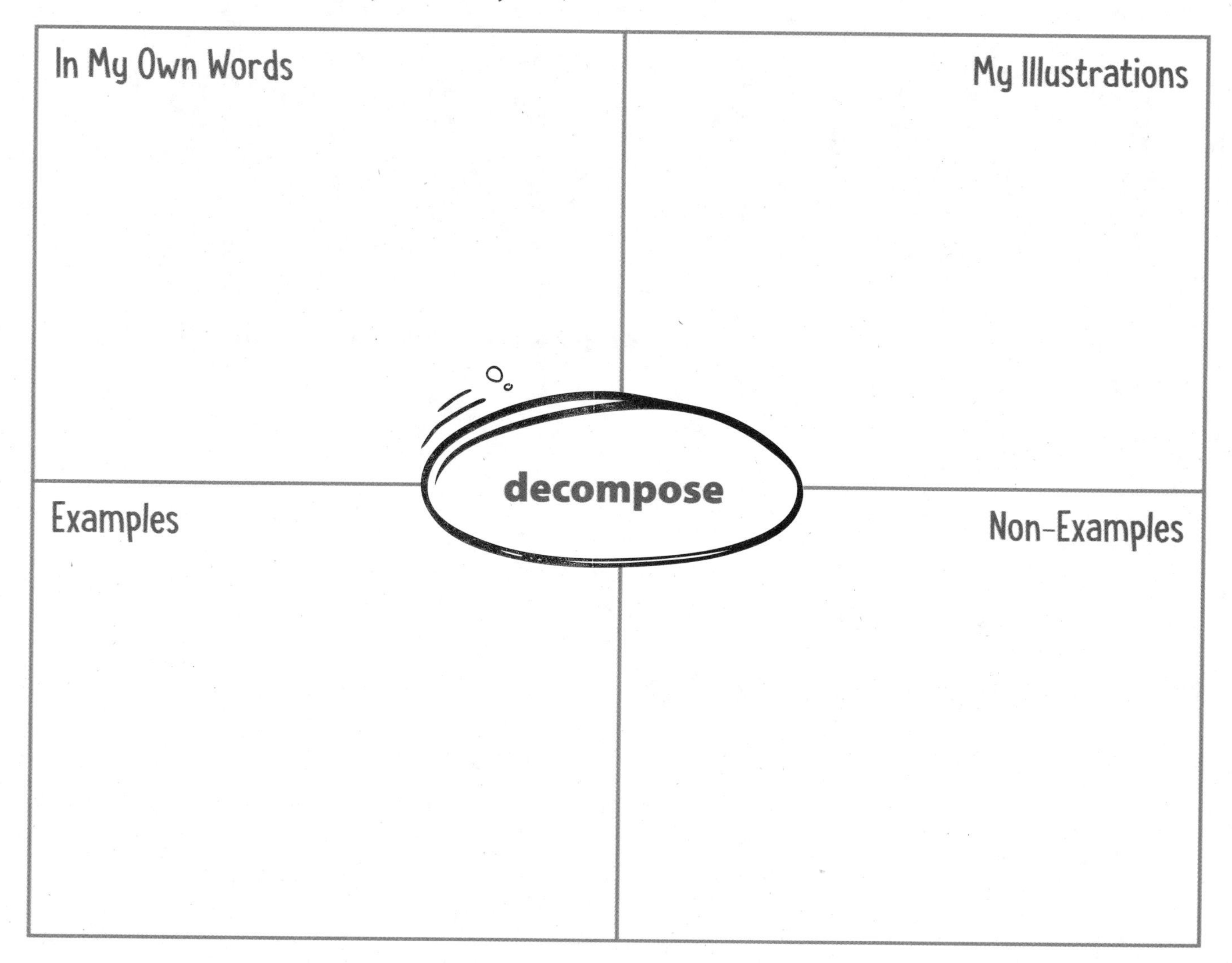

2 Look at one way to decompose a 30° angle. You can write an equation to represent the sum of the measures of the angles that combine to form the 30° angle. Fill in the blanks in the equation.

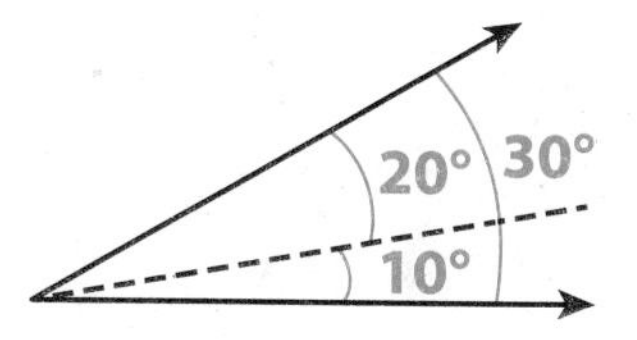

______° = ______° + ______°

3 Solve the problem. Show your work.

Shadi cuts a rectangular strip of construction paper into two pieces on the dotted line.

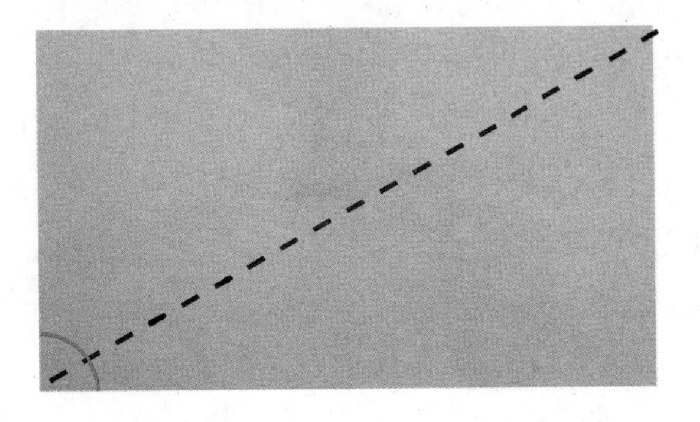

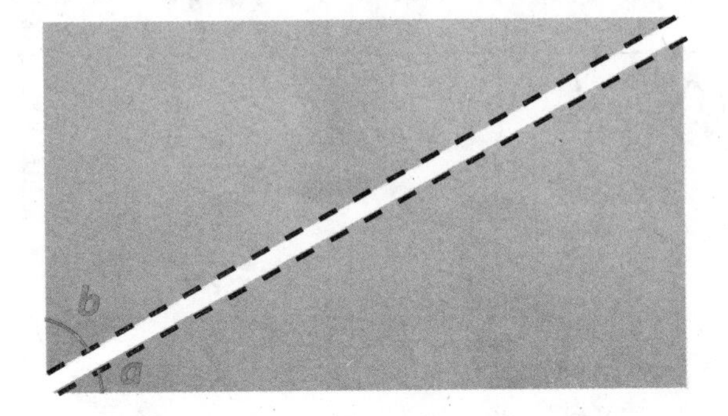

What is the sum of the measures of angle *a* and angle *b*? Explain how you know.

Solution ....

....

....

....

4 Check your answer. Show your work.

Develop Combining Angles

Read and try to solve the problem below.

Waylon and Andres play a puzzle game. The goal is to fill a tray with three same-sized triangular puzzle pieces. There should be no gaps or overlaps between the pieces. What is the measure of the bottom angle of the tray?

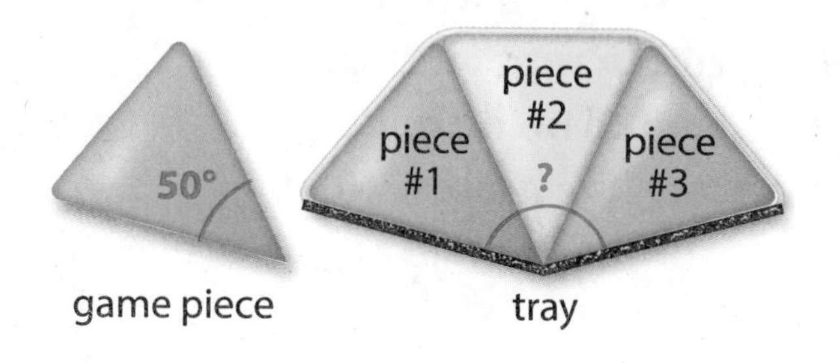

TRY IT

- protractors
- rulers
- toothpicks
- modeling clay
- index cards

Ask your partner: Do you agree with me? Why or why not?

Tell your partner: I disagree with this part because . . .

Explore different ways to understand how to combine smaller angles to form a larger angle.

Waylon and Andres play a puzzle game. The goal is to fill a tray with three same-sized triangular puzzle pieces. There should be no gaps or overlaps between the pieces. What is the measure of the bottom angle of the tray?

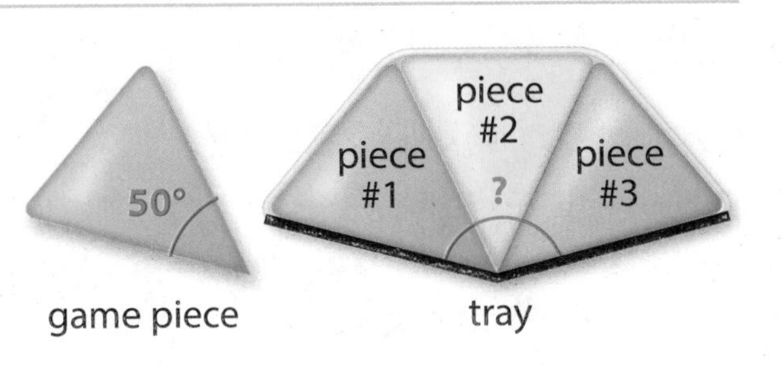

PICTURE IT

You can use a sketch to help understand the problem.

Imagine putting the three pieces together in the tray. The vertices of the 50° angles become the common vertex of a larger angle. This is the angle at the bottom of the tray.

The three 50° angles compose, or combine to form, the larger angle.

MODEL IT

You can also use a protractor to help understand the problem.

Look at a protractor. Start at 0°. Count three jumps of 50° each.

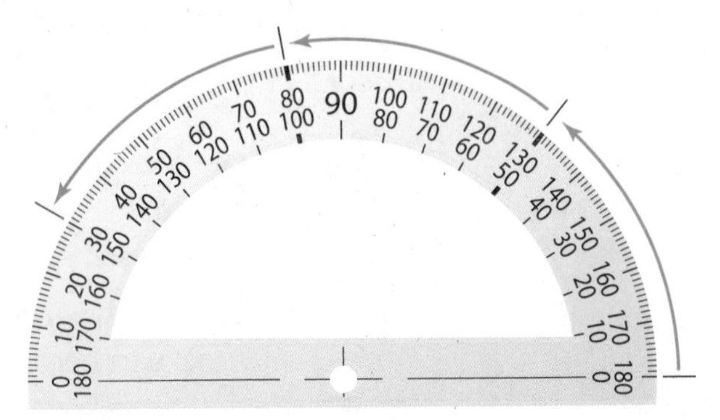

CONNECT IT

Now you will use the problem from the previous page to help you understand how angles combine to form a larger angle.

1 How many 50° angles compose the bottom angle of the tray? ....

2 Does addition or subtraction best express putting two or more angles together to make a greater angle? ....

3 Fill in the blanks to write an equation to combine the 50° angles to compose the bottom angle of the tray.

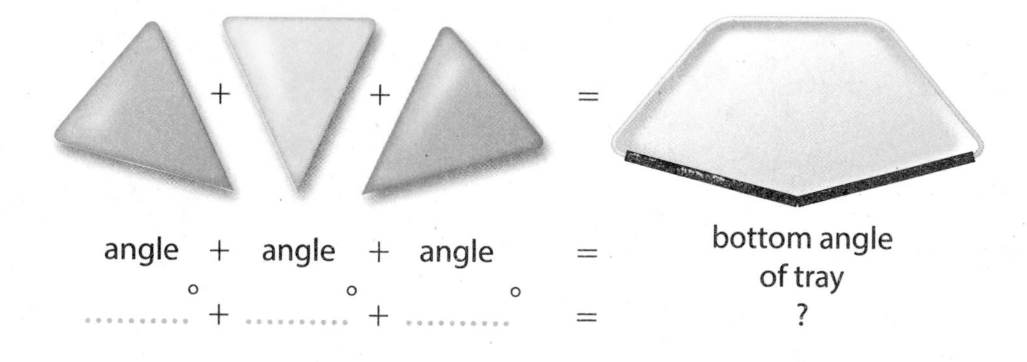

The bottom angle of the tray measures .... degrees.

4 Could you compose an angle that measures 150° from three angles with unequal angle measures? If so, give an example.

5 REFLECT

Look back at your **Try It**, strategies by classmates, and **Picture It** and **Model It**. Which models or strategies do you like best for combining angles? Explain.

....

....

....

....

APPLY IT

Use what you just learned to solve these problems.

6 The angle between each spoke on a wheel of Sophia's bicycle measures 15°. Sophia puts reflectors on two spokes as shown. What is the measure of the angle between the two spokes with the reflectors? Show your work.

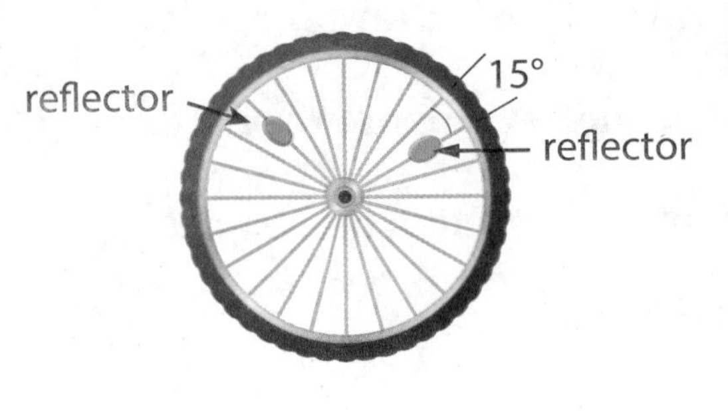

Solution ....

7 Gina sets two floor tiles as shown at the right. What is the measure of the blue angle? Show your work.

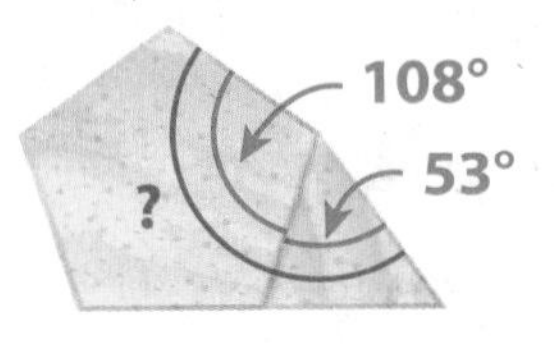

Solution ....

8 What is the sum of the measures of all the angles that are labeled in the figure shown?

Ⓐ 135°

Ⓑ 210°

Ⓒ 245°

Ⓓ 255°

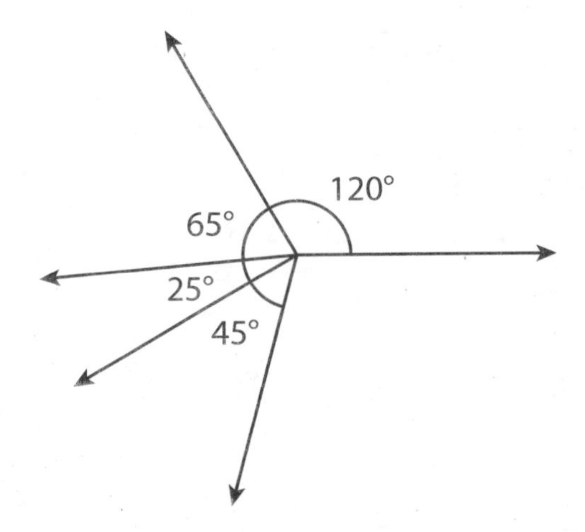

Practice Combining Angles

Study the Example showing how to combine smaller angles to form a larger angle. Then solve problems 1–5.

EXAMPLE

A spotlight in a theater casts a beam that has an angle measure of 24°.

Four spotlights are placed so that they have a common endpoint. What is the measure of the greater angle formed by the beams of all four spotlights?

Four 24° angles compose the greater angle. Use addition to combine the angles.

$24° + 24° + 24° + 24° = \mathbf{96°}$

The measure of the greater angle is 96°.

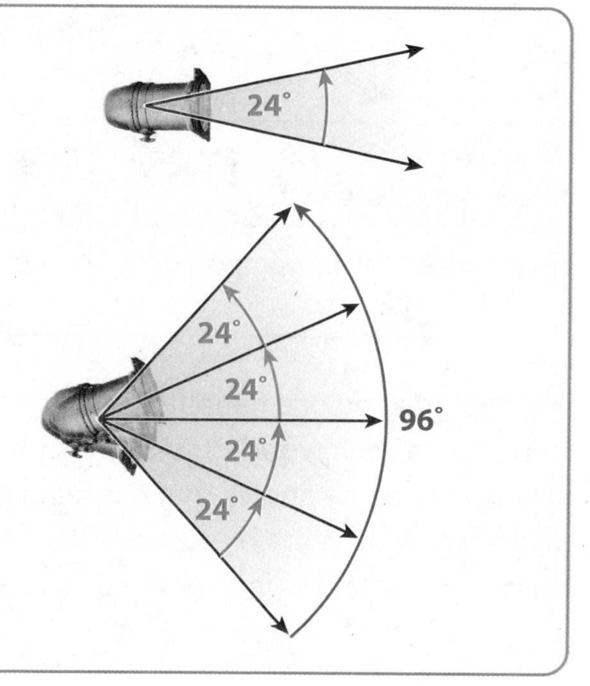

1 Look at the Example above. Suppose three spotlights are placed to have a common endpoint. What is the measure of the greater angle formed by the beams of the three spotlights? Write an addition equation to find the measure of this angle.

Solution ....

2 Another way to compose a 96° angle is to combine two angles: a 90° angle and a 6° angle. Write an addition equation to show why this is true.

Solution ....

3 Tell whether each statement is *True* or *False*.

	True	False
A 20° angle and a 70° angle can be composed into a 90° angle.	Ⓐ	Ⓑ
Three 40° angles compose an angle that measures 340°.	Ⓒ	Ⓓ
A 15° angle and a 60° angle compose an angle that measures 75°.	Ⓔ	Ⓕ
Four 50° angles can be composed into a 200° angle.	Ⓖ	Ⓗ

4 Look at the drawing of a hand fan at the right. The angle between each wooden stick on the fan is 12°. There are 11 of these angles that combine to form the open fan. What is the measure of the blue angle on the open fan? Show your work.

Solution ....

5 Sam lifts the front of his skateboard at a 15° angle to the ground as he gets ready to jump. He lifts his skateboard another 27° when he jumps. What is the measure of the angle that Sam lifts his skateboard from the ground? Show your work.

Solution ....

Develop Finding Unknown Angle Measures

Read and try to solve the problem below.

A door swings open 85° and then gets stuck. Randy pushes on the door, and it opens some more. The door opens 100° in all. How many more degrees does the door open after Randy pushes it?

TRY IT

Math Toolkit

- protractors
- rulers
- straws
- chenille stems
- index cards

DISCUSS IT

Ask your partner: Why did you choose that strategy?

Tell your partner: I knew . . . so I . . .

Explore different ways to understand how to use addition and subtraction to find unknown angle measures.

A door swings open 85° and then gets stuck. Randy pushes on the door, and it opens some more. The door opens 100° in all. How many more degrees does the door open after Randy pushes it?

PICTURE IT

You can use a sketch to help you understand the problem.

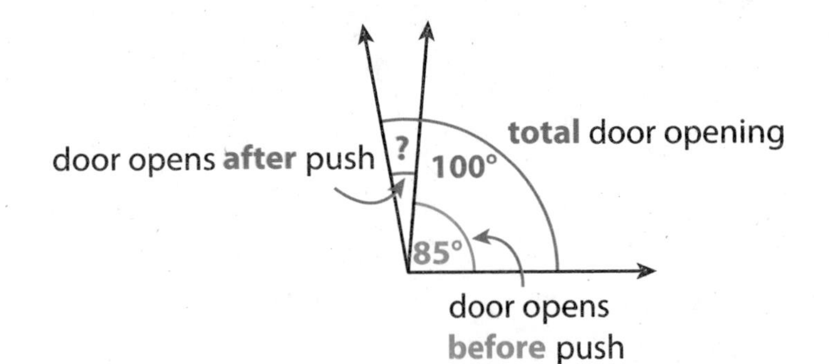

The 100° angle is composed of two smaller angles.
One angle measures 85°, and the other angle measure is unknown.

MODEL IT

You can use a protractor to help you understand the problem.

Look at a protractor. Start at 0°. Count on 85°. How many more degrees do you need to count on to get to 100°?

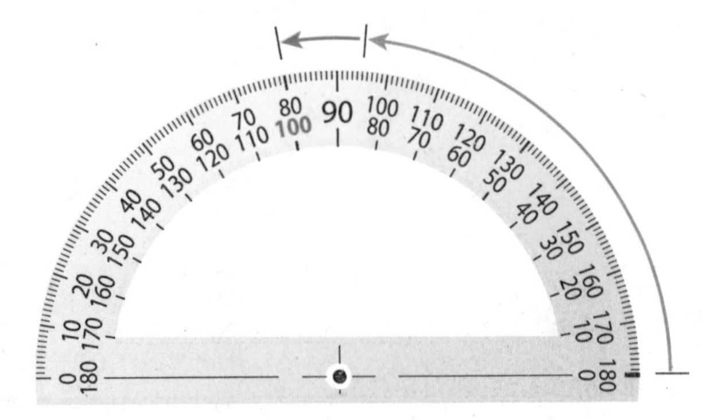

CONNECT IT

Now you will use the problem from the previous page to help you understand how to write and solve addition and subtraction equations to find unknown angle measures.

1. Write a sentence that describes how the unknown angle measure is related to the 85° and 100° angles.

2. Does addition or subtraction best express this relationship? ....

3. Write an equation to represent how the unknown angle measure is related to the 85° and 100° angles.

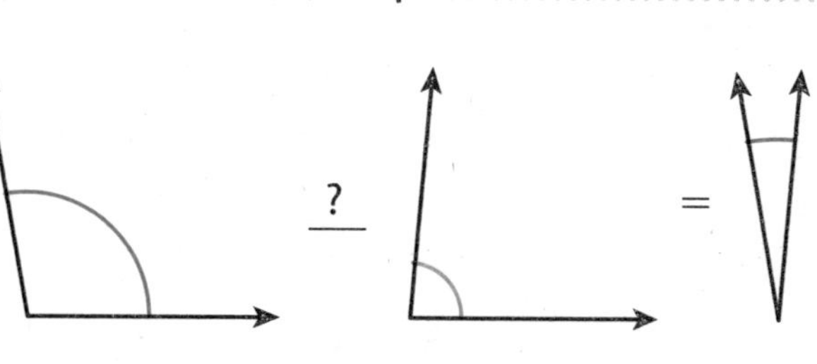

4. How would the measure of the unknown angle change if the door opened a total of 120°?

5. Imagine an angle that is composed of three smaller angles. Suppose you know the measure of the composed angle and the measures of two of the smaller angles. Explain how you could find the measure of the third small angle.

6. ## REFLECT

Look back at your **Try It**, strategies by classmates, and **Picture It** and **Model It**. Which models or strategies do you like best for writing and solving addition and subtraction equations to find an unknown angle measure? Explain.

APPLY IT

Use what you just learned to solve these problems.

7 A game includes an 8-second timer as shown at right. The timer's pointer turns through 135° as it counts down from 8 seconds to 5 seconds. How many more degrees does the pointer have to turn through to complete the full 360° circle? Show your work.

Solution ....

8 A snake's mouth opens to form a 180° angle, a straight line. The snake then partly closes its mouth to form a 60° angle. What is the difference between the measures of the angles formed by the snake's open mouth and partly closed mouth? Show your work.

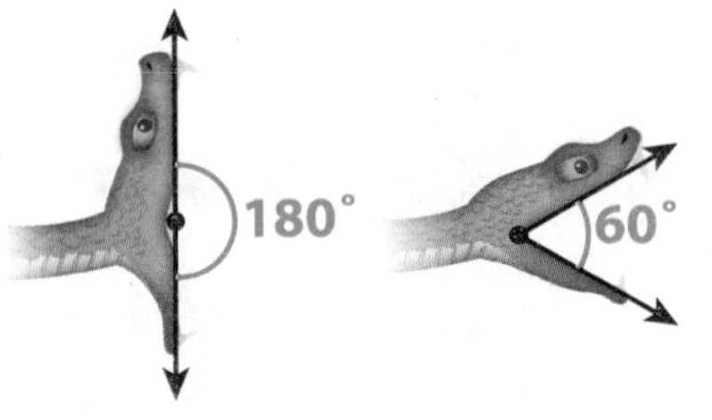

Solution ....

9 A diagram is shown at the right. The bottom line is a straight line. Write and solve an equation that can be used to find the measure of angle *M*. Show your work.

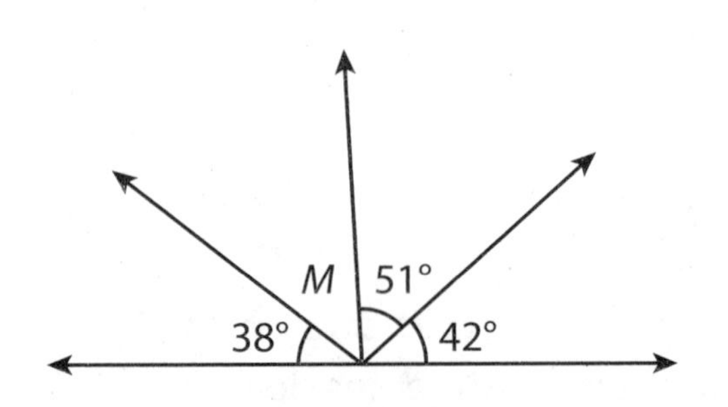

The measure of angle *M* is ....

Practice Finding Unknown Angle Measures

Study the Example showing how to use subtraction to find an unknown angle measure. Then solve problems 1–6.

EXAMPLE

Emma turns the knob on a combination lock 117°. How many more degrees does she need to turn the knob to make one full turn?

Write and solve an equation to find the measure of the unknown angle.

$$360° - 117° = x$$
$$243° = x$$

Emma needs to turn the knob another 243°.

A full turn is 360°.

1 Uma wants to push her brother in a swing. The swing hangs straight down. She pulls the swing back 35° and lets go. The swing moves forward 65°. How many degrees forward from the original straight-down position of the swing did the swing move? Show your work.

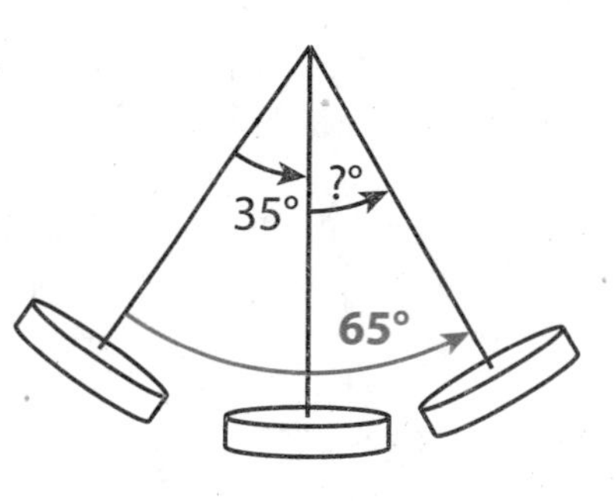

Solution ....

2 A sprinkler in a backyard turns through 180°. The sprinkler has turned 96° so far. How many more degrees will the sprinkler turn through to reach 180°?

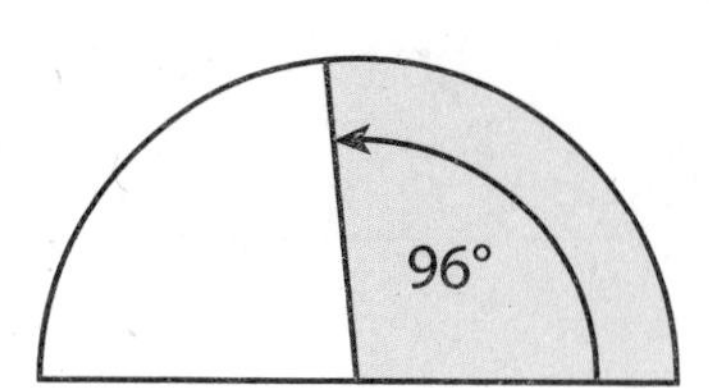

Solution ....

3 A sprinkler turns through 180° every 5 seconds. It turns through 36° every second. Complete the table below.

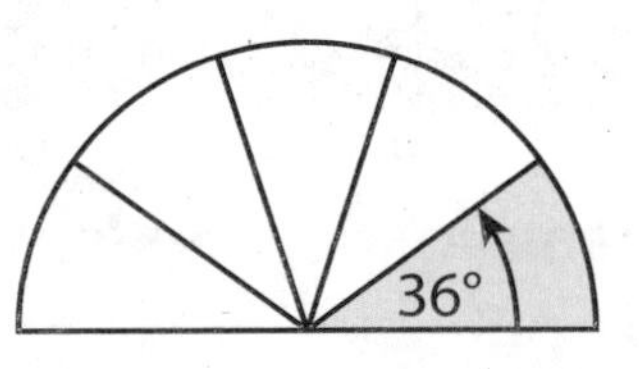

Time (seconds)	Degrees
1	
2	
3	
4	
5	

4 Write the measure of the unknown angle in the box below.

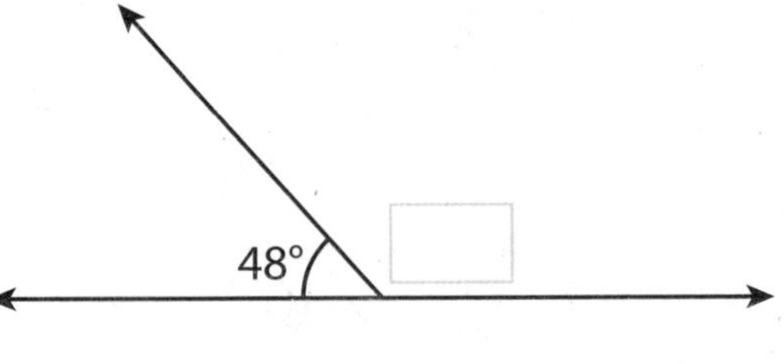

5 Write the measure of the unknown angle in the box below.

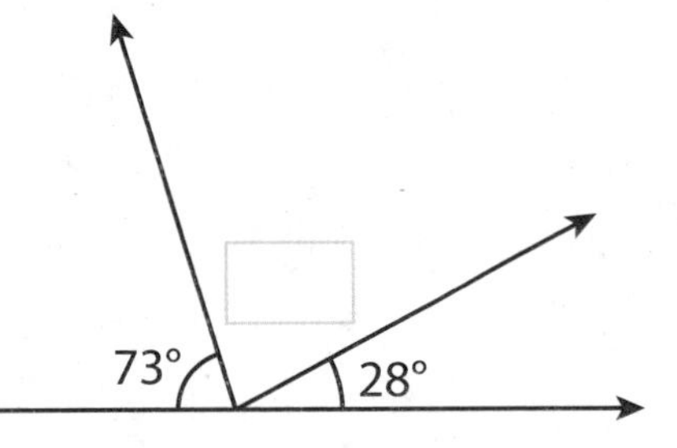

6 Use the angle measures below to fill in the boxes in the diagram with the correct angle measures.

110° 115° 135°

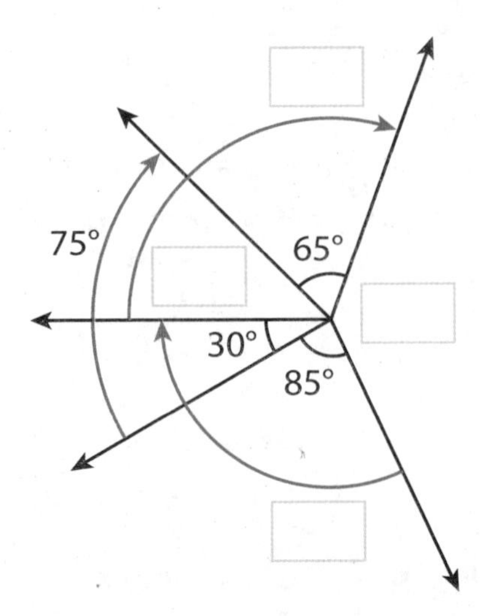

Refine Adding and Subtracting with Angles

Complete the Example below. Then solve problems 1–8.

EXAMPLE

Halah turns a jar lid 60°. Then she turns it 225° more. How many more degrees does Halah need to turn the lid to make one full turn?

Look at how you could show your work using a drawing and an equation.

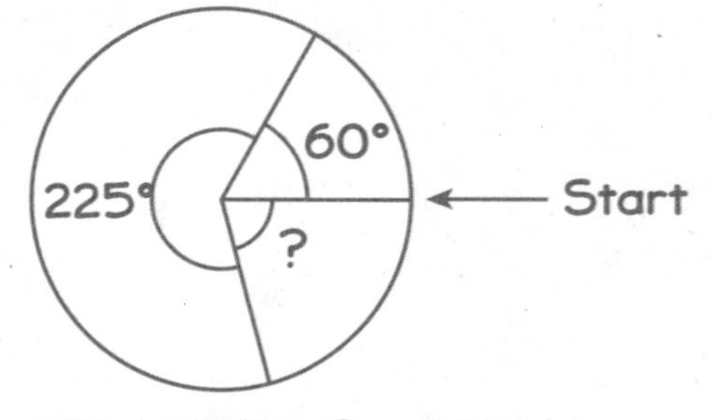

$60° + 225° + ? = 360°$

$285° + ? = 360°$

Solution ....

One full turn is equal to 360°. So the sum of 60, 225, and the measure of the unknown angle is equal to 360.

PAIR/SHARE
What operation did you use to solve the equation?

APPLY IT

1 When the hands of a clock are on 12 and 4, they form a 120° angle. What angle is formed if the hands are on 4 and 6? Show your work.

I know the hands make a 180° angle when they are on 12 and 6.

Solution ....

PAIR/SHARE
Once you know the angle from 4 to 6, how could you find the angle from 4 to 5?

2 Tyra's front door has a half-circle window. What is the measure of the angle of the center piece of glass? Show your work.

?
30° 30°
15° 15°

A circle has 360 degrees, so a half-circle has 180 degrees.

Solution ....

PAIR/SHARE
How could you check your answer?

3 A windshield wiper turns through 140°. The window cleaner sprays across 75°. The wiper turns 40° before it gets to the sprayed area. How many degrees past the sprayed area does the wiper turn?

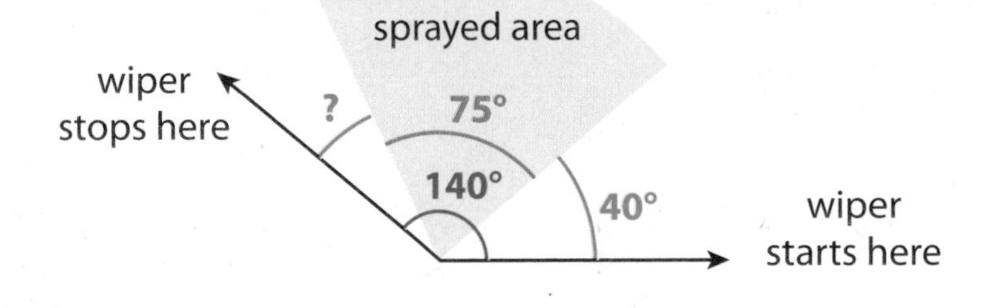

Ⓐ 25°

Ⓑ 35°

Ⓒ 115°

Ⓓ 255°

Ellen chose Ⓓ as the correct answer. How did she get that answer?

The 140° angle is composed of 3 angles: 40°, 75° and ?°. The sum of the measures of these three angles must be 140°.

PAIR/SHARE
Does Ellen's answer make sense?

4 Keith uses a can opener. Each time he twists the knob on the opener, the opener moves 36° around the lid of the can. Which best describes how open the can is after 5 twists?

Ⓐ one-tenth open

Ⓑ one-fifth open

Ⓒ half open

Ⓓ completely open

5 A tire swing hangs straight down. A child gets on, swings forward 50°, and swings back 95°. How many degrees forward must the swing go to return to its starting position?

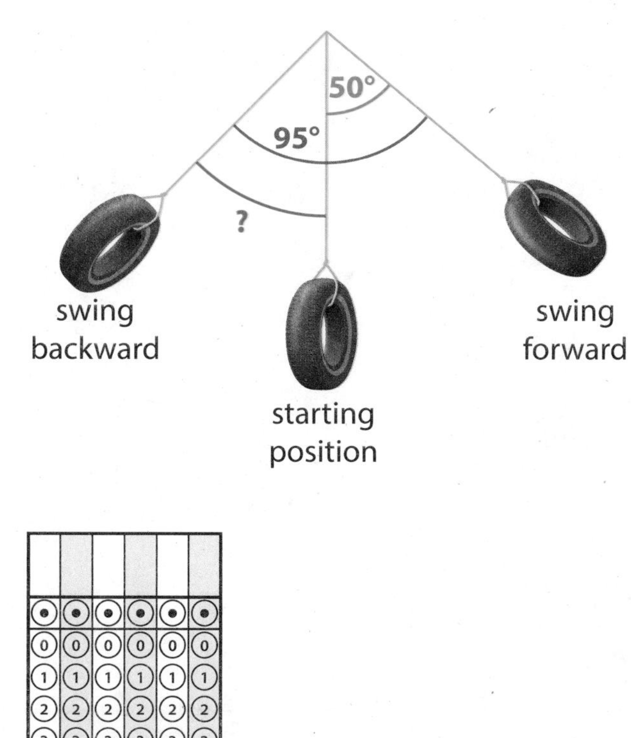

Tell whether there is an angle of each given measure shown in the diagram below.

	Yes	No
225°	Ⓐ	Ⓑ
265°	Ⓒ	Ⓓ
70°	Ⓔ	Ⓕ
320°	Ⓖ	Ⓗ
90°	Ⓘ	Ⓙ

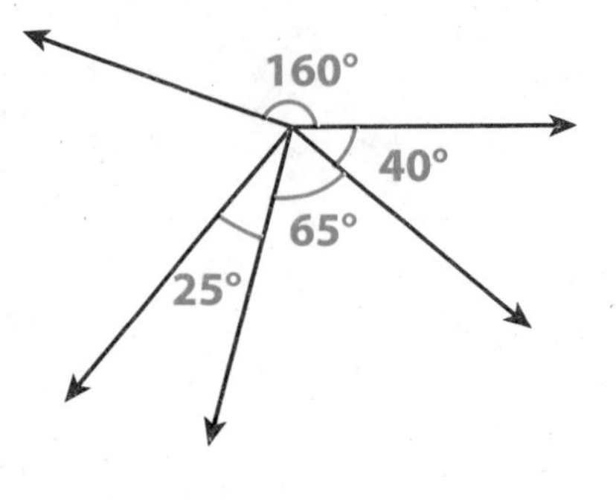

7 The measure of one angle is given in the figure below.

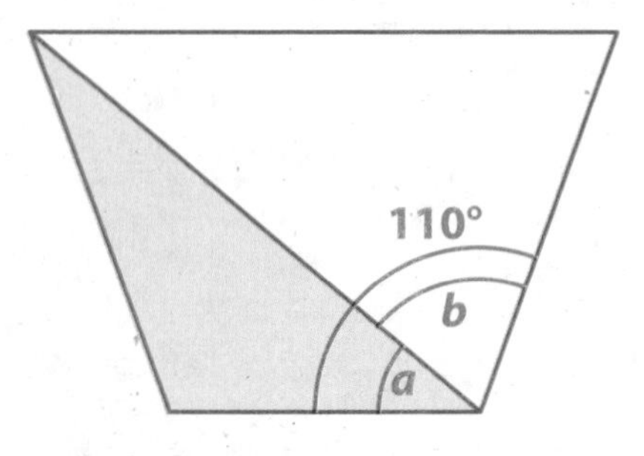

Use a protractor to measure angle *a*. Without measuring angle *b*,

find the measure of angle *b*. ....

8 MATH JOURNAL

Jake wants to make a wooden table top in the shape of a circle. He has three pie-shaped pieces of wood. One piece has an angle of 105°, the second has an angle of 135°, and the third has an angle of 110°. Can Jake use the three pieces of wood to make the table top so that there are no gaps or overlaps between the pieces? Explain.

☑ SELF CHECK Go back to the Unit 5 Opener and see what you can check off.

Classify Two-Dimensional Figures

LESSON 33

Dear Family,

This week your child is learning to classify two-dimensional shapes.

Shapes can be sorted into groups based on the kinds of sides they have and the kind of angles they have. Some shapes your child is classifying are triangles; quadrilaterals such as squares, rhombuses, **trapezoids**, and parallelograms; and **hexagons**.

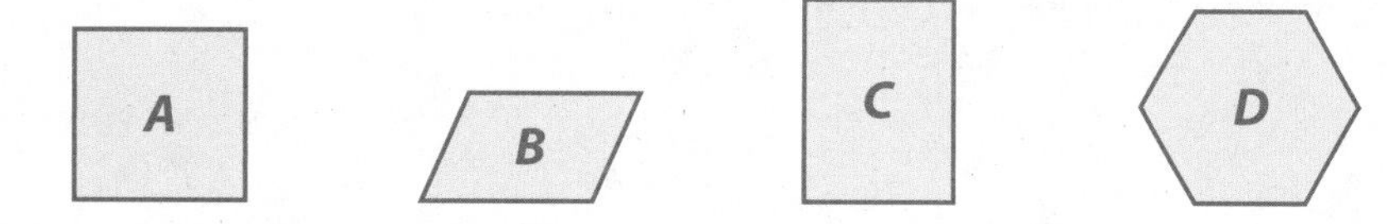

One way to classify shapes is by the kinds of sides they have.

- Shapes *A* and *C* have parallel sides and perpendicular sides.
- Shapes *B* and *D* have parallel sides only.

Another way to classify shapes is by the kinds of angles they have.

- Shapes *A* and *C* have all right angles.
- Shape *B* has some acute angles and some obtuse angles.
- Shape *D* has all obtuse angles.

Triangles can be classified by their sides and angles.

- Triangle *E* is a **scalene triangle**. It has no sides the same length.
- Triangle *F* is a **right triangle**. It has a right angle.

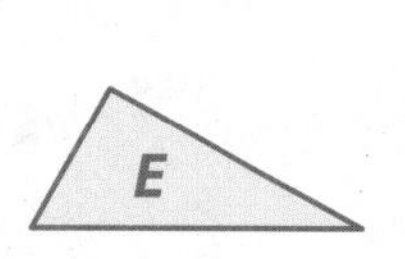

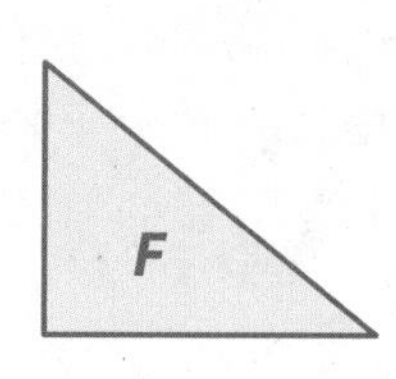

Invite your child to share what he or she knows about classifying two-dimensional figures by doing the following activity together.

ACTIVITY CLASSIFYING TWO-DIMENSIONAL FIGURES

Do this activity with your child to classify two-dimensional figures.

- Use the grid of dots below or make a dot grid on another sheet of paper.
- One person draws a shape. The shape could be a triangle, a quadrilateral, or another kind of shape with straight sides.
- The other person describes the shape. Be sure to talk about any parallel sides and perpendicular sides that the shape has. Describe the angles of the shape, too! Then name the shape.
- Switch roles. Take turns drawing a shape and describing and naming it.

Explore Classifying Two-Dimensional Figures

Learning Target

- Classify two-dimensional figures based on the presence or absence of parallel or perpendicular lines, or the presence or absence of angles of a specified size. Recognize right triangles as a category, and identify right triangles.

SMP 1, 2, 3, 4, 5, 6, 7, 8

You have learned about parallel and perpendicular lines. Use what you know to try to solve the problem below.

Look at the shapes below. Put a check mark on all the shapes that have at least one pair of parallel sides. Put a star on all the shapes that have at least one pair of perpendicular sides. Explain how you could test your choices.

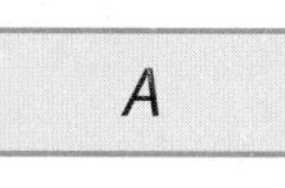

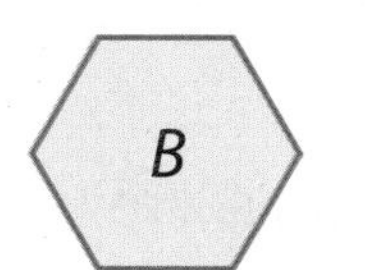

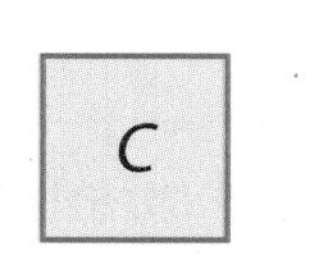

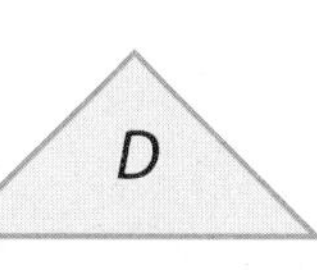

E

TRY IT

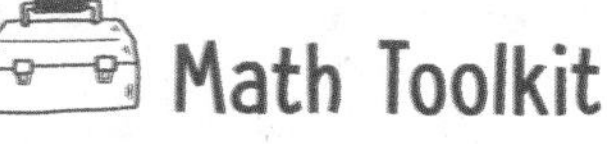

- pattern blocks
- rulers
- index cards
- protractors

STOP

DISCUSS IT

Ask your partner: Can you explain that again?

Tell your partner: I knew . . . so I . . .

CONNECT IT

LOOK BACK

Which shapes have at least one pair of parallel sides and at least one pair of perpendicular sides? Explain.

LOOK AHEAD

Shapes with straight sides, such as triangles and quadrilaterals, are types of **polygons**. There are different ways you can sort these shapes, such as by the number of sides the shape has and by the relationships between the sides. You can also sort shapes by the kinds of angles they have.

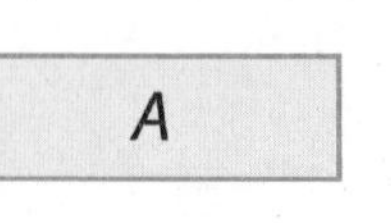

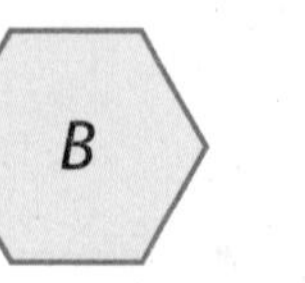

C
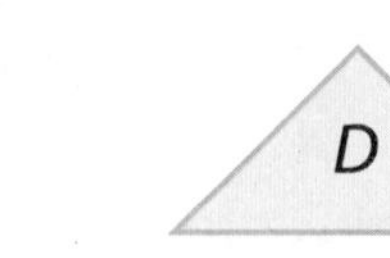

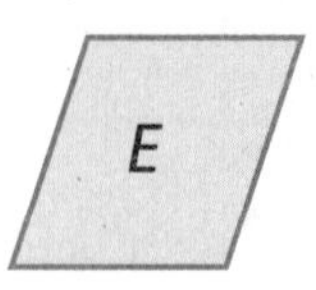

a. Which shapes have at least one right angle? ....

b. Which shapes have at least one acute angle? ....

c. Which shapes have at least one obtuse angle? ....

3 REFLECT

Describe the sides and angles of shape *C*.

....

....

....

....

....

Name: ______________________________

Prepare for Classifying Two-Dimensional Figures

1. Think about what you know about polygons. Fill in each box. Use words, numbers, and pictures. Show as many ideas as you can.

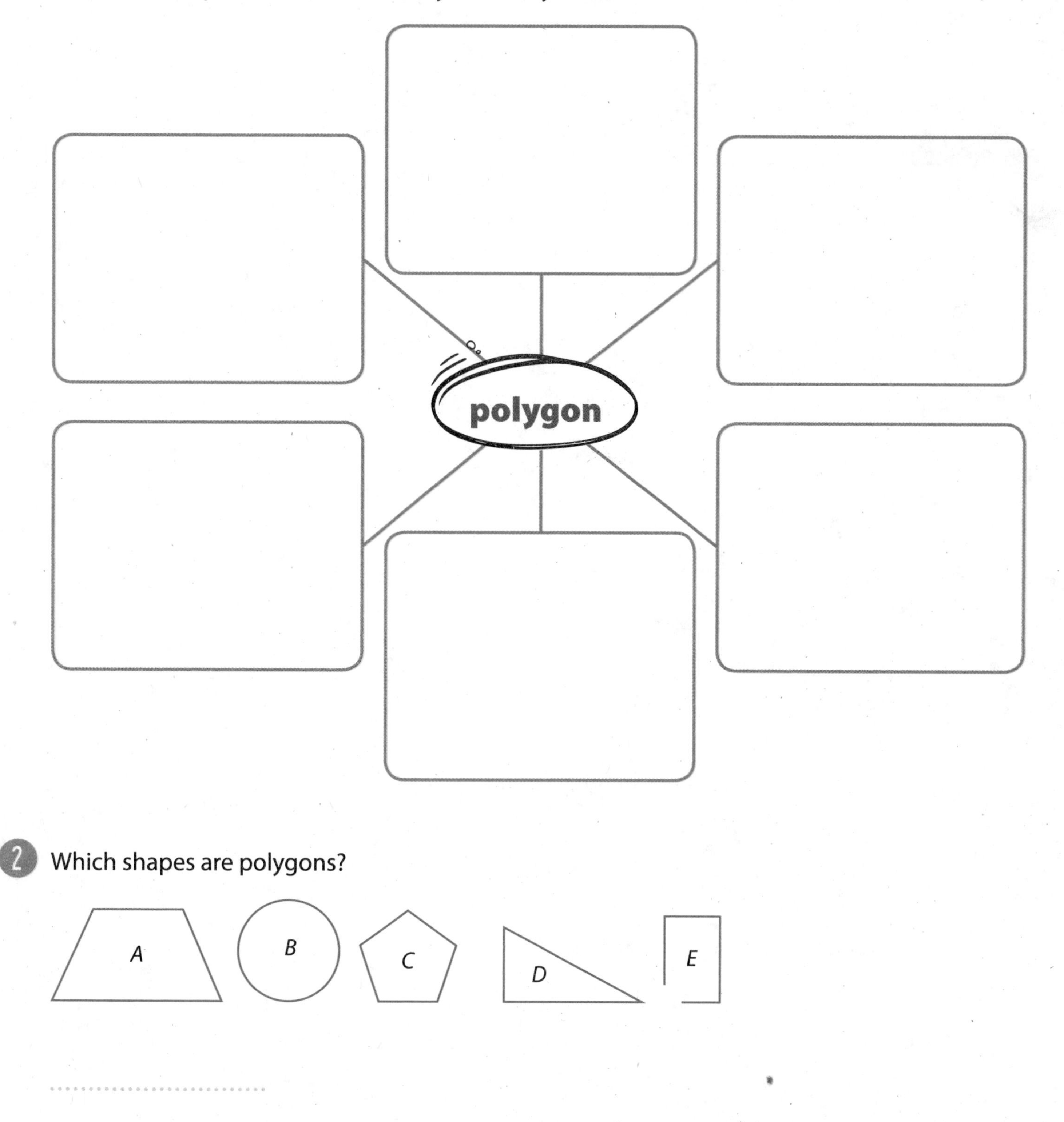

2. Which shapes are polygons?

....

3 Solve the problem. Show your work.

Look at the shapes below. Put a check mark on all the shapes that have at least one right angle. Put a star on all the shapes that have at least one pair of parallel sides. Explain how you could test your choices.

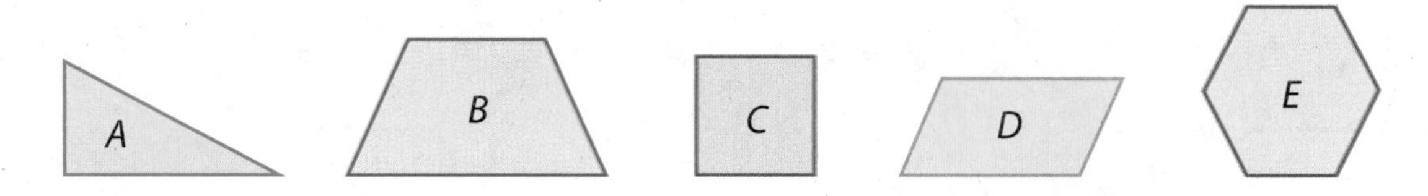

Solution ....

....

....

....

4 Check your answer. Show your work.

Develop Sorting Shapes Based on Sides

Read and try to solve the problem below.

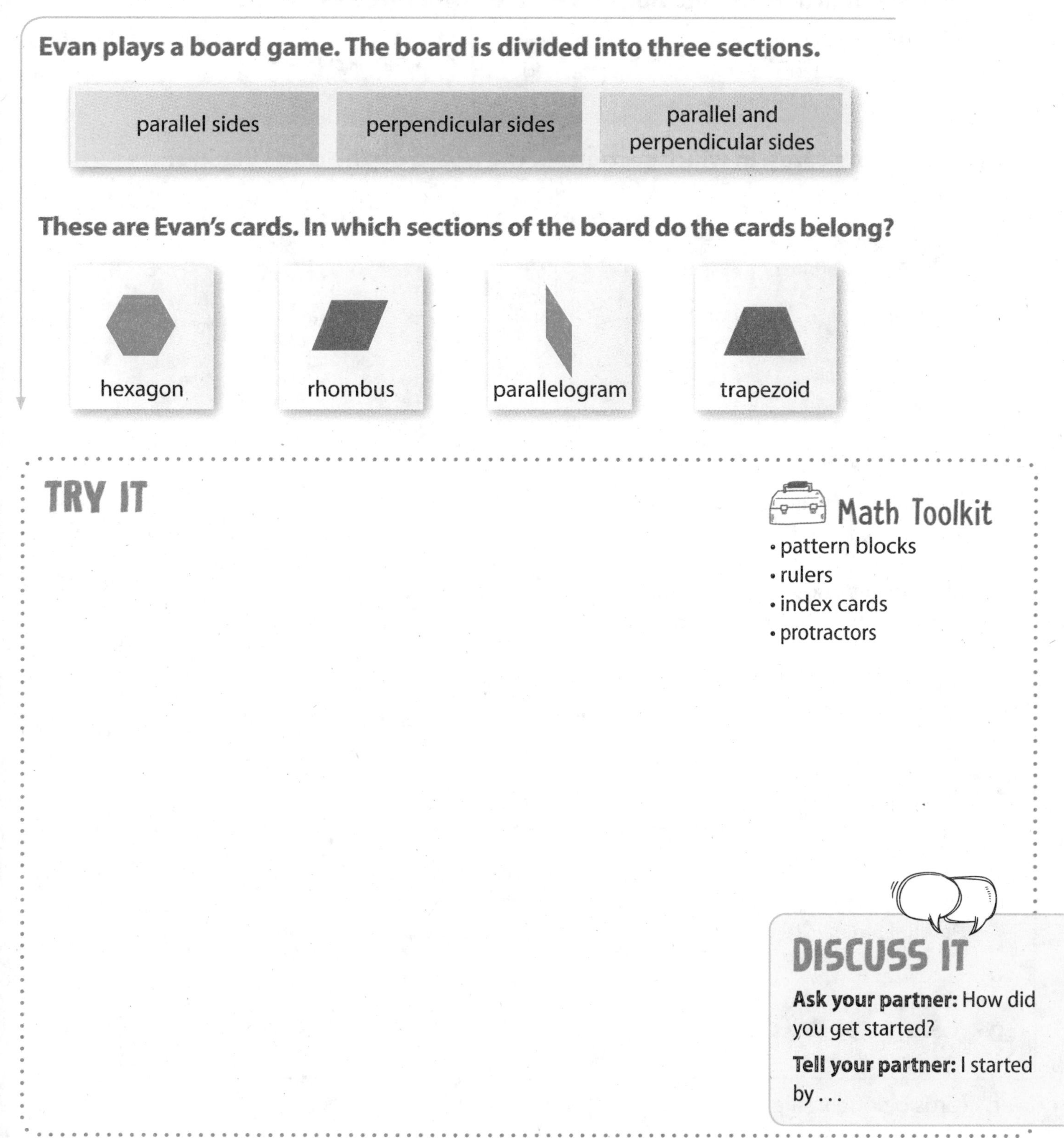

Evan plays a board game. The board is divided into three sections.

parallel sides	perpendicular sides	parallel and perpendicular sides

These are Evan's cards. In which sections of the board do the cards belong?

hexagon · rhombus · parallelogram · trapezoid

TRY IT

Math Toolkit
- pattern blocks
- rulers
- index cards
- protractors

DISCUSS IT

Ask your partner: How did you get started?

Tell your partner: I started by . . .

Explore different ways to understand how to sort shapes into groups based on parallel and perpendicular sides.

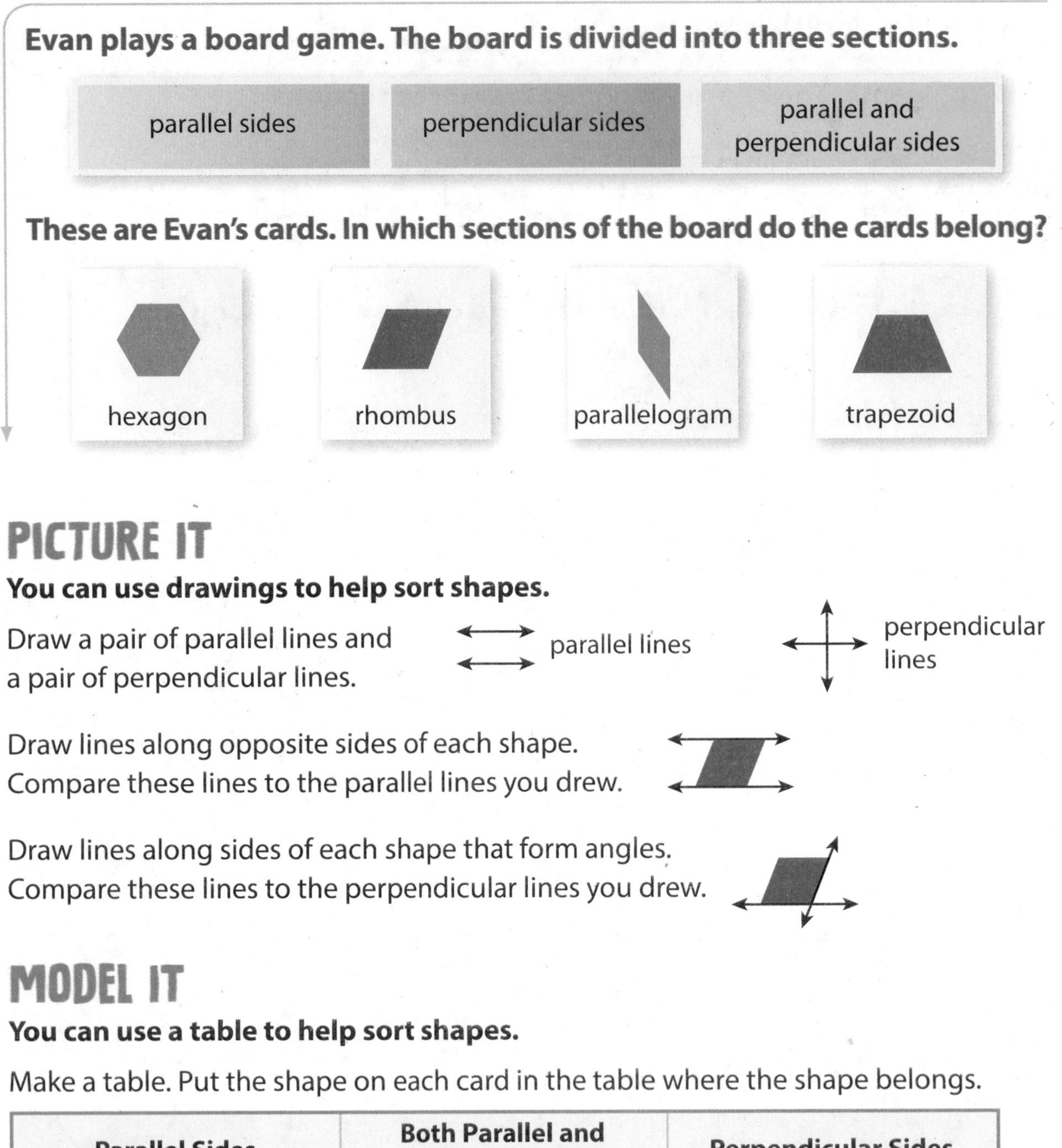

Evan plays a board game. The board is divided into three sections.

parallel sides	perpendicular sides	parallel and perpendicular sides

These are Evan's cards. In which sections of the board do the cards belong?

PICTURE IT

You can use drawings to help sort shapes.

Draw a pair of parallel lines and a pair of perpendicular lines.

Draw lines along opposite sides of each shape. Compare these lines to the parallel lines you drew.

Draw lines along sides of each shape that form angles. Compare these lines to the perpendicular lines you drew.

MODEL IT

You can use a table to help sort shapes.

Make a table. Put the shape on each card in the table where the shape belongs.

Parallel Sides	Both Parallel and Perpendicular Sides	Perpendicular Sides
hexagon, rhombus, parallelogram, trapezoid (shapes)		

Evan's cards belong in the "Parallel Sides" column of the table.

CONNECT IT

Now you will solve a problem similar to the one on the previous page to help you understand how to sort shapes into groups based on parallel and perpendicular sides. Evan gets two more cards. In which sections of the board do the cards with these shapes belong?

square

quadrilateral

1. Evan gets a card with a square. In which section of the board does it belong?

2. Evan gets a card with a quadrilateral. Does the quadrilateral belong to any of the three categories on the board? If not, name a category that can be used to describe this shape.

3. Explain how to sort shapes based on parallel and perpendicular sides.

REFLECT

Look back at your **Try It**, strategies by classmates, and **Picture It** and **Model It**. Which models or strategies do you like best for sorting shapes into groups based on parallel and perpendicular sides? Explain.

APPLY IT

Use what you just learned to solve these problems.

5 Describe the group that the shapes below belong in based on the kinds of sides they have.

Solution ....

6 Circle the shape below that belongs in the group: "no parallel sides."

7 Select all the shapes that always have pairs of perpendicular sides.

Ⓐ hexagon

Ⓑ parallelogram

Ⓒ rectangle

Ⓓ rhombus

Ⓔ square

Ⓕ trapezoid

Name: ______________________________

Practice Sorting Shapes Based on Sides

Study the Example showing how to sort shapes into groups based on parallel and perpendicular sides. Then solve problems 1–4.

EXAMPLE

Sort the shapes below based on parallel and perpendicular sides.
Put the shapes in the table below.

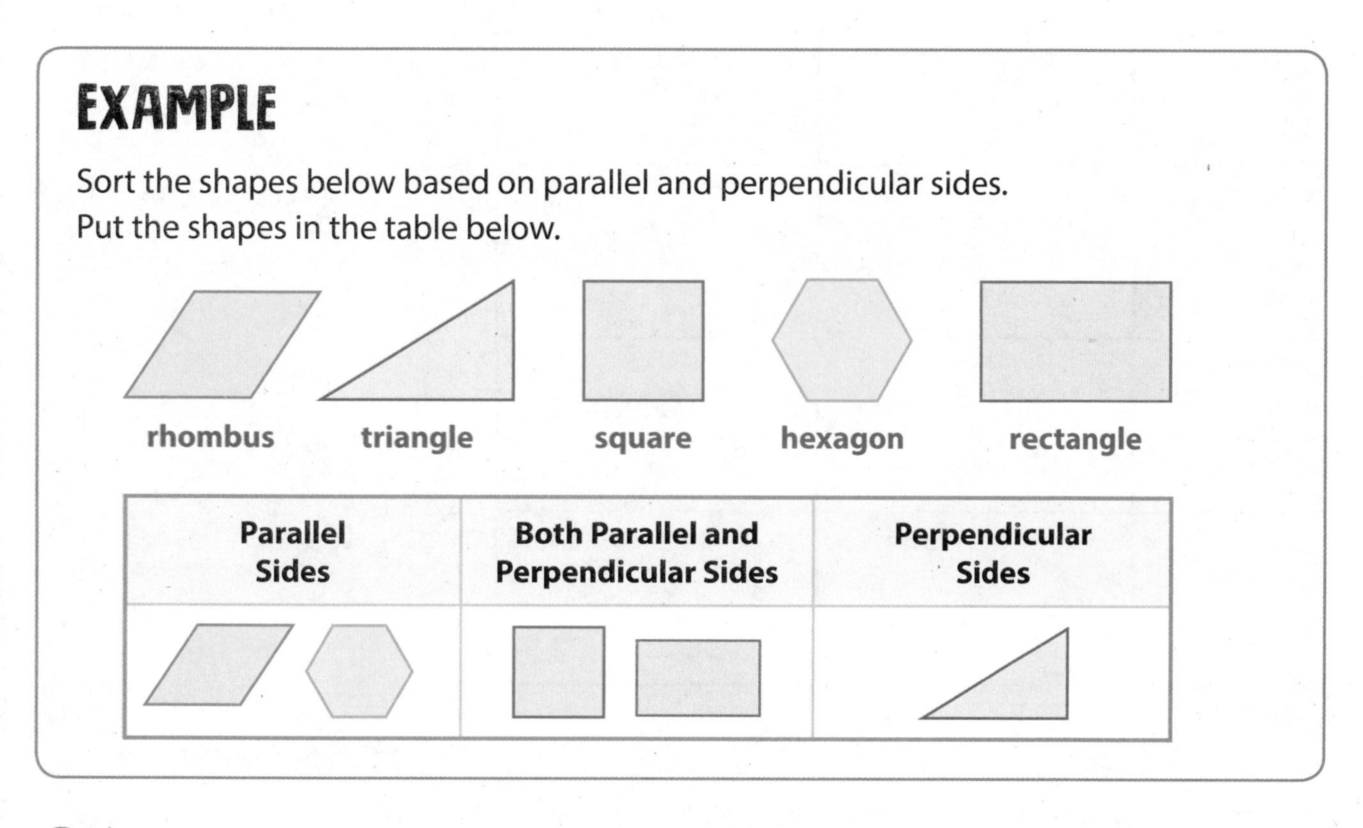

1 Look at how the shapes in the Example above are sorted into groups. Then look at the shape at the right. Which group does the shape belong in?

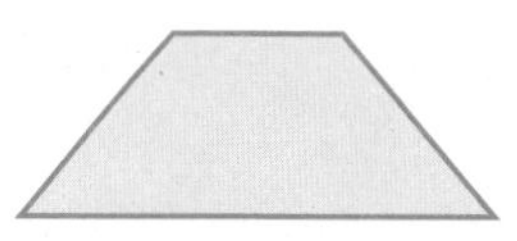

Solution ....

2 Suppose there is another group for shapes: "no parallel or perpendicular sides." Circle the shapes below that belong in this group.

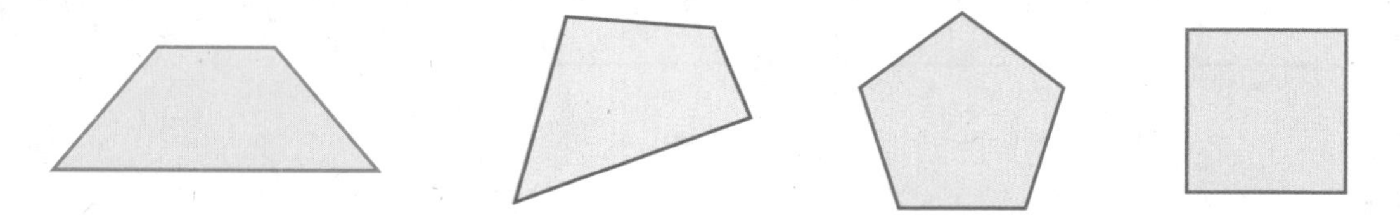

Select the kinds of sides each shape has.

	Parallel Sides	Perpendicular Sides
	Ⓐ	Ⓑ
	Ⓒ	Ⓓ
	Ⓔ	Ⓕ
	Ⓖ	Ⓗ

Select all the properties that always belong to each shape.

	Parallel Sides	Perpendicular Sides
rectangle	Ⓐ	Ⓑ
rhombus	Ⓒ	Ⓓ
square	Ⓔ	Ⓕ

Develop Sorting Shapes Based on Angles

Read and try to solve the problem below.

A classroom computer game shows a set of categories and a set of shapes. The player puts each shape in the correct category. Draw a line from each shape to the category it belongs in.

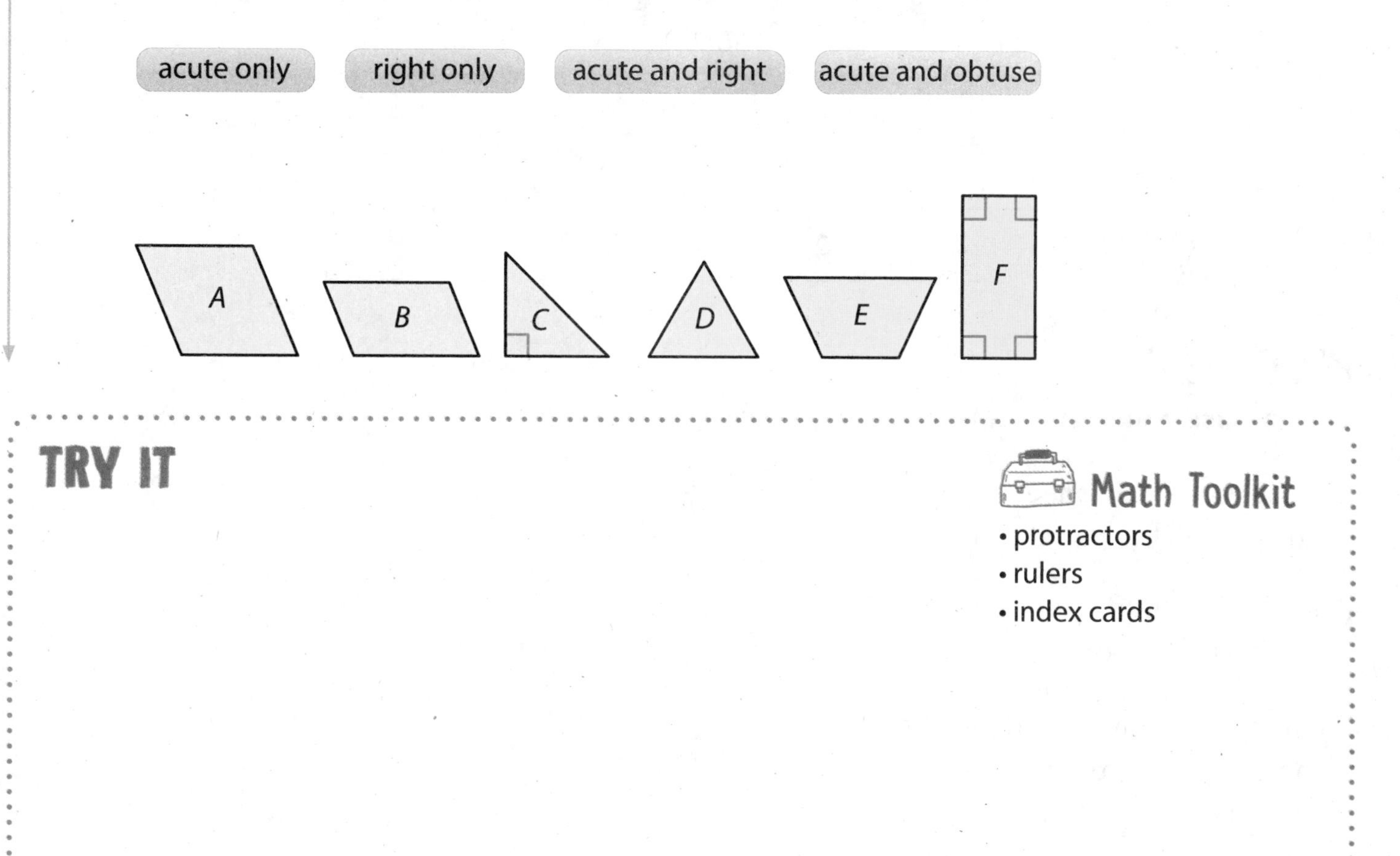

TRY IT

Math Toolkit
- protractors
- rulers
- index cards

DISCUSS IT

Ask your partner: Do you agree with me? Why or why not?

Tell your partner: I agree with you about . . . because . . .

Explore different ways to understand how to sort shapes into categories based on angles.

A classroom computer game shows a set of categories and a set of shapes. The player puts each shape in the correct category. Draw a line from each shape to the category it belongs in.

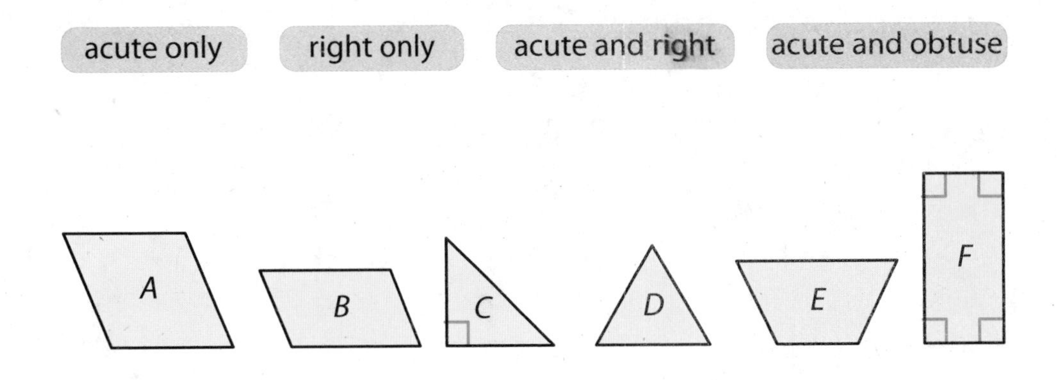

PICTURE IT

You can use a model to help sort shapes based on angles.

Use the corner of a sheet of paper as a model of a right angle. Compare each angle to the paper corner.

For example, hold up the paper corner to the trapezoid.

This angle opens wider than a right angle. The angle is **obtuse**.

Then you can compare the paper corner to each of the other 3 angles in the trapezoid.

MODEL IT

You can label a drawing to help sort shapes based on angles.

Look at each shape. Mark each angle *a* for acute, *r* for right, or *o* for obtuse.

For example, mark the trapezoid like this:

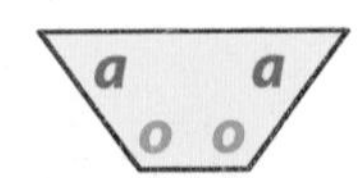

The trapezoid has 2 acute angles and 2 obtuse angles. It belongs in the group "acute and obtuse."

Remember to look at all of the angles in a shape before you put it in a group.

CONNECT IT

Now you will use the problem from the previous page to help you understand how to sort shapes into categories based on angles.

1. Look at parallelograms *A* and *B*. Check that you have drawn lines to the correct group(s). Do the two parallelograms belong to the same group? Explain.

2. Look at the two triangles. Check that you have drawn lines to match the triangles with their group(s). Describe the angles in each triangle.

3. Look at the trapezoid and rectangle. Which has right angles only? ....
Look at **Picture It**. To which group does the trapezoid belong?
.... Check that you have drawn lines to the correct group(s).

4. Explain how to sort shapes based on whether they have acute, right, or obtuse angles.

5. REFLECT

Look back at your **Try It**, strategies by classmates, and **Picture It** and **Model It**. Which models or strategies do you like best for sorting shapes based on angles? Explain.

....

....

....

APPLY IT

Use what you just learned to solve these problems.

6 Which of these groups does the rhombus below belong in: "acute angles only," "obtuse angles only," "right angles only," "both acute and obtuse angles," or "both right and obtuse angles"? Explain.

7 Circle the shape that has an acute angle, a right angle, and an obtuse angle.

 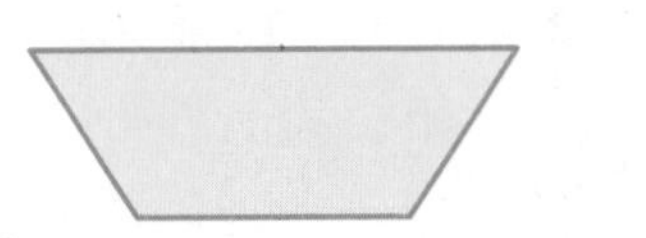 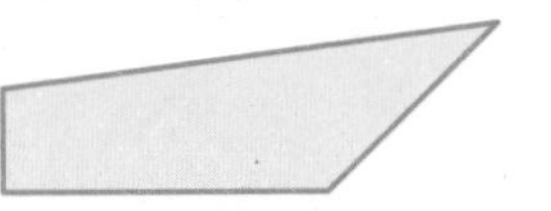

8 The shapes below have been sorted into two groups based on their angles. Explain how the shapes could have been sorted.

Group 1

Group 2

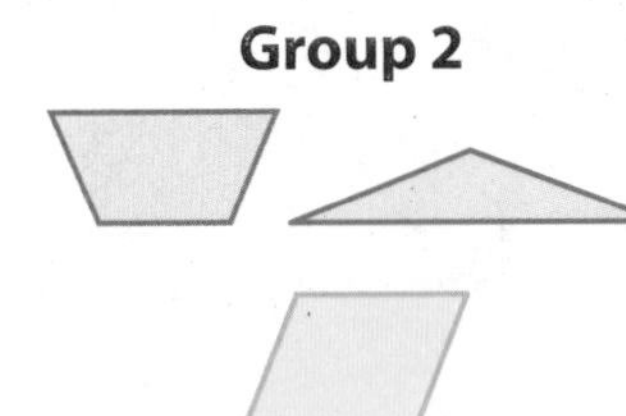

Name: ____________________

Practice Sorting Shapes Based on Angles

Study the Example showing how to sort shapes into groups based on angles. Then solve problems 1–5.

EXAMPLE

Label each angle in the shapes below with *a* for acute, *r* for right, and *o* for obtuse. Then draw a line from each shape to the group it belongs in.

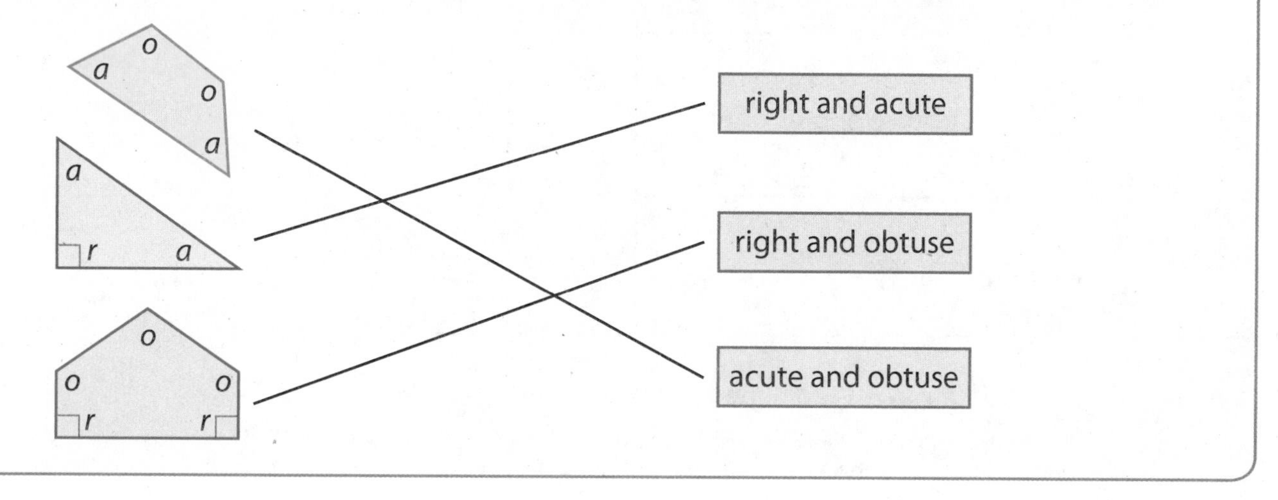

1 Write the number of acute, right, and obtuse angles for each pentagon shown in the table below.

	Acute	Right	Obtuse
X			
Y			

2 Explain how these pentagons are different based on their angles.

Solution ....

....

 Tell whether each shape belongs in the group described.

	Yes	No
all right angles	Ⓐ	Ⓑ
right and acute angles	Ⓒ	Ⓓ
obtuse and acute angles	Ⓔ	Ⓕ
right and obtuse angles only	Ⓖ	Ⓗ
all obtuse angles	Ⓘ	Ⓙ

4 Describe a group that the two shapes at the right belong in, based on the kind of angles the shapes have.

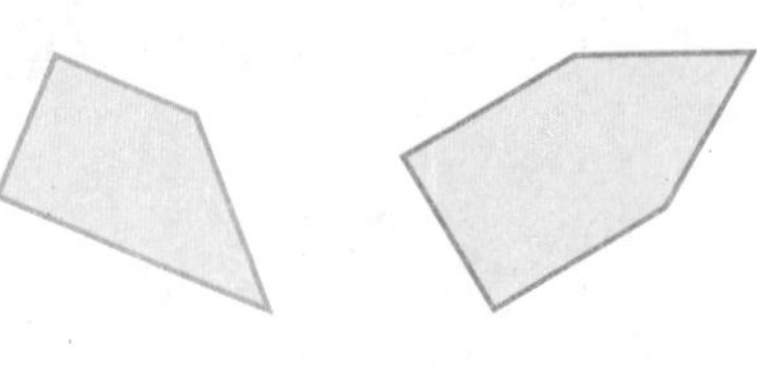

Solution ....

5 Look at the shapes in problem 4. Where do they belong in the table below? Draw each shape in the column in which it belongs. Explain your answer.

Acute and Obtuse Angles	Acute and Right Angles	Obtuse and Right Angles	Acute, Right, and Obtuse Angles

Develop Sorting Triangles

Read and try to solve the problem below.

A website sells 7 kinds of triangular flags based on sides and angles.

Flag	Equal Sides	Angles
1	3	3 acute
2	2	2 acute, 1 right
3	2	2 acute, 1 obtuse
4	2	3 acute

Flag	Equal Sides	Angles
5	0	2 acute, 1 right
6	0	2 acute, 1 obtuse
7	0	3 acute

The triangle at the right is a model for which flag number?

10 in.
7 in.
10 in.

TRY IT

Math Toolkit
- protractors
- rulers
- index cards

DISCUSS IT

Ask your partner: Why did you choose that strategy?

Tell your partner: I do not understand how . . .

Explore different ways to understand how to sort triangles into groups based on kinds of angles and lengths of sides.

A website sells 7 kinds of triangular flags based on sides and angles.

Flag	Equal Sides	Angles
1	3	3 acute
2	2	2 acute, 1 right
3	2	2 acute, 1 obtuse
4	2	3 acute

Flag	Equal Sides	Angles
5	0	2 acute, 1 right
6	0	2 acute, 1 obtuse
7	0	3 acute

The triangle at the right is a model for which flag number?

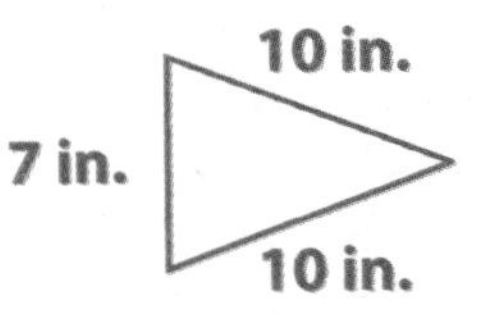

PICTURE IT

You can use a picture to help describe the sides and angles of triangles.

Compare the angles of the triangle to a right angle. The triangle has 3 acute angles.

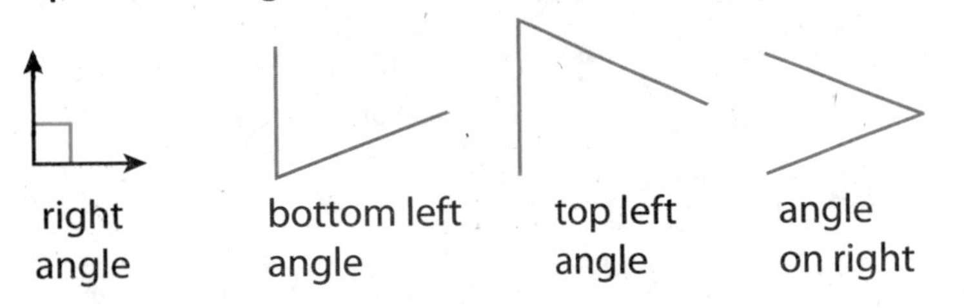

The triangle has 2 sides of equal length (10 in.). Flag 4 has **2 sides of equal length** and **3 acute angles**. The triangle is a model for flag 4.

The tables below show triangle names based on the number of sides of equal length and kinds of angles.

Name	Description of Sides
equilateral	3 equal sides
isosceles	**2 equal sides**
scalene	0 equal sides

Name	Description of Angles
acute	**3 acute angles**
right	1 right angle
obtuse	1 obtuse angle

The triangle has 2 equal sides, so it is an **isosceles triangle**. Since it has 3 acute angles, it is an **acute triangle**.

CONNECT IT

Now you will use the problem from the previous page to help you understand how to sort triangles into groups based on kinds of angles and lengths of sides and how to name triangles.

1. Look back at the model for the triangular flag. Fill in the blanks to name this triangle based on its angles and sides: .... triangle

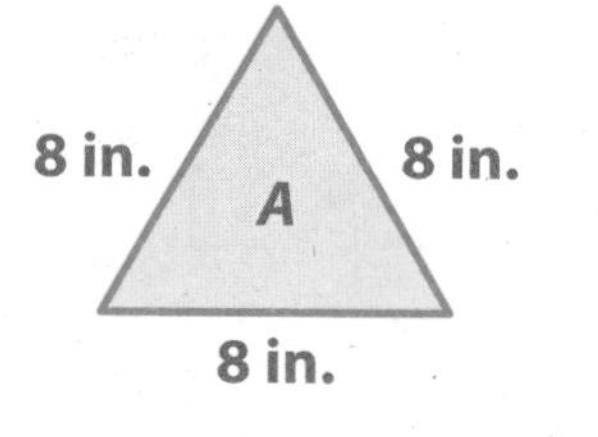

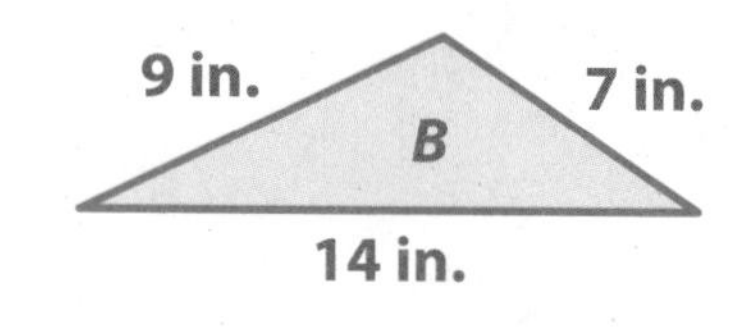

2. Look at triangle *A* above. How many sides are the same length? ....

   What kinds of angles does it have? ....

   What are two names for this triangle? ....

3. What are two names for triangle *B*? ....

   Can triangle *B* also be called an acute triangle? Why or why not?

4. Explain how to give a complete description of a triangle.

5. REFLECT

   Look back at your **Try It**, strategies by classmates, and **Picture It**. Which models or strategies do you like best for sorting triangles into groups based on kinds of angles and lengths of sides and for naming triangles? Explain.

   ....

   ....

   ....

APPLY IT

Use what you just learned to solve these problems.

6 Give a complete description of the triangle below. Show your work.

Solution ....

7 What do the triangles below have in common? How are they different?

Solution ....

....

....

8 Which figure is an acute isosceles triangle?

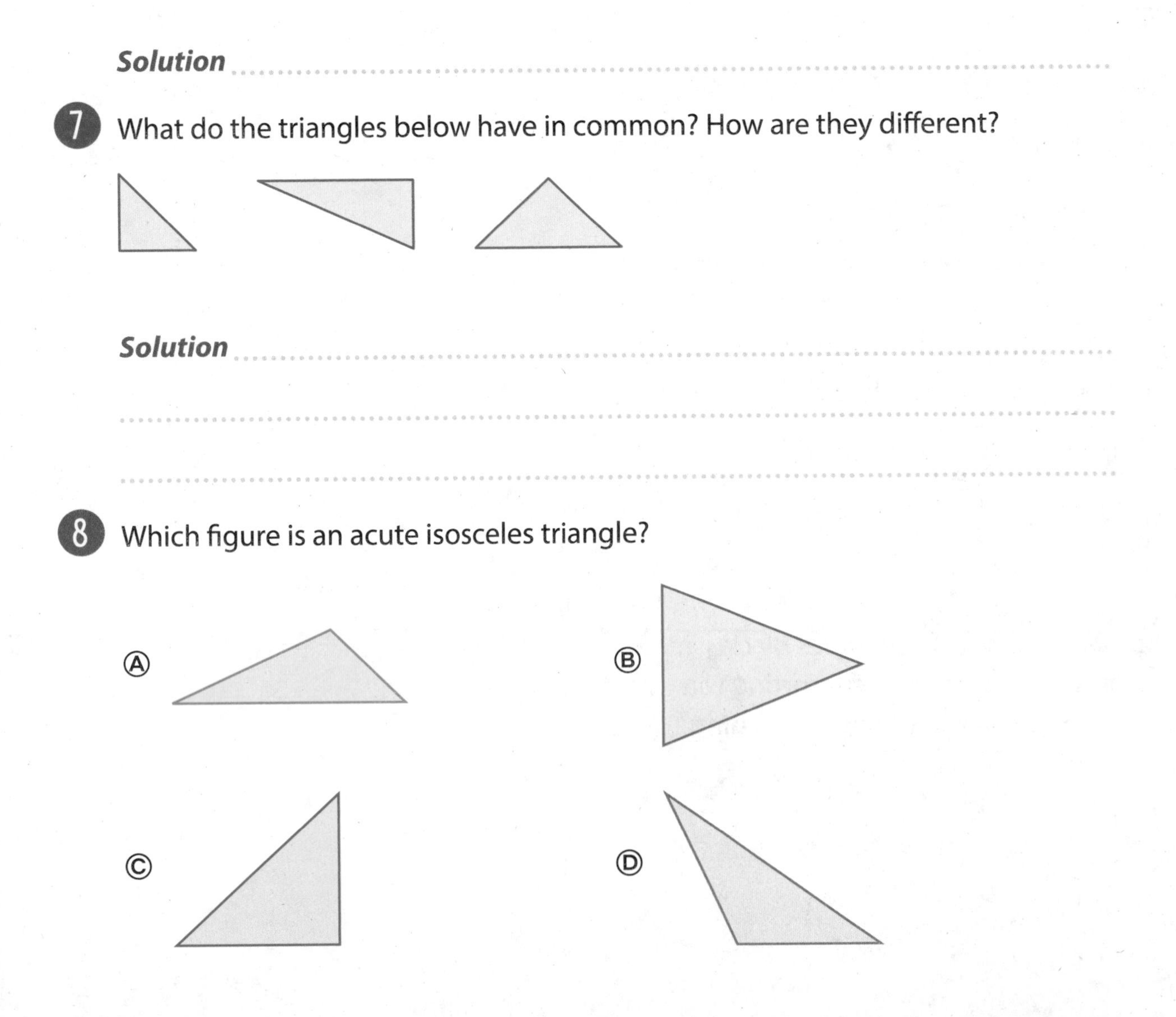

Name: ____________________

Practice Sorting Triangles

Study the Example showing how to sort triangles into groups based on kinds of angles and lengths of sides. Then solve problems 1–4.

EXAMPLE

What is the same about the two triangles shown at the right? What is different?

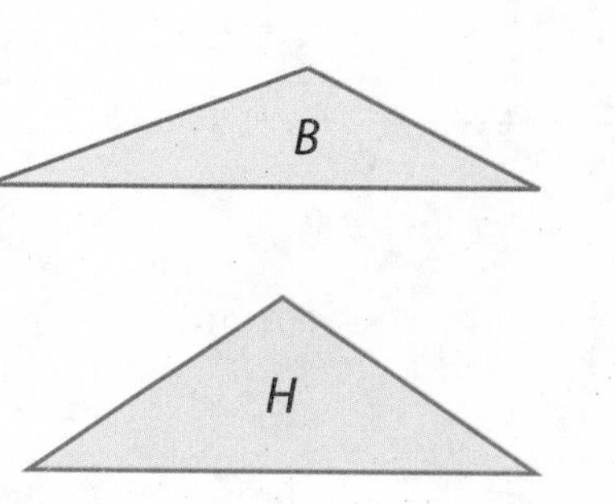

You can sort triangles into groups based on the kinds of angles they have: acute, right, or obtuse.

You can also sort triangles based on the lengths of their sides.

equilateral: 3 equal sides
isosceles: 2 equal sides
scalene: 0 equal sides

Triangles *B* and *H* are the same because they are both obtuse triangles. They each have 1 obtuse angle.

Triangles *B* and *H* are different because triangle *B* is a scalene triangle and triangle *H* is an isosceles triangle.

1. Look at the table. Name each triangle below based on the kinds of angles that it has and the lengths of its sides.

Name	Description of Angles
acute	3 acute angles
right	1 right angle
obtuse	1 obtuse angle

Name	Description of Sides
equilateral	3 equal sides
isosceles	2 equal sides
scalene	0 equal sides

5 m, 13 m, 12 m

14 m, 14 m, 14 m

25 m, 15 m, 15 m

....

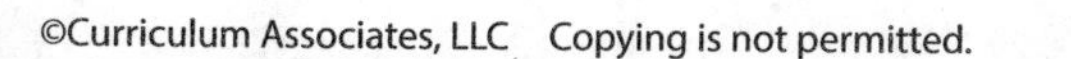

2 Look at the name of each triangle below. Then use the numbers in the boxes to write the missing length for one side of each triangle.

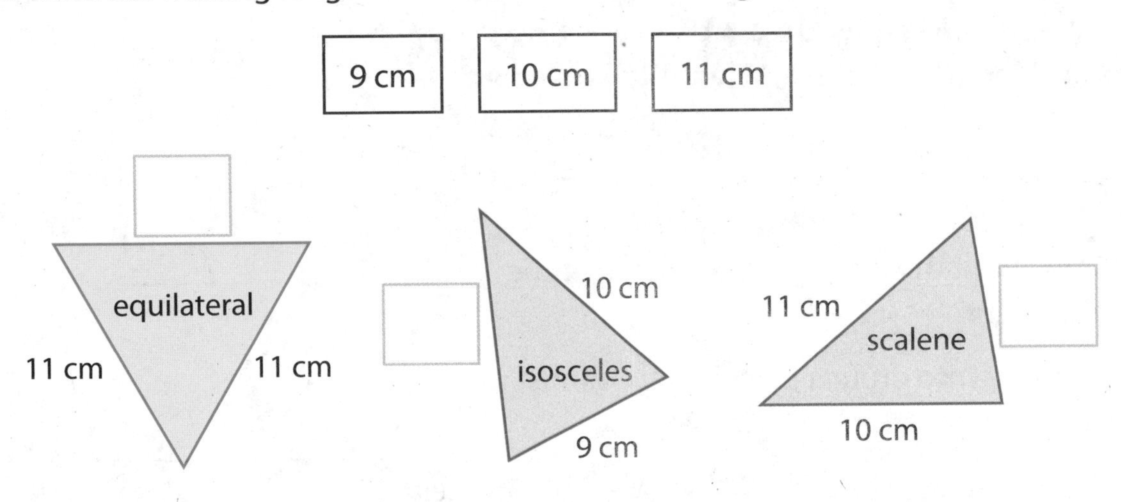

3 Write labels inside each triangle formed by the lines in the drawing below: *a* for acute, *r* for right, *o* for obtuse, *e* for equilateral, *i* for isosceles, *s* for scalene.

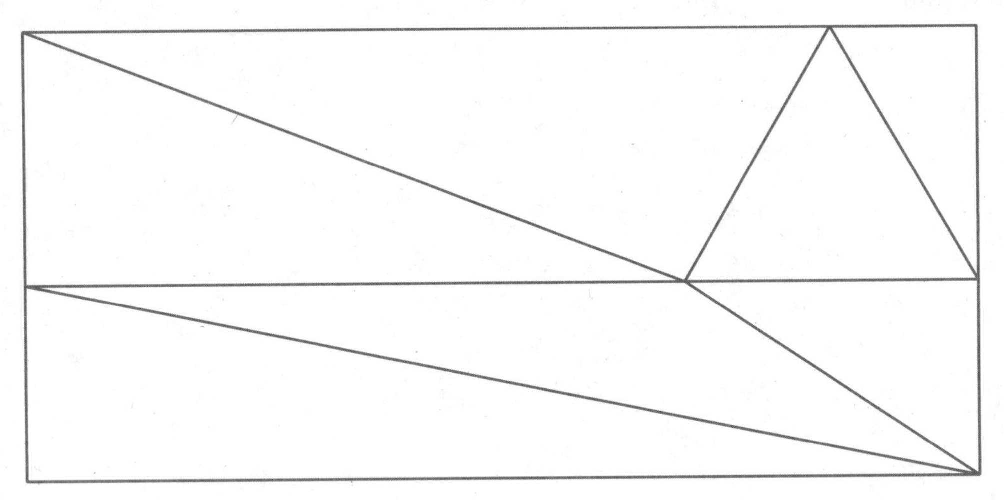

4 Which statements below are true?

Ⓐ An obtuse triangle does not have acute angles.

Ⓑ A scalene triangle can be isosceles.

Ⓒ Equilateral triangles are always acute.

Ⓓ Isosceles triangles can be obtuse.

Ⓔ Right triangles are scalene or isosceles.

Refine Classifying Two-Dimensional Figures

Complete the Example below. Then solve problems 1–7.

EXAMPLE

Do any of the shapes below have at least one pair of parallel sides and at least one right angle? If yes, list the shapes. If no, explain.

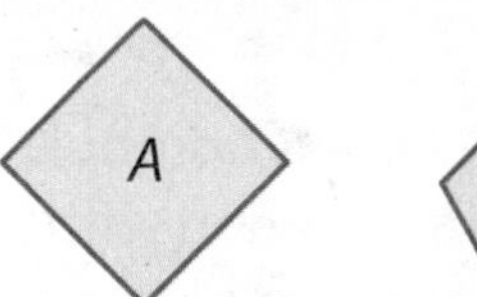

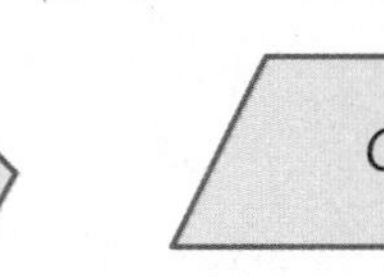

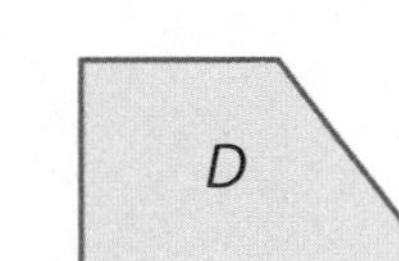

D

Look at how you could show your work using a table.

Shape	Parallel Sides	Right Angle
A	X	X
B		X
C	X	
D	X	X

Solution ....

The student listed each shape in a table and used an X to show that a shape had parallel sides or a right angle.

PAIR/SHARE
How could you test for parallel sides?

APPLY IT

1 Nate and Alicia play Draw My Shape. Nate says: *My shape has 2 pairs of parallel sides, 2 acute angles, and 2 obtuse angles*. Alicia draws the rectangle below. Explain why Alicia's answer is incorrect.

Solution ....

....

You can test the angles to see if they are acute, right, or obtuse.

PAIR/SHARE
Can you have a 4-sided shape with 4 right angles and only 1 pair of parallel sides?

 Tell how the sides and angles of the shapes below are alike and different.

square

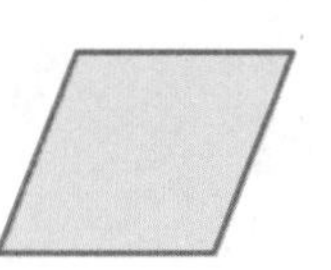
rhombus

All the square's angles look alike, but the rhombus looks like it has two different kinds of angles.

Solution ....

....

....

PAIR/SHARE
What does a rhombus have in common with a parallelogram?

3 Which is the best name for the triangle shown?

How many right angles does a triangle have to have to be called a "right triangle"?

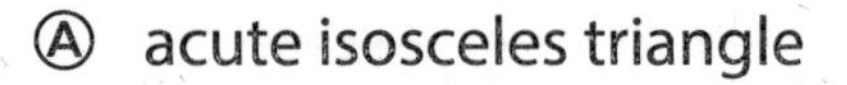

Ⓐ acute isosceles triangle

Ⓑ acute scalene triangle

Ⓒ right isosceles triangle

Ⓓ right scalene triangle

Ricky chose Ⓑ as the correct answer. How did he get that answer?

PAIR/SHARE
Could a triangle ever have 2 right angles?

4 Which is the best name for the group of shapes below?

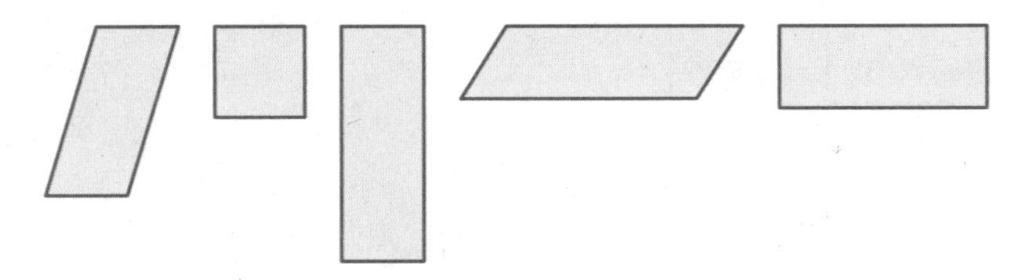

Ⓐ shapes with acute angles

Ⓑ shapes with right angles

Ⓒ shapes with parallel sides

Ⓓ shapes with perpendicular sides

5 Sort the four shapes below. Use the characteristics shown in the table. Draw each shape in each column where it belongs. Some shapes may belong in more than one column.

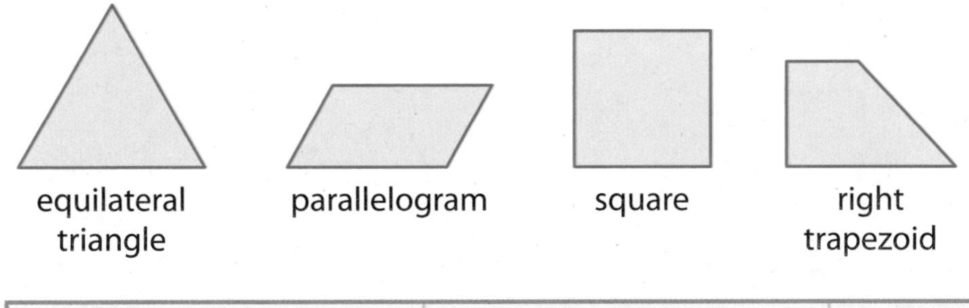

Shapes with at Least One Acute Angle	Shapes with at Least One Pair of Perpendicular Sides	Shapes with at Least One Pair of Parallel Sides

6 Tell whether each sentence is *True* or *False*.

	True	False
A right scalene triangle can have 3 different kinds of angles.	Ⓐ	Ⓑ
A right isosceles triangle has 2 right angles.	Ⓒ	Ⓓ
An equilateral triangle is also an acute triangle.	Ⓔ	Ⓕ
A triangle can have 2 perpendicular sides.	Ⓖ	Ⓗ

7 MATH JOURNAL

Divide the shapes below into two groups. Give each group a title that tells what all the shapes in that group have in common. Then describe another shape that belongs to each group.

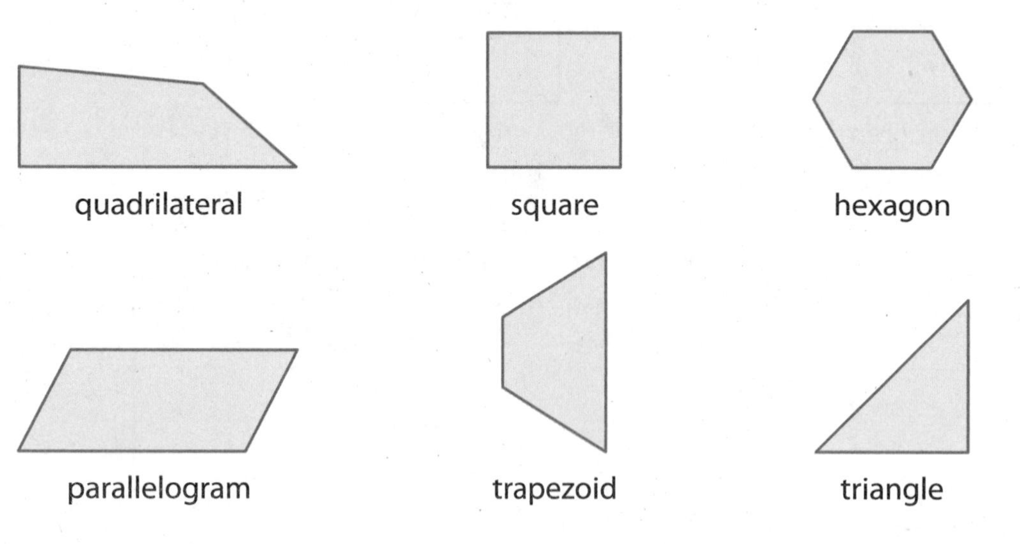

☑ SELF CHECK Go back to the Unit 5 Opener and see what you can check off.

Symmetry

Dear Family,

This week your child is learning about symmetry.

You can find symmetrical shapes in real life, in both natural and man-made objects.

A **line of symmetry** is a line that divides a shape into two mirror images.

Your child is learning to identify lines of symmetry in shapes.

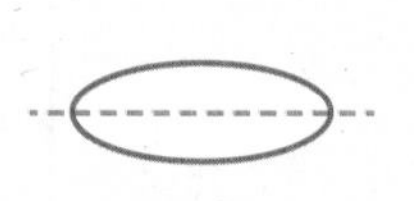

The horizontal line divides the oval into two matching parts. It is a line of symmetry.

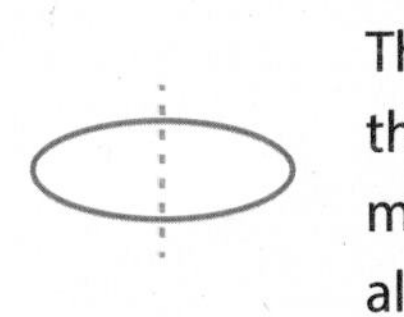

The vertical line divides the oval into two matching parts. It is also a line of symmetry.

Your child is also learning to draw lines of symmetry. One way to do that is to imagine folding a shape in different ways.

To draw lines of symmetry in this shape forming a plus sign, imagine each way it could be folded to form matching parts.

Invite your child to share what he or she knows about symmetry by doing the following activity together.

ACTIVITY SYMMETRY

Do this activity with your child to explore symmetry.

- Look together at the shapes below. Discuss which shapes you think have at least one line of symmetry.
- Describe to each other where the line(s) of symmetry could be drawn.
- Have your child draw the lines of symmetry on the shapes.
- Carefully cut out each shape and fold the shape along the line(s) of symmetry that your child drew.
- Talk about whether each line divides the shape into two matching parts.

Answers: rectangle: 1 horizontal and 1 vertical line of symmetry; square with curved corners: 1 horizontal and 1 vertical line of symmetry, 2 diagonal lines of symmetry; smiley face: 1 vertical line of symmetry; block with arrow: 1 horizontal line of symmetry

Explore Symmetry

Learning Target

- Recognize a line of symmetry for a two-dimensional figure as a line across the figure such that the figure can be folded along the line into matching parts. Identify line-symmetric figures and draw lines of symmetry.

SMP 1, 2, 3, 4, 5, 6, 7

You have learned about shapes and lines. Now you will learn about a line with a particular purpose called a *line of symmetry*. Use what you know to try to solve the problem below.

Each of the shapes below has a dashed line drawn across it. Imagine folding each shape along the dashed line. If the two parts would fit exactly on top of each other when the shape is folded, draw a star on the shape. Explain your answers.

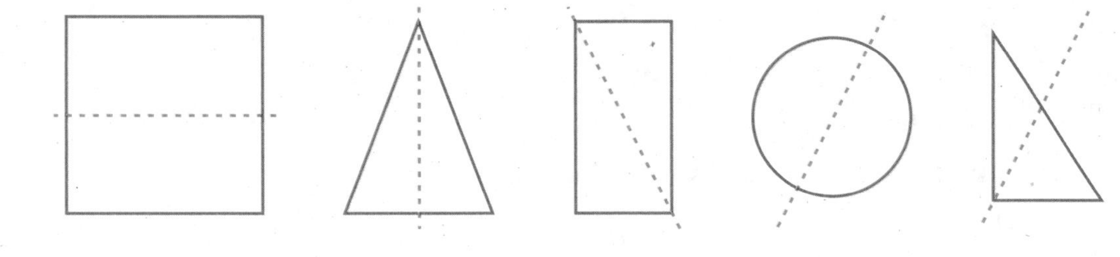

TRY IT

Math Toolkit

- geoboards
- pattern blocks
- rulers
- grid paper
- tracing paper

DISCUSS IT

Ask your partner: Do you agree with me? Why or why not?

Tell your partner: I agree with you about . . . because . . .

CONNECT IT

1 LOOK BACK

Describe how parts that fit exactly on top of each other look and how parts that do not fit exactly on top of each other look.

2 LOOK AHEAD

When you can fold a shape on a line and the parts line up with each other, the line is called a **line of symmetry**. Some shapes have a line of symmetry, and other shapes do not. Shapes can also have more than one line of symmetry.

a. All the lines of symmetry for a square are shown on the square at the right. The lines of symmetry all pass through the center point of the square. How many lines of symmetry does the square have? ....

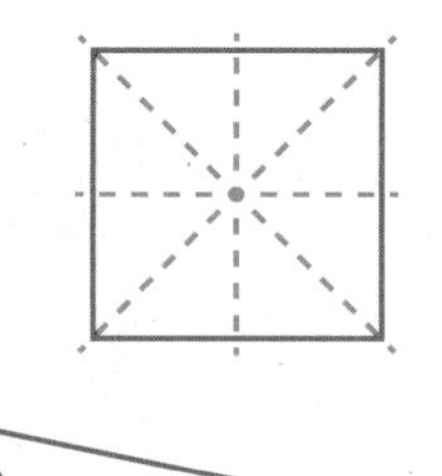

b. Can you draw a line on the scalene triangle so the parts fit exactly on top of each other when folded? How many lines of symmetry does the triangle have? ....

c. Can you draw at least one line of symmetry on each quadrilateral at the right? Explain.

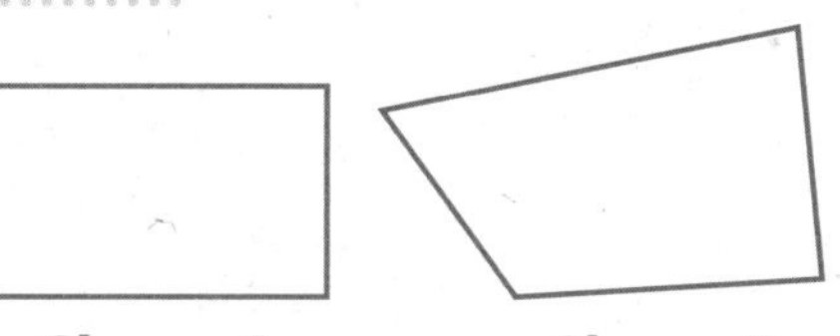

Shape *A* Shape *B*

3 REFLECT

Explain how to tell whether a line that divides a shape into two parts is a line of symmetry.

....

....

Prepare for Symmetry

1 Think about what you know about symmetry. Fill in each box. Use words, numbers, and pictures. Show as many ideas as you can.

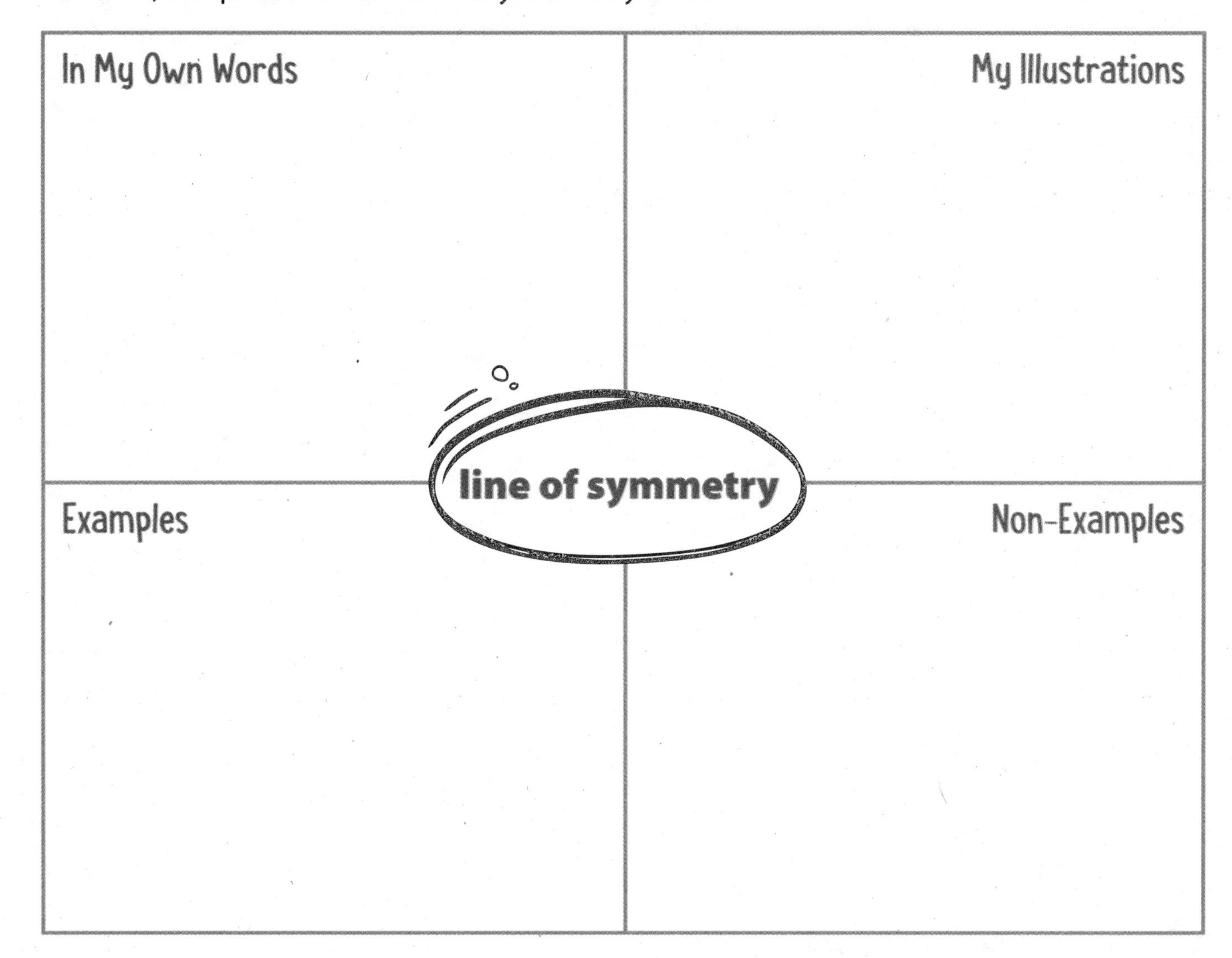

2 Can you draw at least one line of symmetry on each quadrilateral below? Explain.

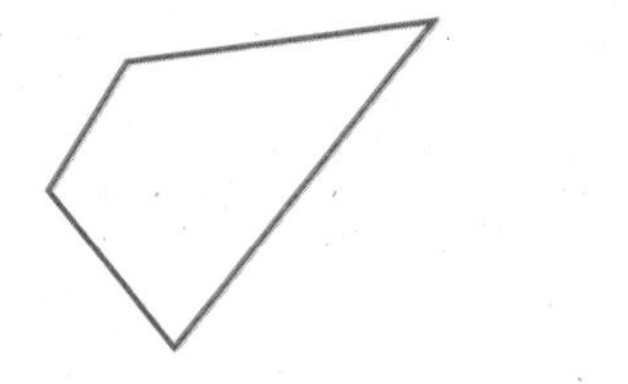

Shape *A*

Shape *B*

3 Solve the problem. Show your work.

Each of the shapes below has a dashed line drawn across it. Imagine folding each shape along the dashed line. If the two parts would fit exactly on top of each other when the shape is folded, draw a star on the shape. Explain your answers.

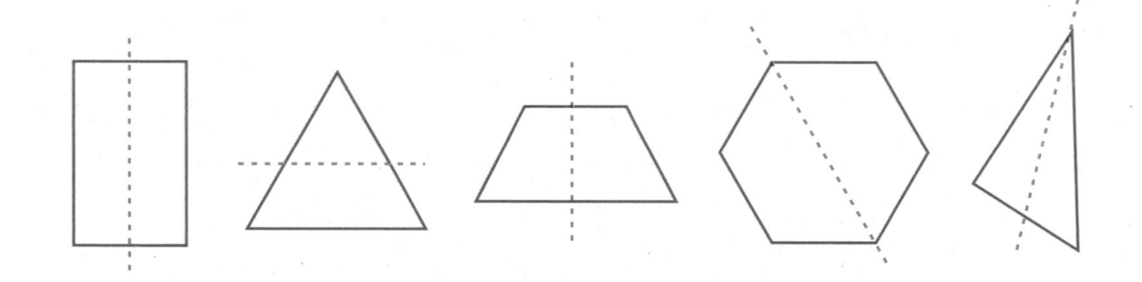

Solution ....

....

....

4 Check your answer. Show your work.

Develop Finding and Drawing a Line of Symmetry

Read and try to solve the problem below.

Draw all of the lines of symmetry for each shape below. How many lines of symmetry does each shape have?

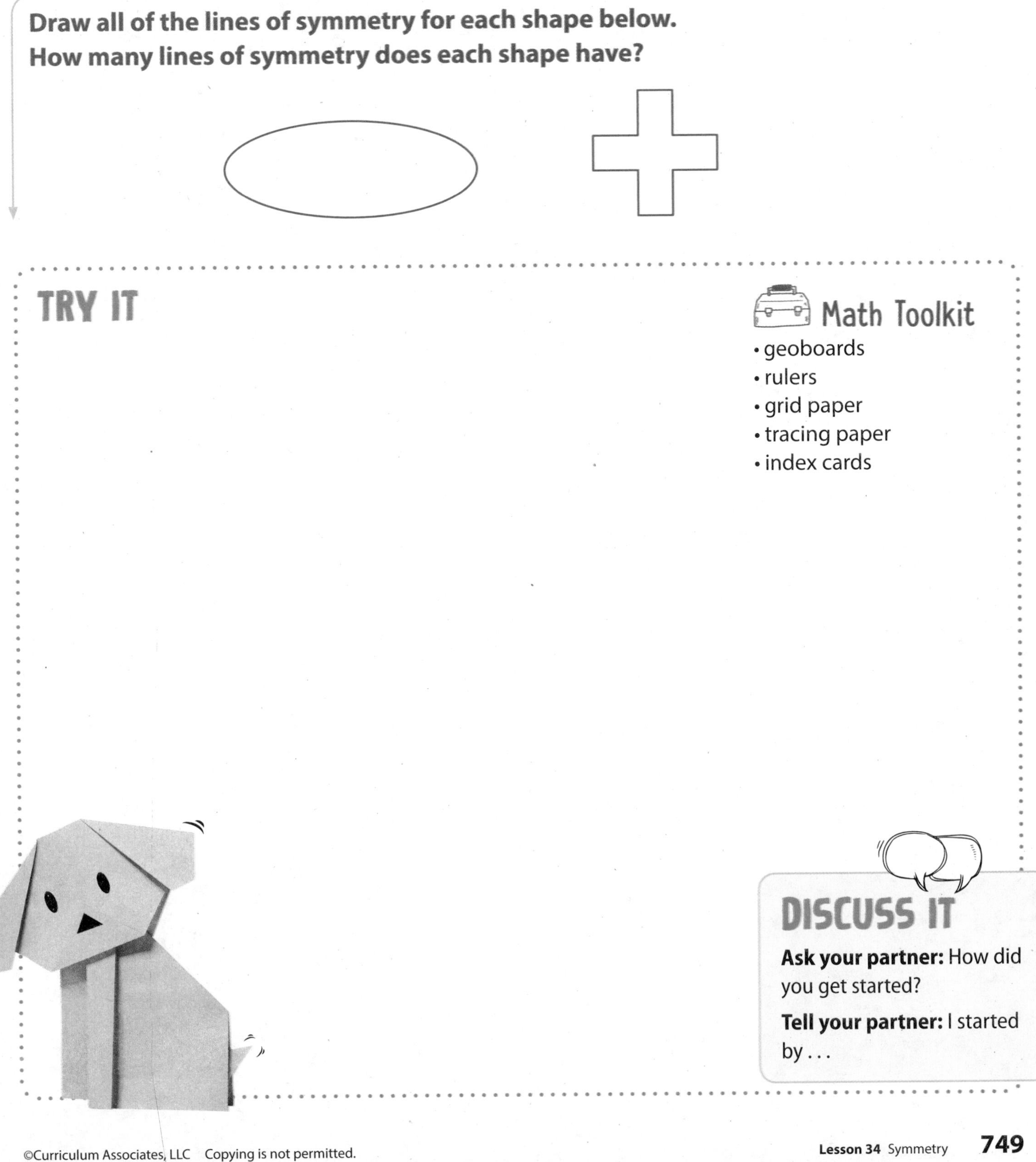

Explore different ways to understand how to find and draw lines of symmetry.

Draw all of the lines of symmetry for each shape below.
How many lines of symmetry does each shape have?

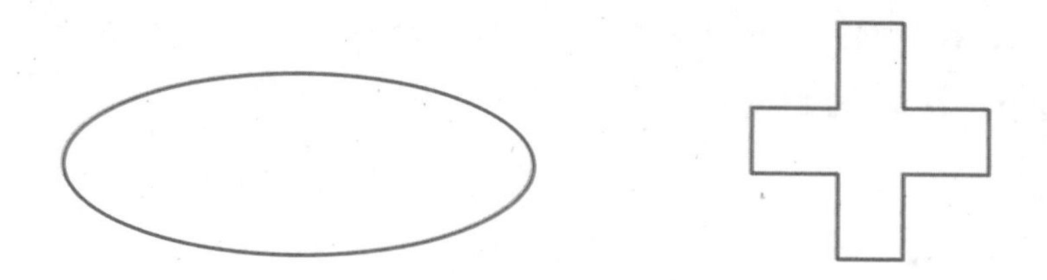

PICTURE IT

You can use drawings to help draw lines of symmetry.

The top and bottom of the oval match, so this shows a line of symmetry.

Another line can be drawn so that the left and right sides of the oval match.

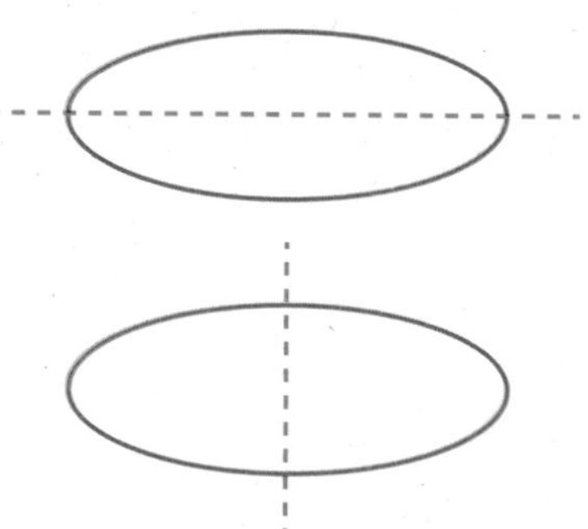

PICTURE IT

You can imagine folding the shape in different ways to draw lines of symmetry.

Look at the plus sign. The lines below show each way it can be folded to form parts that fit on top of each other.

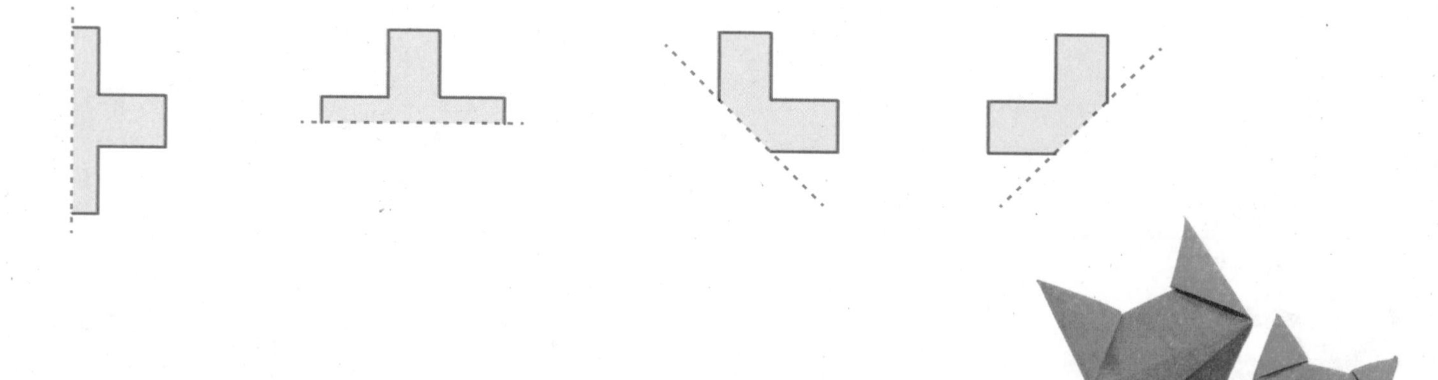

CONNECT IT

Now you will use the problem from the previous page to help you understand how to find and draw lines of symmetry.

1. Check that the lines of symmetry you drew on the oval in **Try It** match the lines shown in the first **Picture It**. What do you notice about the place where all the lines of symmetry cross?

2. Check that the lines of symmetry you drew on the plus sign in **Try It** match the lines shown in the second **Picture It**. Where do the lines of symmetry cross? How does this compare with the oval?

3. How many lines of symmetry does the oval have? ....

4. How many lines of symmetry does the plus sign have? ....

5. Explain how you can decide when you have found all of the lines of symmetry in a shape.

6. **REFLECT**

   Look back at your **Try It**, strategies by classmates, and **Picture Its**. Which models or strategies do you like best for finding and drawing lines of symmetry in a shape? Explain.

APPLY IT

Use what you just learned to solve these problems.

 Circle the shapes below that have a line of symmetry.

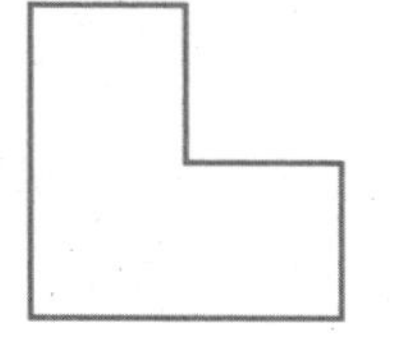  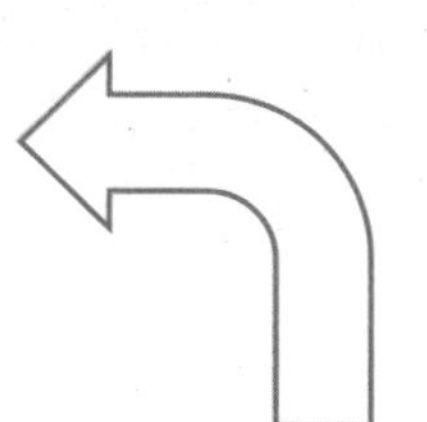 

8 Draw all the lines of symmetry on the tree shape at the right. How many lines of symmetry does the tree shape have?

Solution ....

9 Select all the shapes that show a correctly drawn line of symmetry.

Ⓐ 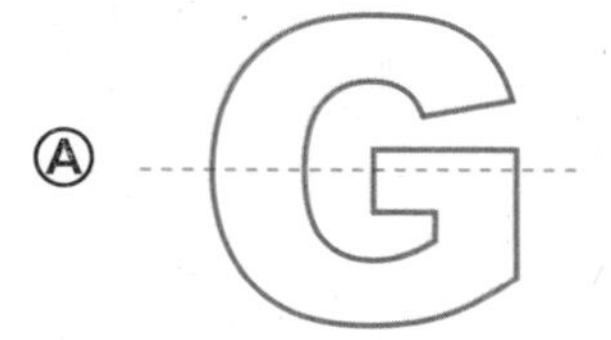

Ⓑ

Ⓒ 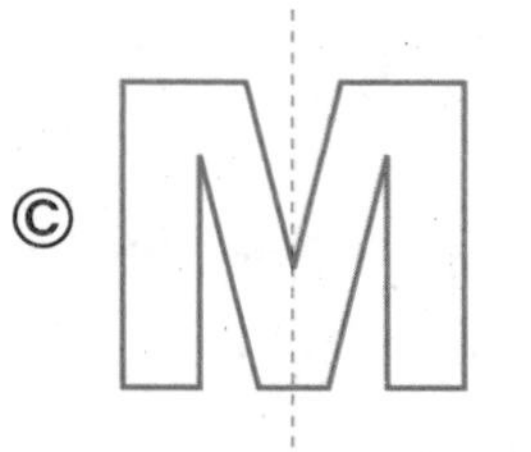

Ⓓ 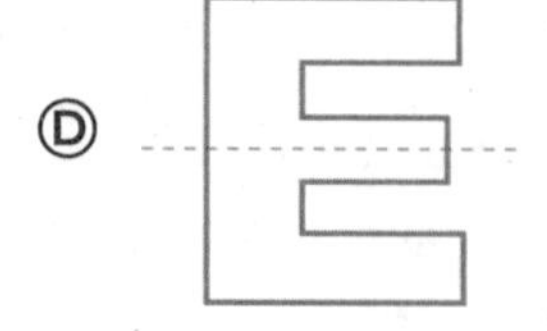

Ⓔ 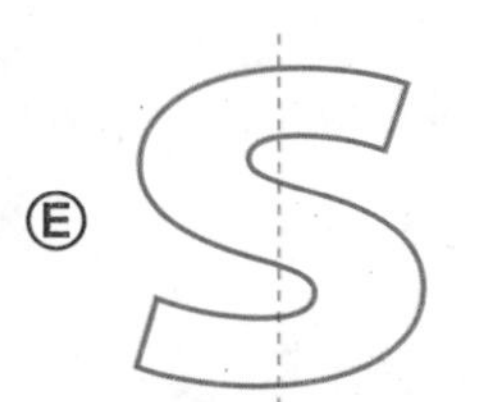

Name: ____________________

Practice Finding and Drawing a Line of Symmetry

Study the Example showing how to find and draw a line of symmetry. Then solve problems 1–5.

EXAMPLE

Find and draw all the lines of symmetry for each star shape. How many lines of symmetry does each shape have? Where do all the lines of symmetry cross?

The 6-pointed star has 6 lines of symmetry.

The 5-pointed star has 5 lines of symmetry.

All the lines of symmetry cross at the center point of each shape.

1. Circle the shape(s) below that have at least one line of symmetry.

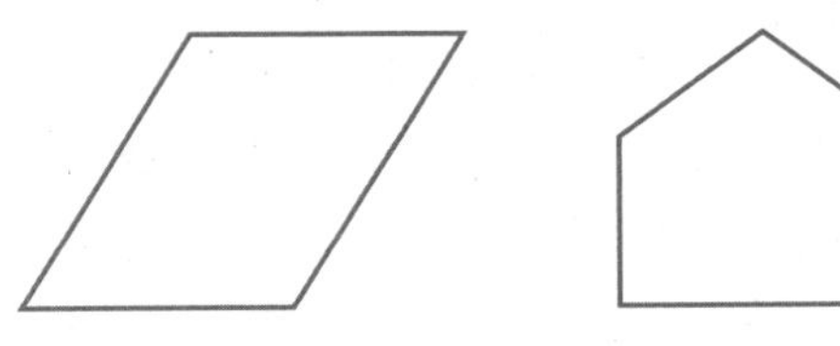

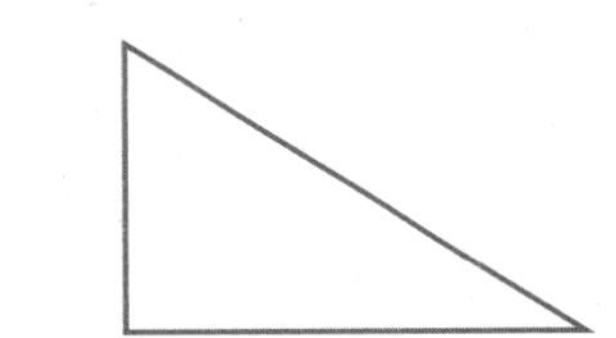

2. Draw all the lines of symmetry on the quadrilaterals below. Circle the quadrilateral that has more lines of symmetry.

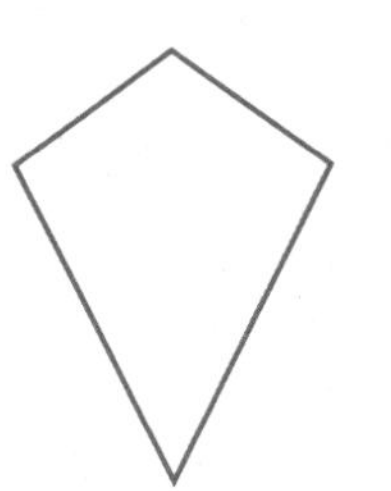

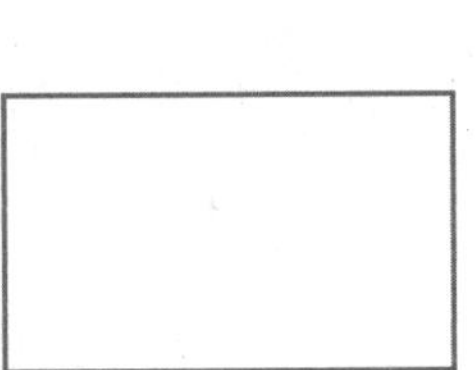

3 Draw all the lines of symmetry on each pentagon below. Write how many lines of symmetry each pentagon has.

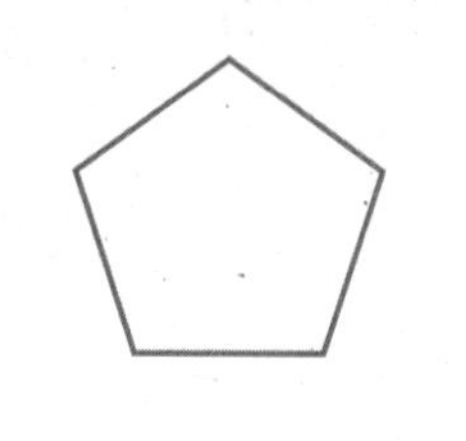

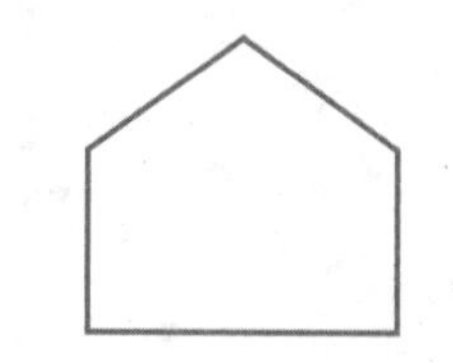

.... line(s) of symmetry

.... line(s) of symmetry

4 Titus draws a hexagon with 6 lines of symmetry. He says that all hexagons have 6 lines of symmetry. Use words and a drawing to explain why Titus's thinking is incorrect.

5 Draw all the lines of symmetry that the design in each flag below has. Then write how many lines of symmetry that the design in each flag has.

line(s) of symmetry

....

line(s) of symmetry

....

Refine Symmetry

Complete the Example below. Then solve problems 1–8.

EXAMPLE

Which of the figures below has fewer lines of symmetry?

Look at how you could explain your work.

The square has lines of symmetry connecting opposite corners and connecting both pairs of opposite sides.

The rectangle only has lines of symmetry connecting opposite sides, not opposite corners.

Solution ....

The student thought about folding the figures to decide where the lines of symmetry are!

PAIR/SHARE
Why do you think that squares and rectangles have different numbers of lines of symmetry?

APPLY IT

1 Name a kind of triangle that has a line of symmetry. Name another kind of triangle that does not have a line of symmetry. Show your work.

Solution ....

....

....

What are the kinds of triangles that are named by their sides?

PAIR/SHARE
What is different about the triangle that has a line of symmetry and the one that does not have a line of symmetry?

 Draw all the lines of symmetry on the hexagon below. How many lines of symmetry does the hexagon have?

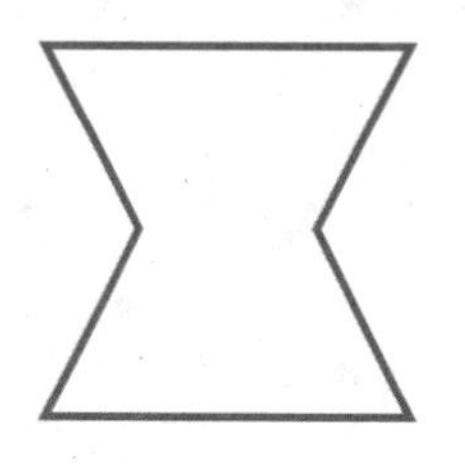

What point in a figure do all lines of symmetry pass through?

Solution ....

PAIR/SHARE
Draw the figure on a sheet of grid paper and cut it out to check the lines of symmetry.

3 Which figure shows the correct line(s) of symmetry?

Imagine folding the figures in half along the lines.

Ⓐ 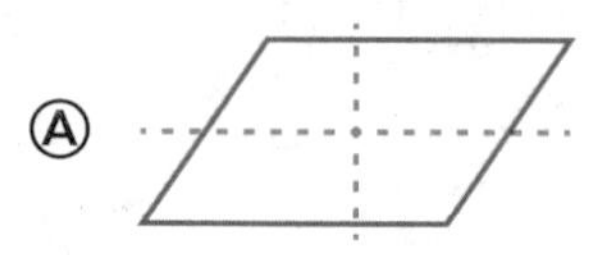

Ⓑ 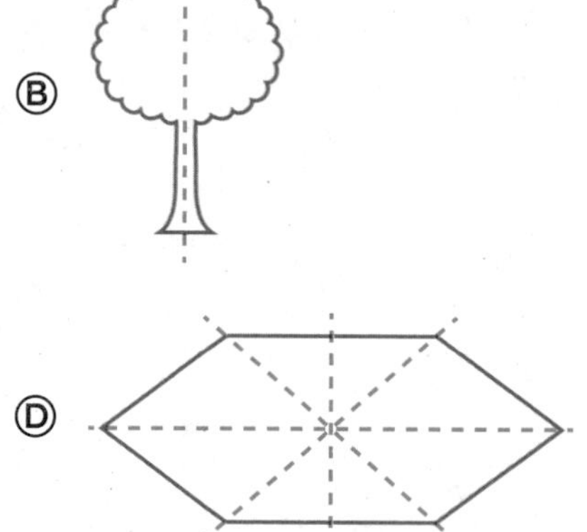

Ⓒ

Ⓓ

Michael chose Ⓓ as the correct answer. How did he get that answer?

PAIR/SHARE
Discuss why the lines of symmetry that are incorrect do not work.

4 Which figure has a line of symmetry?

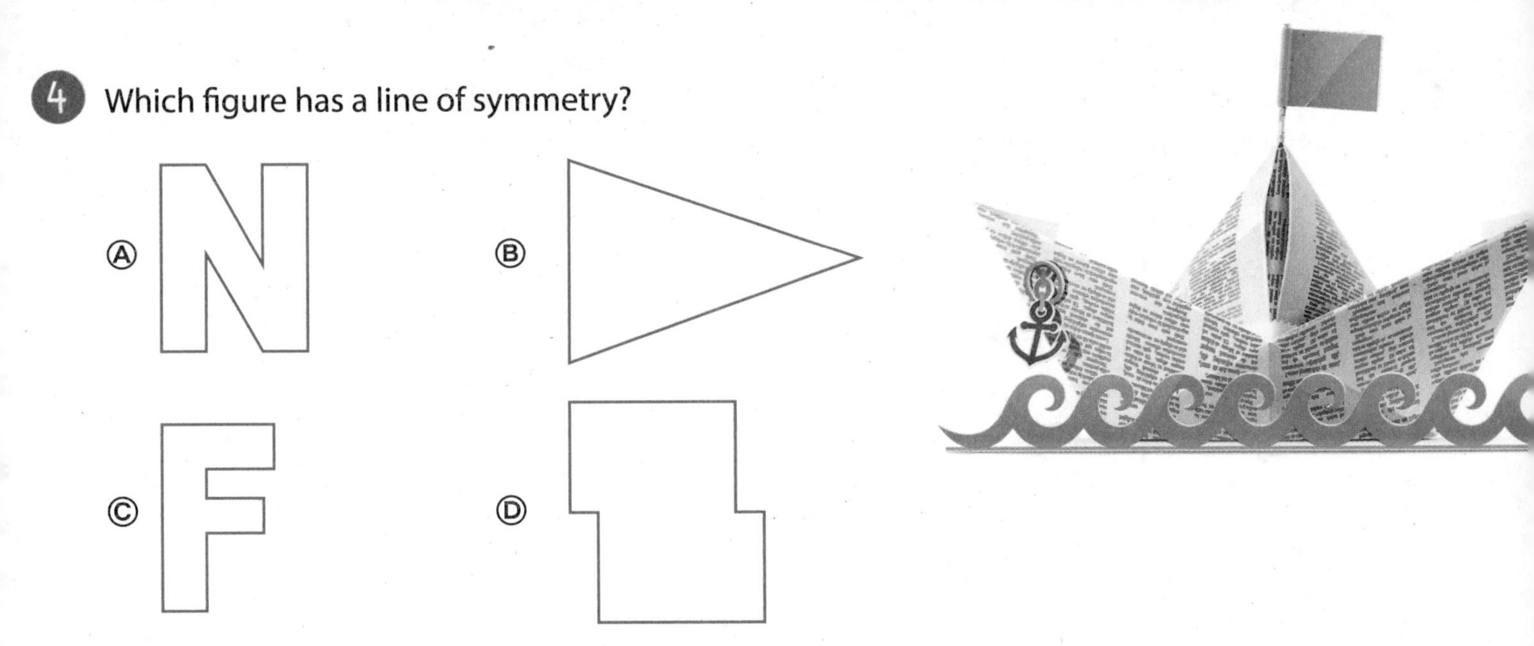

5 Determine the number of lines of symmetry for each figure below. Draw each figure in the correct column of the table. Some columns may have more than one figure. Some columns may not have any figures.

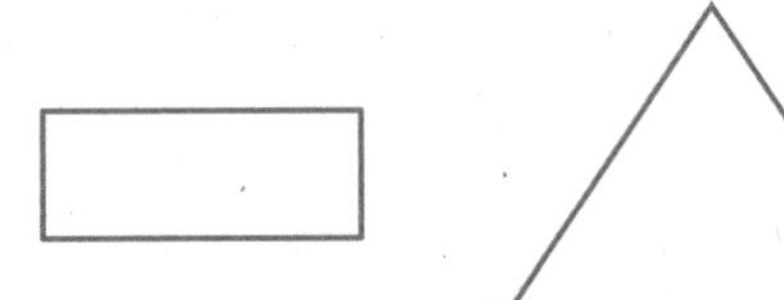  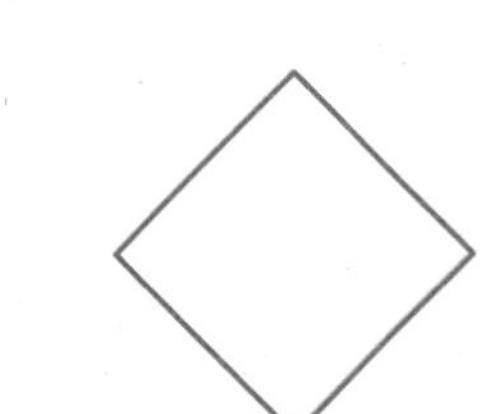

Number of Lines of Symmetry	0	Exactly 1	Exactly 2	Exactly 3	Exactly 4
Figure					

6 Part of a figure is shaded on the grid below. Complete the figure by shading squares. Lines *r* and *s* are lines of symmetry for the completed figure.

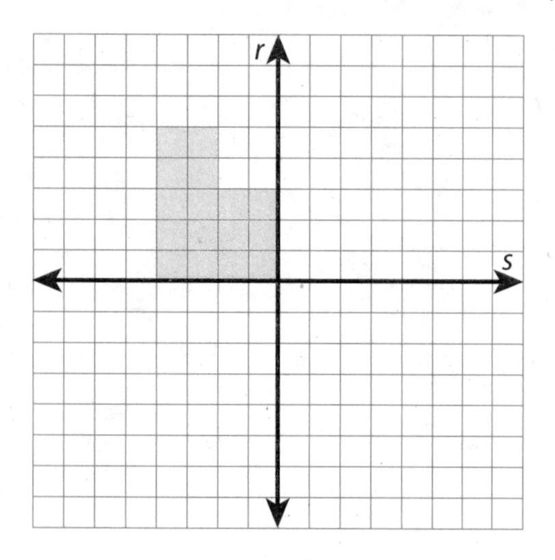

7 Draw all the lines of symmetry on the quadrilateral below. Then draw a different quadrilateral that has more lines of symmetry than the figure shown. Show the lines of symmetry. Explain your work.

8 MATH JOURNAL

Lexi says the line drawn across the circle at the right is a line of symmetry. Is Lexi correct? Explain.

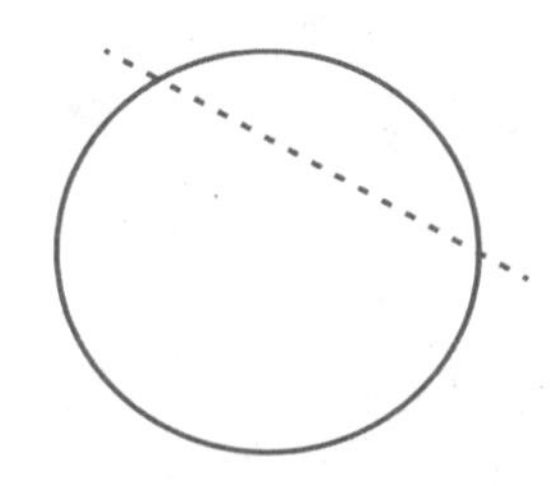

SELF CHECK Go back to the Unit 5 Opener and see what you can check off.

Self Reflection

In this unit you learned to . . .

Skill	Lesson
Identify points, lines, line segments, rays, and perpendicular and parallel lines, for example: a plus sign has perpendicular lines.	30
Measure angles using a protractor, for example: an angle on a stop sign is 135°.	31
Add and subtract angle measures to solve problems.	32
Classify two-dimensional figures based on sides and angles, for example: squares and rectangles have parallel sides.	33
Draw and identify lines of symmetry in shapes, for example: a square has 4 lines of symmetry.	34

Think about what you learned.

Use words, numbers, and drawings.

1. Two things I learned in math are . . .

2. A mistake I made that helped me learn was . . .

3. I could use more practice with . . .

Classify Shapes and Angles

Study an Example Problem and Solution

SMP 1 Make sense of problems and persevere in solving them.

Read this problem about classifying shapes by their sides and angles. Then look at Bella's solution to this problem.

Wood Scraps

Bella cuts scraps of wood into different shapes and saves them to make mosaic art. Sometimes she looks for pieces with certain kinds of sides. Sometimes she looks for shapes with certain kinds of angles. Some of the pieces of wood that Bella needs to sort are shown below.

Show a way to sort all of the shapes. Have at least one category about the shapes' sides. Have at least two categories about the shapes' angles. Put each shape into every category it fits in.

Read the sample solution on the next page. Then look at the checklist below. Find and mark parts of the solution that match the checklist.

PROBLEM-SOLVING CHECKLIST

- ☐ Tell what is known.
- ☐ Tell what the problem is asking.
- ☐ Show all your work.
- ☐ Show that the solution works.

a. **Circle** something that is known.

b. **Underline** something that you need to find.

c. **Draw a box around** what you do to solve the problem.

d. **Put a checkmark** next to the part that shows the solution works.

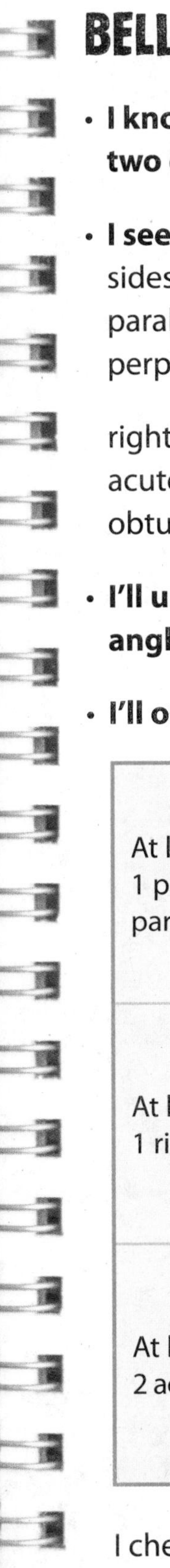

BELLA'S SOLUTION

- **I know I have to find one category for sides and two different categories for angles.**

- **I see some shapes with . . .**
  sides the same length
  parallel sides
  perpendicular sides
  — These describe the sides.

  right angles
  acute angles
  obtuse angles
  — These describe the angles.

- **I'll use the properties to make one side category and two angle categories.**

- **I'll organize the shapes in a table.**

At least 1 pair of parallel sides	
At least 1 right angle	
At least 2 acute angles	

I checked that each shape from the problem is in the table. Each shape is included at least once.

Hi, I'm Bella. Here's how I solved this problem.

I thought of the properties of the shapes. I used these to choose categories.

A shape can be in more than one category.

The table shows my final answer.

Try Another Approach

There are many ways to solve problems. Think about how you might solve the Wood Scraps problem in a different way.

Wood Scraps

Bella cuts scraps of wood into different shapes and saves them to make mosaic art. Sometimes she looks for pieces with certain kinds of sides. Sometimes she looks for shapes with certain kinds of angles. Some of the pieces of wood that Bella needs to sort are shown below.

Show a way to sort all of the shapes. Have at least one category about the shapes' sides. Have at least two categories about the shapes' angles. Put each shape into every category it fits in.

PLAN IT

Answer these questions to help you start thinking about a plan.

A. What are some of the different categories you could use?

B. How can you be sure that the categories you choose will cover all of the shapes?

SOLVE IT

Find a different solution for the Wood Scraps problem. Show all your work on a separate sheet of paper.

You may want to use the Problem-Solving Tips to get started.

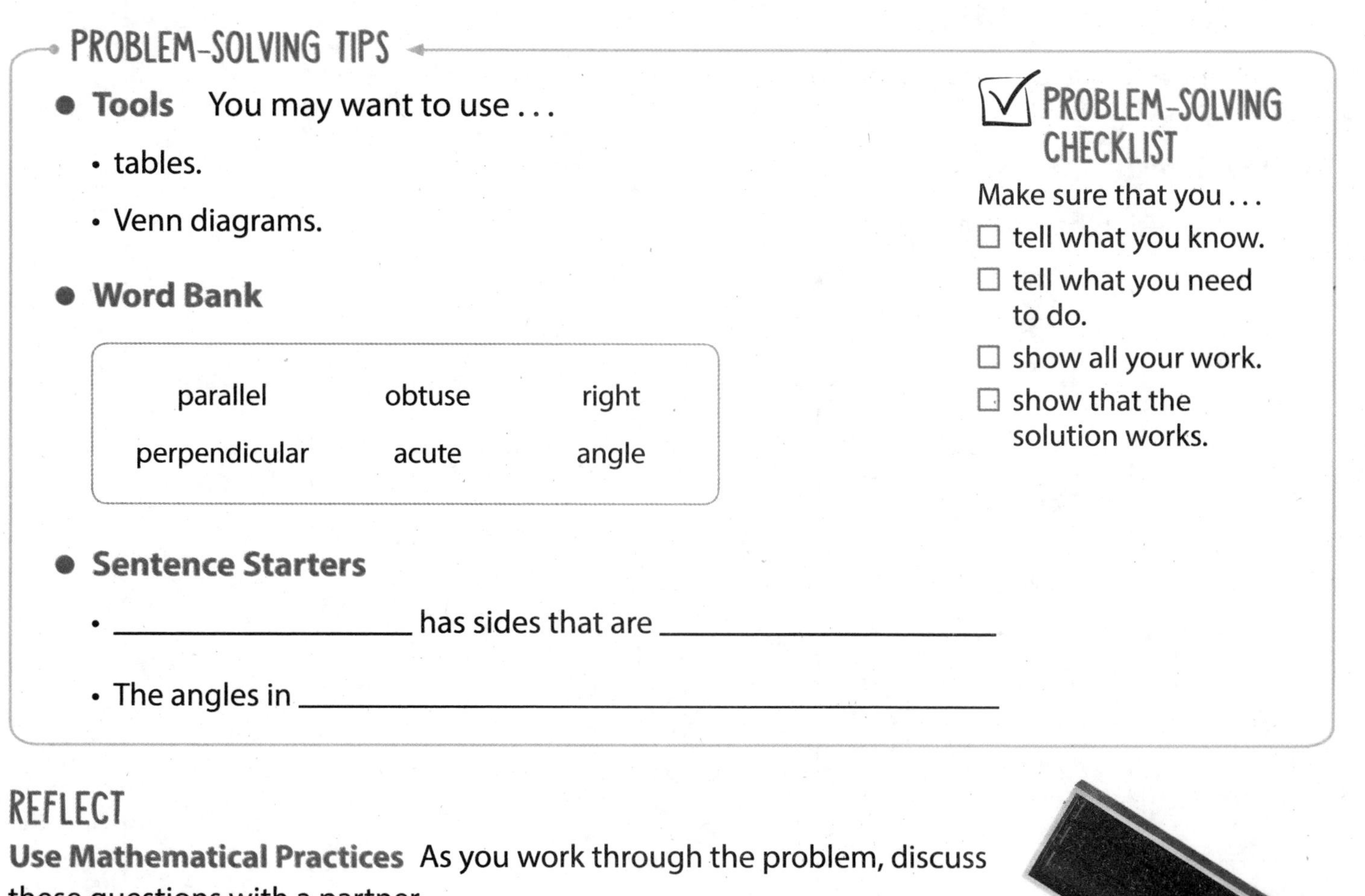

PROBLEM-SOLVING TIPS

- **Tools** You may want to use . . .
  - tables.
  - Venn diagrams.
- **Word Bank**

parallel	obtuse	right
perpendicular	acute	angle

- **Sentence Starters**
  - ________________ has sides that are ________________
  - The angles in ________________________________

PROBLEM-SOLVING CHECKLIST

Make sure that you . . .

- ☐ tell what you know.
- ☐ tell what you need to do.
- ☐ show all your work.
- ☐ show that the solution works.

REFLECT

Use Mathematical Practices As you work through the problem, discuss these questions with a partner.

- **Persevere** How can you use the answers to the **Plan It** questions to decide on the categories to use?
- **Use Repeated Reasoning** Are there shapes that are more likely to fall into more than one category than others? Why do you think this is the case?

Discuss Models and Strategies

Read the problem. Write a solution on a separate sheet of paper. Remember, there are lots of ways to solve a problem!

Symmetric Mosaic

Bella draws designs of different shapes for her mosaic art. This is a drawing she started.

My Notes:

- The design has only 1 line of symmetry.

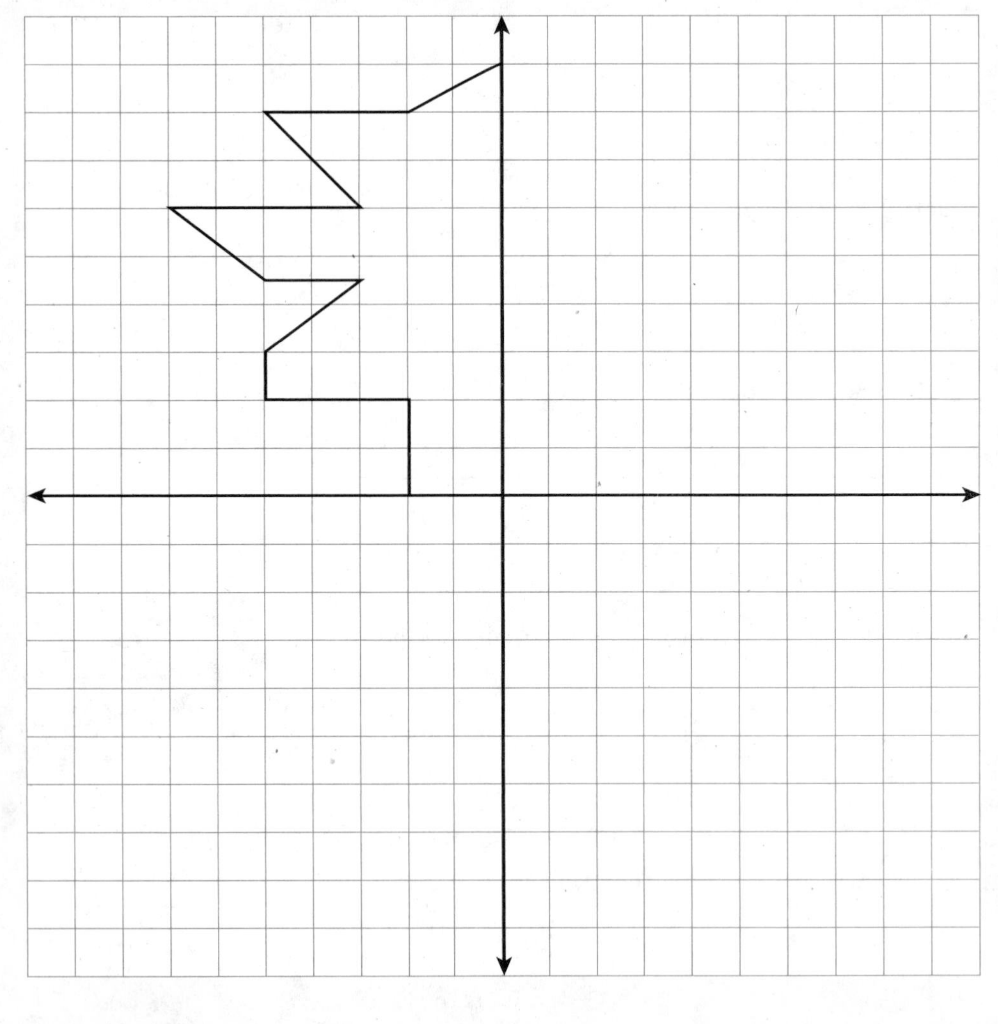

Draw the other half of the design and find ways to make the design with mosaic shapes.

PLAN IT AND SOLVE IT

Find a solution to the Symmetric Mosaic problem.

- Pick a line to use as the line of symmetry. Then draw the other half of the shape.
- Break up the shape into triangles, quadrilaterals, pentagons, and/or hexagons. Use at least three different shapes.
- Write the name of each shape in your design. Tell how many of each shape you used.

You may want to use the Problem-Solving Tips to get started.

PROBLEM-SOLVING TIPS

- **Questions**
  - How can you tell if a line is a line of symmetry?
  - What do the sides and angles of your shapes look like?
- **Word Bank**

right	acute	triangle
rectangle	square	trapezoid

- The line of symmetry ________________________
- I broke the shape into ________________________

PROBLEM-SOLVING CHECKLIST

Make sure that you . . .

- ☐ tell what you know.
- ☐ tell what you need to do.
- ☐ show all your work.
- ☐ show that the solution works.

REFLECT

Use Mathematical Practices As you work through the problem, discuss these questions with a partner.

- **Use Tools** What tools can you use to solve the problem? How could you use the tools?
- **Use Reasoning** How can you decide what shapes to use to make Bella's design?

Persevere On Your Own

Read the problems. Write a solution on a separate sheet of paper.

Mosaic Art

Bella is designing a wood mosaic piece. She wants the outline of the mosaic to be a shape with the features listed below.

My Mosaic Plan

- at least 4 sides
- at least 2 lines of symmetry
- at least 1 pair of parallel sides

What shape could Bella choose for an outline?

SOLVE IT

Suggest a shape that Bella could use as an outline for her mosaic.

Draw a shape that has all of the features listed above.

- Label the shape to show that it has all of the features.
- Use as many geometry words as you can to describe your shape.

REFLECT

Use Mathematical Practices After you complete the task, choose one of these questions to discuss with a partner.

- **Make an Argument** How can you show or explain why your shape has all of the features listed above?
- **Persevere** What different shapes did you try before deciding which one to use in your solution?

Angle Cuts

When Bella cuts pieces of wood for a project, she always saves the scraps. The scraps make good pieces for making mosaics. The cut pieces have different angle measures. Bella sorts pieces by the angle measures. Here are the angle measures of the pieces she has saved.

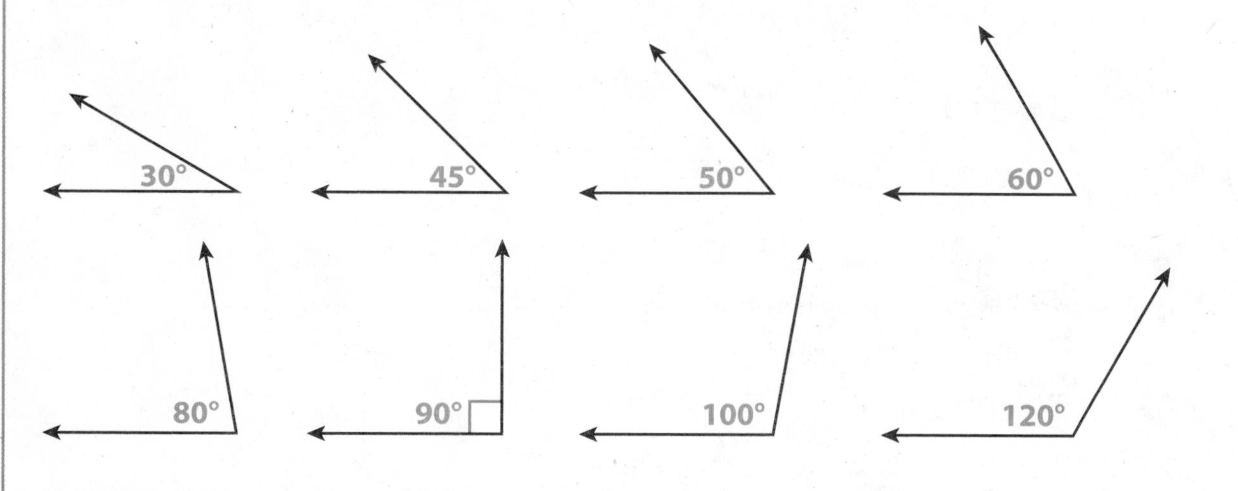

How can Bella put some of these angles together to make a straight line?

SOLVE IT

Help Bella put some of the angles together to make a straight line.

Find a way Bella can put some pieces of wood together to make a 180° angle. Then measure and draw your angles to show that they make a straight line.

REFLECT

Use Mathematical Practices After you complete the task, choose one of these questions to discuss with a partner.

- **Use Tools** How did you use tools to draw and measure angles?
- **Use a Model** What equations could you write to show the total measure of the angles you put together?

Unit Review

1. An angle that measures 163° is composed of three smaller angles. Two of the angles measure 15° and 68°. What is the measure of the third angle? Show your work.

Solution ....

2. Sort the shapes using the categories listed in the table below. Write the letter of each shape in the column for the correct category. Some shapes may belong in more than one category.

A B C D E

Shapes with at Least One Pair of Parallel Sides	Shapes with No Perpendicular Sides	Shapes with at Least One Obtuse Angle

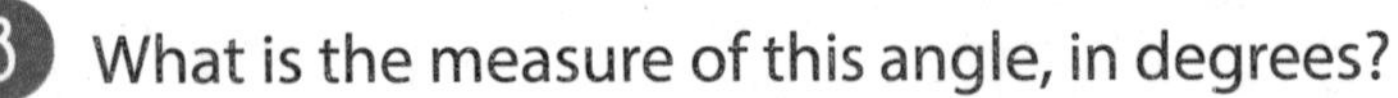

3. What is the measure of this angle, in degrees?

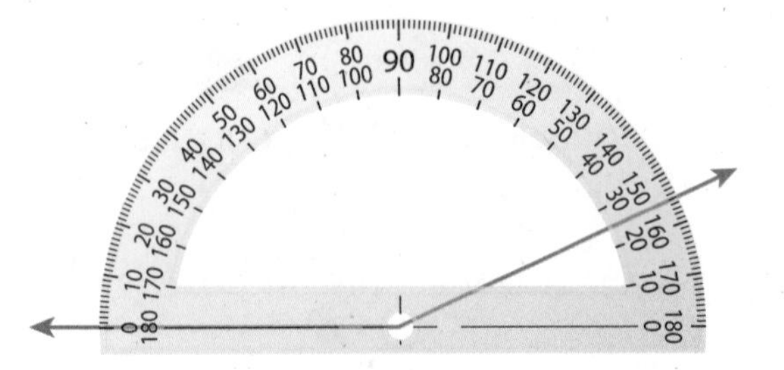

Solution ....

4 Which drawing shows perpendicular lines?

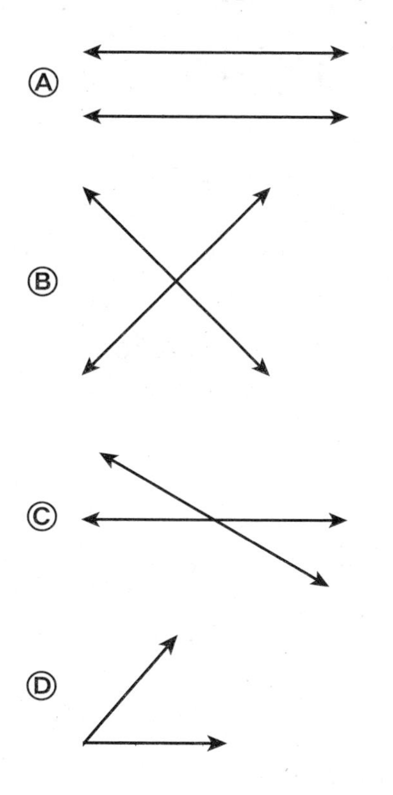

Decide how many lines of symmetry each shape has.

Choose *0 Lines of Symmetry*, *Exactly 1 Line of Symmetry*, *Exactly 2 Lines of Symmetry*, or *More than 2 Lines of Symmetry* for each shape.

	0 Lines of Symmetry	Exactly 1 Line of Symmetry	Exactly 2 Lines of Symmetry	More than 2 Lines of Symmetry
	Ⓐ	Ⓑ	Ⓒ	Ⓓ
	Ⓔ	Ⓕ	Ⓖ	Ⓗ
	Ⓘ	Ⓙ	Ⓚ	Ⓛ
	Ⓜ	Ⓝ	Ⓞ	Ⓟ

Performance Task

Answer the questions and show all your work on separate paper.

Checklist

Did you . . .

- ☐ follow the instructions for the first logo?
- ☐ use a ruler?
- ☐ use vocabulary correctly?

Your Uncle Asher has a new bakery opening soon. He asks you to help him design a logo for the shop sign. The name of the shop is Asher's Sweets. Your uncle described his idea for the shape of the logo:

> My logo is three shapes put together. One shape is a 5-sided figure with exactly two parallel sides, exactly two right angles, and one line of symmetry. The other two shapes are exactly alike. Each one is an isosceles triangle. One side of each triangle—the side that is a different length from the other two sides—matches up to one of the parallel sides of the 5-sided figure.

Draw your uncle's logo on grid paper. Then use geometric shapes to create another logo for him to consider. Draw the logo and describe it in a note to your uncle using the terms *parallel, perpendicular, line of symmetry, acute, obtuse*, and any other geometry vocabulary from this unit.

REFLECT

Use Mathematical Practices After you complete the task, choose one of the following questions to answer.

- **Be Precise** Why is it important that you know the meaning of the geometry terms in your description?
- **Argue and Critique** Suppose you ask your uncle to draw a logo matching your description. Do you think his drawing will match what you had in mind? Explain your answer.

UNIT 5

Vocabulary

Draw or write to show examples for each term.

acute angle an angle that measures more than 0° but less than 90°.

My Example

acute triangle a triangle that has three acute angles.

My Example

angle a geometric shape formed by two rays, lines, or line segments that meet at a common point.

My Example

degree (°) a unit of measure for angles. There are 360° in a circle.

My Example

equilateral triangle a triangle that has all three sides the same length.

My Example

hexagon a polygon with exactly 6 sides and 6 angles.

My Example

isosceles triangle a triangle that has at least two sides the same length.

My Example

line a straight row of points that goes on forever in both directions.

My Example

line of symmetry a line that divides a shape into two mirror images.

My Example

line segment a straight row of points that starts at one point and ends at another point.

My Example

obtuse angle an angle that measures more than 90° but less than 180°.

My Example

obtuse triangle a triangle that has one obtuse angle.

My Example

parallel lines lines that are always the same distance apart and never cross.

My Example

perpendicular lines two lines that meet to form a right angle, or a 90° angle.

My Example

point a single location in space.

My Example

polygon a two-dimensional closed figure made with three or more straight line segments that do not cross over each other.

My Example

protractor a tool used to measure angles.

My Example

ray a straight row of points that starts at one point and goes on forever in one direction.

My Example

right angle an angle that looks like a square corner and measures 90°.

My Example

right triangle a triangle that has one right angle.

My Example

scalene triangle a triangle that has no sides the same length.

My Example

trapezoid (exclusive) a quadrilateral with exactly one pair of parallel sides.

My Example

trapezoid (inclusive) a quadrilateral with at least one pair of parallel sides.

My Example

vertex the point where two rays, lines, or line segments meet to form an angle.

My Example

UNIT 4

Cumulative Practice

Name: ______________________________

Set 1: Multiply by One-Digit Numbers

Multiply. Show your work.

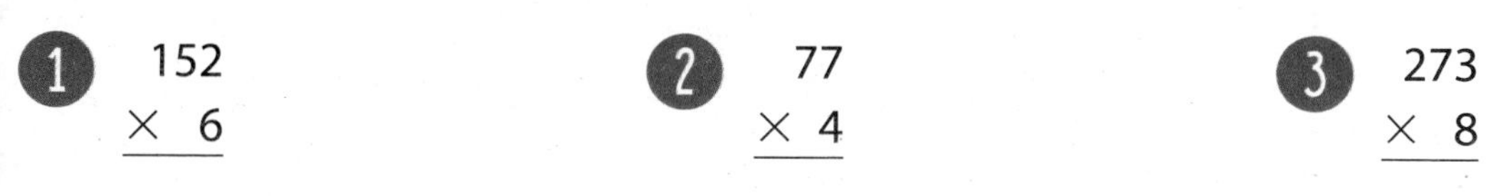

Set 2: Multiply by Two-Digit Numbers

Multiply. Show your work.

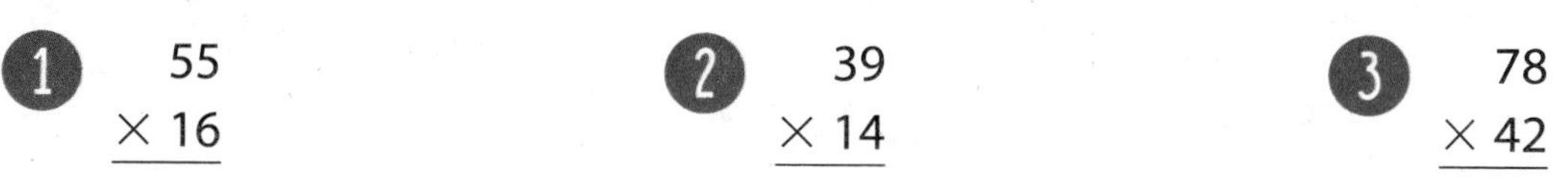

Set 3: Divide Three-Digit Numbers

Divide. Show your work.

1. $108 \div 6$

2. $450 \div 8$

Set 4: Divide Four-Digit Numbers

Divide. Show your work.

1. $4{,}845 \div 5$

2. $2{,}121 \div 7$

3. $3{,}130 \div 6$

Set 5: Multiplication as a Comparison

Write a multiplication equation to represent and solve each problem. Show your work.

1. Zari picked 8 flowers. Her brother picked 3 times as many flowers. How many flowers did Zari's brother pick?

2. Ian earns \$9 babysitting one week. The next week, he earns 4 times as much. How much does Ian earn the next week?

3. Cory swims 6 laps. Jen swims 2 times as many laps as Cory. How many laps does Jen swim?

4. Juana has 7 times as many nickels as dimes. She has 4 dimes. How many nickels does she have?

5. Mireya lives 9 miles from the ocean. Louis lives 7 times as far from the ocean as Mireya. How far from the ocean does Louis live?

Name: ____________________

Set 6: Multiplication and Division in Word Problems

Multiply or divide to solve the problems. Show your work.

1. Kate runs 9 miles in one week. She runs 3 times as far as Jordan. How far does Jordan run?

2. Alejo eats 8 raisins. His brother eats 5 times as many raisins. How many raisins does his brother eat?

3. Colin studies for 5 minutes. Ayana studies for 6 times as long. How long does Ayana study?

4. Cristina buys a jacket and a pair of socks. The jacket costs $32. The jacket costs 8 times as much as the socks. How much do the socks cost?

Set 7: Multi-Step Problems

Write and solve an equation with a variable for each problem. Show your work.

1. In a game, Tom scores 8 points in each of the first four rounds. He scores 2 points in each of the next three rounds. How many points does he score in all seven rounds?

2. Alicia spends 8 hours in a week playing hockey. That is 4 times the number of hours she spends playing basketball. Altogether, how long does she spend playing both sports?

Set 8: Round Whole Numbers

Round the given numbers to each place given below.

Round 92,283

1. To the nearest ten ....
2. To the nearest hundred ....
3. To the nearest thousand ....
4. To the nearest ten thousand ....

Round 215,297

5. To the nearest ten ....
6. To the nearest hundred ....
7. To the nearest thousand ....
8. To the nearest ten thousand ....

Round 8,749

9. To the nearest ten ....
10. To the nearest hundred ....
11. To the nearest thousand ....
12. To the nearest ten thousand ....

Set 9: Add and Subtract Whole Numbers

Add or subtract for problems 1–6. Show your work.

1. 6,152 + 3,726
2. 2,184 + 926
3. 7,651 − 5,421
4. 51,516 + 45,295
5. 63,028 − 32,193
6. 6,103 − 5,945

Fill in the missing digits that make each problem true for problems 7–9.

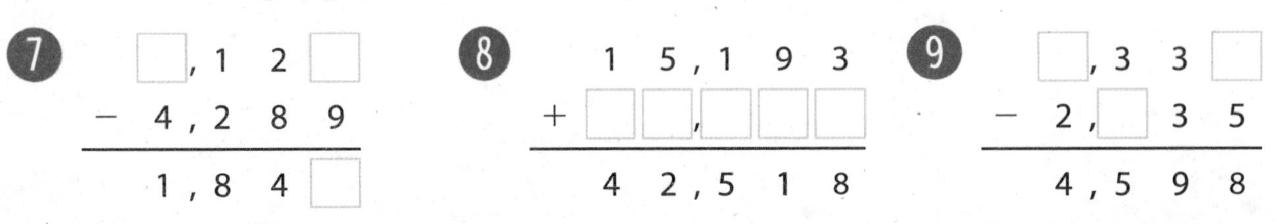

UNIT 5

Cumulative Practice

Name: ______________________________

Set 1: Equivalent Fractions

Write the missing numbers to find equivalent fractions.

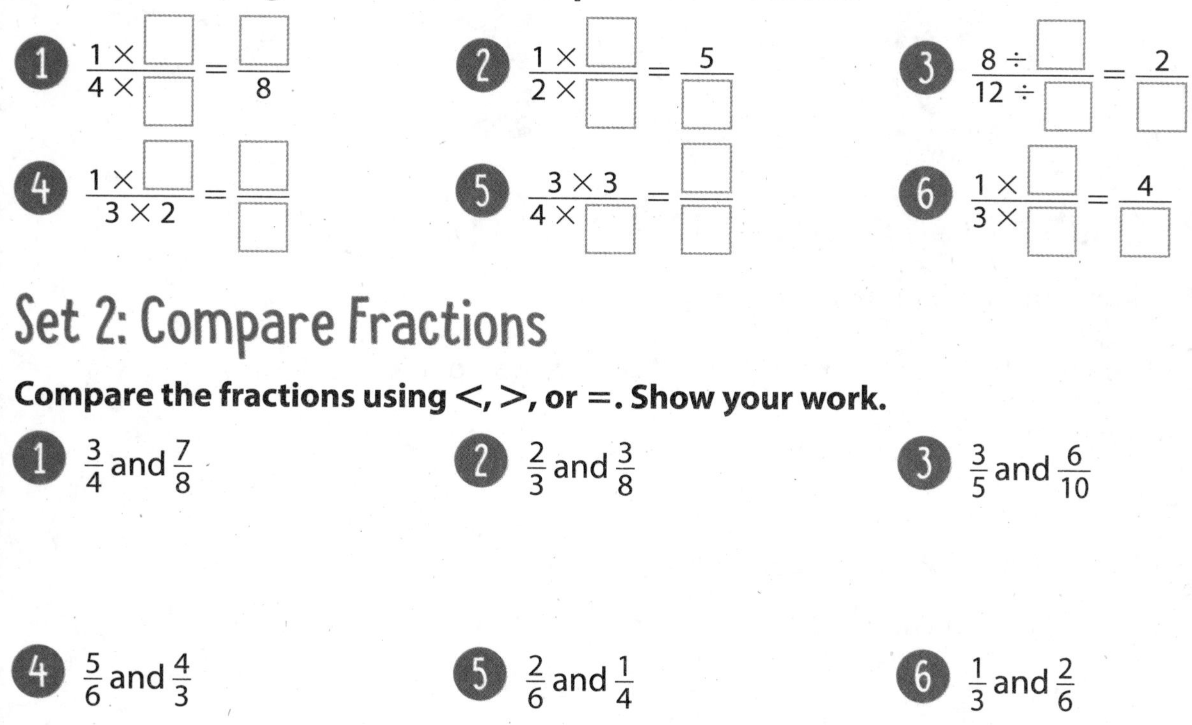

1. $\frac{1 \times \square}{4 \times \square} = \frac{\square}{8}$
2. $\frac{1 \times \square}{2 \times \square} = \frac{5}{\square}$
3. $\frac{8 \div \square}{12 \div \square} = \frac{2}{\square}$
4. $\frac{1 \times \square}{3 \times 2} = \frac{\square}{\square}$
5. $\frac{3 \times 3}{4 \times \square} = \frac{\square}{\square}$
6. $\frac{1 \times \square}{3 \times \square} = \frac{4}{\square}$

Set 2: Compare Fractions

Compare the fractions using <, >, or =. Show your work.

1. $\frac{3}{4}$ and $\frac{7}{8}$
2. $\frac{2}{3}$ and $\frac{3}{8}$
3. $\frac{3}{5}$ and $\frac{6}{10}$
4. $\frac{5}{6}$ and $\frac{4}{3}$
5. $\frac{2}{6}$ and $\frac{1}{4}$
6. $\frac{1}{3}$ and $\frac{2}{6}$

Set 3: Add and Subtract Fractions

Solve problems 1–4.

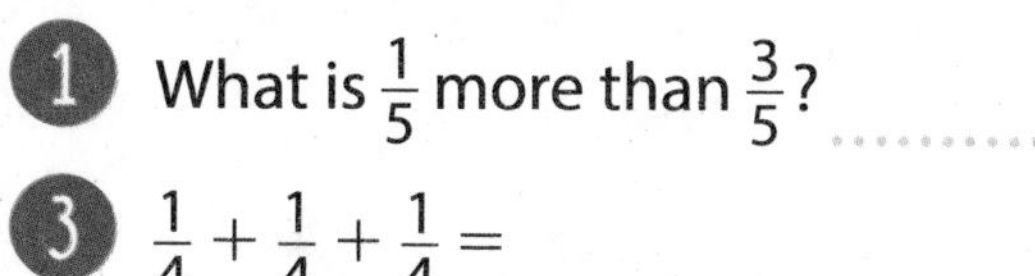

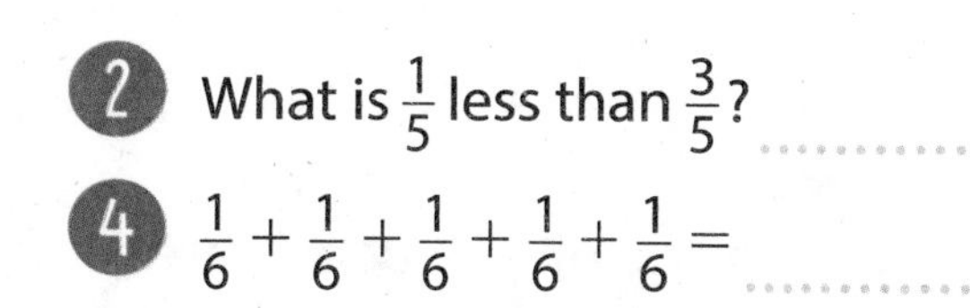

1. What is $\frac{1}{5}$ more than $\frac{3}{5}$? ....
2. What is $\frac{1}{5}$ less than $\frac{3}{5}$? ....
3. $\frac{1}{4} + \frac{1}{4} + \frac{1}{4} =$ ....
4. $\frac{1}{6} + \frac{1}{6} + \frac{1}{6} + \frac{1}{6} + \frac{1}{6} =$ ....

Use the area models to show adding or subtracting fractions for problems 5 and 6.

5. Show $\frac{1}{4} + \frac{2}{4}$.

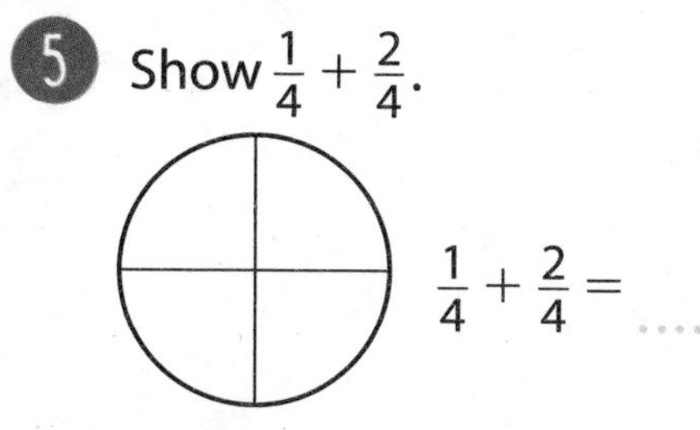

$\frac{1}{4} + \frac{2}{4} =$ ....

6. Show $\frac{5}{8} - \frac{3}{8}$.

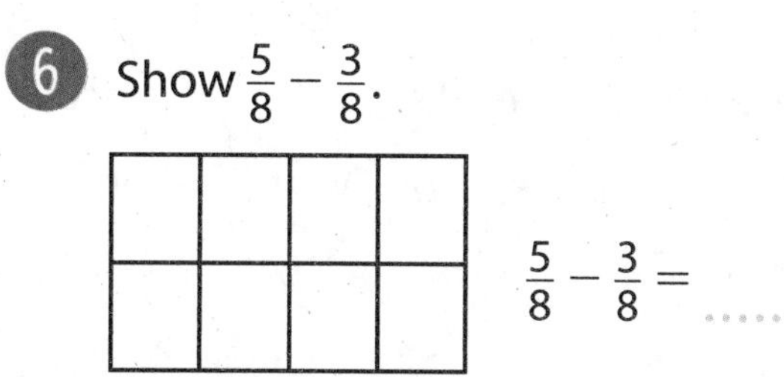

$\frac{5}{8} - \frac{3}{8} =$ ....

Set 4: Decompose Fractions

Complete the equations to show a way to decompose each fraction.

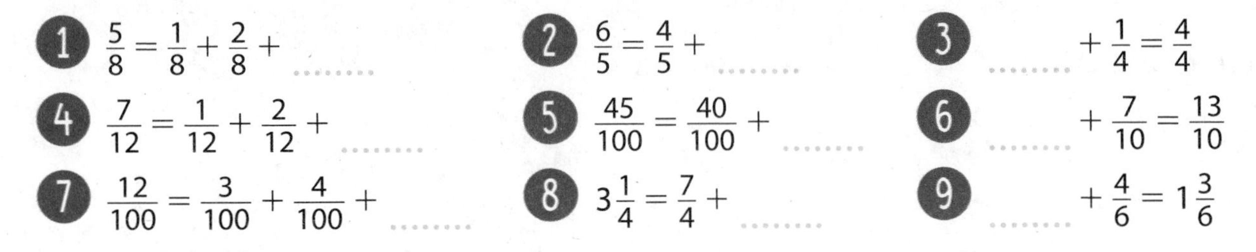

1. $\frac{5}{8} = \frac{1}{8} + \frac{2}{8} + \underline{\qquad}$
2. $\frac{6}{5} = \frac{4}{5} + \underline{\qquad}$
3. $\underline{\qquad} + \frac{1}{4} = \frac{4}{4}$
4. $\frac{7}{12} = \frac{1}{12} + \frac{2}{12} + \underline{\qquad}$
5. $\frac{45}{100} = \frac{40}{100} + \underline{\qquad}$
6. $\underline{\qquad} + \frac{7}{10} = \frac{13}{10}$
7. $\frac{12}{100} = \frac{3}{100} + \frac{4}{100} + \underline{\qquad}$
8. $3\frac{1}{4} = \frac{7}{4} + \underline{\qquad}$
9. $\underline{\qquad} + \frac{4}{6} = 1\frac{3}{6}$

Set 5: Add and Subtract Fractions in Word Problems

Add or subtract to solve the problems. Show your work.

1. Laura eats $\frac{2}{8}$ of a pizza. Hugo eats $\frac{3}{8}$ of the pizza. What fraction of the pizza do they eat altogether?

2. Josefa has $\frac{4}{5}$ of a pound of blackberries. She gives $\frac{1}{5}$ of a pound of blackberries away. How many pounds of blackberries does she have left?

3. Deion has weeded $\frac{7}{12}$ of his yard. Deion wants to weed the whole yard. What fraction of the yard is left to be weeded?

4. Nicole walks $\frac{1}{4}$ of a mile to school and $\frac{1}{4}$ of a mile home. How far does she walk in total?

5. Rodrigo needs $\frac{1}{6}$ of a cup of walnuts to make salad, and $\frac{4}{6}$ of a cup of walnuts to make muffins. How many cups of walnuts does he need altogether?

6. Diane cuts an apple into 8 equal-sized pieces. She eats $\frac{3}{8}$ of the apple. Her friend eats $\frac{1}{8}$ of the apple. What fraction of the apple is left?

Name: ____________________

Set 6: Add and Subtract Mixed Numbers

Add or subtract. Show your work.

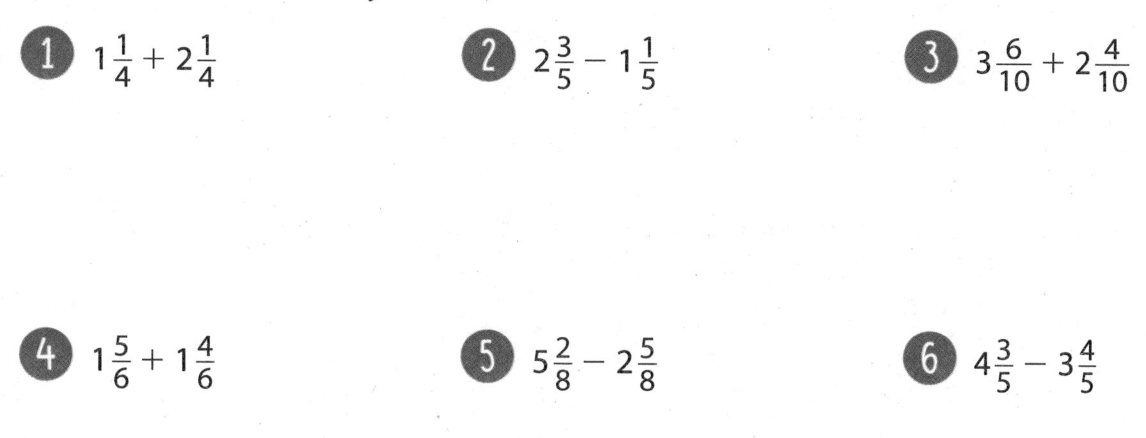

1. $1\frac{1}{4} + 2\frac{1}{4}$
2. $2\frac{3}{5} - 1\frac{1}{5}$
3. $3\frac{6}{10} + 2\frac{4}{10}$
4. $1\frac{5}{6} + 1\frac{4}{6}$
5. $5\frac{2}{8} - 2\frac{5}{8}$
6. $4\frac{3}{5} - 3\frac{4}{5}$

Set 7: Multiply Fractions by Whole Numbers in Word Problems

Write and solve a multiplication equation to solve each problem. Show your work.

1. Marcos walks $\frac{5}{6}$ of a mile each day for 5 days in a row. How far does he walk altogether?

2. Damian is making mini apple pies. One mini apple pie uses $\frac{1}{2}$ of a pound of apples. How many pounds of apples does Damian need to make 6 mini apple pies?

3. Julia plays soccer for $\frac{2}{3}$ of an hour each day for 4 days. How long does she spend playing soccer altogether?

4. Eric drinks 3 full glasses of water. His glass holds $\frac{4}{5}$ of a cup of water. How many cups of water does Eric drink altogether?

Set 8: Relate Decimals and Fractions

Add. Show your work for problems 1–3.

1. $\frac{3}{10} + \frac{9}{100}$
2. $\frac{31}{100} + \frac{4}{10}$
3. $\frac{64}{100} + \frac{8}{10}$

Write each decimal as a fraction with a denominator of 100 for problems 4–6.

4. $0.2 =$ ....
5. $0.04 =$ ....
6. $0.56 =$ ....

Write a decimal equivalent for each fraction or mixed number for problems 7–9.

7. $\frac{7}{10} =$ ....
8. $\frac{8}{100} =$ ....
9. $3\frac{14}{100} =$ ....

Set 9: Compare Decimals

Write $<$, $>$, or $=$ in each circle to compare the decimals.

1. 0.2 ◯ 0.3
2. 0.5 ◯ 0.05
3. 0.25 ◯ 0.52
4. 1.46 ◯ 2.46
5. 0.99 ◯ 0.9
6. 0.1 ◯ 0.11
7. 0.2 ◯ 0.08
8. 1.10 ◯ 1.1
9. 0.72 ◯ 0.36

Set 10: Fraction Multiplication

Complete the multiplication equation represented by each model.

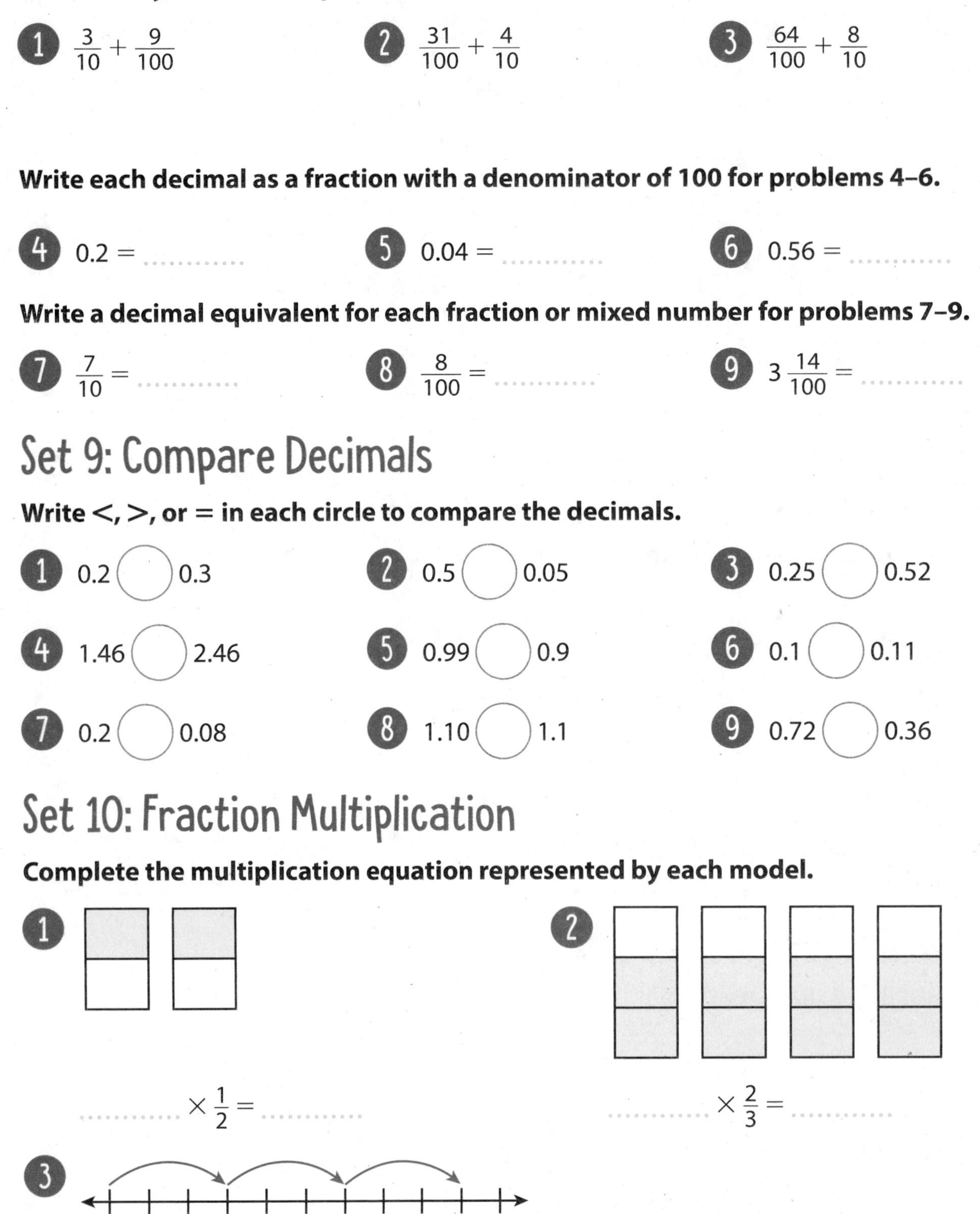

1. .... $\times \frac{1}{2} =$ ....
2. .... $\times \frac{2}{3} =$ ....
3. .... $\times \frac{3}{8} =$ ....

Glossary/Glosario

English	Español	Example/Ejemplo
Aa		
acute angle an angle that measures more than 0° but less than 90°.	**ángulo agudo** ángulo que mide más de 0° pero menos de 90°.	
acute triangle a triangle that has three acute angles.	**triángulo acutángulo** triángulo que tiene tres ángulos agudos.	
addend a number being added.	**sumando** número que se suma.	**24** + **35** = 59 addends
algorithm a set of routine steps used to solve problems.	**algoritmo** conjunto de pasos que se siguen rutinariamente para resolver problemas.	2 26 × 14 104 + 260 364
AM the time from midnight until before noon.	**a. m.** el tiempo que transcurre desde la medianoche hasta el mediodía.	AM 7:20
angle a geometric shape formed by two rays, lines, or line segments that meet at a common point.	**ángulo** figura geométrica formada por dos semirrectas, rectas, o segmentos de recta que se encuentran en un punto.	C A B

English	Español	Example/Ejemplo
area the amount of space inside a closed two-dimensional figure. Area is measured in square units such as square centimeters.	**área** cantidad de espacio dentro de una figura bidimensional cerrada. El área se mide en unidades cuadradas, como los centímetros cuadrados.	Area = 4 square units
array a set of objects arranged in equal rows and equal columns.	**matriz** conjunto de objetos agrupados en filas y columnas iguales.	
associative property of addition when the grouping of three or more addends is changed, the total does not change.	**propiedad asociativa de la suma** cambiar la agrupación de tres o más sumandos no cambia el total.	$(2 + 3) + 4 = 2 + (3 + 4)$
associative property of multiplication changing the grouping of three or more factors does not change the product.	**propiedad asociativa de la multiplicación** cambiar la agrupación de tres o más factores no cambia el producto.	$(2 \times 4) \times 3$ = $2 \times (4 \times 3)$
attribute any characteristic of an object or shape, such as number of sides or angles, lengths of sides, or angle measures.	**atributo** característica de un objeto o una figura, como el número de lados o ángulos, la longitud de los lados, o la medida de los ángulos.	attributes of a square: • 4 square corners • 4 sides of equal length

Bb

English	Español	Example/Ejemplo
benchmark fraction a common fraction that you might compare other fractions to.	**fracción de referencia** fracción común que se puede comparar con otras fracciones.	$\frac{1}{4}$, $\frac{1}{2}$, $\frac{2}{3}$, and $\frac{3}{4}$ are often used as benchmark fractions.

Cc

English	Español	Example/Ejemplo
capacity the amount a container can hold. Capacity can be measured in the same units as liquid volume.	**capacidad** cantidad que cabe en un recipiente. La capacidad se mide en las mismas unidades que el volumen líquido.	2 liters 1 liter capacity of 2 liters

English	Español	Example/Ejemplo
centimeter (cm) a unit of length. There are 100 centimeters in 1 meter.	**centímetro (cm)** unidad de longitud. 100 centímetros equivalen a 1 metro.	Your little finger is about 1 **centimeter** (cm) across.
column a vertical line of objects or numbers, such as in an array or table.	**columna** línea vertical de objetos o números, como las de una matriz o una tabla.	
common denominator a number that is a common multiple of the denominators of two or more fractions.	**denominadores comunes** número que es común múltiplo de los denominadores de dos o más fracciones.	$2 \times 3 = 6$, so 6 is a common denominator for $3\frac{1}{2}$ and $1\frac{1}{3}$.
commutative property of addition changing the order of addends does not change the total.	**propiedad conmutativa de la suma** cambiar el orden de los sumandos no cambia el total.	$3 + 4 = 4 + 3$
commutative property of multiplication changing the order of the factors does not change the product.	**propiedad conmutativa de la multiplicación** cambiar el orden de los factores no cambia el producto.	$3 \times 2 = 2 \times 3$
compare to decide if numbers, amounts, or sizes are greater than, less than, or equal to each other.	**comparar** determinar si un número, una cantidad, o un tamaño es mayor que, menor que o igual a otro número, otra cantidad u otro tamaño.	$6{,}131 > 5{,}113$

English	Español	Example/Ejemplo
compose to make by combining parts. You can put together numbers to make a greater number or shapes to make a new shape.	**componer** combinar partes para formar algo. Se pueden combinar números para formar un número mayor o figuras para formar otra figura.	The three 50° angles compose the larger angle.
composite number a number that has more than one pair of factors.	**número compuesto** número que tiene más de un par de factores.	16 is a composite number.
convert to write an equivalent measurement using a different unit.	**convertir** expresar una medida equivalente en una unidad diferente.	5 feet = 60 inches
cup (c) a liquid volume in the customary system. 4 cups is equivalent to 1 quart.	**taza (tz)** unidad de volumen líquido del sistema usual. Cuatro tazas equivalen a 1 cuarto.	
customary system the measurement system commonly used in the United States that measures length in inches, feet, yards, and miles; liquid volume in cups, pints, quarts, and gallons; and weight in ounces and pounds.	**sistema usual** sistema de medición comúnmente usado en Estados Unidos. La longitud se mide en pulgadas, pies, yardas, y millas; el volumen líquido, en tazas, pintas, cuartos, y galones; y el peso, en onzas y libras.	see tables below

Length
1 foot = 12 inches
1 yard = 3 feet
1 mile = 5,280 feet

Weight
1 pound = 16 ounces

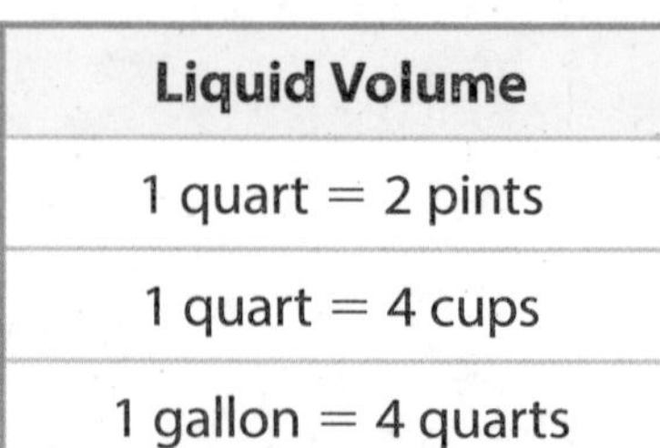

Liquid Volume
1 quart = 2 pints
1 quart = 4 cups
1 gallon = 4 quarts

English	Español	Example/Ejemplo
Dd		
data a set of collected information. Often numerical information such as a list of measurements.	**datos** conjunto de información reunida. A menudo es información numérica, tal como una lista de mediciones.	earthworm lengths (in inches) $4\frac{1}{2}, 5, 5, 5, 5\frac{1}{4}, 5\frac{1}{4}, 5\frac{1}{4}, 6, 6\frac{1}{4}$
decimal a number containing a decimal point that separates a whole from fractional place values (tenths, hundredths, thousandths, and so on).	**número decimal** número que contiene un punto decimal que separa la posición de las unidades de las posiciones fraccionarias (décimas, centésimas, milésimas, etc.).	1.293
decimal point the dot used in a decimal that separates the ones place from the tenths place.	**punto decimal** punto que se usa en un número decimal para separar la posición de las unidades de la posición de las décimas.	1.65 ↑ decimal point
decompose to break into parts. You can break apart numbers and shapes.	**descomponer** separar en partes. Se pueden separar en partes números y figuras.	$\frac{3}{8} = \frac{1}{8} + \frac{1}{8} + \frac{1}{8}$
degree (°) a unit of measure for angles. There are 360° in a circle.	**grado (°)** unidad de medida para ángulos. Hay 360° en un círculo.	There are 360° in a circle.
denominator the number below the line in a fraction that tells the number of equal parts in the whole.	**denominador** número que está debajo de la línea de una fracción. Dice cuántas partes iguales hay en el entero.	$\frac{2}{\mathbf{3}}$
difference the result of subtraction.	**diferencia** el resultado de la resta.	$\frac{3}{4} - \frac{1}{4} = \mathbf{\frac{2}{4}}$
digit a symbol used to write numbers.	**dígito** símbolo que se usa para escribir números.	The digits are 0, 1, 2, 3, 4, 5, 6, 7, 8, and 9.
dimension length in one direction. A figure may have one, two, or three dimensions.	**dimensión** longitud en una dirección. Una figura puede tener una, dos, o tres dimensiones.	5 in. 2 in. 3 in.

English	Español	Example/Ejemplo
distributive property when one of the factors of a product is written as a sum, multiplying each addend by the other factor before adding does not change the product.	**propiedad distributiva** cuando uno de los factores de un producto se escribe como suma, multiplicar cada sumando por el otro factor antes de sumar no cambia el producto.	$2 \times (3 + 6) = (2 \times 3) + (2 \times 6)$
divide to separate into equal groups and find the number in each group or the number of groups.	**dividir** separar en grupos iguales y hallar cuántos hay en cada grupo o el número de grupos.	$2,850 \div 38 = 75$
dividend the number that is divided by another number.	**dividendo** el número que se divide por otro número.	$15 \div 3 = 5$
division an operation used to separate a number of items into equal-sized groups.	**división** operación que se usa para separar una cantidad de objetos en grupos iguales.	Division $12 \div 3 = 4$ total; number of groups; number in each group
divisor the number by which another number is divided.	**divisor** el número por el que se divide otro número.	$15 \div 3 = 15$

Ee

English	Español	Example/Ejemplo
edge a line segment where two faces meet in a three-dimensional shape.	**arista** segmento de recta donde se encuentran dos caras de una figura tridimensional.	edge

English	Español	Example/Ejemplo
elapsed time the amount of time that has passed between a start time and an end time.	**tiempo transcurrido** tiempo que ha pasado entre el momento de inicio y el fin.	The elapsed time from 2:00 PM to 3:00 PM is 1 hour.
equal having the same value, same size, or same amount.	**igual** que tiene el mismo valor, el mismo tamaño o la misma cantidad.	$25 + 15 = 40$ 25 + 15 **is equal to** 40.
equal sign (=) a symbol that means *is the same value as*.	**signo de igual (=)** símbolo que significa *tiene el mismo valor que*.	$12 + 4 = 16$
equation a mathematical statement that uses an equal sign (=) to show that two expressions have the same value.	**ecuación** enunciado matemático que tiene un signo de igual (=) para mostrar que dos expresiones tienen el mismo valor.	$25 - 15 = 10$
equilateral triangle a triangle that has all three sides the same length.	**triángulo equilátero** triángulo que tiene los tres lados de igual longitud.	8 in. 8 in. 8 in.
equivalent fractions two or more different fractions that name the same part of a whole or the same point on a number line.	**fracciones equivalentes** dos o más fracciones diferentes que nombran la misma parte de un entero y el mismo punto en una recta numérica.	$\frac{2}{4} = \frac{1}{2}$ $\frac{5}{10} = \frac{1}{2}$
estimate (noun) a close guess made using mathematical thinking.	**estimación** suposición aproximada que se hace usando el razonamiento matemático.	$28 + 21 = ?$ $30 + 20 = 50$ 50 is an estimate of the sum.

English	Español	Example/Ejemplo
estimate (verb) to make a close guess based on mathematical thinking.	**estimar / hacer una estimación** hacer una suposición aproximada usando el razonamiento matemático.	11×40 is about 400.
even number a whole number that always has 0, 2, 4, 6, or 8 in the ones place. An even number of objects can be put into pairs or into two equal groups without any leftovers.	**número par** número entero que siempre tiene 0, 2, 4, 6, o 8 en la posición de las unidades. Un número par de objetos puede agruparse en pares o en dos grupos iguales sin que queden sobrantes.	20, 22, 24, 26, and 28 are even numbers.
expanded form the way a number is written to show the place value of each digit.	**forma desarrollada** manera de escribir un número para mostrar el valor posicional de cada dígito.	$249 = 200 + 40 + 9$
expression one or more numbers, unknown numbers, and/or operation symbols that represents a quantity.	**expresión** uno o más números, números desconocidos o símbolos de operaciones que representan una cantidad.	3×4 or $5 + b$

Ff

English	Español	Example/Ejemplo
face a flat surface of a solid shape.	**cara** superficie plana de una figura sólida.	face
fact family a group of related equations that use the same numbers, but in a different order, and two different operation symbols. A fact family can show the relationship between addition and subtraction or between multiplication and division.	**familia de datos** grupo de ecuaciones relacionadas que tienen los mismos números, ordenados de distinta manera, y dos símbolos de operaciones diferentes. Una familia de datos puede mostrar la relación que existe entre la multiplicación y la división.	$5 \times 4 = 20$ $4 \times 5 = 20$ $20 \div 4 = 5$ $20 \div 5 = 4$

English	Español	Example/Ejemplo
factor a number that is multiplied.	**factor** número que se multiplica.	$4 \times 5 = 20$ (4 and 5 marked as factors) factors
factor pair two numbers that are multiplied together to give a product.	**pares de factores** dos números que se multiplican para obtener un producto.	$4 \times 5 = 20$ (4 and 5 marked as factor pair) factor pair
factors of a number whole numbers that multiply together to get the given number.	**factores de un número** números enteros que se multiplican para obtener el número dado.	$4 \times 5 = 20$ 4 and 5 are factors of 20.
foot (ft) a unit of length in the customary system. There are 12 inches in 1 foot.	**pie (ft)** unidad de longitud del sistema usual. 1 pie equivale a 12 pulgadas.	12 inches = 1 foot
formula a mathematical relationship that is expressed in the form of an equation.	**fórmula** relación matemática que se expresa en forma de ecuación.	$A = \ell \times w$
fourths the parts formed when a whole is divided into four equal parts.	**cuartos** partes que se forman cuando se divide un entero en cuatro partes iguales.	fourths 4 equal parts
fraction a number that names equal parts of a whole. A fraction names a point on the number line.	**fracción** número que nombra partes iguales de un entero. Una fracción nombra un punto en una recta numérica.	$\frac{3}{4}$

English	Español	Example/Ejemplo
Gg		
gallon (gal) a unit of liquid volume in the customary system. There are 4 quarts in 1 gallon.	**galón (gal)** unidad de volumen liquido del sistema usual. Un galón es igual a 4 cuartos.	4 quarts = 1 gallon
gram (g) a unit of mass in the metric system. A paper clip has a mass of about 1 gram. There are 1,000 grams in 1 kilogram.	**gramo (g)** unidad de masa del sistema métrico. Un clip tiene una masa de aproximadamente 1 gramo. 1,000 gramos equivalen a 1 kilogramo.	1,000 grams = 1 kilogram
greater than symbol (>) a symbol used to compare two numbers when the first is greater than the second.	**símbolo de mayor que (>)** símbolo que se usa para comparar dos números cuando el primero es mayor que el segundo.	6,131 > 5,113
Hh		
halves the parts formed when a whole is divided into two equal parts.	**medios** partes que se obtienen cuando se divide un entero en dos partes iguales.	halves 2 equal parts
hexagon a polygon with exactly 6 sides and 6 angles.	**hexágono** polígono que tiene exactamente 6 lados y 6 ángulos.	
hour (h) a unit of time. There are 60 minutes in 1 hour.	**hora (h)** unidad de tiempo. 1 hora equivale a 60 minutos.	60 minutes = 1 hour
hundredths the parts formed when a whole is divided into 100 equal parts.	**centésimos (fracciones)/ centésimas (decimales)** partes que se forman cuando un entero se divide en 100 partes iguales.	

English	Español	Example/Ejemplo
Ii		
inch (in.) a unit of length in the customary system. There are 12 inches in 1 foot.	**pulgada (pulg.)** unidad de longitud del sistema usual. 12 pulgadas equivalen a 1 pie.	The length of a quarter is about 1 **inch** (in.).
isosceles triangle a triangle that has at least two sides the same length.	**triángulo isósceles** triángulo que tiene al menos dos lados de igual longitud.	8 in. 8 in. 6 in.
Kk		
kilogram (kg) a unit of mass in the metric system. There are 1,000 grams in 1 kilogram.	**kilogramo (kg)** unidad de masa del sistema métrico. 1 kilogramo equivale a 1,000 gramos.	1,000 grams = 1 kilogram
kilometer (km) a unit of length in the metric system. There are 1,000 meters in 1 kilometer.	**kilómetro (km)** unidad de longitud del sistema métrico. Un kilómetro equivale a 1,000 metros.	1 kilometer = 1,000 meters
Ll		
length measurement that tells the distance from one point to another, or how long something is.	**longitud** medida que indica la distancia de un punto a otro, o cuán largo es un objeto.	length
less than symbol (<) a symbol used to compare two numbers when the first is less than the second.	**símbolo de menor que (<)** símbolo que se usa para comparar dos números cuando el primero es menor que el segundo.	5,113 < 6,131

English	Español	Example/Ejemplo
line a straight row of points that goes on forever in both directions.	**recta** fila recta de puntos que continúa infinitamente en ambas direcciones.	
line of symmetry a line that divides a shape into two mirror images.	**eje de simetría** recta que divide una figura en dos imágenes reflejadas.	
line plot a data display that shows data as marks above a number line.	**diagrama de puntos** representación de datos en la cual se muestran los datos como marcas sobre una recta numérica.	Sea Lion Lengths 48 49 50 51 52 Inches
line segment a straight row of points that starts at one point and ends at another point.	**segmento de recta** fila recta de puntos que comienza en un punto y termina en otro punto.	A B
liquid volume the amount of space a liquid takes up.	**volumen líquido** cantidad de espacio que ocupa un líquido.	When you measure how much water is in a bucket, you measure liquid volume.
liter (L) a unit of liquid volume in the metric system. There are 1,000 milliliters in 1 liter.	**litro (l)** unidad de volumen líquido del sistema métrico. 1 litro equivale a 1,000 mililitros.	1,000 milliliters = 1 liter

Mm

English	Español	Example/Ejemplo
mass the amount of matter in an object. Measuring the mass of an object is one way to measure how heavy it is. Units of mass include the gram and kilogram.	**masa** cantidad de materia que hay en un objeto. Medir la masa de un objeto es una manera de medir qué tan pesado es. El gramo y el kilogramo son unidades de masa.	The mass of a paper clip is about 1 gram.
meter (m) a unit of length in the metric system. There are 100 centimeters in 1 meter.	**metro (m)** unidad de longitud del sistema métrico. 1 metro es igual a 100 centímetros.	100 centimeters = 1 meter

English	Español	Example/Ejemplo
metric system the measurement system that measures length based on meters, liquid volume based on liters, and mass based on grams.	**sistema métrico** sistema de medición. La longitud se mide en metros; el volumen líquido, en litros; y la masa, en gramos.	**Length** 1 kilometer = 1,000 meters 1 meter = 100 centimeters 1 meter = 1,000 millimeters **Mass** 1 kilogram = 1,000 grams **Volume** 1 liter = 1,000 milliliters
mile (mi) a unit of length in the customary system. There are 5,280 feet in 1 mile.	**milla** unidad de longitud del sistema usual. 1 milla equivale a 5,280 pies.	5,280 feet = 1 mile
milliliter (ml) a unit of liquid volume in the metric system. There are 1,000 milliliters in 1 liter.	**mililitro (ml)** unidad de volumen líquido del sistema métrico. 1,000 mililitros equivalen a 1 litro.	1,000 milliliters = 1 liter
minute (min) a unit of time. There are 60 minutes in 1 hour.	**minuto (min)** unidad de tiempo. 60 minutos equivalen a 1 hora.	60 minutes = 1 hour
mixed number a number with a whole-number part and a fractional part.	**número mixto** número con una parte entera y una parte fraccionaria.	$2\frac{3}{8}$
multiple the product of a given number and any other whole number.	**múltiplo** producto de un número y cualquier otro número entero.	4, 8, 12, 16, and so on, are multiples of 4.

English	Español	Example/Ejemplo
multiplication an operation used to find the total number of items in a given number of equal-sized groups. See also *multiplicative comparison.*	**multiplicación** operación que se usa para hallar el número total de objetos en un número dado de grupos de igual tamaño. Ver también la *comparación multiplicativa.*	**Multiplication** $3 \times 4 = 12$ number of groups; number in each group; total
multiplicative comparison a comparison that tells how many times as many.	**comparación multiplicativa** comparación que dice cuántas veces una cantidad es otra cantidad.	$7 \times 3 = 21$ tells that 21 is 3 times as many as 7, and that 21 is 7 times as many as 3.
multiply to repeatedly add the same number a certain number of times. Used to find the total number of items in equal-sized groups.	**multiplicar** sumar el mismo número una y otra vez una cierta cantidad de veces. Se multiplica para hallar el número total de objetos que hay en grupos de igual tamaño.	42, 36, 30, 24, 18, 12, 6 $7 \times 6 = 42$

Nn

numerator the number above the line in a fraction that tells the number of equal parts that are being described.	**numerador** número que está encima de la línea de una fracción. Dice cuántas partes iguales se describen.	$\frac{2}{3}$

Oo

obtuse angle an angle that measures more than 90° but less than 180°.	**ángulo obtuso** ángulo que mide más de 90° pero menos de 180°.	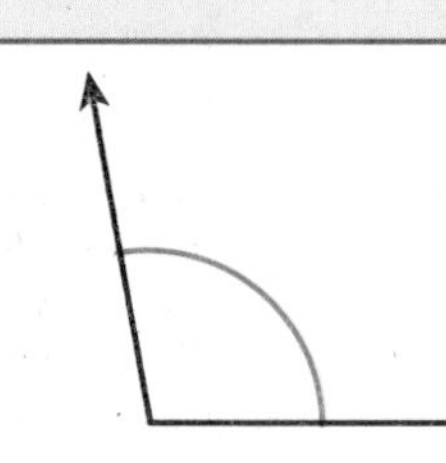

English	Español	Example/Ejemplo
obtuse triangle a triangle that has one obtuse angle.	**triángulo obtusángulo** triángulo que tiene un ángulo obtuso.	
odd number a whole number that always has 1, 3, 5, 7, or 9 in the ones place. An odd number of objects cannot be put into pairs or into two equal groups without a leftover.	**número impar** número entero que siempre tiene el dígito 1, 3, 5, 7, o 9 en la posición de las unidades. Los números impares no pueden ordenarse en pares o en dos grupos iguales sin que queden sobrantes.	21, 23, 25, 27, and 29 are odd numbers.
operation a mathematical action such as addition, subtraction, multiplication, or division.	**operación** acción matemática como la suma, la resta, la multiplicación y la división.	$15 + 5 = 20$ $20 - 5 = 15$ $4 \times 6 = 24$ $24 \div 6 = 4$
ounce (oz) a unit of weight in the customary system. A slice of bread weighs about 1 ounce. There are 16 ounces in 1 pound.	**onza (oz)** unidad de peso del sistema usual. Una rebanada de pan pesa aproximadamente 1 onza. 16 onzas equivalen a 1 libra.	16 ounces = 1 pound

Pp

English	Español	Example/Ejemplo
parallel lines lines that are always the same distance apart and never cross.	**rectas paralelas** rectas que siempre están a la misma distancia y nunca se cruzan.	
parallelogram a quadrilateral with opposite sides parallel and equal in length.	**paralelogramo** cuadrilátero que tiene lados opuestos paralelos e iguales en longitud.	
partial products the products you get in each step of the partial-products strategy. You use place value to find partial products.	**productos parciales** los productos que se obtienen en cada paso de la estrategia de productos parciales. Se usa el valor posicional para hallar productos parciales.	The partial products for 124×3 are 3×100 or 300, 3×20 or 60, and 3×4 or 12.

English	Español	Example/Ejemplo
partial quotients the quotients you get in each step of the partial-quotients strategy. You use place value to find partial quotients.	**cocientes parciales** los cocientes que se obtienen en cada paso de la estrategia de cocientes parciales. Se usa el valor posicional para hallar cocientes parciales.	The partial quotients for 2,124 ÷ 4 could be 2,000 ÷ 4 or 500, 100 ÷ 4 or 25, and 24 ÷ 4 or 6.
partial sums the sums you get in each step of the partial-sums strategy. You use place value to find partial sums.	**sumas parciales** las sumas que se obtienen en cada paso de la estrategia de sumas parciales. Se usa el valor posicional para hallar sumas parciales.	The partial sums for 124 + 234 are 100 + 200 or 300, 20 + 30 or 50, and 4 + 4 or 8.
partial-products strategy a strategy used to multiply multi-digit numbers.	**estrategia de productos parciales** estrategia que se usa para multiplicar números de varios dígitos.	218 × 6 48 (6 × 8 ones) 60 (6 × 1 ten) + 1200 (6 × 2 hundreds) 1308 The partial products for 218 × 6 are 6 × 200 or 1,200, 6 × 10 or 60, and 6 × 8 or 48.
partial-quotients strategy a strategy used to divide multi-digit numbers.	**estrategia de cocientes parciales** estrategia que se usa para dividir números de varios dígitos.	6 25 500 4)2,125 − 2,000 125 − 100 25 − 24 1 The partial quotients are 500, 25, and 6. The quotient, 531, is the sum of the partial quotients. The remainder is 1.

English	Español	Example/Ejemplo
partial-sums strategy a strategy used to add multi-digit numbers.	**estrategia de sumas parciales** estrategia que se usa para sumar números de varios dígitos.	312 +235 Add the hundreds. 500 Add the tens. 40 Add the ones. + 7 547
pattern a series of numbers or shapes that follow a rule to repeat or change.	**patrón** serie de números o figuras que siguen una regla para repetirse o cambiar.	
pentagon a two-dimensional closed shape with exactly 5 sides and 5 angles.	**pentágono** figura bidimensional cerrada que tiene exactamente 5 lados y 5 ángulos.	
perimeter the distance around a two-dimensional shape. The perimeter is equal to the sum of the lengths of the sides.	**perímetro** longitud del contorno de una figura bidimensional. El perímetro es igual al total de las longitudes de los lados.	60 yards 40 yards 40 yards 60 yards The perimeter of the soccer field is 200 yards. (60 yd + 40 yd + 60 yd + 40 yd)
period a group of three places in a number, usually separated by commas. The first three periods are the ones period, the thousands period, and the millions period.	**período** grupo de tres valores posicionales de un número, generalmente separados por comas. Los primeros tres períodos son el período de las unidades, el período de los millares y el período de los millones.	321,987 987 is the first period.
perpendicular lines two lines that meet to form a right angle, or a 90° angle.	**rectas perpendiculares** dos rectas que se unen para formar un ángulo recto, o un ángulo de 90°.	
pint (pt) a unit of liquid volume in the customary system. There are 2 cups in 1 pint.	**pinta (pt)** unidad de volumen líquido del sistema usual. 1 pinta equivale a 2 tazas.	2 cups = 1 pint

English	Español	Example/Ejemplo
place value the value assigned to a digit based on its position in a number.	**valor posicional** valor de un dígito según su posición en un número.	Hundreds / Tens / Ones: 4 / 4 / 4 → 400 / 40 / 4
plane figure a two-dimensional figure, such as a circle, triangle, or rectangle.	**figura plana** figura bidimensional, como un círculo, triángulo, o rectángulo.	
PM the time from noon until before midnight.	**p. m.** tiempo que transcurre desde el mediodía hasta la medianoche.	PM 5:10
point a single location in space.	**punto** ubicación única en el espacio.	A
polygon a two-dimensional closed figure made with three or more straight line segments that do not cross over each other.	**polígono** figura bidimensional cerrada formada que tiene tres o más segmentos de recta que no se cruzan.	Polygons / Not Polygons
pound (lb) a unit of weight in the customary system. There are 16 ounces in 1 pound.	**libra (lb)** unidad de peso del sistema usual. 1 libra equivale a 16 onzas.	16 ounces = 1 pound
prime number a whole number greater than 1 whose only factors are 1 and itself.	**número primo** número entero mayor que 1 cuyos únicos factores son 1 y él mismo.	2, 3, 5, 7, 11, 13, 17, 19 are prime numbers.
product the result of multiplication.	**producto** el resultado de la multiplicación.	$5 \times 3 = \mathbf{15}$

English	Español	Example/Ejemplo
protractor a tool used to measure angles.	**transportador** herramienta que se usa para medir ángulos.	

Qq

English	Español	Example/Ejemplo
quadrilateral a polygon with exactly 4 sides and 4 angles.	**cuadrilátero** polígono que tiene exactamente 4 lados y 4 ángulos.	
quart (qt) a unit of liquid volume in the customary system. There are 4 cups in 1 quart.	**cuarto (ct)** unidad de volumen líquido del sistema usual. 1 cuarto equivale a 4 tazas.	4 cups = 1 quart
quotient the result of division.	**cociente** el resultado de la división.	15 ÷ 3 = **5** ← quotient

Rr

English	Español	Example/Ejemplo
ray a straight row of points that starts at one point and goes on forever in one direction.	**semirrecta** fila recta de puntos que comienza en un punto y continúa infinitamente en una dirección.	*A* *B*
reasonable something that makes sense when given facts are taken into account.	**razonable** algo que tiene sentido cuando se tienen en cuenta los datos dados.	You can estimate to make sure an answer is reasonable. 29 + 22 = 51 30 + 20 = 50
rectangle a quadrilateral with 4 right angles. Opposite sides of a rectangle are the same length.	**rectángulo** paralelogramo que tiene 4 ángulos rectos. Los lados opuestos de un rectángulo tienen la misma longitud.	
regroup to put together or break apart ones, tens, or hundreds.	**reagrupar** unir o separar unidades, decenas, o centenas.	10 ones can be regrouped as 1 ten, or 1 hundred can be regrouped as 10 tens.

English	Español	Example/Ejemplo
remainder the amount left over when one number does not divide another number a whole number of times.	**residuo** en la división, la cantidad que queda después de haber formado grupos iguales.	Remainder $17 \div 5 = 3$ R 2
rhombus a quadrilateral with all sides the same length.	**rombo** cuadrilátero que tiene todos los lados de la misma longitud.	
right angle an angle that looks like a square corner and measures 90°.	**ángulo recto** ángulo que parece la esquina de un cuadrado y mide 90°.	90°
right triangle a triangle that has one right angle.	**triángulo rectángulo** triángulo con un ángulo recto.	90°
round to find a number that is close in value to a given number by finding the nearest ten, hundred, or other place value.	**redondear** hallar un número que es cercano en valor al número dado hallando la decena, la centena, o otro valor posicional más cercano.	48 rounded to the nearest ten is 50.
row a horizontal line of objects or numbers, such as in an array or table.	**fila** línea horizontal de objetos o números, tal como las que aparecen en una matriz o una tabla.	
rule a procedure that is followed to go from one number or shape to the next in a pattern.	**regla** procedimiento que se sigue para ir de un número o una figura al número o la figura siguiente de un patrón.	17, 22, 27, 32, 37, 42 rule: add 5

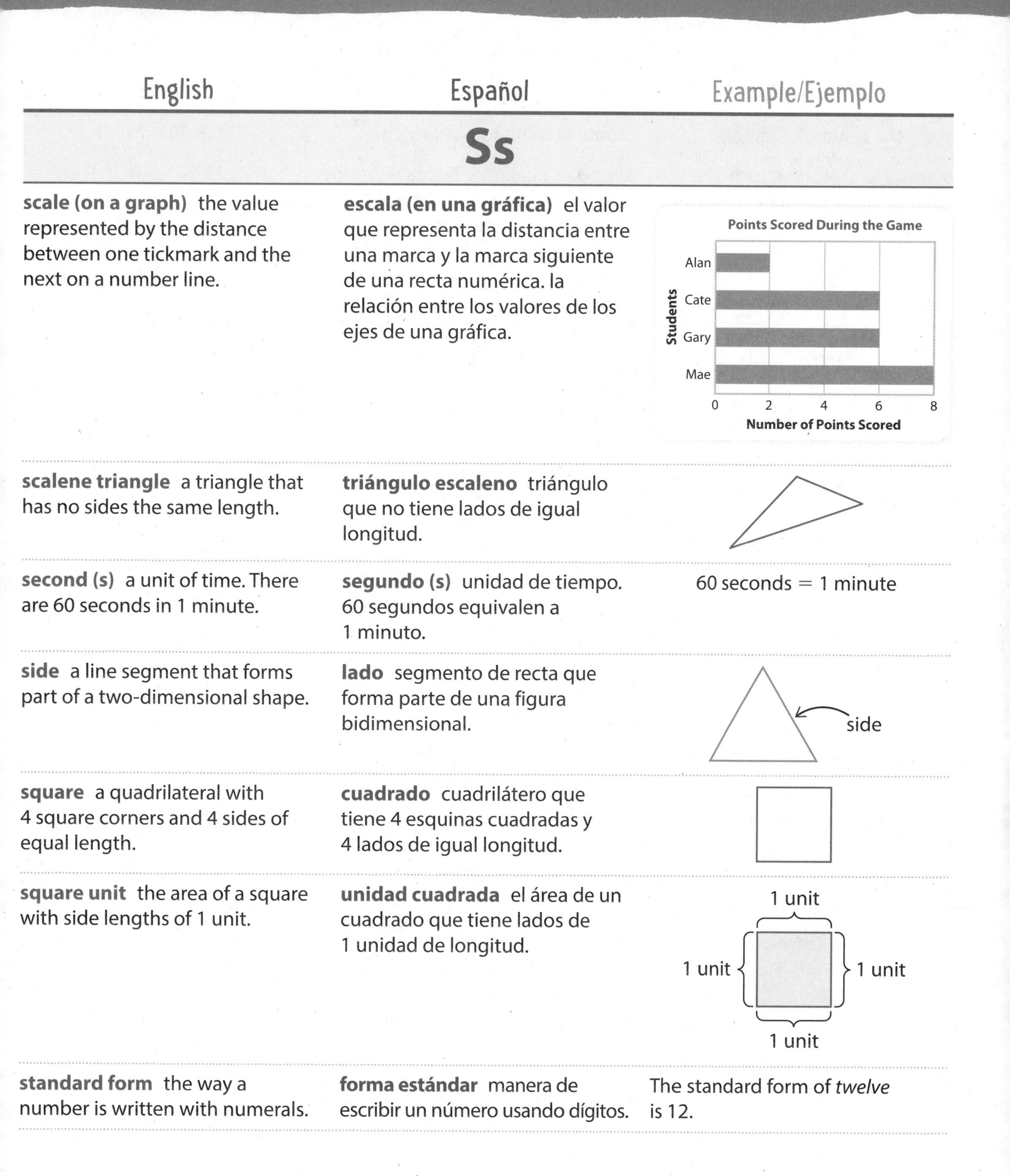

English	Español	Example/Ejemplo

Ss

scale (on a graph) the value represented by the distance between one tickmark and the next on a number line.

escala (en una gráfica) el valor que representa la distancia entre una marca y la marca siguiente de una recta numérica. la relación entre los valores de los ejes de una gráfica.

scalene triangle a triangle that has no sides the same length.

triángulo escaleno triángulo que no tiene lados de igual longitud.

second (s) a unit of time. There are 60 seconds in 1 minute.

segundo (s) unidad de tiempo. 60 segundos equivalen a 1 minuto.

60 seconds = 1 minute

side a line segment that forms part of a two-dimensional shape.

lado segmento de recta que forma parte de una figura bidimensional.

square a quadrilateral with 4 square corners and 4 sides of equal length.

cuadrado cuadrilátero que tiene 4 esquinas cuadradas y 4 lados de igual longitud.

square unit the area of a square with side lengths of 1 unit.

unidad cuadrada el área de un cuadrado que tiene lados de 1 unidad de longitud.

standard form the way a number is written with numerals.

forma estándar manera de escribir un número usando dígitos.

The standard form of *twelve* is 12.

English	Español	Example/Ejemplo
sum the result of addition.	**suma** el resultado de la suma.	34 + 25 = 59
symbol a character, such as a letter or question mark, that can be used to stand for an unknown number in an equation.	**símbolo** cualquier marca o dibujo, tal como una letra o un signo de interrogación, que puede usarse para representar un número desconocido en una ecuación.	18 − ? = 9

Tt

English	Español	Example/Ejemplo
tenths the parts formed when a whole is divided into 10 equal parts.	**décimos (fracciones)/ décimas (decimales)** partes que se forman cuando se divide un entero en 10 partes iguales.	
thirds the parts formed when a whole is divided into three equal parts.	**tercios** partes que se forman cuando se divide un entero en tres partes iguales.	thirds 3 equal parts
three-dimensional solid, or having length, width, and height. For example, a cube is three-dimensional.	**tridimensional** sólido, o que tiene longitud, ancho, y altura. Por ejemplo, los cubos son tridimensionales.	
trapezoid (exclusive) a quadrilateral with exactly one pair of parallel sides.	**trapecio** cuadrilátero que tiene exactamente un par de lados paralelos.	

English	Español	Example/Ejemplo
trapezoid (inclusive) a quadrilateral with at least one pair of parallel sides.	**trapecio** cuadrilátero que tiene al menos un par de lados paralelos.	
triangle a polygon with exactly 3 sides and 3 angles.	**triángulo** polígono que tiene exactamente 3 lados y 3 ángulos.	
two-dimensional flat, or having measurement in two directions, like length and width. For example, a rectangle is two-dimensional.	**bidimensional** plano, o que tiene medidas en dos direcciones, como la longitud y el ancho. Por ejemplo, un rectángulo es bidimensional.	

Uu

English	Español	Example/Ejemplo
unit fraction a fraction with a numerator of 1. Other fractions are built from unit fractions.	**fracción unitaria** fracción cuyo numerador es 1. Otras fracciones se construyen a partir de fracciones unitarias.	$\frac{1}{4}$
unknown the value you need to find to solve a problem.	**desconocido** el valor que se debe hallar para resolver un problema.	18 − **?** = 9

Vv

English	Español	Example/Ejemplo
vertex the point where two rays, lines, or line segments meet to form an angle.	**vértice** punto donde dos semirrectas, rectas, o segmentos de recta se unen y forman un ángulo.	vertex

English	Español	Example/Ejemplo
Ww		
weight the measurement that tells how heavy an object is. Units of weight include ounces and pounds.	**peso** medición que dice cuán pesado es un objeto. Las onzas y las libras son unidades de peso.	**Weight** 1 pound = 16 ounces
word form the way a number is written with words or said aloud.	**en palabras** manera en que se escribe o se dice en voz alta un número usando palabras.	**467,882** **four hundred sixty-seven thousand, eight hundred eighty-two**
Yy		
yard (yd) a unit of length in the customary system. There are 3 feet, or 36 inches, in 1 yard.	**yarda (yd)** unidad de longitud del sistema usual de Estados Unidos. 1 yarda equivale a 3 pies o a 36 pulgadas.	3 feet = 1 yard 36 inches = 1 yard

Acknowledgments

Photography Credits

United States coin images (unless otherwise indicated) from the United States Mint

Images used under license from **Shutterstock.com**.

iii Racheal Grazias, David Herraez Calzada; **iv** Antonia Giroux, tratong; **v** 2happy, Allen McDavid Stoddard; **vi** Gordana Sermek, Thitima Boonnak; **vii** d100, Photoonlife; **1** S. Bonaime; **3** Alex Staroseltsev; **4** Alex Staroseltsev, KaiMook Studio 99, Lano4ka, Mhatzapa; **8** Mhatzapa, NikoNomad; **13** Mhatzapa, Peter Sobolev; **15** Alexsandr Sadkov, Art'n'Lera, Marssanya; **16** Aleksandr Sadkov, Art'n'Lera; **17** piotr_pabijan; **18** Authentic Creations, Pixfiction; **19** Pixfiction; **20** Cheryl Casey; **21** David Lee; **22** Brocreative; **24** Lyekaterina, Super Prin; **29** Khunnoo; **30** Butsaya; **31** Africa Studio; **32** Stratos Giannikos; **33** Africa Studio; **34** Andregric, EkaC; **36** Roman Samokhin; **37** Neveshkin Nikolay; **40** Thodonal88; **44** Antpkr; **45** Kzww; **47** Ann Stryzhekin, dmitro2009, In-Finity, Jason Patrick Ross, Jo Crebbin; **49** Digidreamgrafix, In-Finity, StacieStauffSmith Photos, Steve Bower; **52** Pixeldreams.eu, Zmiter; **53** Racheal Grazias, Redchocolate; **56** Songsak P; **58** Electra, Flipser, Spacaj; **60** Hannamariah; **63** Liskus, Normana Karia; **71** Ekaterina Kondratova, Lotus Images; **74** Bryan Solomon; **75** Ewais; **76** Ericlefrancais; **78** Aperturesound; **79** Dmitry Petrenko; **87** David Herraez Calzada; **89** V J Matthew; **90** Ivonne Wierink; **96** Naruedom Yaempongsa, 3000ad; **105** Lotus_studio; **108** Thodonal88; **115** Cathleen A Clapper; **116** Javier Brosch, olnik_y; **117** olnik_y, Sofiaworld; **118** marssanya, PERLA BERANT WILDER; **119** Efetova Anna; **120** Igor Sirbu, Peyker; **121** tratong; **124** blue67design, Jag_cz; **125–126** Nataliia Pyzhova; **128** Amawasri Pakdara; **130** Denis Belyaevskiy; **131** Elena Schweitzer; **132** Subbotina Anna; **134** Dan Thornberg; **138** Africa Studio, Wonderful Future World; **141** humbak; **142** Sanzhar Murzin; **143** blue67design, Leigh Prather; **146** Eans; **147** Sarah Marchan; **148** ILEISH ANNA, Kaiskynet Studio; **149** Jiri Hera; **150** Good Shop Background; **152** Nata-Lia; **153–154** Narong Jongsirikul; **159** James Steidl; **160** elbud; **169** Kaspri, LDDesign, Maaike Boot, Travelview, Vibe Images; **170** PowerUp; **171** T Cassidy; **175** design56, Kolopach; **176** Ostill; **178** Elena Voynova; **179** Nataliia Pyzhova, RedHead_Anna, Venus Angel; **181–182** Antonia Giroux; **191** Julie Vader; **192** Nikita Biserov; **196** OmniArt, TeddyandMia; **197** EDMAVR, FernPat; **198** Mon Nakornthab; **201** Erik Lam; **202** Vladyslav Starozhylov; **203** Billion Photos; **204** Issarawat Tattong, Levent Konuk; **206** Axio Images; **208** alfocome; **210** Mlorenz; **211** Dmitry Petrenko; **214, 216** Domnitsky; **218** Videowokart, Koncz, Arsentyeva E, Barbol, oksana2010, tr3gin, Pavel Vakhrushev, Stephen B. Goodwin; **220** Evgenyi; **221** Marilyn Barbone, Smspsy, I'm Friday, Temastadnyk; **227** eyal granith; **229** Allen McDavid Stoddard; **230** Owatta, Pandapaw; **241** ravl; **242** Orla; **248** Sashkin; **249** David Franklin, WhiteDragon; **250** Ewapee; **252** PrimaStockPhoto; **257** vdimage; **258** Room27; **261** RemarkEliza; **262** ZanyZeus; **264** Elena Elisseeva; **268** ConstantinosZ, IB Photography; **270** 2happy; **272** Denis Rozhnovsky; **273** Africa Studio; **274** 5 second Studio, Natasha Pankina; **276** Roman Samokhin, Subject Photo; **278** M. Unal Ozmen; **279** Igor Polyakov; **280** Potapov Alexander; **282** Daniela Barreto, Evgeny Karandaev; **284** Beata Becla; **286** GoBOb, Ponsawan saelim; **287** SOMMAI; **288** kolopach; **290** Artem Shadrin; **301** Lori Martin; **304** YolLusZam1802; **306** Ravl; **308** Philip Lange; **309** Heymo; **310** Hong Vo; **312** Art24hrDesign; **317** Alexey Boldin; **322** Sosika; **325** Seregam; **326** Andrei Dubadzel; **327** Jiang Zhongyan; **328** Marco Scisetti, v.s.anandhakrishna; **329** Graph, Vasily Kovalev; **332** JIANG HONGYAN, olnik_y, Visual Generation; **333** Cynoclub, Monica Click; **334** Eric Isselee, olnik_y, Natasha Pankina, Visual Generation; **336** Stephen Orsillo; **339–340** horiyan; **344** Peter Wollinga; **346** Worraket; **348** Lucy Liu, olnik_y, Vilax; **350** Eric Isselee; **352** Igor Zh; **354** Rtimages; **356** Maerzkind; **357** Bas Nastassia, Marekusz, WachiraS, vovan, Vlabo; **363** Ocskay Bence; **365** Tim UR; **366** Gayvoronskaya_Yana; **377** Tatyana Vyc; **378** DenisNata; **379** Andy Dean Photography; **382** HelgaLin, Mark Herreid, Padma Sanjaya; **383** Protasov AN; **384** happymay; **386** Madlen; **389** Africa Studio; **390** kolopach; **397** Davidoff777; **398** Images.etc; **399** PhotoMediaGroup; **400** Lurii Kackkovskyi; **401** Theo Fitzhugh; **402** IB Photography; **405** Naruedom Yaempongsa; **409** Duplass, Stephen Mcsweeny; **410** cynoclub; **411** LittlePigPower; **412** MaraZe, Rodrigobark, Wealthylady; **413** Victor Habbick, Aphelleon, Marc Ward, Niko Nomad, NASA, NASA/JPL-Caltech, NASA/JPL/Cornell University/ Maas Digital, NASA/JPL, NASA, ESA, and M. Livio and the Hubble 20th Anniversary Team (STScI), NASA/Ames **414** Bestv, blue67design; **416** Christian Musat, Don Mammoser, Florida Stock, Gary powell, Jayne Carney, Moosehenderson, Sandy Hedgepeth, Schalke fotografie | Melissa Schalke, Steven Blandin; **417–418** Sergej Razvodovskij; **419** blue67design, Gino Santa Maria; **420** Bernashafo; **421** Africa Studio, Ffolas, Strannik_fox; **422** blue67design, Halfpoint; **423** 3777190317; **424** Mariyana M; **425** Kolopach; **426** Robert_s; **427** Jaroslav74; **428** Africa Studio; **429** Hong Vo; **433** RusGri; **437** John Kasawa; **438** Carlos E. Santa Maria; **439** CameraOnHand; **440** Butterfly Hunter, Lucky-photographer, Luria; **441** Danielle Balderas; **442** showcake; **444** HelloRF Zcool, Wonderful Future World, Yellow Cat; **445** Photo Melon; **446** Lunatictm; **448** bonchan; **449** Gordana Sermek; **451** Zheltyshev; **452** ZoranOrcik; **455** Nattika; **456** Viktar Malyshchyts, Wonderful Future World; **457** Inhabitant; **459** Hurst Photo; **460** Tiger Images, Wintakorn Choemnarong; **461** bonchan; **462** Alfocome; **463** Nataly Studio; **464** Kzww; **466** Gita Kulinitch Studio, smilewithjul; **467** Valentina Razumova; **468** Wk1003mike; **470** Bonchan; **472** Natasha Pankina, Scorpp; **474** Aopsan; **476** olnik_y; **477** Aleksandr Simonov; **479, 480, 482** Manbetta; **483** kolopach; **487** Kalamurzing; **488** Africa Studio; **490** Elizabeth A. Cummings; **499** Sarah Marchant; **501** EG_, RedHead_Anna; **502** gowithstock, M. Unal Ozmen, Padma Sanjaya; **503** Richard Peterson; **506** lineartestpilot, Yellow Cat; **507** Tyler Olson; **508** Sevenke, Thitima Boonnak; **511** Pockygallery; **512** Baishev, RedHead_Anna; **514** Billion Photos; **515** victoriaKh; **516** Mtsaride; **517** Aperture51; **519** Luminis; **522** Daniela Barreto, Gelpi; **523** Jeffrey Sheldon; **526** Ivinni; **527** Matt Benoit; **530** schankz; **532** C-You, hchjjl; **535** Aperture51; **536** Thodonal88; **538** Sharon Day; **539** Daniela Barreto, Jezper; **545** Andrey Yurlov, Eugene Onischenko, ostill; **546** Eugene Onischenko; **549** Natalia D.; **553** 3D_creation,

Front Cover Credits

©Bill Reitzel/Digital Vision/Getty Images

Maaike Boot; **556** HstrongART, Ljupco Smokovski; **557** design56; **558** Bborriss.67; **560** baibaz; **561** karen roach; **565** Tim UR; **566** Africa Studio; **567** Dionisvera, irin-k; **568** irin-k, Trofimov Denis; **571** Tiger Images; **574** PrimaStockPhoto; **577** Coprid; **578** Heymo, Monticello; **579** Elena Elisseeva; **582** Jaroslava V; **583** Sasha_Ivv, Myimages-Micha; **586** picamaniac; **588** Mega Pixel; **589** Motorolka; **590** Fotoksa, nimon, Pete Spiro; **592** Africa Studio; **594** Chones, Keith Wilson; **597** CWIS; **598** Evangelos, Gemenacom; **600** Montego; **601** Swardian; **602** Swardian; **605** Garantiopa; **606** Olga Nayashkova; **608** Africa Studio; **610** Eugene Onischenko; **611** GrigoryL; **612** Minur; **614** KarSol; **616** Fascinadora; **617** Heymo; **618** Ulrike Welsch; **620** VAV; **622** New Africa; **626** Peter Zvonar; **627** Steve Mann; **628** Deniza 40x; **630** Marieke Feenstra; **631** Deniza 40x; **632** Sanit Fuangnakhon, OnlyZoia; **633** Vilaiporn Chatchawal; **634** Ksokolowska; **635** JoemanjiArts; **638** Anastasia Sergeeva, M. Unal Ozmen, Hurst Photo, Gts, design56; **641** carlos castilla; **644** Akura Yochi, Ann_saowaluk, Megaflopp, YK; **654** Photoonlife; **656** Optimarc; **659** Ian Scammell, liskus; **661** Mega Pixel; **665** d100, denisik11; **666** PloyBuraphon; **668** equinoxvect; **671** Veniamin Kraskov; **672** MR. RAWIN TANPIN, photka, Sergiy Kuzmin; **677** Veniamin Kraskov; **683** Artem Shadrin; **684** Hayati Kayhan; **693** Veniamin Kraskov; **694** DiamondGT, Gmlykin; **702** Dmitry Naumov; **703** Twin Design; **704** Photo Melon; **705** Mtlapcevic; **708** kamnuan; **713** Arthito; **715** grmarc, Petr Malyshev; **717** Farah Sadikhova, Zsolt Biczo; **718** Shah Rohani; **724** Elnur, hchjjl; **730** Farah Sadikhova, Vitezslav Valka; **736** photogal; **738** YaniSinla; **742** Farah Sadikhova, RusGri; **743** Butterfly Hunter, Mr. Alien; **749** George_C; **750** Andrii Cherniakhov; **752** Claudio Divizia, Kriangx1234; **753** wacomka; **754** Murat Irfan Yalcin, Nata9; **757** Aleksangel; **759** Tatiana Popova; **760** Nico99; **762** Nortongo; **763** Laborant; **A3** Prostock-studio; **A11** Trinacria Photo

Student Handbook, appearing in Student Bookshelf and Teacher Guide only:HBi ArtMari, Rawpixel.com, Pixfiction, Disavorabuth; **HB1** Africa Studio, opicobello; **HB2** iadams; **HB3** Palabra; **HB5** Havepino; **HB6** Tatiana Popova; **HB8** Chiyacat; **HB9** Kyselova Inna, Markus Mainka; **HB10** ArtMari; **HB11** Disavorabuth; **HB12** ArtMari, Disavorabuth; **HB13-HB14** ArtMari; **HB16** Rawpixel.com